Philosophy and Life

Professor A. C. Grayling is Principal of the New College of the Humanities at Northeastern University, London, and a Supernumerary Fellow of St Anne's College, Oxford. He has written and edited over thirty books on philosophy, history, science and current affairs. For several years he wrote columns for the *Guardian* newspaper and *The Times* and was the chairman of the 2014 Man Booker Prize.

Philosophy and Life

Exploring the great questions of how to live

A. C. GRAYLING

PENGUIN BOOKS

PENGUIN BOOKS

UK | USA | Canada | Ireland | Australia
India | New Zealand | South Africa

Penguin Books is part of the Penguin Random House group of companies
whose addresses can be found at global.penguinrandomhouse.com.

First published by Viking 2023
Published in Penguin Books 2024

002

Typeset by Jouve (UK), Milton Keynes
Printed and bound in Great Britain by Clays Ltd, Elcograf S.p.A.

The authorized representative in the EEA is Penguin Random House Ireland,
Morrison Chambers, 32 Nassau Street, Dublin D02 YH68

A CIP catalogue record for this book is available from the British Library

ISBN: 978–0–241–99320–0

www.greenpenguin.co.uk

Penguin Random House is committed to a
sustainable future for our business, our readers
and our planet. This book is made from Forest
Stewardship Council® certified paper.

For Georgina, *filia mea:*
in lumine tuo lumen videmus

Contents

viii   *Contents*

Preface

There is a question everyone has to ask and answer – in fact, has to keep on asking and keep on answering. It is 'How should I live my life?', meaning 'What values shall I live by? What sort of person should I be? What shall I aim for?' The great majority of people do not *ask* this question, they merely *answer it unthinkingly*, by adopting conventional views of life and what matters in it, and moving along with the crowds of unasking, unthinking answerers in the direction that the crowds take them.

I call this question the 'Socratic Question' because it was Socrates who, at least in philosophy's recorded history, was the first thinker we know who systematically asked it to prompt a search for *reasoned* answers – that is, answers formulated independently of some antecedent traditional or religious viewpoint.

To say that in our time, as in Socrates' time – indeed in all times – the great majority of people do not ask themselves his question but answer it unthinkingly, is to say that whereas everyone has a philosophy of life, the great majority of people are not aware of having one. The philosophy of life they have is adopted from the society around them, and shared with most other people. They acquired it from parents, school, friends, television, social media, church or mosque, society at large, absorbing it unconsciously. Indeed they work hard – also in largely unconscious ways – to be as like other people as possible, and to behave in ways acceptable to them. Almost everyone copies everyone else in their social circles, and cleaves to the values and aims held in common there, reinforcing the shared philosophy of life they thus adopt.[1] As Oscar Wilde observed, 'Most people are other people. Their thoughts are someone else's opinions, their lives a mimicry, their passions a quotation.'

And yet there are times in most lives when something – a feeling of confusion, a sense of unformulated questions pushing at the back of one's mind, perhaps moments of depression, illness, grief, failure – suddenly forces a halt, a pause, and prompts one to think, giving one a desire to make sense of things. And at those times the unconsciously acquired philosophy one lives by does not seem enough.

But it does not take bad times only to make one pause and think. If you, reading this, were to think about the philosophy – the values, aims, attitudes – that makes you live as you do and choose the things that you choose – and I mean *really* think about it, to see whether you fully agree with it once you know what it is, what justifications you can give for its values, and what it prompts you to aim for – is it possible that you might find yourself wishing to change some things about it? If so, why? And if not, why not?

The theme of this book is 'philosophy of life', *Lebensphilosophie*. Its importance as something we should all consider announces itself in its name. Yet it is almost wholly neglected in the study of philosophy as an academic subject in universities. Academic philosophy focuses upon questions of reality, knowledge, truth, reason, and the principles (not so much the practice) of ethics.[2] These are deep and important matters, and some of history's most brilliant minds have investigated them, from ancient times to our own day, with great consequences – for from these enquiries have sprung the natural and social sciences and the political and social developments that characterize the modern world. But the other half of philosophy – the philosophy of life, of living, of being human in a complicated world – has in the past century and more vanished from what came to be called 'Analytic' philosophy (the technical academic philosophy of most *universities* in the English-speaking world), while in 'Continental' (mainly French and German) intellectual debates philosophy has diversified into many forms in association with sociology, literary theory, the history of ideas, psychoanalysis, film criticism and general *critique*, not necessarily if at all anchored to universities. The various contributors to Continental philosophy are described as *philosophes*, a category broader than that denoted by the English word 'philosopher' because *philosophe* in French essentially means 'thinker', 'enquirer', 'intellectual'. That indeed is what 'philosopher' meant in English too, until philosophy became a professional university discipline with a specialist technical jargon, a curriculum and examinations.[3]

Sequestering philosophy in universities and intellectual coteries has the effect of shutting out those who have not gained the requisite credentials of admission. Among the excluded are significant numbers desirous of knowing what are the best, the deepest, the most insightful and helpful things that have been said and thought about life, as materials for reflecting on that question for themselves. Note that I do not reserve the implied strictures here to philosophy in the Analytic tradition alone; those *philosophes* of sociology, film criticism, psychoanalysis and the rest deserve censure too when what they do degenerates into wordplay, pose-striking and sophistry, with incomprehensibility masquerading as profundity, and wilful paradoxes offered as the currency of debate. The clean, clear, life-enhancing insight is a rare thing in both these ways of doing philosophy.

But the important point I seek to make is that in this 'other half of philosophy' – the philosophy of life – the philosophers, the *philosophes*, are not just philosophers or *philosophes* as such, they are also the novelists, historians, dramatists, essayists, poets and scientists whose explorations and thoughts are likewise about life and how we do, and should, live it. This is because reflection on life, exploring its complexities and possibilities, seeking routes to survival at least and flourishing at best – finding the good that is in things bad and wrestling with the bad that is in things good, and deciding what really matters in the end – is everywhere the business of intelligent minds when they apply themselves, whether directly or indirectly, to answering for themselves the Socratic Question.

The period in the history of Western philosophy when the question of how to live was most actively pursued – and the results applied in life itself – was the Hellenistic and Roman period in which Stoicism, Epicureanism and other approaches took their classic form: between the fourth century BCE and the fourth century CE.

In Indian philosophy the connection between understanding the nature of reality and what to do as a result was never severed. The dominance of Christianity over intellectual life in the West which began in the fourth century CE and lasted until the seventeenth century CE, and over moral life which still lingers today either actively in some quarters or as general backdrop, was the major factor in the loss to culture of the ethical schools of antiquity, although in fact Christianity adopted many of their teachings and insights and made them – often disguised them – as its own.

There has of late been a revival of interest in the ideas of the ancient ethical schools, Stoicism chief among them. As the persuasiveness of religious doctrines evaporates, interest in philosophical approaches to life increases among those who think. This is a welcome development. It is somewhat hampered by the fact that too much of what is, in consequence, offered as accounts of philosophical approaches to life is thin and shallow, in the 'rules for life' or 'what such-and-such a great name can teach you about life' genre. The proffered nostrums rarely stick, and readers of them might think, 'If this is all, it's not much use' – and thus be put off the quest. To assemble materials for formulating one's own individual answer to Socrates' question requires more, therefore; the pages that follow are a contribution to that 'more'.

It has been my good fortune to have the opportunity – the privilege, really – provided by a career as a professor of philosophy, to study much and write often about the answers given to the Socratic Question by philosophers, scientists, poets, thinkers of all kinds from all ages and cultures. A major part of the aim in doing this was to contribute to the conversation that we have, or at least should have – both with ourselves as individuals and with each other in society – about the challenge that the Socratic Question poses. Another part of the aim was to educate and encourage myself; with the poet Paul Valéry I might say, 'Others make books; I am making my mind' – of course (given human nature) with only partial success.[4] Indeed it might be argued that the most important insights in this arena come from one's failures and turpitudes, as Clavdia Chauchat tells Hans Castorp in Thomas Mann's *Magic Mountain*.[5]

In what follows here I gather and discuss the responses offered by the great traditions of debate, to provide materials to anyone who will make use of them to reflect on his or her own views. The endeavour justifies itself, for I believe as strongly now as I ever did that Socrates' question is the most important anyone can be asked to answer.

Introduction

The Socratic Question – which can be posed in several alternative but
equivalent ways: 'What sort of person should I be?' 'What values
shall I live by?' 'What shall I aim for?' – is both an invitation and a
challenge. As the discussions in the following chapters show, there is
no one-size-fits-all answer, but instead a serious invitation to each
individual to formulate a personal answer. A powerful aid to doing so
is reflection on the debate that Socrates initiated two and a half millennia ago and which has continued since. There are many insights
and suggestions in this debate which any of us can take and put to
work for our own purposes; we can help ourselves to them, for wisdom is free and belongs to everyone.

This book has three sections. Part I clarifies the Socratic Question
and puts in place two important preliminaries required by Part II,
these being a consideration of human nature – who are the 'we' who
answer Socrates' question? – and a survey of the main schools of ethical thought since Socrates' time. The ideas and principles of these
schools – Cynic, Peripatetic, Stoic, Epicurean and others – will be
mentioned often in the following two sections. A detailed example
of Stoic and Epicurean ideas being applied in practice is given in
Appendix 1, along with an illustration of the 'faith and reason' contrast in thinking about ethics.

Part II considers the great matters of death and love, happiness,
grief, success and failure, courage, compassion, altruism, good and
bad, right and wrong, the challenge of life's inevitabilities, and the
ultimate question of meaning. All lives, from the most ordinary to
the most extraordinary either in positive or negative senses, are
marked by these things, making them the focus of philosophical
reflection; they are what a philosophy of life is a philosophy of.

Death and love are such big matters for human beings that
each deserves a thorough examination in itself, and receives it. The

virtues – to use a term most often associated with the 'cardinal virtues' of courage, wisdom, temperance and justice (very different from the 'theological virtues' of faith, hope and charity) – provide a significant point of departure for thinking about the ideas of what sort of person one would like to be, and of how one should behave in the different conditions and circumstances of life. These conditions (for example: is one healthy or unhealthy?) and circumstances (for example: does one live in a poor strife-torn country or a wealthy one?) make an important difference to some aspects of what is possible in one's philosophy, as in one's life, but reflection also shows that some things are perennially significant, independently of circumstances.

There is a genre of literature which has encouragement and solace as its chief purpose in discussing these matters, usually presented in small-format books with pastel covers. The concern they prompt is that many who read them might think, 'Is that it? Is that all that philosophy says?' and be put off. One does better to dig deeper, more thoroughly – and with honesty, accepting that there are more questions than answers in philosophy and that we have to seek the latter for ourselves. There is no reason why this cannot be done accessibly and engagingly. What follows here does not belong to the pastel genre. Where philosophy provides either encouragement or solace, it does so for deeper reasons; and for deeper reasons sometimes it does neither. The aim here is to display some of the best that has been said and thought about the matters mentioned, so that all who wish to do so can make use of it to formulate a philosophy of their own.

Readers may wish to go straight to Part II, leaving the preparatory discussions of Part I to be read afterwards; but these preparatory discussions are essential to making optimal use of Part II, which is why they are offered.

Part III surveys the way that philosophies have been and are lived, especially consciously chosen philosophies, though it is also important to note how unconscious philosophies function, and the problems that can arise in them from unclarity, or internal contradictions, or conflicts between a society's currently prevailing philosophy and an ideological commitment – religious, political or other – that a person simultaneously tries to apply. In the penultimate chapter, having been largely dispassionate throughout the discussion to that point, I sketch a life in philosophy: the philosophical choices I have made, and my reasons for them.

To dramatize the importance of finding one's own answer to Socrates' question, I like to cite a story told by Herodotus in his *Histories* of the visit made by Solon of Athens to King Croesus of Lydia at the beginning of the sixth century BCE.[1] Solon, one of the Seven Sages of Greece, had been asked by his fellow Athenians to give them a new set of laws. He did so, then – wishing to avoid being asked to change the laws until they had time to prove themselves – he went on ten years of travels in Egypt and Asia. In the course of those travels he visited King Croesus' court at Sardis in Lydia, in what is now Anatolia. Croesus was fabulously wealthy, the richest person of ancient times, and he liked to show off his store of treasures to visitors. He would then ask them who they thought was the happiest man in the world, expecting that they would nominate him because he was a king and so rich.

When Croesus asked Solon this question he was very surprised by the answer, for Solon – after mentioning a minor king who had lived an unexceptionably normal life of the kind approved by convention – nominated a pair of brothers, Kleobis and Biton, who had been rewarded for a display of filial piety. Their mother, Cydippe – a priestess of the temple of Hera, queen of the gods – urgently needed to attend a great festival honouring the goddess, but there were no oxen available to pull a cart to take her. So the brothers hitched themselves to the cart and pulled her to the temple, a distance of six miles. Cydippe prayed to Hera to give her sons the best reward that anyone could have; Hera responded by giving them, right there and then, a quiet and easeful death.

Solon explained to Croesus his choice of the brothers by saying, 'Call no man happy until he is dead.' He meant that you cannot judge whether a life is a happy one until it is over, because of chances and changes, uncertainties, the brevity of good fortune and the ever-present possibility of trouble. By 'happy', incidentally, Solon – and everyone until very recent times – did not mean a pleasant and satisfied emotional state, 'all smiles' as one might say; indeed he did not mean an *emotional* state at all, but a *condition of life*: if you are generally secure, fed, warm and dry, then you are in a happy condition even if at this particular moment you are annoyed about something or suffering with toothache. The American Declaration of Independence talks of 'Life, Liberty and the pursuit of Happiness', and by 'happiness' it does not mean 'all smiles' but what Solon meant: secure, fed, warm and dry – a good and satisfying condition of life.

And then Solon came to the really important part. He said to Croesus, 'I do not know whether you are happy, but I do know that it is important to think about what would make you so. Because a human lifespan is very brief; it is less than a thousand months long. A large part of it has gone even before we realize its brevity.'

Less than a thousand months. Think of it. If you live until the age of eighty, you live 960 months. Unless you are an insomniac or an avid partygoer, you are asleep for a third of this time, 320 months. Of the remaining 640 months much time is spent shopping for groceries, paying electricity bills, waiting at bus stops, suffering from flu or relationship breakdown, watching television, playing games on your phone, recovering from a hangover, working at a desk, making plans, standing in queues. By the time you have reached the age of twenty you have already had 240 months out of your 960.

This is why an unknown Aztec poet said, 'That we come to this earth to live is untrue. We come but to sleep' and why the great poet of ancient Greece, Pindar, said that a human being is 'but a shadow in a dream'. A stroll through a cemetery is a poignant reminder that when one's brief span of months is over, even one's existence as a memory lasts no longer than the span of months left to those who remember you.

These are sombre thoughts. But! – let us suppose, while we are still in arithmetical mood, that the shopping-queuing-influenza-etc. months amount to half of the waking months, thus leaving us 320 months to use effectively. Three hundred and twenty months is roughly twenty-six years, so matters are actually not too bad: these are twenty-six years available to live, really to live, to do things deeply worthwhile, to find meaning, to justify one's existence, to stand up and look at the world and both give it and receive from it the best of what we can do and be.

And there is yet better news. One can even forget talk of a thousand months and of twenty-six years, because in one important sense *there is no such thing as time, there is only experience*. How long you live is not measured by quantity but by quality, and quality determines quantity, like this: suppose you go somewhere with someone you really like for a romantic weekend. While you are there, time stands still. When you return home, the weekend seems to have passed in a flash. Time is thus elastic around experience, expanding and contracting in such a way that if you live a life rich in experience, you do not live one lifetime but many; a thousand lifetimes, perhaps, as measured by the wealth and depth of experience you have.

Another way of seeing this truth is to consider this: suppose you do exactly the same thing at exactly the same moment every day of your life. You get up at the same hour, eat the same things for breakfast and all other meals, read the same words on the same page of the same book – every single day. How many days do you live? The answer is: one. Just one, the same one, over and over. This proves that time is measured in experiential terms, not by the mere ticking of a clock.

Some people think that 'experience' denotes wild parties, drinking, uproariousness, excitement (the Chinese expression for a good time is *rinao*, literally 'hot and noisy'). These are certainly good escapes, while they last, from anything that does not have itself as the only goal of the activity. Schopenhauer observed that whereas all other animals live in the present moment, humans live in the past and future, and this is the source of what he saw as their misery. Wild parties are graspings of present moments, and such moments can consist in exhilaration, laughter, high pleasure. They are about achieving happiness in today's emotional sense of the term. The liberation from self and from the more drudging or difficult aspects of life thus provided is welcome. There are some who make the quest of such moments their purpose in life; they live to party. There are some among these some, in turn, who find that the kind of out-of-self experience involved is injectable – literally.

These considerations prompt one to ask why, if happiness is the goal of life and if by 'happiness' we now mean a pleasant, pleased, positive – even exhilarated – emotional state, we do not simply pump Prozac or (for that matter) opium into the mains water supply. Another way to frame this thought is to invoke the old trope, 'Which is better: to be a happy pig or an unhappy Socrates?' And here *the* point that lies at the heart of Socrates' question leaps out: what is meant by 'better' in this question? What would one mean by 'the better, or the best, life for me to live'?

Whatever answer one gives, it will be an answer to Socrates' question.

It is undoubtedly easier to accept the implicit, mainly unconscious, philosophy of life widely assumed in one's society in the current phase of its history, than to think about how to answer Socrates' question. Thinking about what one really believes and values, justifying these values to oneself, maybe choosing different values – and with them, perhaps, new goals – and setting oneself to live by them, probably seems like hard work. One might think about these matters and decide in the end to accept what current social norms prescribe. One might examine the tenets and doctrines of this religion or that, and decide to accept and believe, and to live accordingly. Provided one does this seriously and authentically, at least one would have used one's power to think and one's will to choose. It is a fair bet that scrutiny of social norms – or where these differ, and they mostly do, religious teachings – will prove productive for any enquirer, one way or another. It is a yet better bet that a serious endeavour to answer, for oneself, the Socratic Question could be an enhancing life-changer.

Philosophy far too often deals in generalizations and abstractions alone. In the pages to follow, general questions and abstract ideas will be exemplified by particularities. This is important because everyone has a philosophy, everyone *lives* a philosophy, but – as already mentioned – most people do not know they have and live a philosophy, and do not know that they have and live a philosophy devised for them and decided for them by society's conventions and history, and by the expectations of others. We might, once we have examined what we assume and believe and do, decide that we are happy to go along with those conventions and expectations. But we might decide to think and live a bit differently, or even a lot differently, once we have examined our assumptions and beliefs, and thought about how we live and why we live that way.

Whatever we decide, it will be on the basis of having thought about things: we will have *answered* the Socratic Question.

PART I

1. The Question

The Socratic Question, 'What sort of person should I be?' – and its variants, 'What kind of life should I lead?' 'What values shall I live by?' 'What shall I aim for?' – asks any reflective person, at any point in life, to pause and consider *what really matters*, and as far as practically possible to live according to the answers. The Stoic philosopher Epictetus pointed out that a person might be struck by the force of this Socratic challenge even in the last hours of advanced old age, and at that moment 'begin', as he put it, 'to be wise'. It is never too late.[1]

It might strain optimism to think that a philosophy of life could be arrived at early, in the sense that a youth might consider Socrates' question, come to a decision, and thereafter live in conformity with that decision. Yet although it is never too late to consider one's philosophy of life, neither is it ever too soon. Life is a winding road, littered with the debris of experience, and the challenge to consider one's answers to Socrates' question is a recurring one. We have to be able to change when circumstances require it, but that does not imply that a life can be lived without a theme, consisting in a view of what matters and what aims one sets oneself, even if the theme adds new notes or modulates to a new key in response to what is learned along the way. The theme might change from time to time, but there is a theme always.

To *not* think about how to answer the Socratic Question is to betray one's own intelligence. It is to be lazy. Worse, it is to put oneself in the hands not merely of convention but of those who, knowing that most people do not think about this matter, can therefore too easily manipulate them. Advertisers and politicians, partisan media, purveyors of every form of charlatanism trade on this fact. Above all, to ignore the Socratic Question is to waste one's life; it is to live asleep, to miss opportunities. A Russian proverb says, 'We are born in an open field, but we die in a forest' – one interpretation of which is that many possibilities lie before us when we set out in life, but if we are not active choosers we are progressively limited in our options as the years pass, until we find ourselves with no options left in the final enclosure, darkly pressed about by thickets of inevitability.

'Active choosers' – but yes, admittedly, convention and the conditions of society already make many choices on our behalf which, in general, we can do little about. We have to earn a living, we generally have to behave in socially acceptable ways; standard expectations are operative even in our private lives. What is seen as desirable in the way of success – wealth, fame and influence, getting to the top of the ladder; even the lower rungs glitter with invitation to lesser degrees of these – is dangled hypnotically before our eyes. But walk down any city shopping street and consider: only the very richest could buy much of what entices in the shop windows, which means that the great majority of people live in a state of unsatisfied desire, not least the desire to be a person who possesses and is seen to possess such things. Yet! – even so, choice remains, as proved by the existence of the *ultimate* choice: whether to continue living. For the philosophers of antiquity this fact was the guarantee of freedom. They said, 'To learn to philosophize is to learn to die,' meaning that once they ceased to fear death and instead saw it as the final and complete palliation of the worst that could happen, they could live with liberty and courage in the face of all things. In light of this fact, however much heroism it might take to throw off the bonds of convention and enforced obligation, the possibility of doing so genuinely exists – and that means there are senses in which, and ways in which, we can indeed be active choosers in the answer we give to Socrates' question.

But wait: 'the possibility of choosing genuinely exists; we can indeed be active choosers' – who are 'we', and is it true that we possess a power of ultimate choice, meaning that we have 'free will' in the full sense of this term? Socrates' question makes no sense if the answer to this last question is 'No'. And answers to the question about who 'we' are turn out to be highly relevant. In due place below, powerful reasons are given for assuming that the answer to the free-will question is 'Yes', and all the more powerful for relating to the 'we' at issue.

Given this, one can proceed to ask: where does one start to answer Socrates' question? Here is where being on one's guard against wrong answers matters. At the outset one has to understand certain simple but deep assumptions already present in asking the question. First: we have to *think*, and *for ourselves*, because second: the answer to the question is individual to each person who seeks to answer it. This is a supremely important point. *There is no one-size-fits-all answer.* This is what the ideologies (again: religions mainly, but all ideologies) offer, and in their very nature their nostrums demand a oneness, a commonality, a lack of diversity in humanity, because the nostrums only work if people renounce their individuality and submit to – conform to – the model required, so that 'one-size-fits-all' will fit all. Note that if one *chooses* to submit and conform to a model, after genuinely examining the tenets and promises of what one is handing oneself over to, then: fine. But most followers of a one-size-fits-all ideology did not choose or reason their way into giving themselves over to it (which means giving themselves over to those in charge of it: the priests, mullahs, demagogues); no, it is almost always upbringing, social pressure, emotional drivers that slotted them into the model, independently of their own rational choice. For one example: how many would, if encountering the Christian story for the first time when intellectually mature, give it any credence? It is in essentials the same as any number of other ancient Near-Eastern and Greek myths, such as the story of Zeus fathering Hercules on Alcmene – Hercules, the worker of marvels, who visits the underworld and then joins his father on Olympus – exemplifying the pattern 'God fathers a son on a mortal woman, the son works wonders, descends into hell then ascends into heaven' and in supplementary or analogous versions dies and resurrects, as do Osiris in Egypt, Baal and Mot in the ancient Levant, Jesus in the more recent Levant, and numerous other tales in that genre.

The discussion in what follows, accordingly, is premised on the idea that each individual has to think and choose, for himself or herself, what answer to give the Socratic Question and its variants, because the fact of human diversity by itself tells us that one-size-fits-all ideologies by their very nature can never wholly satisfy anyone without self-denial or self-deception.

This discussion is *ethics*. Not 'morals', not 'morality', but *ethics*. Ethics is about the answer we give to the Socratic Question; 'ethics' comes from ancient Greek *ethos*, meaning 'character', and therefore concerns what we are, what we value and what we aim for. Morality is different. It is about behaviour, and almost exclusively about inter-personal behaviour – keeping promises, not telling lies, staying sexually faithful to your spouse. Moralities wax and wane over time in their degree of strictness or liberalism: some things regarded as immoral ceasing to be so (e.g. homosexuality, at least among liberal-minded people); some things once regarded as acceptable coming instead to be abhorred (e.g. slavery). The word 'moral' derives from a coining by Cicero, who adapted the term *mos, moris* (plural *mores*) – variously connoting 'custom', 'manners', 'etiquette' – to form *moralis*, from which our term 'moral' descends.

So: ethics is about character, about what sort of person you are and the nature of your life; morals is about aspects of your behaviour. Your morals will flow from your ethics, but they are not the same thing, and it is important to keep the distinction clear.

In connection with the point made above about what confronts us as 'active choosers', I have to nominate a word to describe the important phenomenon which, in that respect, is at work in people's lives. This phenomenon, already alluded to, is *currently (for any 'currently') prevailing social sentiment, opinion, custom, tradition and expectation* – the net, woven out of place, history and other people, in which we are stuck like flies in a spider's web. Despite the negative connotations of this simile, entanglement in the net has good aspects: it gives definition and structure to life (there is some truth in T. H. Huxley's remark that 'A man's worst difficulties begin when he can do as he likes'), and not just to its externals but to the way we think, which is significant because the way we think helps us to navigate the net and to understand other people also entangled in it. But entanglement in the net has bad aspects: it is limiting, constraining, sometimes stifling and often burdensome. It is a vexation to some to reflect that, having not asked to come into the world, nevertheless upon arrival in it – at least: upon arrival at the stage in life when they become aware of their entanglements – they have obligations and duties, there are expectations, they are almost inescapably caught in the mesh of society, law, custom and other people. *Almost* inescapably: some do head out into the desert to live alone in a cave, figuratively more than literally these days, becoming hippies, dropouts, all the way from antisocial solitaries behind closed curtains to tramps on the street.

The word I will use to capture this net of *currently prevailing social sentiment, opinion, custom, tradition and expectation* is 'normativity'. This is an unaesthetic word, granted, but it is preferable to alternatives such as 'spirit of the age' and 'mind of the time', which the shallow slipperiness of human thought too easily interprets as an agent of some sort, like a genie or god – a dangerous slippage because society is not an agent but a dumb power made up of tens of millions of units, each only barely aware, if aware at all, that they are imposing those sentiments and expectations on themselves and others. The unawareness is part of the problem. The weight, the sometimes-crushing weight, of the burden of normativity is largely responsible for the way so many – perhaps most – lives diminish as the years pass; the bright hopes of youth, and its ambition, being eroded away by disappointment, mortgages, domestic responsibilities, realization of the large forces that stand in the way of the (by comparison, puny) efforts of individuals.

So, to repeat: by 'normativity' I mean *prevailing sentiment, conventions and expectations*, and one reason for placing the fact of normativity, thus understood, front and centre in thinking about life is that it is – alongside the benefits noted – one of the two principle sources of obstruction to fully living the answers one gives to Socrates' question. The other principle source, already mentioned, is the metaphysical question of whether there is such a thing as 'free will'. Note that even if we humans have free will in an ultimate, metaphysical sense, it could remain that normativity wraps such a powerful set of chains around us that in practice our metaphysical freedom cannot be exercised. Indeed, a sceptic about society might say that it is precisely normativity's aim to deny our metaphysical freedom as much as possible, even to eliminate it, to squash people into sardine cans of conformity as tightly and inescapably as possible.

But one must not forget that many people – again: perhaps most people – *welcome* the effect of normativity on life. It has made their choices for them; it tells them most of what they need to know about what to think and what to do and be in life. It stipulates what a normal life looks like: you get an education, you get a job, you marry, buy a house, have a family, go on annual holidays, pay into a pension, retire, potter about for a bit, die. In the meantime you vote for the same political party most of the time, shake your head in disapproval over some of the things normativity definitely does not like, though you daringly disagree with normativity about one or two things, especially when the party you did not vote for is in government. And through it all you cope with the pain of relationships that break down, grief at the death of parents or others you care about, anxiety about your income, your weight, your career prospects as these dwindle with the years; you might turn to ready nostrums for support in those times when the difficulties are eating at you, sucking at your resolve: alcohol, religion, an affair, an acceptance of and compromise with defeat. Meanwhile there are genuinely some things you enjoy: that TV series, that book, that beer, that holiday beach. These things keep you going, after a fashion; a little something to look forward to, week to week, year to year. And there is always the lottery ticket, and certain dreams you have – vague perhaps, but dreams. When you stop hoping, you can still have dreams; when you stop dreaming, the last of life's colour drains away.

On the outer edges of the life that normativity has ordained and that most people accept, there are those whose health cracks apart under the strain, who go insane, commit suicide or murder – in short, who fall out of the spider's web by madly wriggling and twisting in ways that normativity cannot and will not endure. Prisons and mental hospitals sequester those who do not keep to the paths laid out. But this is at the outer edge, note; there is no inevitability that these are the only ways a person can be free while being what all normal human beings are, viz. *social* beings, actively in need of love, friendship, community membership and a sense of belonging. For even in the journey along normativity's laid-out paths, most especially in what can be the vast inner universe of a life and mind, there is great scope for a life worth living, for meaning, for things that make existing better than not existing.

Some societies are essentially pluralistic, allowing variety in styles of life, and some are essentially monistic, requiring great conformity of practice and belief, and usually just one set of belief practices. The latter are almost all societies in which the principal source of normativity is a religion. Monistic normativity is exemplified by a Mennonite village, an ultra-Orthodox Jewish community, a Muslim-majority country. In pluralistic normativities there are more opportunities for choice in the pursuit of individual paths in life, and more opportunities for escape for those who wish to escape. But normativity remains the norm even there. It even defines the nature of the escape from it, by negation; to be a hippy, for example, is to 'tune in, turn on and drop out' as the old phrase had it – tune in and turn on to the theme of the alternative lifestyle, and drop out of society. Into what? – a new normativity. It might be that the one true kind of escape is inward: into the mind, either into its potential for madness or into the universes of thought it is capable of creating and exploring. One interpretation of the deep bass note sounded by so many philosophies of life is that the ultimate freedom of the individual is to be found within.

It is timely now to add a word both satirical and sceptical about what we are doing here. The essay 'On Not Being a Philosopher' by the Irish writer Robert Lynd is a must-read for anyone beginning the quest for a philosophy of life.[2] It is a salutary corrective to the idea that one could take in hand a volume of the classical philosophers and find there, ready-made, the answers one seeks to the questions one asks, as if it were a book of divination like China's *Yi Jing*. Lynd's amusing essay records how he heard someone extolling the wisdom of the Stoic philosopher Epictetus: 'I became interested, curious, for I had never read Epictetus, though I had often looked at his works on the shelf – perhaps I had even quoted him – and I wondered if here at last was the book of wisdom that I had been looking for at intervals ever since I was at school.'

Accordingly he got hold of a volume of Epictetus and settled down in an armchair: 'I read him. I confess I read him with considerable excitement. He is the kind of philosopher I like, not treating life as if at its finest it were an argument conducted in difficult jargon, but discussing, among other things, how men should behave in the affairs of ordinary life.' And Lynd found himself agreeing with everything Epictetus said. 'Indifference to pain, death, poverty – yes, that is eminently desirable. Not to be troubled over anything over which one has no control, whether the oppression of tyrants or the peril of earthquakes – on the necessity of this also, Epictetus and I are as one.'

But, as he read, Lynd came to feel that although he and Epictetus were at one in their opinions, Epictetus was wise but he, Lynd, was not wise. He could agree with Epictetus' opinions but not for a single instant could he live by them when faced with 'death, pain and poverty', which Epictetus says we must be indifferent to but which Lynd regarded as 'very real evils, except when I am in an armchair reading a book by a philosopher. If an earthquake happened while I was reading a book of philosophy, I should forget the book of philosophy and think only of the earthquake and how to avoid tumbling walls and chimneys. This, though I am the staunchest admirer of Socrates, Pliny, and people of that sort. Sound though I am as an armchair philosopher, at a crisis I find that both the spirit and the flesh are weak.'

And yet, Lynd continues, almost everyone accepts that the philosophers are right that 'most of the things we bother about are not worth bothering about'. Here, therefore, a paradox arises. For even as it is admitted that the philosophers are right, 'most of us would be alarmed if one of our dearest friends began to put the philosophy of Epictetus into practice too literally. What we regard as wisdom in Epictetus we should look on as insanity in an acquaintance. Or, perhaps, not in an acquaintance, but at least in a near relation . . . I am sure that if I became as indifferent to money and comfort and all external things as Epictetus, and reasoned in his fashion with a happy smile about property and thieves, my relations would become more perturbed than if I became a successful company promoter with the most materialistic philosophy conceivable.'

Indeed. Normativity and the wisdom of the philosophers appear to diverge rather sharply – if one's understanding of what Epictetus and others are saying is superficial enough. For let's examine what Lynd understood Epictetus to mean in preaching a Stoic attitude to material possessions and the things over which we have no control, such as earthquakes and death. The Stoics did not suggest sitting calmly in your armchair while your house tumbles around your ears. They would have regarded it as rational to flee to safety, just as you and I would; because it is preferable to be alive and well than injured or dead. But they argued that you do yourself a great favour by schooling yourself to recognize – and to act accordingly – that what ultimately matters in life is not wealth or social status, but whether you have been courageous and true to yourself and your principles.

A direct contrast to Lynd is offered by the English essayist and novelist Llewelyn Powys, who not only read the philosophers but lived according to the tenets of one whose views he properly understood in their original intention: Epicurus.[3] His application of the rational materialism of the Epicurean view is the more striking because of the way it supported him throughout a positive, creative life lived in the permanent shadow of death; stricken with pulmonary tuberculosis as a young adult, coughing up blood for the next thirty years of a hampered and frequently bed-bound existence – a vexation to one who had been a great walker and lover of the countryside as a youth – he both championed and lived the Epicurean philosophy. Note well that the modern meaning of 'Epicurean' to denote someone committed only to careless pleasure-seeking, a bon vivant lifestyle, is not at all what Epicurus or Powys meant, as we shall see.

To think about life is to think about possibilities and inevitabilities, good and bad. It is to think about that litany of fundamental things already mentioned and worth repeating: love and death, striving, triumph, defeat, success, failure, desire, despair, gain and loss, grief, joy, hope, pain, happiness. These are commonalities of the human condition, and not just philosophers and poets but reflective people everywhere have pondered them, struggled with them, and either succumbed to them or won victories over them, throughout recorded history. The universality of the great themes – their timelessness; their irremovable lodgement in the human condition – is very easy to demonstrate. We see, and feel, the deep human experiences from across all recorded millennia. Think of grief-stricken Achilles mourning his beloved Patroclus on the beach of Troy:

> A dark cloud of grief fell upon Achilles. He filled both hands with dust from the ground and poured it over his head, and flung himself down, huge and hugely at full length, tearing his hair with his hands. The bondswomen of Achilles and Patroclus screamed aloud for grief, beating their breasts, their limbs failing them for sorrow. Antilochus bent over Achilles the while, weeping and holding both his hands as he lay groaning for he feared that he might plunge a knife into his own throat.

Writing nearly three thousand years after *The Iliad*, Tennyson mourned his friend Arthur Hallam in *In Memoriam*:

> O Sorrow, cruel fellowship,
> O Priestess in the vaults of Death,
> O sweet and bitter in a breath,
> What whispers from thy lying lip?
> [. . .] Never morning wore
> To evening, but some heart did break.

As to love and desire – on a Mesopotamian cuneiform tablet dating from the age of Sumer in the fourth millennium BCE we read:

> My sweetheart brought me into his house
> He lay me down on the honey-fragrant bed
> And when my dear sweetheart had lain very close to me
> One-by-one, making tongue, one-by-one,
> As if dumb struck I moved toward him,
> Trembling below, I pushed quietly to him,
> My sweetheart, my hand placed on his thigh,
> So did I pass the time with him there![4]

We meet the same themes in the *Song of Solomon* two thousand years later:

> He brought me to the house of wine,
> And his glance toward me is love;
> Support me with raisin-cakes,
> Spread me among the apricots;
> For I am sick with love.
> His left-hand is beneath my head,
> His right-hand embraces me.

– and in Ovid a thousand years after that:

> Such lovely hips, such silken thighs,
> Why itemise further? All was perfection;
> I pressed her naked body to mine:
> Who does not know the rest?
> Afterwards we slept entwined:
> May many such afternoons again be mine![5]

Much might change as the great wheels of history turn, in the way of customs, institutions, manners, moralities, the appearance and configuration of things; but underneath all these changes the fundamentals of human experience remain, like grief and the pleasures of love just described. Few people like to be cold, hungry, in pain, afraid, ill, grief-stricken, lovelorn, oppressed, caged; most people like the feel of the sun's warmth on their faces, the sound of a running stream, the laughter of friends, the taste of good food, a lover's touch, the prospect of a day free from labour and care. From these basic facts we can infer much about how we should respond when we encounter people who are in pain or in need, for we know well how little we like either state ourselves. And we know what kinds of things enhance life, liberate it, bring pleasure into it. There are few excuses for being morally blind, given these simple facts.

But when we encounter the negatives of existence, how are we to respond? And as we seek its positives, how are we to determine – each of us in our individuality – which to pursue, and why? Answering these questions is answering the Socratic Question. Answering the

Socratic Question is *doing philosophy*. In light of the facts — assorted examples of which are that we are social animals; we have built-in instincts, needs and desires; our choices and actions are mainly governed by our emotions; most resources are scarce; we have, or are capable of exercising, intelligence; we are all going to make mistakes; we are all going to die — *doing philosophy* is not an option, it is a necessity.

2. 'We' and Human Nature

There has already been mention of 'we' in these pages, and there will be more. Who are 'we'? This is a question which, already complex enough, has become a focus of conflict.

There is also the question of what 'human nature' is, and even whether there is anything sufficiently uniform about the varieties among human cultures, communities and individuals to be definable as such. By itself this suggests that taking 'we' to mean 'we human beings in general' is problematic.

In considering who 'we' are we have to take into account the related questions of *intersectionality* and *positionality*. Take each of the adjectives in the description 'white heterosexual middle-class fully employed female citizen' and ring the changes on them, substituting one by one, then in combinations of two and three, and finally all, the words 'black/non-white, gay/transgender, working-class, unemployed' and add remarks about education level, disability, age, immigration status, and membership of minority ethnic and/or religious communities. Then ask: who are 'we' in a highly diverse world?

And then there is the fact that most if not all human beings do not consist of a single self, in just one clearly defined referent of the pronoun 'I', but in a number of selves projected to the world – to different people, in different circumstances – and even inwardly, introspectively, to themselves, depending on mood and the prevailing condition of their lives at a given point. Many people engage in constant or at least frequent efforts to modify themselves, or to develop a dominant self that will master other but self-betraying selves they find within – the self-betraying selves that cannot concentrate, sleep, combat fears, face realities, maintain the discipline to persist in reaching a goal. In this regard one can forget 'Who are we?' and ask, 'Who am I? *Which* am I?'

But on the other hand, there are indeed generalizable facts about human beings. As noted above, almost all human beings, just as such, are capable of experiencing cold, hunger, pain, loneliness and fear. They are also capable of experiencing pleasure, happiness, satisfaction and comfort. Most human beings have a reasonably good idea of what, given the various circumstances they can find themselves in, conduces to experiences of the first and the second kinds, at very least in basic respects. What conduces to the second kind includes shelter, warmth, food and safety, together with some assurance of the continuity of all four, and in addition companionship and a sense of living a worthwhile life with at least reasonable hopes for the future. These facts are the groundwork of thinking about moral obligations and the justification of regimes of law and human rights. Indeed *without* such generalizable facts it would be impossible to explain the point of discussing intersectionality and positionality – if we did not care about justice or rights, we would not care about discrimination and suffering – and at the same time *with* them we can ground some useful further generalizations about human beings and what counts among the fundamentals of good and worthwhile lives.

Answering Socrates' question – 'What sort of person should I be?' – begins from this latter thought. But what it abstracts from must always be remembered. The temptation to see a human being as an idealized, naked individual entity, detached from society and physical nature, has to be resisted most of the time in thinking about others, and at least half the time in thinking about oneself. Immediately this seems to make it hard to see, through the veils of entanglements and dependencies that constitute living in society and the world – and which therefore constitute most of a person's normativity-constituted selves – what possibilities of choice individuals have in their lives. For the most part, the truth about 'who I am' is a function of a story, a historical and social setting and its constituent net of relationships, because a mind – a personality, a character – is the product of many settings and encounters.[1]

But on the other hand – yet again – there is indeed also room for the thought of an *individual as such*, as a point within reflection and self-consciousness, the 'I' among the constellation of selves which is a reference for the unfolding narrative of these selves' experiences – the 'I' which we take to be what remembers, feels shame or pride, knows joy and despair; the 'I' which is the prisoner not only of outer circumstance but more poignantly of its own emotions, and indeed the most primal of them when they make themselves felt: fear, grief, greed, yearning, lust, anger, envy, hatred, pity, love, desire. I – 'I' – might wish to learn ancient Greek or master the calculus (I might wish these things ardently) but this 'I' is not the 'I' of my fears and inchoate yearnings. It is a self I privilege to myself as what I take to be, or wish to be, *the* 'myself'. It counts as the particular private self, the *moi profond* of which Proust spoke, doubtless elusive to others and sometimes to itself, but the least artificial of all the selves out of which one's being in the world is formed. So, at any rate, we hope and believe.

However sceptical one might be about the existence of such a 'true self' as an actuality – or better: as what we seek, or seek to create, through answering Socrates' question – the assumption that such a thing exists is, as the logicians say, undischargeable; we cannot do without it. For without it, all else falls apart, nothing makes sense. The world and life within it would then just be an inchoate sequence of momentary impressions, nothing more. Yet mysteriously it *appears* that the impressions that constitute our experience are linked in a generally coherent way, which makes us ask: appear to whom or what? And why?

This essentially assumed central, private self is the self which the motto on the gate to Delphi commanded visitors to seek: *gnothi seauton*, 'know thyself'. It is not easy to obey this injunction, given that the usual first victim of one's widely successful efforts at deception is oneself.

In searching for (or creating) this deep personal self, people have to be aware that their autobiographical selves are by no means guaranteed to be this self, because their autobiographies are constructs, constantly revised and adjusted for presentation to the outside world – constructs they must themselves find almost completely credible in order to make them seem plausible to others. In any case, people *wish* to believe their autobiographies; their autobiographies contain all the excuses, self-justifications and exculpations needed to shore up their self-respect and shift the blame for the messes they have made. Procedures such as psychoanalysis represent attempts to evade the propaganda of autobiography and to reach the self that underlies and motivates all the other selves. Answering the Socratic Question can be construed either as seeking or making that underlying, ultimate self.

In light of the foregoing remarks, 'we' and the 'self' which every 'I' is taken to denote are to be understood as follows in this book: the instances of 'I' who make up the 'we' to whom its remarks are addressed are in each case the underlying, fundamental, private selves lurking among the historically and socially constructed selves which are presented to the world as a public 'myself'. And the ideal of philosophical reflection aimed at answering Socrates' question is to make the fundamental self this public 'myself', or at very least its governor.

At the same time, it would be incorrect to say that the 'we' of this book is the human species in general, for in truth it is at most the people who do or might read a book such as this, and who therefore constitute a minority. In all their diversity otherwise, these 'we' are people who at some point pause to reflect on Socrates' question, and who might make choices as a result.

But these last remarks raise an important question. Although the reference of 'we' is restricted in the way just described, it is important nevertheless to have a sense of what is meant by talk of human nature in general, because – to repeat, and now dropping the 'scare quotes' around 'we' – we are fully part of nature and society and their respective evolutionary histories, and the degree to which we are not governed by their deterministic aspects matters to the question of whether we can in fact make choices, instead of only thinking that we do. On this crucial point the entire question of whether we can give individual answers to Socrates' question turns.

To put this point in its simplest and crudest terms as a question: do we have 'free will', the ability to choose without prior irresistible restriction or compulsion of any kind, at least on significant occasions, between genuine alternatives – or is everything we do the outcome of deterministic causal processes in the sense that what we do cannot have happened otherwise, given antecedent conditions? Are we ever *agents*, acting in and on the world – or are we ever only *patients*, passive recipients of events being passed along through time, our doings not doings but happenings, links in a causal chain begun long ago?

The thrust of biology and in particular neuropsychology answers 'No' to 'Are we agents?' and 'Yes' to 'Are we causal patients?' They say that if the idea of 'free will' is the idea that we can initiate wholly novel causal sequences, or can intervene in the causal realm from outside it and redirect causal flows, then there is no such thing as free will.

And this is a major problem, which threatens to bring what this book seeks to do to a shuddering halt right here. Given that we think that we make choices, that we believe we can change things as a result of deciding to do so, that the whole of our picture of humanity and the moral universe turns fundamentally on the idea of free will – which means: on commitment to the idea that we are responsible for what we do, and can be praised and blamed accordingly, because we have genuine, ultimate, novelty-introducing choice over alternatives in the situations meriting either – then if we are wrong about this we have to see ourselves as the victims of a massive and systematic error. And if so, evolution has played a mighty trick on us in endowing us with this false view. (But again: if this is indeed so, there would presumably be some kind of evolutionary advantage achieved by nature's deluding us in this way; on the supposition that everything living is ultimately impelled by the aims of surviving and reproducing – of surviving long enough to reproduce – one might be able to construct a story in which believing that we have free will enhances that project.)

One can see assumptions and risks at work on either side of the division between thinking that people are genuinely able to choose among real (not just apparent) alternatives, and seeing them as passive recipients and transmitters of causally determined processes. Thus put, the contrast between the two views, *agent* versus *patient*, is stark.

The *agent view* attributes at least some degree of malleability to human nature, such that experience, education, culture – in general:

the 'nurture' side of the nature-nurture pairing, including self-nurture and endeavour – enters into the formation of individual character. Humanity bases its vast investments in education, morality, law, indeed almost all social institutions and practices – in short: in everything that has a possibility of influencing what people think and do – on the premise that they can be educated, influenced, persuaded, and can change accordingly.

The *patient view* attributes most if not all to our genes and their hardwiring of our brains. Studies of identical twins suggest that preferences, including even political inclinations, are genetically predisposed, and studies of brain activation in experimental observations of people making choices appear to show 'the brain deciding' before the people themselves are conscious of making a decision.[2] On this view, humanity's investment in the belief that people can be persuaded and can choose differently as a result of such endeavours as education and persuasion, even punishment, is wasted. What, for example, would be the point of a prison system aiming to punish or reform if criminals are literally incapable of acting otherwise than they do? It is a very ancient Greek idea that an individual can be inescapably fated to commit a crime but merit punishment for it anyway. (Such was the fate of Oedipus, who to the modern mind suffered a cosmic injustice.) And if criminality is a predeterminedly fixed aspect of a person's character, what hope is there of reform?

Needless to say, there is a large philosophical debate – one might say: industry – devoted to the free-will question, for it is one of the hardest of all questions in philosophy, and one of the most important.[3] Roughly speaking there are three positions available: pro-free will plus anti-determinism; pro-determinism plus anti-free will; and 'compatibilism', which as the label suggests is the attempt to reconcile the idea that we are responsible agents with the fact of our being physical entities in a causal universe. On this latter view it is reasonably pointed out that we wish, as agents, to be causally connected to what our actions produce, so that we can be praised for them when appropriate – and we wish to hold others (sometimes ourselves, in fits of honesty) accountable when things go wrong, as being the cause of their being so. So here our agency is itself in need of being part of the causal realm. The persistent difficulty is that these acts are themselves the effects of preceding causes – and without an originating novel cause, a Very First cause (and what would such a thing be: an uncaused cause?), the regress of causes appears to run unstoppably back to the Big Bang – in which case whatever happens has precious little to do with our or any agency.

Before cutting the Gordian Knot of this problem, one thought that bears noting is that the free-will dilemma is *essentially* predicated on regarding the world as a causal realm. All our ordinary thinking about the way the world works is based on this idea. Yet note that the world as it appears to us in our ordinary experience of it is a virtual reality, a projection from the way the faculties of our cognitive psychology handle the input data of experience. Kant long ago observed that the conceptual categories we apply in managing experience create a world for us consisting of property-bearing particular things standing in causal relationships to each other in space and time. But all these concepts – 'particular thing', 'space', 'time', 'causality' – are imposed by our minds on the raw data of experience to give them shape and coherence; they are *our* constructs, and Kant was of the view that by definition therefore they are not descriptive of reality as it is in itself – what he called 'noumenal' reality to distinguish it from the way the world appears to us, this being 'phenomenal' reality.[4] On this view, the concept of causality is a cognitive convenience, not a fact about ultimate reality.

Two further thoughts add considerable weight to this view. One is that, in our currently best theories in physics, the concept of causation plays at best an equivocal role – if any role at all – as shown by the (already experimentally observed) occurrence of 'quantum entanglement'. The other is that the concepts we apply in our experience of the world around us are 'paraconsistent' – that is, only consistent within their own bubbles of application, and inconsistent with others in other bubbles. We have inconsistent notions of time and space: we think of the space of visual and tactual perception as a three-dimensional continuous Euclidean realm, but it is in fact neither Euclidean nor continuous; some of the standard visual illusions (such as the parallel arrows, duck-rabbit and 'gorilla video') amply illustrate the way the brain makes up a lot of what we think we see.[5] Our perceptual apparatus and the concepts associated with them, causality among them, are sometimes mutually conflicting conveniences, helpful illusions, pragmatic falsehoods. At very least, therefore, *rejecting* an interpretation of ourselves as agents – capable of choosing, of initiating and intervening in and thereby changing events – because we accept instead that causality is an unbreakable iron law of ultimate reality, is to make a dramatic choice of world view indeed.

But in any case the Gordian Knot can be, and in fact has to be, sliced through. Taking ourselves to be 'free-willed beings' in the full sense of this term – genuinely able to make choices between genuine alternatives; agents; initiators of and interveners in events; responsible, accountable – is every bit as much an undischargeable assumption as the assumption that we are each possessors of a 'true' self. As with this latter assumption, denying that we have free will means that we stop right here; there is no room for further discussion. Socrates' question assumes both that there is an 'I' and that it can make real choices, can change and thereby self-create.

But – another 'but'! – 'free-willed beings in the full sense of this term'? These words immediately ring a different set of alarm bells. For an important example: some people who are hostile to homosexuality claim that it is a choice, not a natural endowment, and that boys can be 'turned into' homosexuals by being interfered with when young. Gay people themselves deny that their sexuality is a matter of choice. Much sorrow and tragedy has been inflicted on people who have struggled to deny their sexual nature in the belief – other people's belief – that they could 'choose' to be, or could be psychoanalysed into being, heterosexual. The same applies more generally to questions of sex, sexuality and gender across a wide spectrum of possibilities. This is a sharp reminder that considerations of nature, genetics, the hard-wired aspects of the brain, are not to be swept blithely aside by the assertion of humanity's self-perception as free, and by the compelling truth that this is a principle on which civilization itself is built. Thus the dilemma is reintroduced in a slightly different guise. In this new guise it presents as a question about the *nature* in 'human nature' – in particular about the contribution of genes and their evolutionary development to what constitutes human beings.

Every theory of human nature apart from the obviously false one – if there is such a one, viz. that human beings have no nature at all but at birth are completely plastic and blank (tabula rasa) – entails that there is *some* degree of determinism, or at very least a strong inclining pressure implicit in the facts of that nature. All such theories premise themselves on identification of something taken to be the essence of humanness, and thus by definition are 'essentialist' to some degree. Determinists are hard essentialists; soft essentialists are what we might call 'inclinationists'. Those who think that our genes set strong parameters to what we can be and how we can act are at the hard essentialist end of the spectrum. A view such as Aristotle's, namely that possession of reason is defining of humanness, is at the soft essentialist end of the spectrum, in that it premises the idea that reason makes it possible for us to choose well if we put our reasoning powers to work.

The difference between hard and soft essentialism, obviously enough, concerns the respective degrees of the influence of nature and nurture in the formation of individual character. But note that the undischargeable free-will assumption is not just about the degree to which an individual can defy the impulsions of genetic endowment (for pertinent examples: the impulses to aggression, lust, and the like), but also the strong inclinations formed by nurture (by upbringing, education, community pressure to conform, and the like again). The assumption thus cuts across the nature-nurture binary too.

Until the advent of sociobiology and its successor as applied to human beings, viz. evolutionary psychology – both these enquiries near-contemporaneous with genetics and closely followed by neuropsychology, all of these pursuits grounded in empirical science – theories of human nature were variously based on experience, reflection and doctrine; in the case of the last of these, as often reflecting theorizers' wishes as their observations. For brevity let us distinguish the recent science-based theories from their philosophical predecessors by grouping the former as 'biological' and the latter as 'aspectual' (because they focus on some aspect of human psycho-logical endowment or proclivity that seems to the theorist to be characteristic).

Consider the aspectual theories first. Ancient Greek philosophers all accepted that human beings (or at very least, *men* : human males) are distinguished from the rest of the universe – except for its gods – by possession of reason and free will, and therefore by the capacity to master the negative and harmful impulses of their nature and to dir-ect themselves into paths of virtue instead. They recognized that this required effort, given natural propensities to laziness, cowardice and the like, but they did not question the assumption that having a rea-son for acting one way rather than another was a sufficient motive for doing so. This view was directly controverted by David Hume many centuries later; he argued that only emotions motivate actions, and that having a reason is never enough by itself. These two views mark the opposite ends of a scale in aspectual theories about the place of reason and emotion as sources of action.

There was an equally sharp division of opinion, though on a differ-ent matter, within the Confucian tradition in China. The view attributed to Confucius himself, as recorded in the *Analects*, is idealistic and optimistic about human nature and the possibility of its cultivation of *ren*, 'gentlemanly virtues'. Mencius, the second master of the Con-fucian tradition – he lived a century after Confucius' time – agreed that human nature is fundamentally good and that therefore the prospects for developing an ideal society are likewise good. Two generations later, the third Confucian master, Xunzi, disagreed emphatically on this point; he regarded human beings as fundamentally wicked.[6]

Mencius explained wrongdoing as the result of external forces such as poverty and hunger, arguing that it is hard times that make people commit crimes, because they are struggling to survive. It is not natural for people to be like this, he said, but the experience of suffering 'sinks and drowns their hearts'. As proof of innate goodness Mencius cited such phenomena as the distress people feel when they see a child in danger of falling into a well; they do not feel this because they wish to please the child's parents or to get social approval; the sentiment arises naturally in their *xin*, 'heart'.

Xunzi, by contrast, held that people are by nature inclined to be bad, from which it follows that being good takes conscious effort. People are greedy, they seek personal profit, they regard others as rivals; and as a result, envy and enmity arise, causing crime and betrayal. The very fact that people are born with sense organs makes them seek dissolute pleasures. Therefore, said Xunzi, education is required, based on models of upright behaviour. Only then can courtesy, refinement and loyalty develop. 'Thus,' he wrote, 'a warped piece of wood requires the press-frame, steam to soften it, and force applied to straighten it. A blunt piece of metal must be whetted on the grindstone to make it sharp.'[7]

All the Indian traditions of thought, whether 'orthodox' *astika* or 'heterodox' *nastika* (the latter including Buddhism and Jainism), share some or all of the themes of suffering, liberation from suffering by extinction, this liberation following upon understanding the illusory nature of what is encountered in ordinary experience and through asceticism, meditation and the accumulation of good karma to achieve release from the cycle of rebirth. These ideas recur in all the schools, and focus attention on the central aim they share: escape from suffering.[8] They are *soteriologies*, teachings about salvation – in their case, salvation achieved by escape from the pain and distress that is the essence of existence. Another common feature of the Indian traditions is that they are gnostic: liberation follows the attainment of *knowledge*, for the source of suffering is ignorance. Despite what these remarks and the various practices constituting Hinduism historically and at present suggest, most of the Indian schools are non-theistic; their teachings are philosophies, not religions.

Given the Indian schools' concentration on the source of suffering as the essence of existence, and their recipes for escaping it, a view of human nature is implied rather than explicit. References to the capacity to suffer, to be deluded by appearances, to desire, and to cling to things and people, together portray a creature both extremely vulnerable and yet – in the possibility of achieving understanding and thereby repudiating the false appearances of things, and of overcoming desire and attachment by severe self-discipline – capable of great efforts at liberation.

Christianity is another soteriology, this time predicated on humanity's helplessness and frailty, its inability to save itself. A doctrine of salvation requires that there be something to be saved from. The Indian traditions in effect say that we need to be saved from ignorance; Christianity says that we must be saved from our own inborn sinful nature and the weakness which makes it impossible for us to save ourselves from its dictates. We are born sick, sick with sin – Adam's sin, for which all mankind is condemned – and have to be saved. We can be saved if we believe that at a moment in fairly recent history the deity took human form and offered himself as a blood sacrifice to expiate the sins of humankind. We need the 'grace of God' to be saved, and we achieve it by believing and obeying, submitting our will wholly: 'not my will, but thine, be done' says the universal prayer of Christianity, the *Pater Noster*, 'Our Father'. The two young religions of the world – Christianity and Islam – both share this obeisant, self-negating outlook; *Islam* literally means 'submission'.

Yet implied in this view is that people can rebel against the edicts of the deity, which means that they have free will and enough power as individuals to defy, at least for a time, threats of severe punishment and pressures to submit. This, the sin of pride, is an acknowledgement of human autonomy. Other foci of religious anxiety relate to the powerful drives and instincts that underlie much human motivation. For reasons that are not clear without supplementary argument, questions especially about sex take up a great deal of bandwidth in religious ethical thinking – fornication, adultery and homosexuality are far hotter trigger topics than war, injustice, wealth accumulation, slavery, the subordination of women, and a host of other matters that one might think of greater moment. Indeed, both Christianity and Islam, far from opposing such things as war and the subordination of women, have historically been active in perpetrating both, along with slavery and social inequality. Again, however, the religions thereby acknowledge human capacity to act autonomously; moral behaviour consists in large part in resisting the demands of human nature – in taming it, controlling it, extirpating it – which would not be possible unless people had the power to do it, however much effort it takes.

For all their differences, these various outlooks share a view of human beings as creatures who can reason and, however much they might be constrained by society and other factors – even when these include some powerful natural urges and instincts – have free will. Even the cynic who thinks that most people are stupid and lazy, that they do not use their powers of reason much or at all, that they are content to let others do their thinking for them, that they want to be told what to do instead of thinking for themselves, thereby assumes that they have reason and a will that they could use if only they would.

The latest and most scientific view of the matter is that the cynic is at best only partly right on this last point, on the grounds that human nature – human psychology – is the product of evolution. On this view the repertoire of human behaviours such as mate choice and competition, formation of social hierarchies, instinctive responses to snakes and spiders, disgust (for example at rotting food), incest aversion, and much more, are the outcome of natural selection over at least the two million years of the Pleistocene era, which ended twelve thousand years ago (when the current Holocene era began). But long before the Holocene began, the psychological equipment of pre- and emerging *Homo sapiens* had reached 'fixation' in the adaptations that resulted from dealing with the challenges – over those two million years and more – posed by the 'environment of evolutionary adaptedness' (EEA) set by Pleistocene and doubtless even earlier conditions. As one slogan encapsulating this view has it, our skulls therefore contain Stone Age minds, an idea invoked by some to explain what they see as the maladaptive nature of human life and experience in post-Stone Age conditions.

Evolutionary psychology ('evopsych') is controversial. In the first couple of decades of evopsych theory the controversy was especially bitter. The concept, and the reasons for the controversy, are as follows.[9]

It was for a long time thought that the mind is almost a blank slate, equipped with a few basic capacities enabling it to receive impressions from experience and, from them, to form beliefs and develop mental functions. These capacities are latent until stimulated by input; they need experience to furnish them with their content and endow them with powers – or at least, to awake the activity of those powers.[10] This was the view of the empiricist philosophers of the seventeenth and eighteenth centuries, and it remained an underlying assumption even as philosophy and psychology developed more elaborate metaphors of the mind, for example as functioning like a telephone exchange or like a general-purpose computer. But the 'general purpose' notion was key; the ability to learn, remember, reason, imbibe a culture, and so on, was regarded as what brains have a general ability to do, such that everything they acquire in the way of these things is the result of the experiences they are exposed to. This theory appears to be supported by the empirical datum that if you place a baby in any linguistic and cultural environment other than the one in which it was born, it will grow up shaped by that culture, not by its birth mother's culture – illustrating the brain's broad plastic capacity.

On this 'domain-general' view of the brain's operations, such abilities as interpreting others' emotions, learning a language, understanding the purpose and value of reciprocity, and almost all the rest, are taken to employ the same basic mental faculties, regarded as having no content in themselves but dependent on experience for their various special characters and functioning. But as psychology, neurology and evolutionary explanations in biology and ethology (the study of animal behaviour) progressed, this view came increasingly to seem inadequate. In particular, the fact that the brain is an important organ in a body that has evolved under the pressure of natural selection over long periods of time made it compelling to think that it too has evolved its various functions in ways specific to their tasks, so that instead of the brain's capacities being 'domain-general' they are highly 'domain-specific', there being an evolved module for language, a separate evolved module for facial recognition, a separate module for the disgust reaction, and so for each of the rest of the mental, perceptual and psychological competences.

The basic principle of evolutionary psychology, accordingly, is that as a physical system the brain's structure has been 'designed' by evolutionary pressures to deal with the challenges it faces in surviving and reproducing itself. Because for 99 per cent of their history, humans and their ancestors have been hunter-gatherers, the human brain has evolved to deal with that form of life. As two of evolutionary psychology's chief proponents (Leda Cosmides and John Tooby) write:

> The key to understanding how the modern mind works is to realize that its circuits were not designed to solve the day-to-day problems of a modern American – they were designed to solve the day-to-day problems of our hunter-gatherer ancestors. These stone age priorities produced a brain far better at solving some problems than others. For example, it is easier for us to deal with small, hunter-gatherer-band sized groups of people than with crowds of thousands; it is easier for us to learn to fear snakes than electric sockets, even though electric sockets pose a larger threat than snakes do in most American communities. In many cases, our brains are *better* at solving the kinds of problems our ancestors faced on the African savannahs than they are at solving the more familiar tasks we face in a college classroom or a modern city. In saying that our modern skulls house a stone age mind, we do not mean to imply that our minds are unsophisticated. Quite the contrary: they are very sophisticated computers, whose circuits are elegantly designed to solve the kinds of problems our ancestors routinely faced.[11]

In its early days, evolutionary psychology was confronted by formidable critics, not least among them Stephen Jay Gould and Richard Lewontin.[12] Gould's fundamental objection was to what he saw as the underlying implication of hard determinism, in which the only operative factor is natural selection tending to fixation over long timescales, arguing instead that evolution can occur also through cultural pressures and as a result of 'spandrels' – these being the consequence of two unrelated developments interacting and creating the conditions for novelty. While acknowledging the importance of biology to psychology, he argued for potentiality as against determinism – for flexibility in adaptation that 'permits us to be aggressive or peaceful, dominant or submissive, spiteful or generous . . . Violence, sexism, and general nastiness *are* biological since they represent one subset of a possible range of behaviors. But peacefulness, equality, and kindness are just as biological – and we may see their influence increase if we can create social structures that permit them to flourish.'[13]

As the tenor of this remark implies, there was a subtext to objections to evolutionary psychology. It involved what critics of Gould described as 'politically correct' objections to the idea that such aspects of human behaviour as aggression, male dominance and cruelty are baked into human nature, so that war is inevitable, hierarchies and inequalities unavoidable – even that rape is 'natural'. On the view of those who deny the genetic component in the formation of behaviour, the propensity of little boys to be noisy and destructive and little girls to play with dolls is attributed entirely to socialization, and efforts to correct the socializing tendencies by giving little boys dolls and little girls plastic guns were earnestly made.

Richard Dawkins' 'selfish gene' and the so-called Santa Barbara school of evolutionary psychology (this being the location of the University of California campus at which Tooby and Cosmides taught) might be interpretable as deterministic, but another defender of the view that there is such a thing as biologically evolved human nature, Steven Pinker, is somewhat more conciliatory, acknowledging the interplay between environment and genetic endowment in the formation of *individual* character while demonstrating that a portmanteau 'blank slate' view is untenable.[14] Among the advantages of recognizing the powerful empirical evidence for this, while simultaneously demonstrating the inadequacies of different versions of a 'blank slate' thesis (including the 'Noble Savage' and 'Ghost in the Machine' alternatives), he cites recognition of the 'psychological unity of our species beneath the superficial differences of physical appearance and parochial culture'. The view that the human species has an underlying, genetically determined psychological commonality contributes to explanation of the 'theory of mind' that people so successfully operate in identifying and predicting the intentions, desires and behaviour of others, across as well as within cultures – the facial expressions of crying, laughing and feeling acute pain are simple examples.

The hard determinism implicit in early evolutionary psychology, with its commitment to the 'Stone Age minds' view, is predicated on the idea that natural selection operates over large timescales. The mere twelve millennia since the beginning of the Holocene (roughly contemporaneous with the beginning of the Neolithic period in the development of human culture) seems a mere flash of time compared to the three and a half billion years over which nature has repeatedly experimented with evolutionary strategies. But this view is tempered by the fact that some evolutionary processes are observed to develop much faster; for example, lactose tolerance in humans – the ability to digest non-human milk – has evolved in some populations only since the late Palaeolithic, and most notably since the beginning of the domestication of milk-yielding animals such as horses, goats and cows (twenty thousand years or less).

But arguments about the pace of evolution are not a decisive issue in this connection. A more relevant question is whether acceptance of the 'modularity' theory of mind, which says that the mind is a large collection of specific capacities each dedicated to just one function, entails that there are *no* general competences – that is, broad abilities of the kind that allow individuals to adapt themselves to new conditions, rapid changes in circumstances and radically different environments within the scope of their lifetimes. Consider that anatomically and behaviourally modern humans emigrated from Africa about sixty thousand years ago, and by fifteen to twenty thousand years ago had occupied every climate and ecosystem on the planet, from permanently frozen wastes to dense jungles to sweltering deserts. This bespeaks great adaptability in timescales far shorter than slow evolutionary determinism allows. Life in the Arctic and life in the Australian outback, life in the Amazon jungle and life predicated on canoeing vast distances between Pacific islands, life high in mountains and life in fertile valleys, these all require applications of intelligence to very different things: different conditions, different tools, different strategies for utilizing different types of resources and avoiding different types of dangers – in short, remarkable flexibility of mind, imagination and skill. And this is manifested in what, in terms of evolutionary time, is a blink of an eye. If cultural evolution

happens very much faster than biological evolution, then what biological evolution has endowed in the way of the human brain's
capacities to make it apt for such rapid cultural evolution – indeed,
cultural *re*volution – cannot be fixed to the challenges of the African
savannah half a million years ago.

So even granting that human mental capacities are evolved and are
modular, it would seem that in marked contrast to the largely inflexible patterns of behaviour evidenced in almost all other animals,
human minds have ways of combining, sometimes overriding, and
frequently generalizing their capacities. Perhaps a clinching example
is the fact that humans are hard-wired for language, but what
language individuals speak depends on what they are exposed to in
early life, manifesting with great clarity the interaction between
neurology and the environment outside the head – in short: the
nature-nurture interaction.[15]

It is usual for evolutionary psychologists to dislike talk of nature-
nurture, plasticity, flexibility, generalized capacities, and the like, as
too vague and as unconformable to the clean idea of specific adaptations for specific purposes. The examples of arachnophobia, incest
aversion, disgust, cheater detection, mate preferences, and more, fit
well with the 'massive modularity of mind' paradigm that main-
stream evolutionary psychology proposes. On the other hand, the
examples of human adaptability to extremely different environments
and new challenges, and the ability almost every individual displays
to learn complicated culturally propagated skills from scratch, suggests that there is something to be said for general capacity too,
consistent with modularity of most functions, either alongside them
or supervenient upon them.

If a conclusion can be drawn from debates about evolution and
psychology for the 'human nature' question itself, it is what was
described above as a 'soft essentialist' one – that is, it is one that
acknowledges the evolved nature of the human mind and grants the
modularity of at least many of its capacities, but makes room for the
empirical datum that it also manifests significant degrees of plasticity
and domain-generality. Both are themselves of obvious evolutionary
advantage to a creature dependent on intelligence – rather than claws

or teeth, fur or scales, size or speed – to survive and flourish. And both underlie the universal self-perception of humans as volunteers in at least some of what they do, capable of personal change in at least some important respects, and able to adapt to new conditions and changed circumstances most of the time. For the purposes of the enterprise here – answering Socrates' question – this is more than enough.

So to conclude: *we* – readers of books like this – are ultimately free, despite our many entanglements in history and society, to make choices about how we should live and what values we should live by. We are able to answer Socrates' question, each one of us for ourselves in the interests of the best and truest self we can each individually find or make – *make* being the chief goal of the Socratic quest. On these undischargeable assumptions the following discussions rest.

3. The Schools of Life

Beginning in the latter half of the twentieth century, and increasingly since, there has been a revival of interest in the ethical teachings of the ancient philosophers, principally the Stoics and to a lesser extent the Epicureans. Perhaps 'revival' is not quite the right term, given that the various philosophical schools have always been of interest since antiquity itself, though latterly restricted to those who have had an opportunity to learn about them. Yet it is true to say that this interest has widened, with more people taking note and more articles and books – some of a popular character, some detailed – being published. One major part of the explanation for this phenomenon is the shape of history in Western civilization over the last two and a half thousand years.

For the first thousand years of that span, from the beginning of recognized philosophy in ancient Greece in the sixth century BCE to the moment in the late fourth century CE – to be precise: the year 380 – when Emperor Theodosius I issued the Edict of Thessalonica establishing Christianity as the official religion of the Roman Empire (simultaneously banning all others), ethical discussion and reflection was a secular matter, in the sense that it did not premise itself on what a deity commanded but was a matter of people working out, for themselves and in discussion with others, how best to live. The respectively monopolistic advents of Christianity in the fourth century CE and Islam three centuries later dramatically changed that.

Both these religions were (and theoretically remain) hegemonistic ideologies requiring everyone to believe the same doctrines and behave in the same ways – the doctrines claimed to be handed down from heaven, and the behaviour crucial to whether posthumous existence will be idyllic or punitive. Whereas ethical reflection in the pre-Christian era had been a matter for debate and choice, with different philosophical schools emphasizing different principles and requiring people to think about them and act accordingly, the religions specifically and categorically *banned* thinking *for oneself* in the relevant respects. This sounds like a merely polemical point but as noted earlier it is literally true.[1] Unquestioning belief – faith – in the teachings, and obedience and conformity to the requirements were (and for purists remain) the essence of each, and are regarded as virtues. In Christianity 'pride' (thinking for oneself; standing on one's own feet and not relying on the deity's saving grace) is a great sin – 'thy will, not mine, be done' – and recall that, likewise, *Islam* literally means 'submission'.

The religions are therefore one hundred and eighty degrees different from antiquity's philosophical schools in these very germane respects. Where philosophy said 'think', Christianity and Islam said 'accept and obey'. Where philosophy said 'question', Christianity and Islam said 'believe'.[2] Religion's achievement in subduing tens of millions of people to conformity of belief and practice is remarkable, though perhaps the human propensity to superstitious anxieties and unrealistic hopes makes such manipulation less difficult than one might think. It is a striking fact that power, not least as evidenced by grand buildings (cathedrals, mosques) – along with wealth, pomp, ceremonies, robes, the commissioning of beautiful paintings and music – can make miracles, contradictions and meaningless formulae ('three-in-one', 'conceived by the holy ghost', etc.) acceptable or unnoticeable. But so it is.

The power in question was not always exercised through advertising by means of buildings, art and ceremony. It reached all the way to the flames of the stake, where heretics – those who would not conform – were burned. While religion maintained a hold over temporal authorities, coercion was available to it; the brutal effects of the Reformation in the sixteenth-century Wars of Religion and seventeenth-century Thirty Years' War put an end to that resource in Christendom, though there has yet been no comparable reformation, and hence no comparable loosening of grip, in the Islamic world.

Note the arc of history in Christianity: in Theodosius' time, the Church Fathers wrote 'apologetics', which is literature designed to persuade. They were, after all, speaking to a sophisticated and

advanced civilization whose educated elites were disinclined to too
much magical thinking. The Church's eventual triumph succeeded in
plunging this civilization into what is – not entirely misleadingly –
described as the 'Dark Ages'; literacy, knowledge, skills and social
organization all dramatically declined, their slow recovery beginning
again only under Charlemagne in the late eighth century CE.[3] At the
height of its power in the later medieval era, the Church no longer
needed to persuade because now it commanded. 'Believe or die' was
the bottom line; it had become a criminal offence not to believe. By
the mid-seventeenth century at the latest – the prosecution of Galileo took place in 1633 – Christianity had lost its power to coerce, and
was obliged to return to apologetics. Since the Enlightenment, therefore, persuasion (a famous example is William Paley's *Evidences of
Christianity* with its 'watchmaker' argument for creationism; there
are numerous others) has again been its only recourse.[4] 'Believe or
die' remains a live option in fundamentalist Islam, as apostates (those
who no longer believe) and *kafirs* or infidels (those who have never
believed) can find to their cost.[5]

The decline of religious belief in the modern West explains today's
returning interest in the ethical schools of antiquity. As mentioned,
this interest never went away among the educated; think, for just a
couple of illustrative examples, of what was said of Cicero by Erasmus in the sixteenth century and Hume in the eighteenth century:
Erasmus said he should be renamed 'Saint Cicero', and Hume said he
wished that he had been given Cicero to read rather than devotional
tracts.[6] The Renaissance recovery of the literature, philosophy, science and medicine of antiquity was a recovery of what, from the
Renaissance perspective, was literally the latest and most advanced
thinking in these fields, because so little independent enquiry had
been allowed under the hegemony of the Church, apart from those
aspects of philosophy that subserved theology.[7] Likewise, today's
return of interest in Stoicism, Epicureanism and the other schools of
thought is a return to the latest and most advanced *secular* thinking
about the matters here summarized under the rubric 'Socrates'
question'.

Think of that! – Stoicism, Epicureanism and the other schools

literally constitute *the latest and most advanced secular thinking* about
how to answer Socrates' question – 'What sort of person should I be
and how should I live?' – in a world whose Western part, at least, has
only become significantly, consciously, publicly more secular in matters of morality and personal life since the middle of the twentieth
century.[8] This is why the Stoics and Epicureans are of renewed interest; because in this newly secular-morality world the need for answers
to Socrates' question emerges from the unsatisfactory and temporary
satisfactions offered by so many different agencies – no longer just the
churches but advertisers, political parties, conspiracy theorists, dieticians, fitness experts, pundits of every stamp; a babel of competing
outlooks, most of them superficial and one-trick in their preoccupa-
tions, overwhelming us with their nostrums for happiness (such as
material possessions, trim waistlines, low taxes, cheap holidays). And
where is one to look for aids to reflection? Answer: among the rich
resources of a thousand years of thinking and practice in the philosophical schools, *still* therefore *the latest and most advanced secular thinking*
available on these matters.

One must add that there are resources in the Indian traditions too,
principally Buddhism and Yoga, the latter in the form of its early
association with Samkhya as developed by the sage Kapila; and in
China's Daoist teachings. More on them later; but their attraction for
Westerners is itself a mark of the situation here described.[9]

Here, therefore, is a survey of the latest and most advanced thinking,
offered by the philosophical schools of antiquity, about how to
answer Socrates' question. In Part II many of their ideas will find
application. As this remark suggests, there is no question here of urging the claims of any one school. To think for oneself is, in part, to
cherry-pick from everywhere any insights and suggestions that res-
onate and which help one to work out one's own views. Starting
with Socrates himself, this survey will take us, in order of their
appearance in the century after his death, through the views of the
Cynics, Cyrenaics, Aristotelians, Epicureans and Stoics.

It is no accident that we begin with Socrates himself. Before him,
almost all the philosophers of antiquity addressed themselves to

questions about the nature of reality (in Greek, *physis*) and what can be known about it.[10] Only Pythagoras and his school added teachings about how to live, chiefly dietary restrictions based on their belief in metempsychosis, the transmigration of souls; they believed that the souls of the dead migrated into beans, which therefore they did not eat, and into animals, which made Pythagoreans (non-bean-eating) vegetarians.

But Socrates turned his attention exclusively to ethics, having sampled the various 'physical' schools and found that they disagreed with each other inconclusively, and – worse – that they neglected what he regarded as the much more urgent and immediate question of *how one should live*. He was a man of powerful personality and charisma – principled, kind, humorous, fiercely intelligent, challenging; a celebrity in Athens loved by some but annoying to others – and though he left no writings he had an enormous impact on the philosophical schools that came after him. One can see how the different aspects of the example he set influenced them: his indifference to wealth and worldly goods was imitated by the Cynics; his self-discipline and steadfast commitment to civic duty was followed by the Stoics; his extolling of the 'considered life' inspired Aristotle's view that the application of reason to ethics is the basis of the best kind of life.[11] And he was the starting point for his famous pupil Plato, who, though developing his own much further-ranging philosophical views on a wider range of subjects, retained a key Socratic idea about the relation of knowledge and virtue – namely, that knowledge *is* virtue.[12]

Athens in the central decades of the fifth century BCE was at its apogee. It was the Athens of Pericles; it had led the way in repulsing the massive Persian invasion of Greece under Xerxes in the early part of the century; and it was the centre of a Greek world that stretched from southern Italy to the coastal regions of what is now Anatolia in Turkey. Although the city states of Corinth, Sparta, Thebes and the rest were independent, a number of them affiliated themselves with Athens in such a way that the phrase 'Athenian empire' is not a misdescription. In this great epoch Athens erected beautiful temples, public buildings, theatres and statuary, and enjoyed a period of democracy – a democracy of adult male citizens only, of course – in which the rotating obligation to hold public office, and the skills needed for debate, led to an explosion of higher education offered by sophists. This was not the only reason; knowledge and intellectual skill were coming to be valued as highly as, if not more highly than, the physical beauty and skill that Greeks had always admired. 'Old education' in ancient Greece had focused on gymnastics and 'music' (the arts of the Muses, chiefly poetry) – the former for health and fitness of body, the latter to imbibe the culture-forming traditions provided by Hesiod and Homer. It lasted only until adolescence began. From the middle of the fifth century BCE a more general interest in philosophy – enquiry, knowledge – prompted continuing and higher education, at first by famous individual sophists such as Gorgias, Protagoras, Hippias and Critias, but by the fourth century BCE and thereafter taking shape in formally organized schools such as Isocrates' school of rhetoric, Plato's Academy, Aristotle's Lyceum, Epicurus' Garden, and the Stoa of Zeno of Citium.[13]

The term 'sophist' now has a pejorative connotation because of the bad press sophists received from Plato, who disliked the fact that they taught debating techniques rather than austerely dedicating themselves to the quest for truth – and (worse still) that they charged money for doing so. But he was not quite fair to them. Sophists were professional instructors in the arts of public discourse and forensic skill, and in the knowledge of such matters as history and law required alongside. Moreover, as the relevant sayings have it, 'a man must live' and 'the labourer is worth his hire'. They earned their wages.

Socrates was, literally speaking, a sophist too, but although part of this situation he was in significant ways a sharp contrast to it. He was a part of it in gathering pupils about him, and a contrast to it because instead of teaching the skills required for success in public life, he challenged his pupils to think about the fundamental concepts of ethics such as courage, honesty, justice, self-restraint, wisdom and the nature of virtue itself. He did not charge fees, and he did not seek to impose any doctrines on his pupils, except to urge them to think for themselves. Indeed there are only two positive teachings we know Socrates offered: that worthwhile lives are those that have been carefully considered and chosen by the individuals living them; and that 'knowledge is virtue', in the sense that when one knows what is the right thing to do, it is impossible to do the wrong thing.

This second point is unpersuasive; it is a commonplace of human experience that we know what would be the right thing to do and yet do not do it, and indeed might even do the wrong thing – a minor example would be eating chocolate cake despite being on a diet. Aristotle, who was more realistic than Socrates on this point, recognized this as *akrasia*, 'weakness of will'. But on the first point, about the *considered life*, Socrates makes a major contribution. In fact he put the point like this: the *unconsidered* life is not worth living because it is not one's own life, it is at best someone else's idea of what life should be. To live according to others' ideas of how to live is to be a football in someone else's game, and one's direction of travel is the result of being kicked in that direction by other people's choices. A life worth living is a life one *owns* because one has *chosen* it deliberately. And 'deliberately' means: on the basis of thinking about it.

This simple-seeming point is in fact both deep and subversive. It is deep because it places conscious examination of questions of value – of what really matters, both in itself and to the thinker himself or herself – at the foundation of living. And it is subversive because in saying that individuals must think and choose for themselves, it contests the one-size-fits-all ideologies under which most people for most of history have lived; the ideologies – mainly religions – which claim to have the one-size-fits-all answer that applies to anyone and everyone irrespective of the many differences that make individuals what they are in their time, place and particularity.

All the schools of thought after Socrates agree with him that the good and worthwhile life is one that is consciously chosen on the basis of reason. Like him, therefore, the teachers and adherents of these schools accept the assumptions that we are free to choose, that we can change ourselves, and that there are things worth doing and being in life. These assumptions are, to employ the term used in discussion of these points in the previous chapter, undischargeable. Socrates' contribution was to move ethics to a central place in philosophical thought, and because these assumptions are undischargeably involved in it, he thereby set the terms for all thinking about ethics since.

What especially impressed Socrates' followers was that his view of happiness, 'the health of the soul', was – as this phrase itself implies – radically internalist, a perspective which led some, not least Epicurus, to treat philosophy as a practical *therapy* for the soul. In their writings Plato and Xenophon both emphasized Socrates' ability to master the appetites that are a source of disturbance for most other people – appetites for food, comfort, sex – because they are chief among the drivers of bad conduct. Xenophon wrote, 'Socrates was the most self-controlled of all men over sex and bodily appetite, the most resilient in relation to winter and summer and all exertions, and so trained for needing moderate amounts that he was satisfied when he had only little.'[14]

Plato's early dialogues doubtless give a fairly accurate portrait of Socrates' method of challenge and questioning, often not reaching a conclusion but considerably illuminating the topic nevertheless. Plato himself had more, and larger, fish to fry over his long philosophical life, and the 'Socrates' who appears in the majority of his dialogues is a mouthpiece only – in some cases not even on the winning side of the argument. But, as noted, Plato never questioned either the point about the considered life or the 'knowledge is virtue' claim, indeed even expanding the latter into his elaborate view that knowledge, genuine knowledge, concerns only what is perfect, unchanging and eternal, these being the 'Forms' in the 'Realm of Being' which we only *know* when our disembodied souls are in direct communion with them.[15] A critic might point out that if genuine knowledge is not possible in the course of our embodied life in the ordinary world – Plato called the ordinary world the 'Realm of Becoming' because everything in it is ever-changing, always becoming something else, and therefore we can have mere opinion about it only – then it seems hard to see how anyone could do more than aspire to live a good life but not actually live it in full. Indeed, this might be what Plato in fact thought, at least for all but philosophers.[16]

*

The first of the ethical schools after Socrates is Cynicism, if 'school' is not too elaborate a name for it; perhaps 'movement' is more accurate, if a relatively small, marginal but persistent outlook can be called such.[17] It began with one of Socrates' associates, Antisthenes, who admired Socrates' rejection of social norms and expectations, his hardiness and indifference to material comforts, and his unyielding independence of spirit. In Greek *kyon* is 'dog' and *kynikos* 'dog-like', and the label was attached to Antisthenes' even more famous successor Diogenes for good reason, which is that he literally lived as stray dogs do. The Cynic tenet was 'live according to nature', and Diogenes obeyed it to the letter: he dispensed with clothes, slept in a barrel, urinated, defecated and masturbated in public (saying of the latter practice that he wished hunger was as easily appeased by rubbing the stomach), and carried a lit lantern in the sunlight, saying, when asked why he did so, that he was 'looking for a man' and adding that he had 'once seen some boys in Sparta', his point being that the tough Spartan way of life was commendably less effete than the Athenian way.

Antisthenes, the accredited founder of the movement, was born in Athens in the mid-fifth century BCE and lived for eighty years, which meant that he was in his forties when Socrates was put to death in the year 399 for 'corrupting the youth of Athens' (by making them think and question; there was at that time a nervous and authoritarian regime in power in Athens, a consequence of the political breakdown that followed defeat in the Peloponnesian War). Antisthenes first studied with the celebrated sophist Gorgias, becoming as a result an accomplished orator, but then transferred his allegiance to Socrates, by whom he was inspired to think that virtue is the basis of happiness, and that virtue consists in self-restraint and frugality. In line with Socrates' view about the relation of knowledge and virtue – namely, that 'knowing what is right means one cannot do what is wrong' – Antisthenes believed that virtue can be taught; to learn it, he said, one needs only the 'strength of a Socrates', by which he meant courage and self-discipline. Virtue is manifested in actions, not words – indeed it requires very few words. How one lives should be dictated by the principles of virtue, irrespective of whether they conform to the state's laws. For that reason Antisthenes taught that 'the good deserve to be loved', which is in effect to urge solidarity with those whose adherence to virtue brings them into conflict with the state's laws, as happened with Socrates.

Rejecting convention and disciplining oneself to hardihood are thus the defining features of the Cynic outlook. Antisthenes demonstrated this by embracing poverty and asceticism wholeheartedly. What came to be the symbols of Cynicism in all the following centuries – a staff, a small bag or 'wallet', and a ragged cloak (he remarked that the only thing you need by way of a bed is a folded cloak) – are said to have originated with him.

Antisthenes wrote many books, but hardly anything he wrote survives. His influence both on those who followed him and those who developed his ideas further was great. They include Diogenes, Crates of Thebes and Zeno of Citium, the latter being the founder of Stoicism. Diogenes Laërtius, the historian of the lives and opinions of the ancient philosophers, wrote in the third century CE that Antisthenes 'gave the impulse to the indifference of Diogenes, the continence of Crates, and the hardihood of Zeno'.

The most notorious of the Cynics, Diogenes, took the idea of rejecting all conventions to its logical limit. He was not born in Athens but in the town of Sinope on the Black Sea, and lived to the age of ninety, dying in 323 BCE. This meant that he was thirteen years old when Socrates died. He was banished from Sinope for a crime which he and his father committed together – namely, debasing the town's coinage (his father ran Sinope's mint). When he arrived in Athens, Diogenes attached himself persistently to Antisthenes even though the latter did not want any pupils and tried to shake him off. One suggested origin for the name 'Cynic' – from a more positive interpretation of 'dog-like' – is Diogenes' dogged pursuit of Antisthenes, faithfully following him everywhere.

Diogenes enthusiastically embraced the idea of the simple life. Not only – again, 'dog-like' – did he perform his natural functions wherever and whenever he felt the need, including eating whenever he felt hungry, but he observed no taboos about what could be eaten, even taking food from temple sacrifices. He described himself as a *cosmopolitan*, a 'citizen of the world'. He denounced his contemporaries for their artificial lives, saying their minds were befogged or 'smoky' because of their foolish desire for status and wealth. He insisted that the goal of life should be contentment and clarity of mind (his word for which was *atuphia*, which literally means 'unsmokiness'), to be achieved through asceticism, which gives self-sufficiency, strength and therefore *ataraxia*, tranquillity. This meant living without shame and rejecting any laws of state and society which conflicted with a simple and natural life.

Others in different periods of history who, in their quest for virtue, have rejected society and its artificialities – think, for example, of the Christian hermits and anchorites – went to the desert to escape temptation. Diogenes challenged temptation right in its midst, in the rich and flourishing capital city. He and later Cynics did not take themselves into the wilderness in search of simplicity, but sought it and lived it where temptation most abounded. Their point was to challenge people to embrace the Cynic way by showing them an example of it. And they did so not just by example, but by criticizing, poking fun at, embarrassing – even horrifying – people, to get them to think.

One story says that, later on, Diogenes was kidnapped by pirates and sold into slavery at Corinth, where he was bought by a man called Xeniades who made him tutor to his sons. Here Diogenes became a much-loved member of the family, remaining with them for the rest of his life. Among many different accounts of his death, one has it that he was fatally poisoned by a dog bite – a too-obvious end for a Cynic. Although Diogenes is said to have written plays and books, his teachings are chiefly conveyed by anecdotes about his life, many of them no doubt apocryphal. One such is that Alexander the Great visited him and offered to grant him any request, to which Diogenes – whom we must imagine as curled up in his barrel with his royal visitor's shadow falling over him – replied, 'You can stand out of my sunlight.'

One might think that Diogenes had nothing to lose, given that he was a criminal exile and later a slave, by advocating and living a dog's life. The opposite is true of the next leading Cynics, Crates of Thebes and his wife, Hipparchia of Maroneia, who were both born to wealth but gave it away after they heard Diogenes lecture and witnessed his commitment. Crates described himself as a 'fellow-citizen of Diogenes' – meaning, a citizen of the world and an adherent of the Cynic way. He and Hipparchia accordingly chose to live as beggars. They came to be well known in Athens, respected for their good humour, kindness and principled stance, and were welcomed everywhere, not least in their role as soothing conciliators of family quarrels. Their version of the Cynic life was far less confrontational than Diogenes', focused more on the peace of mind achieved by freedom from conventional attitudes than on attacking people for having such attitudes.

Crates' philosophical letters were said to be as beautifully written as Plato's dialogues, but none survive. He advocated the philosophical life because, he said, it liberates you from troubles and dissatisfactions – when you have money you can share it freely; when you have none, the fact that you do not want it anyway means that you will not repine at being poor, but will be content with whatever you have. He advised a simple diet of lentils, on the grounds that luxurious living leads to strife because status and wealth are necessary to gain and maintain luxury, obliging people to compete with each other.

Crates and Hipparchia are attractive advocates of the view that the simple life is the route to happiness. It is not implausible to suppose that they succeeded in their journey because they had each other's company on the way.

Cynicism was always a minority view, even a marginal one; the Cynics were the original hippies, living an alternative lifestyle orthogonal to social norms. But it was a very long-lasting movement – there were still self-described Cynics eight centuries later, such as Sallustius of Emesa. Although some (such as Sallustius himself) were of the barking, snarling persuasion, others were more like Crates and Hipparchia – for example Demonax the Cypriot, who lived in Athens in the first century CE and, like them, became beloved for his peace-making and kindness. A distinctive fact about the school was its commitment to the equality of all people, a striking example being the way the Cynic Heraclius addressed the emperor Julian on the occasion of a discussion between them in 362 CE, prompting Julian to write in his Seventh Oration that philosophers should be more respectful.

The early Cynics disliked the aristocratic and wealthy Plato. Antisthenes charged him with pride and conceit, once saying to him, on seeing a showy horse capering in a procession, 'If you were a steed you would be just like that.' Diogenes likewise had a prickly relationship with Plato, criticizing him for attending banquets and having carpets in his house. Stamping on Plato's carpets one day, he said, 'I trample on the pride of Plato,' to which Plato responded, 'Yes, Diogenes, with pride of another kind.' There was evidently some class feeling at work in this: Plato was a well-connected member of the Athenian upper class; Antisthenes was a *nothos* or 'bastard', in the literal sense of having unmarried parents – and anyway his mother was not Athenian but a Thracian immigrant, so he was barred from Athenian citizenship. And Diogenes had, as mentioned, a somewhat dubious background in his deportation from Sinope for a criminal offence.

But philosophical commitments did not themselves follow class lines. Crates and Hipparchia began as wealthy scions of the elite, and the highly influential school that grew out of Cynicism, namely Stoicism, became the outlook of reflective people right across society, from slaves (like Epictetus) to patricians (like Seneca) to an emperor (Marcus Aurelius).

The Stoics shared with Cynics the view that happiness comes from living in agreement with nature, and that this agreement is achieved by self-mastery and discipline. The things of civilized life (wealth, possessions, status, power) have no value in nature; they are artificial products of society. False beliefs about what is important cause emotional disturbance and weakness, and are the source of unhappiness. They therefore adopted from the Cynics a commitment to continence and self-discipline, but differed markedly in that they cared about their duties to society whereas Cynics refused to engage with society. In sharing the Cynics' cosmopolitanism, a commitment to the fraternity and equality of all people, they added to it a sense of duty: if you are a citizen of the cosmos in common with all others, you cannot ignore the obligations this entails. The Cynics lived their virtues in public; the Stoics internalized them – and instead of regarding wealth and status with aversion, the Stoics treated them with indifference, in the sense that, although they recognized that most people, including themselves, would prefer to have them rather than not, they did not see the lack of them as a barrier to what really mattered, which was to live honourably, with courage towards what is inevitable or unavoidable (inevitabilities such as ageing and death; unavoidables such as earthquakes) and with self-mastery over what lies within ourselves, such as desires, appetites and fears.

Another major difference between Stoics and Cynics is that the former developed philosophical views about the nature of the universe and about logic and reason, making them a full-blown philosophical school, which Cynicism was not. The crucial aspect of Stoic metaphysics (their view of the nature of the universe) is that it is material, and that it exemplifies *logos* – this being a highly significant and heavily loaded term in Greek philosophy which literally means 'word' but by extension means 'reason', 'principle', 'what is rational', 'ordered'. Several centuries after the founding of Stoicism, its later adherents – the Roman philosophers of the imperial period, chief among them Epictetus, Seneca and Marcus Aurelius – had ceased to debate metaphysical and logical ideas, concentrating on the ethical aspects only, and at the same time interpreting *logos* as a providential agency – a god, though a rather abstract god, which was not regarded as having handed down the Stoic teachings or promised posthumous rewards if they were followed, so it was not a god in the Christian or Muslim sense. Nevertheless, Christianity – when after several centuries it found itself in need of a morality more liveable than the Gospels' 'give away all your possessions and make no plans' – found Stoicism and other Greek ethical schools a handy resource of ideas.

Stoicism's founder, Zeno, was born at Citium, a Greek colony on the island of Cyprus, in 334 BCE. He started life as a merchant, but after reading about Socrates in Xenophon's *Memorabilia* he turned his attention to philosophy. On visiting Athens he looked for a philosophy teacher, and legend has it that, just as he was asking a bookseller where he might find one, the Cynic Crates walked by and the bookseller pointed him out.

Zeno acquired from Crates his dedication to the Cynic virtues of simplicity and continence, but his modesty prevented him from public display, especially from living in the Cynic's preferred manner of 'shamelessness', so he sought to internalize the virtues instead. Besides modesty he had a strong sense of civic responsibility, and believed that one should accept one's duties as a citizen. He demonstrated the sincerity of this conviction when Athens, out of admiration for his life and teachings, offered him citizenship – a greatly prized possession – and he refused it so that he could remain loyal to his native Citium, where he had endowed the public baths and was held in high esteem.

In addition to learning from Crates, Zeno studied at the Megarian school of logic and attended philosophical discussions at the Academy, the institution founded nearly a century earlier by Plato. Cynicism inspired his ethical views, but it was from these other sources that he developed theories in logic and physics. He set up his own school in the Stoa (*stoa poikile*) – the painted colonnade of the Athenian agora – which is how his school got its name. When he died in 262 BCE his pupil and colleague Cleanthes succeeded him as head of the school. It was Cleanthes and his own successor, Chrysippus, who most thoroughly developed the logical and physical teachings of Stoicism.

But it was the ethics of Stoicism that made it such a great influence for so long, especially among Romans. The fundamental Stoic idea is that happiness consists in achieving inner equilibrium, and this in turn is achieved by 'living in accordance with nature'. What accords with nature is good – by 'good' meaning what benefits us in all circumstances, unlike things which are good only in some circumstances but not in others (as, for example, wealth; being rich might usually be a benefit but it can also cause problems). The Stoics gave the label 'indifferents' to things that are sometimes good and sometimes bad. The things that are always good are prudence, courage, moderation and justice. Given that wealth can sometimes be good, though unlike prudence it is not an unqualified good, we must distinguish between what is good *always and as such* and what can sometimes have value. One will usually prefer things which can sometimes have value over their opposites – obviously enough, health, wealth and honour are preferable to illness, poverty and dishonour – because they are usually of advantage to us, which is why we have a rational tendency to seek them. But if they interfere with what is wholly and unqualifiedly good, they are not to be preferred, and their absence will not negate what is wholly and unqualifiedly good.

The well-lived life consists in choosing those things that are unqualifiedly good, together with those things that are appropriate when consistent with what is good. The choices themselves should be governed by seeking what is in accordance with nature. We might not succeed in achieving some of the 'indifferents' which, rationally and appropriately enough, we pursue, such as wealth; but if nevertheless we have what is always good in itself – courage, prudence, moderation – we will achieve equanimity, peace of mind: *ataraxia*.

A crucial principle in this attitude is that we should master what lies within our control, in particular our appetites and fears; but as regards things we can do nothing about – for example growing old, or suffering the inflictions of illness or natural disaster – we must face them with courage. What is at stake here is the difference between action and passion: action is what we do, passion is what we undergo as recipients without a choice. To bear the passions, *pathe*, courageously means not letting them overmaster us; we must be *apathetic* with regard to them. That is the original meaning of this word. The slogan that encapsulates this principle for the Stoics is *abstine et sustine*, 'forebear, and bear'.

The ancient philosophers thought that emotions we now regard as active, such as anger and love, and which we now paradoxically call 'passions', were really indeed *passions* in the sense of passively received impositions upon us as recipients of them. Lust, for example, was thought to be an infliction, even a punishment. Because excessive passions are 'disobedient to reason' it is necessary for us to school ourselves to be ready for them, so that we can be – well, *stoical* about them.

The Athenians were immediately impressed by Zeno's teaching. The philosophies of Plato and Aristotle were technical and difficult, the Cynics were entertaining but their teachings were unliveable; here was a philosophy that made great good sense and the Athenians admired it and the man who taught it. A statue of Zeno was raised bearing the inscription 'Zeno of Citium – a man of worth – he exhorted the youth who were his pupils to virtue and temperance, affording by his own conduct a pattern in perfect accord with his teachings'. It was a popular philosophy, gaining widespread recognition and including among its admirers King Antigonus Gonatas of Macedon, who had attended Zeno's lectures in Athens as a young man and who tried unsuccessfully to get Zeno to move to Macedon to tutor his son. The ruler of Sparta, Cleomenes, introduced reforms in line with Zeno's teaching, and by the first century BCE Stoic ideas had become a significant feature in patrician education in Rome; Octavian, who became the emperor Augustus, had a Stoic tutor, Athenodorus Calvus, when he was young.

The leading Stoics of the first two centuries CE were Epictetus and Marcus Aurelius, who wrote in Greek; and before them Seneca, who wrote in Latin. Whereas Epictetus taught, and Seneca published, Aurelius' Stoicism was privately practised; he kept a diary while with his army on the dangerous Danube frontier in the years 170–180 CE. He called the diary *To Himself* (now known as the *Meditations*) and wrote it in Greek for privacy's sake (only the most educated in the Latin world knew Greek). The humanity and Stoic dedication to service exemplified in it have been admired from the time of its first publication.

It is a more striking fact than it first appears that an emperor should be a Stoic, not just because the temptations of power, wealth and luxury that wrecked the characters of lesser men such as Caligula and Nero made them bywords for the opposite of Stoic virtues, but because, in the second half of the first century CE, under the Flavian dynasty of emperors, Stoics did not hide their displeasure at their rulers' unvirtuous conduct. Eventually, in exasperation, in 93 CE the Flavian emperor Domitian banned the teaching of philosophy and banished the philosophers themselves from all Italy. That is why

Epictetus moved to Nicopolis in Greece in that year, re-establishing there the school he had founded in Rome. Domitian was assassinated in 96, and under the ensuing and successful Nerva-Antonine dynasty, of which Marcus Aurelius was a later member, philosophy returned to Rome.

As these events suggest, Stoicism was a major presence in Roman life; it was the outlook of many if not most educated Romans, chiming well with the traditional republican sense of virtues associated with Rome's rise into pre-eminence in its world. One indication of this is the esteem in which a great exponent of Stoic philosophy was held: Seneca the Younger.

Seneca – known as 'the Younger' to distinguish him from his father, who was also an author – was born at Córdoba in Spain in 4 BCE into a wealthy and talented family. His father wrote treatises on rhetoric and a (now lost) account of the period in Roman history contemporary with his own lifetime. Seneca's brother became a provincial governor, and his nephew Lucan achieved fame as a poet. Seneca the Younger himself attained greater fame than all of them, becoming first the tutor and then the advisor and – in effect – prime minister of the emperor Nero. In the first five years of Nero's reign Seneca and his colleague Sextus Afranius Burrus, prefect of the Praetorian Guard, ran a steady and effective government, but when Nero started to involve himself in affairs of state more actively, and with ill effect, Seneca's influence waned. His attempts to moderate the increasing instability and cruelty of Nero's rule failed, prompting him to try to retire on two occasions, Nero both times refusing to let him go.

Eventually, in 65 CE, Seneca was accused of involvement in a plot to assassinate Nero – the Pisonian conspiracy – and was ordered to commit suicide, a form of execution reserved to members of the senatorial class as being the most dignified. Tacitus the historian gives a graphic description of what happened; because of his age and frail health Seneca was unable to bleed to death despite cutting open several veins – the blood trickled too weakly from the wounds – so he took poison also, and eventually immersed himself in a hot bath to try to induce more haemorrhaging. Tacitus rather improbably says that, in the end, he was 'suffocated by the steam'.

Seneca was a copious writer, producing essays, moral letters, dialogues and plays, most of them published in his lifetime, all of them popular and widely read. He was deeply versed in Stoic philosophy, and applied it thoughtfully to the project of living a fortitudinous, reason-governed life. His standing as a philosophical thinker in his generation was high; there is a double-bust of him and Socrates, carved back to back out of a single block of marble, illustrating the equivalence accorded the two of them by Seneca's contemporaries. Some examples of his practical approach are these: 'No doubt troubles will come; but they are not a present fact, and might not even happen after all – why run to meet them? . . . More things make us afraid than do us harm . . . Do not be unhappy before the crisis comes . . . Some things torment us more than they ought, some torment us before they even happen; some torment us which should not torment us at all. We exaggerate, or imagine, or anticipate sorrow, unnecessarily.' These sentiments capture a central Stoic teaching that it is our own attitudes that make life good or bad, a theme often recapitulated, as in Hamlet's 'There is nothing either good or bad but thinking makes it so' and Antoine de Saint-Exupéry's 'The meaning of things lies not in things themselves, but in our attitudes to them.'

As an example of a man of staunch Stoic principles Seneca cited Cato the Younger. Cato had bitterly opposed Julius Caesar's attempt to become Rome's lifelong dictator and, when his side of the conflict was defeated, took his own life rather than lose his liberty and see the old republican virtues of Rome betrayed – these virtues very much mirroring Stoic ones. He was a famously stubborn individual, who apart from his resolute opposition to Caesar was known for his integrity and his attacks on corruption. Although born into wealth he lived austerely, training himself to endure cold and discomfort; for much of his adult life he kept privately to himself and only engaged in public affairs when circumstances obliged. Seneca admired him for preferring death to the loss of liberty, and for retaining his dignity and equanimity despite repeated defeats in seeking election to the high offices of praetorship and consulship. 'You see that man can endure toil,' Seneca wrote in one of his moral essays known as the *Letters to Lucilius*:

Cato, on foot, led an army through African deserts. You see that thirst can be endured: he marched over sun-baked hills, dragging the remains of a defeated army without supplies, suffering lack of water and wearing a heavy suit of armour. He was always the last to drink at the few springs they chanced to find. You see that honour, and dishonour too, can be despised: for it is reported that on the very day Cato was defeated in the elections, he played a game of ball. You see also that a man can be free from fear of those above him in station: for Cato attacked both Caesar and Pompey simultaneously, at a time when no one dared fall foul of one of them without trying to oblige the other. You see that death can be scorned as well as exile: Cato inflicted exile upon himself, and finally death too.[18]

Epictetus, a younger contemporary of Seneca – he was fifteen when Seneca died – was born a slave at Hierapolis in Phrygia. His name literally means 'bought' or 'owned'. He was taken to Rome as a youth, where his owner, Epaphroditos (himself a freedman – a former slave – who had been in service to the emperor Nero and had grown rich), allowed him to study philosophy with the Stoic teacher Musonius Rufus. After gaining his freedom, Epictetus set up a school of his own. He wrote nothing himself, but his teachings have been preserved in the *Discourses* and, for a more popular readership, the *Enchiridion* ('Handbook'), both written by his pupil Arrian.[19]

The two key related ideas in Epictetus are *self-knowledge* and *self-mastery*. He argued that the distinction between what is within our power and what is outside our power shows where the good is to be found – namely, within ourselves. Self-knowledge reveals to us our frailties, our liability to self-deception and weakness of will, and thus identifies for us where our efforts at living a worthy life must be directed. We have reason and freedom of choice, which together allow us to consider what is happening in our lives and to ask, 'Can I do something about this?' If the answer is 'Yes', then act; if the answer is 'No', then say, 'It is nothing to me'; this is the *apatheia*, 'apathy' in its original sense, entailed in the idea of enduring – 'being stoical about' – what is unavoidable or inevitable. This reprises the theme insisted upon by Seneca and the whole Stoic tradition, that everything turns on our attitudes, and that these lie under our own reason-guided control. As Epictetus put it, acceptance of inevitabilities is freedom; it is 'the price paid for a quiet mind'.

These ideas reflect the mature-minded attitude that won Stoicism's founder Zeno so much respect. There is, however, a tincture of something else in Epictetus, four centuries after Zeno; a tincture of fatalism, which one suspects enters with the later Stoics' interpretation of the *logos* as a kind of 'providence' or governing principle in the universe, bringing with it a motif of judgment as if by an (impersonal) god. This is suggested by Epictetus' saying (as Arrian reports): 'Ask not that events should happen as you will, but let your will be that events should happen as they do, and you shall be at peace . . . Behave in life as you would at a banquet. A dish is handed round and comes to you; put out your hand and take politely. It passes you; do not stop it. It has not reached you; do not be impatient to get it, but wait until your turn comes.' This suggests not 'apathy' in the Stoic sense, but actual passivity. More characteristic of Stoicism in its central doctrines is what Epictetus goes on to say: 'Remember that foul words and blows are no outrage in themselves; it is your judgment that they are so that makes them so. When anyone makes you angry, it is your own thought that has angered you. Therefore make sure not to let your impressions carry you away.'

Stories are told of Epictetus that illustrate the conformity of his life to his teaching. He lived with great simplicity in a hut for most of his life, though in old age, with the help of a woman who might have been a consort, he adopted and raised a child whose parents had either died or were in too great poverty to manage. He walked with a limp, as a result – so one legend has it – of having his leg broken by the son of an owner when he was a slave; the son twisted his leg more and more to see how long he would bear the suffering. The legend says that Epictetus never uttered a cry. This story is an example of how simplifications of philosophical views occur, for although Stoicism of course advocates fortitude when undergoing physical discomfort, its chief aim is to inculcate psychological fortitude, in which bearing with bodily suffering is only one and perhaps the lesser part.

Among the most graceful and inspiring expressions of Stoicism is

Marcus Aurelius' *To Himself* (the *Meditations*). It says much about Aurelius' independence of mind that two of his tutors – Herodes Atticus, who taught him Greek, and Marcus Cornelius Fronto, an expert on Latin grammar (and second only to Cicero as a Latin stylist) – were strongly opposed to his inclination to Stoicism, Atticus because he hated the Stoics and Fronto because he despised philosophy in general. Atticus and Fronto were also at odds with each other – it seems they had a bitter legal dispute at one point – though Aurelius remained friendly with Atticus, and was deeply attached to Fronto, with whom he exchanged what read like fulsome love letters, though historians are divided over whether they were actually lovers. Aurelius' Stoic teachers were Apollonius of Chalcedon and Quintus Junius Rusticus; for the latter especially he retained a lifelong admiration and profound respect. Rusticus, a grandson of one of the Stoics who had been persecuted by Domitian, was regarded as Seneca's successor as Stoicism's leading exponent. Aurelius was so attracted to Stoic principles that he found the ceremonies and luxuries of court life a burden, and he remained a student all his life – right up to his last years taking instruction from the Stoic thinker Sextus of Chaeronea, a descendent of Plutarch.

The heavy task of administering a great empire, and the constant military demands along its borders, make it no surprise that Aurelius died relatively young, aged only fifty-eight. But he was sustained throughout by his philosophy. The *Meditations* were written not as instruction to others but, exactly as their earlier title has it, to himself; it was a work of self-adjuration, self-encouragement, an expression of continuous resolve to fortify himself to his duties by taking the right attitudes to what confronted him. As we will see in a later chapter, the book records his *practice* of philosophy – exercises in philosophical self-fortification and advice, like the 'spiritual exercises' of Jesuits and others, centuries later.[20]

The *Meditations* opens with Aurelius recalling the principal lessons he learned from his Stoic teachers. Rusticus, who introduced him to the teachings of Epictetus, had encouraged him to look within and understand himself better – not least his failings – and 'to read with diligence, not to rest satisfied with a light and superficial knowledge,

nor quickly to assent to things commonly spoken of'. From Apollonius he said he learned 'true liberty, and unvariable steadfastness', to
pay attention only to the claims of reason and what is right, and to be
'the same man' through all experiences whether good or bad. He lists
also lessons learned from his father and brother and from friends and
colleagues, and acknowledges the good fortune surrounding his start
in life.

Thereafter the *Meditations* consists in exercises of instruction and
admonishment to himself, for example to remind himself when he
wakes each morning that he is sure to meet someone that day who
through ignorance of the good is 'unthankful, a railer, a crafty, false
or envious man', but that he must remember that this transgressor is
his kinsman 'not by blood and seed, but by participation of the same
reason' (this is the Stoic principle of the kinship and equality of
humanity), and that nothing such a person can do will harm him if he
does not let it.[21]

As all the foregoing shows, there is nothing merely theoretical
about Stoic ethics. For the Stoics philosophy was a practical matter,
aimed at guiding conduct and maintaining personal standards. They
argued that self-understanding and a clear-eyed, dispassionate grasp
of how things are in the world is liberating because it puts the means
of happiness into our own hands: we can choose *apatheia* towards
what we cannot influence while rationally governing our own feelings. Cicero, who although a follower of the Academy was attracted
to aspects of Stoicism in ethics, found a striking way to encapsulate
the outlook by citing one of Socrates' observations: 'To learn to
philosophize,' he wrote, 'is to learn how to die,' meaning that a right
understanding of death frees one from the fear of it, therefore enabling one to live courageously and autonomously; for whoever is
unafraid of death is ultimately and completely free, always having an
escape from anything intolerable. Freedom from anxiety and fear,
and from useless hankering after what one cannot have, is happiness.

But generalizations are never enough by themselves. Seneca sensi-
bly remarked that practical examples and precepts are necessary to
show how Stoic principles can be applied in particular instances,
hence his reason for citing Cato as an example of a Stoic in action.

For Aurelius the question of how to treat others was provided by the metaphor of the cosmos as a city in which all human beings are fellow citizens, which means that considerations of *justice* will guide us. Correlatively, bad actions are those that run counter to the interests of the cosmopolis. The justification for this view is drawn from the Stoics' 'live according to nature' precept, in this case because in the same way as it is natural to care about the welfare of one's family, so is it natural to treat everyone well because all people are kin – all people are one's family too: 'the brotherhood of man'.

In the eighth book of the *Meditations* Aurelius summarizes the central Stoic tenets by which he lived: 'Every nature is satisfied with itself when it goes along its path well, and the rational nature does this when it assents to nothing false or unclear among its impressions, when it directs impulses to communal actions, when it generates desires and inclinations for only those things that are in our power, and when it welcomes everything apportioned to it by common nature.' The only slight novelty in this formulation is the idea that good actions are those that promote the common good, but this is a novelty of expression not of doctrine; no Stoic would regard actions that do not promote the common good as acceptable. No doubt because he was an emperor, Aurelius thought in collective terms; other Stoics focused principally on the individual.

Stoicism and its partial parent Cynicism stemmed directly from one aspect of Socrates' example, this being his indifference to convention, his hardiness and simplicity of life, and his adherence to principle. Admiration for these qualities inspired Antisthenes and his Cynic followers, and it inspired Zeno of Citium and the many who adopted his Stoic views. A different aspect of Socrates' outlook was the inspiration, in rather different ways, for two other great schools of thought: his commitment to reason, his demand that people *think*, his challenge to live the 'considered life'. One was the Peripatetic school of Aristotle, the other Epicureanism. Some commentators point out that Epicurus was more influenced by Democritus and the Atomists than by Socrates, and as regards Epicurus' physics, which have an important bearing on his ethics, this is true. But in advocating a considered life Epicurus is very much in the tradition of the example set by Socrates.

Aristotle's commitment to the idea that reason is the dominating human characteristic, and that a good life – the considered life – is one based on reason, is quintessentially Socratic. Aristotle's ethical theory is closely connected with his political theory because he believed that discussion about the best kind of life has to proceed in tandem with discussion about what kind of society is best for individuals to live in. The ethical aspect of his views has proved more enduringly interesting than their political aspect, but it is informative to see how these two facets of what Aristotle called 'practical philosophy' connect.

It is also informative to see how Aristotle reasoned. He begins by clarifying the concept of the 'end' – the *telos*, 'goal, purpose, aim' – of any activity. The goal of a gunsmith is to make guns, and the production of a gun is thus the 'end' (in both senses) of his activity. But to a soldier the gun is merely instrumental to a different end, which is fighting and conquering his enemy. Soldierly activity, in turn, is instrumental to the ruler's more inclusive goal, which is to defend the state. The ruler tells the soldier whom to fight, and the soldier tells the gunsmith what he requires of a gun. The ruler's art is directed at the highest end in this particular sequence – namely, protection of the state. What the gunsmith and the soldier do, each working to achieve his own more specific end, is instrumental to this highest end. Accordingly, Aristotle describes politics as the highest art, aimed at the overall flourishing of society. Note that by 'politics' Aristotle specifically meant statecraft, the art of government, of running a good *polis*, not party-politicking; today the terms 'politics' and 'statecraft' no longer mean the same.

Among the various arts that help to achieve the flourishing of society is education. Education, for Aristotle, is about forming character; recall that the Greek word for 'character' is *ethos*. Character is the combination of moral and intellectual qualities which together make a person what he or she is. Ethical theory, therefore, is enquiry into what constitutes the best kind of character, because people with the best kind of character will live the best kind of lives.

Aristotle's method was to consider commonly held views about things and the disagreements that arise about them, and to work out a way of resolving the disagreements. In his *Nicomachean Ethics* he begins by observing that everything people do – carpentry, writing books, growing vegetables, governing a state – aims at achieving whatever counts as a good outcome for the pursuit in question. This means that there are as many different kinds of good outcomes as there are things people do. Each pursuit requires various subsidiary goods to be achieved first – to build a house, one must make bricks and dig foundations, and each of these has to be done well so that the house itself will be well built. Each good outcome in brick-making or foundation-digging serves the purpose of achieving the higher good of a satisfactory house.

So, what is the *supreme good*, the ultimate overall good, which all subordinate goods serve? Aristotle points out that the supreme good will be what is desired absolutely for its own sake and not as a means to anything beyond itself. What end or goal is desired only for its own sake? This is *the* key question; but in fact there is, he says, 'very widespread agreement' about the answer: 'both the general run of people and those of superior refinement concur in saying that the highest good is *happiness*'. ('Happiness' is a rather inadequate translation for the term Aristotle uses, namely *eudaimonia*, which is better translated as 'well-being and well-doing', 'flourishing'.)

But then, alas, people disagree about what 'happiness' is. Some say it consists in having wealth, others nominate honour, others again talk of pleasure. Moreover people's opinions vary according to how things are with them; the pauper says wealth is happiness, the sick person says it is health.

However, even just a little thought shows that wealth, health, honour and pleasure are not ends in themselves; they are in fact instrumental to whatever is genuinely the highest good. This highest good is indeed *eudaimonia*, which is not to be identified with any individual instrumental end. Instead, Aristotle says, it will be what is attained when we live in accordance with the 'function of human beings'.

So what is the 'function of human beings'? In his customary

manner Aristotle formulates an answer by using analogies. What makes a good lawyer? Someone skilled in legal practice. What makes a good doctor? Someone who cures or cares for her patients well. Each is 'good' because she does her work – performs her function – well. To do her work well is the virtue or excellence (*arête*) of a lawyer qua lawyer or doctor qua doctor. What is the *arête* of a human being qua human being? Answer: it is to do the 'work of being human' well – and the 'work' of a human being is to live according to what is both distinctive about and defining of humanity; namely, the possession and exercise of reason. A fully human person is one who lives and acts rationally. Implicit here is the idea that a person who acts according to instincts and appetites merely, without thought, is not living up to the potential of being human, because she is governed by the same impulses as direct other animals, and therefore lives no differently from them.

But a *good* person does not only act rationally, she acts 'rationally in accordance with virtue', Aristotle says. Now, therefore, we must understand what *virtue* is. He tells us there are two kinds of virtue: one of mind, namely wisdom or prudence; and three of character, namely courage, temperance and justice. Everyone[22] is born with the capacity to develop the various virtues belonging to these four categories, but this depends on education – on acquiring good habits in childhood with the eventual aim, on attaining maturity, of consistently being wise in practical matters. By 'good habits' Aristotle meant a settled disposition to feel and act in ways appropriate to circumstances, an important point for him because, given the phenomenon of *akrasia*, 'weakness of will', he could not agree with the Socratic claim that 'virtue is knowledge'. Aristotle says *akrasia* is caused by ungoverned emotions, which is why acquiring habits of self-discipline is important.

Aristotle's next question concerns how to identify what is virtuous on any given occasion. The answer is that virtue is the middle path or 'mean' between opposing vices, one being a vice of deficiency and the other a vice of excess. Thus, courage is the mean between cowardice (deficiency) and rashness (excess); generosity is the mean between meanness (deficiency) and profligacy (excess). The lawyer and the doctor know how to steer a middle course between the deficiencies and excesses that would spoil their efforts; likewise anyone can acquire what resembles their technical skill in knowing how to steer between vicious extremes whose mean is the appropriate virtue.

Is there a general, invariable rule about the middle path in all cases? No; individual circumstances determine what the mean is. Take gentleness; you might think that, as a virtue, gentleness implies never being angry, and that staying calm in the face of – for example – injustice is the mean between anger and indifference in response to it. But Aristotle says that anger is sometimes justified; to be angry 'in the right way, to the right degree, for the right reason' is in fact virtuous. (But of course not to such an extent that it overthrows reason.)

In Aristotle's view 'virtue makes the goal right, practical wisdom teaches how to reach it'. Character-forming habits will help us to recognize the right goals, and if we do not – or do not yet – know how to recognize them or have the practical wisdom to know how to reach them, we must follow the example of those who do have such wisdom.

Aristotle was realistic enough to concede that luck plays its part in living a virtuous life, for those in fortunate circumstances generally find it easier to achieve *eudaimonia* than those who have to struggle with poverty, illness or oppression. But, as Primo Levi and Viktor Frankl showed millennia later in their remarkable writings about experiences among victims of the Holocaust, the exercise of virtue is possible even in appalling circumstances.[23]

It would be a mistake to regard Aristotle's 'doctrine of the mean' as entailing that every goal is a mere compromise. The doctrine is about how to act appropriately, not about seeking halfway houses. The critics who say that Aristotle's 'middle way' is by its very nature 'middle-class, middle-aged and middle-brow' are confusing action with outcome. Reflecting on the best course of action in a given situation, taking all its details into account, is aimed at achieving the best outcome; but the best outcome is not necessarily whatever is intermediate between the possible outcomes associated with either of the flanking extremes. For example: suppose someone in need asks you for money. The flanking extremes are to give him nothing and to give him everything you have – or at least, to give him simultaneously 'more than he needs and more than you can spare'. If you misunderstand Aristotle's doctrine of the mean you might conclude that however much money you have, you should give him *half* of it. That might be appropriate if you only have a little, but not if you have a lot – though in the latter case, to match the generosity exemplified in the former case you would have to give him quite a bit.

Aristotle said that human beings are 'political animals' – that is, beings for whom it is natural and right to live together in communities. He thought of the polis, a small self-governing community – small enough for the town crier to be heard from one end to the other – as the ideal setting for human flourishing, provided that the community was a cooperative and harmonious one. But for Aristotle life in the polis was not the absolute best; the absolute best life was a life of contemplation, the philosophical life. Whereas a citizen's life in the polis is a life of activity and business, a philosopher's life is one dedicated to thinking, to enquiry, and thus a life lived in accordance with *the* distinguishing feature of humanness – the exercise of reason.

It follows from this view, for Aristotle, that a good state will provide opportunities for leisure so that people can discuss and meditate, not relying for their happiness on minor instrumental desiderata such as status and material possessions, but on personal independence and the exercise of intellect, which is the purest of pleasures. That is the real reason why we educate ourselves, Aristotle says; it is so that we can make 'a noble use of our leisure'.

These points illustrate again why Aristotle connected ethics with politics. In his *Politics* he argues that the original reason why the polis came into existence was 'to ensure that men might live' by benefiting from mutual aid and protection. But then, as the polis matured, its point became 'to ensure that men might live *well*'. He meant that it is in the circumstances of a flourishing state that people can have the opportunity to develop their intellectual interests, thereby giving them what makes life most worthwhile.

Aristotle would be hard-pressed to deny that a life of contemplation would be pleasant. The pleasure enjoyed in such a life would be an inseparable aspect of its point. But pleasure merely as such could not *be* the point, on his view, because then the life of a well-situated pig – that is, one with plenty of mud to wallow in and plenty of swill to eat – would be a *good life* in the best philosophical sense. And yet, on the basis of reason, a view that appears to accept just such a conclusion was the chief rival both to Stoicism and to Aristotle's ethics. That view is Epicureanism.

In fact Epicureanism's commitment to the idea that the best life is one in which pleasure is pursued and pain avoided is not at all what such a blunt statement of it suggests. Instead the 'pig' criticism would apply to the view known as Cyrenaicism. Founded in the fourth century BCE by Aristippus of Cyrene, this school promoted the active search for pleasure, especially physical pleasure – food, drink, sex – to be enjoyed in the moment, right *now* and to the full, because present pleasure is a vastly stronger experience than pleasure remembered or anticipated. Epicureans regarded Cyrenaicism's pleasures as a source of pain, given the degree of indulgence it extolled. Remarkably, Aristippus had been a pupil of Socrates, and appears to have fastened onto an observation made by the latter that pleasure is a secondary good, which encourages one to seek other and higher goods. Reflecting on this, Aristippus decided that, just as current perceptual experience is the only guaranteed source of truth, so current experience in general is the only reality. Given that pleasurable current experience is greatly preferable to unpleasant current experience, it follows that what is good is currently experienced pleasure. He said there is no general or overall goal for life; there is only a particular goal for each particular thing we do, and this is to get the greatest degree of pleasure from it. The Cyrenaics therefore rejected the Epicurean view of pleasure as *aponia*, 'absence of pain', saying this is the condition of a corpse. And they rejected the Epicurean view that the pleasures and pains of mind are greater than physical ones.

Aristippus' daughter Arete and her son, Aristippus the Younger, promoted this view, and the outlook gained a following – although not as large or as long-lasting as that of the more refined philosophy of Epicureanism.

Epicurus was born at Samos in 341 BCE, and came to Athens at the age of eighteen when he and the island's other Athenian colonists were expelled following the death of Alexander the Great. He studied with Nausiphanes, a pupil of Democritus the Atomist, before going first to Mytilene and then Lampsacus, in each place gathering pupils and developing his ideas. Eventually he returned to Athens and bought a garden as a site for his school, living there with his pupils until his death at the age of seventy-one. His school was known as the Garden accordingly.

Epicurus, who shared Aristotle's empiricism and pragmatism, was greatly influenced by Democritus' atomistic physics, which he saw as having deep ethical implications. Atomism is the view that all reality consists of material atoms (*atomos* means 'uncuttable' or 'indivisible'); for Democritus, atoms were the smallest components of matter, their combinations and interactions as they swirled in the void giving rise to all the phenomena of perceived reality.[24] Epicurus accordingly took as his starting point the idea that atoms and the void are all that there is, and argued that this fact removes any reason to fear either death or what superstition calls 'fate'.

Diogenes Laërtius devoted an entire book of his *Lives of the Philosophers* to Epicurus, quoting extensively from three letters in which Epicurus summarized his views. Other sources for his philosophy are collections of his sayings; documents preserved in the library of the Epicurean philosopher Philodemus (found under the Vesuvian ashes at Herculaneum); and Lucretius' superb poem *De Rerum Natura* ('On the Nature of Things'), which gives a comprehensive account of Epicurean theory.[25]

Lucretius' poem is a verse adaptation of Epicurus' book *On Nature*, since lost. Cicero, writing in the same era as Philodemus and Lucretius – the first century BCE – subjected the Epicurean philosophy to a critical examination in his *De Finibus*, *De Natura Deorum* and *Tusculan Disputations*. The reputation of Epicureanism in the Hellenic and Roman imperial periods is demonstrated by the fact that its chief teachings were inscribed for public benefit on the wall of a portico in the Lycran city of Oenoanda, placed there in the second century CE.

One of the striking things about Diogenes Laërtius' life of Epicurus is the detailed report it contains of the hostile attacks he suffered at the hands of his enemies. He was accused of practising magic and casting spells for a fee, writing scandalous letters, consorting with prostitutes, flattering influential people and plagiarizing other philosophers; of devoting himself to luxury and sensuality even to the point of bulimia – self-inducing vomiting so that he could keep on eating large quantities when at a feast – and being so enfeebled by excess that he could scarcely get out of his chair; and of insulting other philosophers such as Aristotle and Heraclitus, accusing Aristotle of wasting his inheritance and making money by selling drugs, and describing Heraclitus as a 'muddler'.

Diogenes Laërtius was an admirer of Epicurus. He wrote that those who said these things about Epicurus were 'mad' because all other sources testified to his kindness, goodwill, generosity, gentleness, consideration for others, humility, restraint and frugality, and that the moderation of the Garden's lifestyle was famous. Part at least of the hostility felt by Epicurus' enemies doubtlessly arose from his rejection of religion, and in confusing his 'pursuit of pleasure and avoidance of pain' principle with Cyrenaic ideas.

The real meaning of Epicurus' doctrine is explained by clarifying its source. The Atomist theory accepted by Epicurus says that perception (seeing, hearing, tasting, touching) arises reliably from the interaction between the atoms constituting the world and the atoms constituting our sense organs. It follows from the fact that the world is wholly physical that there are no non-physical souls or minds (the word for both is the same: *anima*). Our bodies and minds affect each other, which could not occur, Epicurus pointed out, if they were not made of the same stuff. When the body dies, the atoms constituting the mind are dispersed, and thought and sensation accordingly cease; there is no life after death. This was a key point for Epicurus. Because death is the end, there is nothing to fear about it. 'Death is nothing to us,' he wrote, 'for good and evil imply sentience, and death is the cessation of all sentience.'

Epicurus' view that 'the alpha and omega of a blessed life' is pleasure – that 'pleasure is our first and native good' – has given rise to the modern meaning of 'Epicureanism' as 'luxurious indulgence in the pleasures of the senses' because of an erroneous interpretation of what he meant by these remarks. For immediately after them he went on to say:

> We often pass over many pleasures when a greater annoyance arises from them, and we often regard certain pains as preferable to pleasures when as a result they bring a greater pleasure to us later . . . We regard being independent of outward things as a great good, not in order to be content with little but so that we are not inconvenienced when we do not have much; for they most enjoy luxury who have no need of it, and we know that what is natural is easily procured, while only vain and worthless things are hard to get. Plain food gives as much pleasure as a costly diet, bread and water confer the highest pleasure when conveyed to hungry lips . . . To habituate ourselves to a simple and inexpensive diet supplies all that is needful for health, and enables us to meet all life's necessities without shrinking.

These ideas are encapsulated in the Epicureans' classification of desires into three kinds: those that are natural and necessary, such as eating, sleeping and friendships; those that are natural but not necessary, such as sex; and those that are both unnatural and unnecessary, the principal examples of which include wealth, power and status. The Epicureans point out that efforts to acquire these latter are stressful, causing anxiety and problems, which are easily avoided by rejecting them as goals.

The definition of pleasure as 'the end and aim' of life is accordingly this: 'We do not mean the pleasures of profligacy or sensuality, we mean the absence of pain in the body and trouble in the mind; what produces a pleasant life is sober reasoning, searching out the grounds of every choice, and banishing those things that cause anxiety and fear.' Understanding the nature of the world is what underwrites this rational view; when we know that the universe is a material realm we are no longer afraid – as Lucretius puts it in his poem – of 'our foes' religion and superstition, but instead base our views on reason and a clear understanding of reality.

The Epicurean view, therefore, is that pleasure is *the absence of pain and anxiety*. The absence of physical pain, *aponia*, and the absence of psychological pain, *ataraxia*, 'peace of mind', yield the happiness that comes from a life of reason, because reason dispels the various irrational fears that disturb us and directs us to courses of life that keep us healthy. To do wrong is to burden ourselves with guilt and worry about reprisals; to eat and drink too much is to invite the discomforts that overindulgence brings; to live an unhealthy life is soon to suffer the pains that result. So the 'pursuit of pleasure' is the pursuit of moderation, continence, a rationally chosen way of life. Sobriety, friendship and discussion are among the central components of the good life, and the greatest liberation comes from realizing that death is not an evil. Inscribed on the gravestones of many of Epicurus' followers is his saying 'I did not exist, then I existed, now I exist no more; I am untroubled' (in Latin the saying more succinctly reads *non fui, fui, non sum, non curo*). The Epicurean prescription for happiness is summed up in the *tetrapharmakos*, the 'fourfold remedy': 'religion presents no fears, death is no cause for alarm, it is easy to pursue what is good, it is easy to endure what is evil'. The first two points follow from the Epicureans' view that the universe is material. The third point is true if one is willing to live on little and with little, for here the truth that 'he is rich who has enough and desires no more' plays its part. And the final point is true also, for if one has given few hostages to fortune in the way of debts and commitments, and has lived soberly and healthily, and above all if one tranquilly accepts that death – as the ultimate palliation even for the worst conceivable ills and sufferings – is nothing to fear, then one is safe from evils because one can readily escape them.

Aristotle placed a very high value on friendship, *philia*, and Epicurus shared that view, regarding it as the source of one of the greatest pleasures.[26] He saw the growth of individual friendships as recapitulating the evolution of society; in the beginning people were solitary creatures, but over the course of time they formed families and communities. The idea prefigures Locke's and Rousseau's theories of civil society's emergence from a 'state of nature'. In a way that more closely anticipates Rousseau, Epicurus argued that the benefits of cooperation eventually came to be negated by the fact that, because of society's increasing complexity, kings and tyrants appeared, and religion, and fears of punishment. But the true source of justice lies in recognizing the mutual benefit that arises from keeping promises and honouring agreements, and because a prudent and honourable life is the most pleasant one. In utopian mood – though it is hard to disagree – Epicurus held that if everyone lived by this ideal there would be no tyrannies, and no need of religion to act as a kind of police agency, because life in society, and society itself, would be good.

For Epicurus, the chief purpose of philosophy is to help people understand what the best kind of life is, and why it is so. It is both an education and a therapy for the soul. 'If philosophy does not heal the soul,' he said, 'it is as bad as a medicine that does not heal the body.' Rational reflection leading to moderation and the enjoyment of what gives real and lasting pleasure is liberating, and what it liberates us into is tranquillity. 'Neither drinking-parties nor continual revelling, nor the enjoyment of boys and girls, or fish and all that a lavish table can offer, can provide a life of pleasure – only sober reason.' The continence of Epicurus prompted Nietzsche to remark in his *Human, All Too Human*, 'A little garden, some figs, a piece of cheese, plus three or four good friends – that was the sum of Epicurus' extravagances.'[27]

Epicureanism was at its most popular and widespread during the first several centuries of the first millennium CE. The austere and conservative Stoics were disdainful of it, Cynics thought it was a soft option, and when Christianity became dominant from the late fourth century onwards their vigorously hostile attitude to it – conflating it either ignorantly or propagandistically with Cyrenaicism – sent it into eclipse. Following its recovery in the Renaissance it again exerted influence: on John Locke, Denis Diderot, Voltaire, Thomas Jefferson, Jeremy Bentham, Karl Marx, Nietzsche, and others. Catherine Wilson, a leading scholar of the history of ideas, has convincingly argued that Epicureanism lay at the foundations of modernity in the seventeenth and eighteenth centuries, by prompting the revival of atomistic physics, criticism of superstition and religion, and focus on the possibility of a good life in this world rather than relying on promises of felicity in an afterlife.[28] In his admiring article on Epicurus in the *Encyclopédie*, Diderot describes him as 'the only one of all the ancient philosophers who knew how to reconcile his moral code with what he understood to be man's true happiness, and his precepts with the appetites and requirements of nature. He therefore had and will have at all times a great number of disciples. One can become a Stoic, but one is born an *Epicurean*.' Examples of the influence of Epicurean sentiment on outlooks in and since the Enlightenment are easy to find. The characters in Voltaire's *Candide* bring their tumultuous adventures to a peaceful close by cultivating a garden, while Llewelyn Powys is an explicit Epicurean in the full sense of the term; so almost certainly (even if unconsciously) are many others today, at least by general tendency – which is to say that they would be Epicureans if they were made aware of the irrationality of much of what troubles them.

It is useful to take a moment to reflect on the survey just given. The multiple and diverging influence of Socrates apparent in it is striking. Within a century of Socrates' death in 399 BCE all the major schools of ethics had come into existence: chronologically, the Cynicism of Antisthenes and the Cyrenaicism of Aristippus, Aristotle's Peripatos, Epicurus' Garden, and the Stoicism of Epicurus' younger contemporary Zeno of Citium. Note that the first two movements, both of them rejecting convention and opposing social norms, were radical inheritors of aspects of Socrates' life and teaching and, perhaps more to the point, were radical responses to the society that Socrates himself had challenged and which had therefore put him to death. Aristotle was not as impressed by Socrates as were others – and as was his teacher Plato – when he met with the legend of the man on beginning his studies at the Academy thirty or so years after Socrates' death. This was doubtless because of Socrates' lack of interest in science and his scepticism about whether humankind would ever profit from studying it. If Aristotle lived today he would almost certainly be a scientist, probably a biologist, so he did not find this attitude endearing. Nevertheless, he wholeheartedly agreed with what Plato had learned from Socrates: the supreme importance of reason. Socrates' motivating idea was that the chief task of philosophy is to provide a rational basis for an individual's happiness. The idea of a 'rational foundation' for life is opposed to the view that there are non-rational (including irrational) foundations: emotional feelings, superstitious beliefs, divine commandments, tradition, ancestors, romantic appeals to the tribe, race, blood, nation, history, a *Führerprinzip*, all of which have been (and still are) invoked as a reason for regarding one sort of life, one set of values, as better than others. All the ethical schools after Socrates sought a rational foundation for life; they are all examples of answers to Socrates' question.

One thing to note about Aristotle's ethical theory is that it is both practical and realistic. He acknowledged that happiness is vulnerable to misfortune and chance, luck playing a significant part in life; that virtue can be learned but also lost; that to become possessed of 'practical wisdom' requires learning and experience; that those who cannot be wise on their own account should follow the example of those who are wise. His pragmatism and common sense are here on full display. But aspects of this view, not least its 'middle way' method of choosing the right thing to do in any given situation, drew – as mentioned earlier – the criticism that it is a 'middle-class, middle-brow, middle-aged' conservative philosophy, an opinion reinforced by Aristotle's picture of the ethical man: namely, the stately and self-composed megalopsychos who walks with unhurried step. The rather alarming-looking term *megalopsychos* means 'great-souled', and we get 'magnanimous' in English from it via Latin's *magna anima*. Our contemporary idea of magnanimity is an attractive one, so this could be a saving feature of Aristotle's view, though it is again tempered by the fact that the constituency to which he specifically addressed his views – populated by those he thought best capable of profiting from them – was restricted to male citizens, where 'citizen' meant a legitimate member of a polis; not an immigrant, slave, illegitimate offspring or foreigner. So, at its harshest, the criticism someone might today make of the Aristotelian view is that it is racist or at least xenophobic, sexist and conservative, even reactionary. Without contextualization this is of course anachronistic – except as regards the universally applicable truth about the position of women in his society (as in practically all societies in all recorded history) – because it looks down the wrong end of the telescope at what he is seeking to say. His ideal is a community (the polis) comprised of responsible, thoughtful members who *think* about what to do when faced with making a choice, which is what constitutes them as ethical individuals because they are thereby living in conformity with the fact that possession of intelligence is the distinguishing feature – the essence – of being human.

For Cynics, Epicureans and Stoics alike, as well as for Aristotle, a highly significant feature of Socrates' thought was that *eudaimonia comes from within*. A commonplace before Socrates was that justice consists in obeying rules, whether divine or human, and that happiness accrues from receiving the gods' approval for doing so. But it is an obvious empirical fact that the reward of happiness does not reliably follow from obeying the rules, whoever makes them; indeed it seems haphazard whether or not obedience to the gods is attended by *eudaimonia*. The only way to ensure one's own happiness, so Xenophon in his *Memorabilia* records Socrates as saying, is by achieving it through self-mastery and resilience. Diogenes Laërtius describes Crates the Cynic as 'most like Socrates' as Xenophon portrays the latter in that book; Zeno of Citium likewise claimed direct intellectual descent from Socrates in this depiction of him. The importance of this aspect of Socrates' example is indirectly illustrated by Plato's remark about Diogenes: that he was 'Socrates gone mad'. What Plato perhaps overlooked is that living a Cynic or, to a not much lesser extent, Stoic life takes a great deal of self-command and a constant exertion of effort.

Indeed here lies the most problematic aspect of all the ethical schools' teachings: their commitment to the idea that by schooling and then consistently applying one's inner individual resources of character, one can be invulnerable to the contingencies of life. This is at best a tall order, especially in the first period – perhaps many years – of seeking to live by the principles in question. But it is not impossible, and the many examples of individuals cited by the likes of Seneca, Diogenes Laërtius and others as exemplary in their philosophical lives is proof enough.

The chief point to note is that what Socrates represents, through the Socratic Question and these various responses to it, is a tremendously significant moment in the development of humanity. Because of the anchor dropped by the world's young religions – Christianity and Islam – the voyage Socrates set going has been much hampered and delayed, and therefore we are still only at the beginning of it. But the anchor chains are rusted through, and the tide might at last be right to set full sail – each of us his or her own captain.

The Chinese and Indian philosophical traditions are also rich in suggestions about how the Socratic Question might be answered.[29] In the Chinese case it is not the major philosophical schools, Confucianism and Legalism, which do this, because they are chiefly interested in socio-political theory, in which individuals are considered almost exclusively as inseparable components of collectives (society and family), which are therefore the units of interest in these outlooks.[30] Instead, in Chinese philosophy it is Mohism and especially Daoism to which one looks for suggestions about how to live.

In Indian thought a central theme of the major schools, whether orthodox (*astika*) or heterodox (*nastika*) – this distinction turning on the degree to which respect is paid to the earliest texts of Indian culture, the Vedas – is that the world is an illusion, that desire and attachment to this illusory world is the source of suffering, and that the aim of both enquiry and practice is to escape the cycle of rebirth and thus achieve nirvana. *Nirvana* literally means 'extinction', as when a candle is snuffed out, though it is controversial whether it means actual annihilation or instead absorption – perhaps blissful – into whatever constitutes ultimate reality. But either way it means the end of the ego and personal consciousness. The heterodox schools of Buddhism and Jainism are the best-known workings-out of this idea from a Western point of view.[31]

The founder of China's Mohist school, Mozi, was a direct contemporary of Socrates. His teaching rests on two principles. The first is benevolent concern for others, which he called 'brotherly love'. Its absence causes harm; 'all the disorder in the world' arises from the lack of it, whether between members of a family, between rulers and people, or between one state and another. His second principle is the utilitarian-anticipating idea that our actions should be based on a comparison of the benefits and the deficits that might follow from them. Applying this rule makes life more rational. One example he gives concerns mourning; in Mozi's day, observance of obsequies for deceased parents included not working for three years. Reflection on the benefits or otherwise of this practice, given the responsibilities one might have to living family members, suggests that other ways of honouring the dead could be better.

We are to 'elevate the worthy individual' and 'follow the standard he sets', according to Mozi – a suggestion rather like Aristotle's advice to follow the example of the man of practical wisdom until we are ourselves wise. One reason is that when people of high standards run the government, society is more apt to flourish. This is because they will exercise 'impartial concern', which means equal consideration for all, thus promoting harmony. Mozi associates this with a further principle, 'seek peace' (in the specific sense of avoiding resort to aggression, not least military aggression), as a way of solving problems, for the obvious reason that the disadvantages flowing from conflict are much more likely to outweigh the benefits, and anyway in the case of actual war the motivation is almost always lust for wealth and power, which is unworthy.

'When we enquire into the causes of harms, what do we find?' Mozi asks. 'Do they come from loving others and trying to benefit them? Certainly not! They come, rather, from hating others and trying to injure them. Such actions are motivated by partiality and selfishness, and this gives rise to all the great harms in the world.'

There is a flavour of familiarity about these doctrines, heightened when one sees what Mozi described as the alternative to them – namely an anarchic situation in which people think only of themselves and disregard, even trample upon, the interests of others; a situation which in the worst case resembles Hobbes' 'nasty and brutish' state of nature where life is a 'war of all on all'. In Hobbes' view the answer is to set up an all-powerful authority that can repress and control the selfish propensities that threaten society.[32] In Mozi's view, the answer is to promote mutual concern by 'elevating the worthy' and sharing high standards. Obviously enough, trying for the latter while prudently arranging for the former is how most societies in fact manage.

Note that Mozi made his appeal to individuals, focusing on what their attitudes and practices should be, convinced that private virtue conduces to public good. That appears to be a reasonable assumption until one recalls Bernard Mandeville's *Fable of the Bees*, in which the argument is that private *vices* conduce to public good.[33] This is not just because consumption and excess stimulate economic activity – butchers and wine merchants benefit from greed; lawyers earn fees from prosecuting or defending criminals; doctors earn fees from patients with the diseases of overindulgence – but because the greed and suspicion of individuals, their mutual envy and competitiveness, obliges them to maintain a socio-legal system in which hypocritical adherence to seeming virtue maintains, so Mandeville argues, the social structure.

Mohist ethics, not least because of its somewhat wistful idealism, is an attractive and sympathetic outlook; so too, though in a rather different way, is Daoism (once written 'Taoism'[34]). Readers might recognize the aphorism 'The world is won by those who let it go; when you try and try, the world is beyond winning.' Zen Buddhism (in China called Chan Buddhism) likewise recommends this attitude – it is in effect the technique of not concentrating on the methodology of whatever you are doing, because self-consciousness is inhibiting, but instead of just 'going with the flow'. It works well for sporting activities, but it is of doubtful value in a surgical operation or the cockpit of a jet airliner. But in any case, this idea could well have been derived from Daoism, the philosophy of the Way (*dao* means 'way') because this is precisely Daoism's central tenet.

In fact several Chinese movements invoke the concept of a Way. Confucius, for example, spoke of the Way that leads to becoming a 'superior man', *ren*, but this is nothing like the Daoists' conception. For these latter the Way is what leads to tranquillity, detachment, escape from the futile demands and restraints of society. It is very like Cynicism in this respect, without the 'shamelessness' of a Diogenes. The text regarded as central to this outlook is the *Daodejing* (*Tao Te Ching*), sometimes also named for its supposed author, Laozi (a name that literally means 'Old Master').

Laozi is either a legendary figure, as indeed his name suggests, or he was a man called Lao Dan who lived in the sixth century BCE and was – according to some traditions – a teacher of Confucius. Some proponents of Daoism claimed that their teachings originated in the remotest antiquity, attributing them to the Yellow Emperor whom fable placed in the third millennium BCE as the founder of Chinese civilization. Sima Qian, author of the *Records of the Grand Historian*, says that Confucius was awed by Laozi, calling him a 'dragon' (dragons being the grandest of China's mythological creatures). From early pre-Han times Confucianism and Daoism were regarded as rival – indeed opposed – outlooks, a view promoted by the later Daoist classic the *Zhuangzi*, which in the course of extolling Daoism's relaxed flexibility of outlook remarks that Confucius lacked this quality.

Scholars have shown that the *Daodejing* is a compilation from a multiplicity of authors, just as is the Judaeo-Christian bible. It provides the core of a set of ideas called *daode* (literally 'the virtue way' – *de* means 'virtue', also 'power', 'potency') and Sima Qian gives the name *Daojia* to those who lived by these ideas – *jia* meaning 'family' or 'tribe'. A number of *Daojia* emerged over time, now distinguished from one another by such labels as 'Huang-Lao' (a term combining the names of the Yellow Emperor, Huang, and Laozi) 'philosophical Daoism', 'religious Daoism', and several more. But they all draw on the central concepts, adding to that of the Way and its virtue the idea of *wuwei*, 'do-nothing', *ziran*, 'naturalness', and the 'Three Treasures' of compassion, moderation and simplicity. The *Daodejing* itself (*jing* means 'classic') is in two parts: the classic of *Dao* and the classic of *De*.

The concept of *dao* is complex and rich. The *Daodejing* opens: 'The *dao* that can be explained is not the eternal *dao*.' The second sentence is 'The name that can be named is not the eternal name.' These remarks seem rather dismaying, as stating at the outset that one cannot define the Way, which means that one cannot understand what it is. This is especially dismaying if the implication is that there is *one* correct eternal Way, as suggested by the reference to its eternal character. Some indeed interpret these sentences thus. But others argue that it is left open by the original Chinese that there are many Ways – the original of the first sentence is *dao ke dao fei chang dao*, literally 'Dao possible to say [is] not ever-enduring Dao', which does nothing to imply a 'the', the definite article, necessary if uniqueness is intended.

And indeed the *Daodejing* then proceeds to describe *dao* as *wanwu*, 'ten thousand things', which implies that the reason it cannot be defined or uniquely named is because it is so multiple. *Wanwu* suggests that *dao* transcends comprehension because it is inexhaustible. Various suggestions accordingly arise, for example that *dao* is the source of reality and sustains everything in being, and is inaccessible to understanding precisely because it is so fundamental. Of course such metaphysical interpretations are suppositious, since *dao* is ineffable. Some commentators go further, giving it religious connotations and associating it with divination and mysticism.

The translation of *de* as 'virtue' in the sense of moral goodness is reinforced by the 'Three Treasures' idea, but recall that another reading of it is 'power' and 'potency', in the sense of a life force that drives towards self-realization. Thus understood, to follow the Way is to unleash and apply one's potential. 'To follow the Way' echoes the early understanding of *dao* as a teaching, a doctrine; the Chinese character for the word has two parts, one meaning 'walking' or 'journey' and the other 'following', as in following a path, a route – a way.

The compilers of the *Daodejing* regarded its doctrines as greatly superior to those of other schools, which in their view were evidence of a decline from an age when the Way was properly followed: 'When the great Dao declined, the doctrines of humaneness and uprightness arose. When the ideas of knowledge and wisdom came along, hypocrisy arose. When relationships are out of harmony, ideas of filial piety and love for children arise. When the country is disordered, praise will arise for good ministers. Abandon these ideas, and there will be wisdom, and uprightness, there will be filial piety, and love.' The idea implicit here is that in the era before organized society, people behaved naturally and spontaneously, with effortless (*wuwei*) goodness. With society comes the need for *effort* to be humane, honest and filial – effort that too often fails, not least because in 'trying too hard' effortfulness is self-defeating.[35]

Wuwei, literally 'non-action', does not literally mean doing nothing at all; as just suggested, 'effortlessness' is the more accurate interpretation, to mean doing things in a relaxed, non-striving manner. In the *Zhuangzi* it denotes non-attachment and serenity. (Later Legalist philosophers took a hint from this and advised rulers to observe *wuwei* in the sense of 'masterly inaction', letting things take their course without interference.) Daoist masters use various analogies to explain the idea, typically likening *wuwei* to water flowing around rocks in a stream. 'The wise man acts without effort, teaches without many words, produces without possessing, creates but is indifferent to the outcome, lays claim to nothing, and therefore has nothing to lose.' In the term for 'naturalness', *ziren*, the *zi* component means 'self' and *ren* means 'thus', 'as it is'. The idea is that what one is and does comes from within, from inner nature.

Daoism's other great classic, the *Zhuangzi*, is named for its author, Zhuangzi ('Master Zhuang'). He was born in the year that Socrates died, 399 BCE, and lived a very long time – a good advertisement for the Way's unstressful approach to life. The *Zhuangzi* is more playful than the *Daodejing*, more sceptical, more critical, and full of entertaining anecdotes drawn from animal and insect life. It poses questions and puzzles but teasingly leaves them unanswered. Among the tales is the story of the man who dreamed he was a butterfly, and on waking wondered whether he was a man who had dreamed he was a butterfly, or a butterfly dreaming that he was a man.

Some commentators regard the *Zhuangzi* as more sophisticated both in its writing and teaching than the *Daodejing*. It sees the Way less as a means to worldly success and more as a personal inward journey. It is not clear what the respective dates of composition of the two works are, nor therefore what their relationship is – is one a development from the other, or an alternative, or are the differences between them simply of emphasis and tone?

The *Zhuangzi* advises its readers to eschew politics and practical life. Striving and overthinking things is wrong, Zhuangzi says; conventional values are a distraction. The ideal is just to *wander along the Way*.

From early in the first millennium CE and for a thousand years afterwards, a form of Daoism known as 'Highest Clarity Daoism' – the Shangqing school founded by Lady Wei Huacun – was popular among the elite. One of her followers, Yang Xi, 'almost certainly under the influence of cannabis' according to the historian Joseph Needham, claimed that the texts setting out the school's doctrines were dictated to him by spirits. The role of cannabis in developing the school's theories is mildly implausible given that the school was expressly opposed to the use of drugs and potions for achieving enlightenment, instead advocating meditation. But in any case, as shown by the role accorded to 'spirits', what Shangqing yet again demonstrates is that the evolution over time of schools of thought is not guaranteed to improve them. Consider Buddhism in its migrations from northern India; what began as a philosophy soon accumulated superstitions, spirits, apsaras, bodhisattvas, gods and elaborate rituals and legends, clouding and degrading the original inspiration. When it comes to ethical schools, it would seem that the purest water is to be found at the spring.

Despite the elaborate accretions that now envelop Buddhism's various versions, its original ideas remain steady at their centre: the doctrine of the Four Noble Truths and the Eightfold Path to liberation from existence by attainment of nirvana. The Four Noble Truths are that life is suffering, that suffering arises from ignorance and desire, that suffering can be escaped, and that one can achieve liberation by living an ethical life and by meditation. The Eightfold Path of the ethical life is Right Vision (understanding), Right Emotion, Right Speech, Right Action, Right Livelihood (work that does not harm others), Right Effort, Right Mindfulness and Right Meditation. When one reflects on these ideas one sees that, in essentials, they summarize the teachings of all the ethical schools already described. The single tweak, so to speak, might be meditation, though the withdrawal from conventional activities, and particularly from absorption in futile distractions of the moment, is paralleled in the Hellenistic schools; and as we will see in Chapter 12, there is a highly plausible view that followers of Hellenistic schools regarded 'living philosophically' as a practice requiring exercises in which repeating the doctrines and meditating on them were key. This brings the Eastern and Western philosophies even closer together.

The difference between Buddhism as a heterodox (*nastika*) school and the orthodox (*astika*) schools of Indian philosophy lies less with the ethical practices enjoined as in their respective underlying views of reality. The *astika* schools share a common point of departure in the concept, central to the Upanishads, of the relation between Atman (the individual self or soul) and Brahman (reality as a whole, 'the Absolute', the universal soul). In the classic Upanishadic view, Atman and Brahman are two sides of the same coin, subjective and objective respectively; the Advaita 'non-dualist' form of Vedanta specifically teaches that they are one and the same. This is the meaning attached by Advaita to the *mahavakya*, the 'great saying', of the Upanishads: *tat tvam asi*, 'that thou art', interpreted to entail 'I am that' ('Atman is Brahman') and hence 'I and the universe are one'. The soteriological point – achieving liberation from suffering – is that understanding this, overcoming our ignorance, will free us from attachment (and, via endless rebirths, reattachment) to this illusory world.

Buddhism agrees with the soteriological point, but not with the underlying metaphysics. Instead Buddhism asserts that there is no Atman, no Brahman; there is not only no such thing as *self* but no permanence of any kind. In short, there is no reality at all. Postulating the existence of a permanent self is not merely a mistake, it is the very source of suffering. When we see that the things we take to be real in the course of ordinary experience have no substance – that they are empty, a mere flow of nothings – we understand why they are not worth the craving we have for them. As long as we believe that they are substantial we will continue to suffer.

The purpose of meditation in Buddhism is understood variously in its different schools, but generally its purpose is to still the mind, to empty it of the tumult of distractions that prevent enlightenment entering, and to promote mindfulness. According to the Madhyamaka school it is not a reaching-down into fundamental layers of reality, because *ex hypothesi* there are none; there are only illusions. The Yogacara school, however, argues that if appearances (as 'secondary existents') are illusory, there must be something real which the illusory appearances hide from us (a 'primary existent'), and they nominate consciousness – not ordinary phenomenological consciousness, but the deep stream of fundamental, ultimate consciousness itself – as fulfilling this role: 'mind only', or *cittamatra*. Meditation enables us to reach this fundamental level. The next step is to see that reaching it is to achieve *emptiness*, given that pure consciousness is not divided into itself and something else, a duality of subject and object, so the vanishing of a putative self into the undifferentiated stream of consciousness is extinction. Yogacara accordingly reaches the same terminus as all other versions of Buddhism, but provides itself with a justification for placing yoga at the centre of its practice.

One of the most attractive schools of ethics in any tradition, East or West, is Jainism, though it is a hard one to live. Its teachings are owed to the sage Mahavira, who lived in the sixth century BCE, but Jains say their doctrines were formulated long before him; indeed they regard him as the twenty-fourth Tirthankara or 'discoverer of a ford across the sea of endless births and deaths' (*samsara*), and as having not devised but revived and refreshed the teachings. Tirthankaras are those who attain a true understanding of the self and thus are able to cross *samsara*, leaving guidance behind them for others to follow so that they can likewise achieve liberation (*moksha*) from existence.

Jainism's name derives from *jina*, 'victory' – victory over the suffering that is existence. It teaches asceticism and *ahimsa* (doing no harm), detachment, and acceptance of the fact that reality is infinitely complex and many-sided, which makes it impossible to give a single definitive description of anything. This means that everything we think or say can at best be only partly true, and even then 'only from a certain point of view', which implies that every point of view might have some truth in it.[36]

A common feature of all Indian soteriologies is that they are gnostic: liberation from suffering, whose source is ignorance, is achieved through knowledge. Once again the analogies with the Western schools is striking. Although the Western schools do not regard the world of ordinary experience as unreal, they do regard the conventional values attached to it as illusory, and therefore a right understanding of what really matters is liberating, leading to *ataraxia* and *eudaimonia* in this life. The slogan that applies across the whole compass, geographical and philosophical, is therefore *the truth will set you free*. The key thing, obviously, is to identify what the truth is.

I would guess that quite a few readers who combine having come this far with honesty might regard Cynics and Daoists with nervous dislike (their counterparts today being hippies and dropouts); would wish others to be Stoics (well-behaved and sober) while themselves being Epicurean (undisturbedly enjoying the good things of life), though believing themselves to be Aristotelian (reasonable, sensible); and would regard Buddhists and Jains with distant admiration but no desire to adopt their outlook or ways.[37] Such at any rate would likely be the case for any *homme moyen sensuel*. On the other hand, of course, given that the 'we' of this book is a self-selected minority, we might be any of these things with sincerity, and quite likely a chosen amalgam of the best of most of them.[38]

But the point of this survey is not to set out a menu of doctrines to choose from, as if the option is to choose just one of the '-isms' mentioned (in fact, the invitation is to cherry-pick from among them all), but to provide background for the discussion in Part II of the pressing matters that need to be addressed in answering Socrates' question. In those discussions we shall frequently see, as part of the process, what these schools of thought might contribute.

4. Avoiding a Wrong Turning

The premise of the discussion in this book, in line with the implication of Socrates' challenge, is that individuals have to choose their values and goals for themselves and take responsibility for living accordingly. No one says that doing so is easy or that the result will be perfect; rather the contrary, on both counts. Among the big advantages, however, is that one can truly 'live with oneself' – have self-respect – because the endeavour to live a chosen and self-directed life is a noble thing. Provided, of course, that the choices one makes include respect for others' right to choose and to live lives worth living, for to choose to live in ways that self-regardingly exploit or harm others is as ignoble as it is wrong. That should be obvious.

But what of views that explicitly or implicitly reject the premise of this book? As already acknowledged, the majority of people do not think about what answer to give the Socratic Question, but live according to a predetermined answer to it – namely, the beliefs and conventions of the society into which they are born: normativity. The majority of this majority live according to the outlook of one or another religious tradition, falling on a spectrum between, at one extreme, a vague 'there is a power greater than us' view – useful as a resource in moments of psychological distress and as an indistinct anchorage for conceptions of right and wrong – and at the other extreme the totalizing commitment of the fundamentalist in which the tenets of the religion dictate thought and action so completely that each such epigone of each such faith is indistinguishable, in all but inessentials, from every other. Most believers are situated somewhere along this spectrum, generally speaking closer to the first in traditionally Christian 'Western' society, and closer to the second in orthodox Jewish, Islamic and Hindu societies. But it is not many centuries since Christian societies were much more like these latter.

Perhaps, however, many will ask: why not adopt a religion as your philosophy of life? After all, having a philosophy of life is meant to provide not only guidance and values but to help one through diffi-cult times, and for the great majority of people religions provide exactly this; they are ready-made philosophies of life that obviate the necessity of working one out for oneself. For practical reasons hav-ing to do with their viability over time – by reinventing themselves to suit historically local conditions – some religions allow their fol-lowers a degree of latitude in choosing which parts to believe and practise, against a general background that differentiates them from other religions, so that Hinduism, Christianity, Judaism, Islam and so forth can be told apart; though Islam generally, and more enthusiastic versions of other religions, continue to be highly prescriptive, shap-ing the daily lives of devotees quite closely. Nevertheless, one thing they all have in common is that they provide meaning, strength, con-solation and solace. So, why not adopt a religion?

The straightforward answer – to pull no punches: a much more detailed answer is referenced in this endnote[1] – is that adherence to a religion requires accepting a particular problematic collection of claims, fables and meaningless formulae as true or at least especially significant, and it also helps continue and even promote the serious harm that religions cause in the world, which the good they do in art, music and charity – good also done by the non-religious – does not excuse. You could ignore both points and continue to rely on a reli-gion as your philosophy of life by thinking – as regards the first point – that the important thing is comfort, and comforting myths are better than uncomfortable truths; and, as regards the second point, that you consider interreligious conflict, wars, pogroms, inquisitions, persecution of homosexuals, subordination of women, brainwashing of children, denial of science, and so forth, to be a price worth paying so long as you and some other people feel comfort-able.[2] It is not too difficult to do this if you deploy the argument that what humans do with their religions is not the fault of the gods; but in this case you have to justify why our sources of information about the gods – texts like the Bible – have to be highly cherry-picked to preserve us from their currently unpalatable parts (like the instruction to stone to death adulterers, homosexuals and those who do not go to church on the Sabbath).

It is not impossible that you might study the claims and doctrines of a religion and conclude that the claims are true and the doctrines appealing, and hence become an adherent of it; in which case you will at least have satisfied a demand that the Socratic challenge makes, namely to think things through, to use your reason, to evaluate and critically examine. This relates in a crucial way to the cherry-picking point just made. For example, you might find that there are rationally disciplined ways of deciding which assertions in the documents of your chosen religion are to be treated literally and which metaphorically, and how to render the literally interpreted ones as consistent with apparently competing claims, for example in physics, palaeontology and biology. Take the case of a commitment shared by Judaism, Christianity and Islam: that a deity created the world: as follows.

There is first the question of what a 'deity' is. We can agree at the outset that it is at least supposed to be some kind of supernatural agent, the nature and properties of which are unknown other than by negation on the properties of human beings: humans are mortal, limited, finite, so a deity is immortal, unlimited (omniscient, omnipotent), infinite. Humans (until very recently) are confined to the surface of the earth, move slowly, can only access a limited range of the electromagnetic spectrum through vision and hearing, need to ingest food and water by mouth – whereas by contrast deities fly, can be everywhere (or at least many places) at once and instantly, see through walls, consume the sacrificed oxen on the altar by inhalation of its fumes or by mystical means, and so on. Of course modern theology has dispensed with these primitive ways of conceiving of deity, despite the only sources for speculation about them being writings set down a long time ago, giving us these – our only available – descriptions of what is being talked about. The extremely refined speculations of modern theology have taken recourse to abstractions and gestures such as 'god is love', 'god is life', 'god is the essence of all things', some of which (e.g. 'god is love') are difficult to square with natural evils – cancer, tsunamis – and moral evil (as creator of all things and, being omniscient, able to foresee or at least infer the consequences of the creation, a deity would not just have had Hitler, Pol Pot, Stalin and Mao on the radar, but intended them). Yet despite the sophistications of modern theology, the churches continue to read out the texts and preach as if the original descriptions still apply. Challenged, theologians fall back on their refined abstractions, excusing the continued literalist usages on the grounds that as symbolic or figurative means to a relationship with the deity they are suitable for (the lesser intellectual powers of) non-theologians. Challenged in turn on these refined abstractions, they fall back yet again, this time to their last line of defence: our finite minds cannot capture the infinite nature of god, god is ineffable, it's a great mystery, there is nothing more to be said; just believe in – whatever it is.

If there is one such entity as a deity there is no logical reason why there cannot be more, even an infinite number of them, so the reduction in the number of deities over the course of history (except in Hinduism, although some now say that the different Hindu gods and goddesses are emanations of a single godhead) is interesting, even if the need to turn a small pantheon into a monotheism (Christianity's 'three-in-one') requires a special act of not thinking too critically. (Roman Catholicism is unapologetic about being pantheistic – apart from the trinity there is Mary, a goddess figure, and a football-stadium-full of saints, all of whom can be solicited in prayer for favours and intercessions.) The reduction in the number of deities conforms to the increase in human knowledge of nature; originally all natural processes, not being understood, had a deity at work in them: the wind and the thunder, the movement of the sea and the change of the seasons, were produced by divinities; each tree had its dryad and each stream its nymph; Zeus hurled the thunderbolt and Poseidon shook the earth to make earthquakes. As nature became more naturalistically understood, the gods withdrew from it – first to mountaintops (Olympus; Moses' burning bush on the summit of Mount Horeb); then, when mountains had been climbed, to the sky, which to a flat-earther is 'up', so when the earth was accepted as spherical with no preferred up and down directions, heaven became abstract – not a place but a condition of non-physical being. By this process of successive abstractions and distancings, heaven and deity will, like the Cheshire Cat, eventually vanish altogether.

Making any sense of the notion of 'deity' is the first and largest step. One might think that, having achieved it – on the grounds of 'if you can believe *that* you can believe anything' – all else would follow smoothly. But in fact this is not the end of the problems. For next there is the question of what 'creation' is. Considered as an act of – in some sense – making, building, constructing, producing, originating, which requires no pre-existing materials but is an emanation of thought or will, explicable on the basis of an imputation to the creator of unlimited powers of an inscrutable kind, it depends on leaving two enormous questions undefined: whence and how the creator itself exists, and what these creation-competent powers are. Both points can of course be left aside under the blanket of ineffability ('our finite minds cannot understand these mysteries' again). But the claim that there was an act of creation by a conscious agency is taken literally by almost every adherent of almost all religions.

I leave aside the complication that 'deity' and 'creator' might not be the same thing, though almost all religions assume they are. Enlightenment deists (despite their name) did not think that a creator agency is the same thing as the god or gods of any revealed (textual) religion, or even perhaps a god at all. But this is a distraction, like arguing whether Western astrology is better than Chinese astrology.

In the founding texts of the three linearly connected religions, Judaism, Christianity and Islam, 'the world' (in the sense of 'the universe') is restricted to planet earth and things in the sky visible from it, all taken to be relatively nearby. The texts give no indication of the universe being something very much larger than appearances suggest. Unaided observation indeed appears to show that all the objects in the sky rotate around the earth, and observation also appears to suggest that the earth is flat; the scriptures of the three religions rest content with both observations, even though they claim as the source for this information the omniscient agency supposed to have constructed the universe and who might therefore have known differently. Of course, it could be that current astronomy, cosmology and space flight are massively and systematically mistaken – or are an elaborate conspiracy – or the creator, knowing that the universe is very much larger than the region of space around earth, has to be regarded as having wished humankind to be misled for a time, for reasons which (again owing to our finitude) are opaque to us.

The 'six days' of creation can be regarded by most believers as figurative, though some – the 'Young Earth' creationists – boldly continue to accept this timescale literally. Their literalism requires them to exercise ingenuity in explaining what appears to be a geological and fossil record of billions of years of earthly existence, by invoking the crushing weight of a great flood of water.

Having accepted creation literally, having found a way of accommodating the incorrect description of the heavens, and having selected which of the most obviously implausible aspects – the six days, the creation of Adam and Eve, and so on – to treat as merely figurative, the faithful then have to deal with miracles. Miracles are local and temporary suspensions of the laws of physics and biology, from relatively minor examples (a jug of oil which never empties, water turning into wine) to considerable and wondrous examples (animals talking, the sun standing still, the seas parting, the earth splitting open on being struck by a staff, fire pouring from heaven to destroy a city, flying chariots, virgins giving birth, the dead resurrecting, a journey to heaven on a winged horse, and many more). It is not clear what believers make of such things, unless they actually believe they happened given that the deity's omnipotence entails that there is no barrier to anything whatsoever happening. Or, perhaps, many current believers do not believe they happened, and impute reports of them to the credulity of earlier times, while still somehow managing to 'believe in' the religion even though what persuaded the earlier believers was precisely the evidence putatively offered by the miracles, for miracle stories were to earlier times what advertising claims are to our own – an application of an 'our god washes whiter than other gods' logic. Remember that these religions were then in a competitive marketplace of superstitions.

The foregoing just scratches the surface of what has to be accepted if a religion is to pass muster as the basis for a philosophy of life.[3] It is a heavy price to pay for guidance and consolation – not least because, quite literally, it entails that *any falsehood or myth will do if it is consoling to believe it*. Consider the question of whether one should tell someone that he has terminal cancer: is it better to lie to him about his situation in order to protect him from anxiety? Or would it be wrong to do so, even if well intentioned? Leaving aside the question of giving someone an opportunity to make final dispositions and farewells, is the truth subordinate to comfort? If it is in this case, in what other cases is it likewise so? Might it indeed be so generally? Would not a policy of infusing the public water supply with a heavy tranquillizing drug be supported by the same logic as saying that because religions provide comfort they are therefore acceptable?

The question can be reframed more specifically. In seeking a world view, shall we aim to adopt one, any one, that gives us most consolation even if it consists in a string of myths and unintelligibilities, or shall we seek one that stands up to critical scrutiny in the light of reason?

It is an assumption of this book that the question just asked answers itself.

There is a simple way to demonstrate that the great majority of people who follow a religion do not *choose* it as their answer to the Socratic Question. It is to point out that almost all believers hold the religious beliefs of their parents. Indeed this is enough to demonstrate that they do not even ask themselves the Socratic Question. However, some people claim to think about the claims of Islam or Christianity and to choose to accept them, either being 'reborn' into the religion they were born into or converting under what they see as the compelling logic (more likely, what they feel as the emotional impact) of the faith in question. Obviously, this book is not for such people, or for those whose commitment to their faith – or its grip on them: the same thing – is unshakeable. But there is another reason, not yet touched upon, why religion is no substitute for a philosophy that is the result of thought and choice. It is as follows.

If the basic claim of all religion is correct – namely, that there are one or more supernatural agencies in or associated with the universe, possessed of powers sufficient to suspend any law of nature at will, and which have an interest in human affairs on this planet – then to put matters simply and bluntly but with complete accuracy: all bets are off; there is no point in thinking about anything other than whether or not to do whatever these agencies want, in light of the rewards or penalties on offer. That is the bottom line, and the oceans of ink and hurricanes of hot air applied to the complexities and niceties of religious life, devotion, prayer, the struggle with doubt, the dark nights of the soul, the bliss of accepting a saviour into one's life, and so forth, are window dressing.

This remains true despite what has already been mentioned – the beautiful art and music, and the equally beautiful acts of charity, inspired by religious faith; for beautiful art and music, and equally beautiful acts of charity, are inspired by many things other than religious faith too, and are created and enacted by non-religious as well as religiously motivated people. Religion – a man-made thing – has a lot of strife, murder and oppression to compensate for, and it would be a subtle calculation indeed that worked out how much torment and how many dead people a gallery-full of paintings of Annunciations and Depositions, or the *St Matthew Passion*, or a Blue Mosque, is worth. We would like to have these things without the cost they incurred, of course we would; but the same *human* emotions are at work behind the good and the bad things alike, a fact to be borne in mind.

To repeat the essential point: if there is an inescapably all-powerful supernatural agency in control of the universe, the only point to existence is to do, as a matter of prudence, whatever it requires. It makes thinking about life meaningless other than by asking, 'What do I do in response to the fact that I am the powerless creature of an all-powerful agency?' The deity's standard requirement, as the religions present it, is self-abnegation ('not my will but thy will be done') and submission ('Islam'), expressing not obedience – which presupposes the genuine practicability of the alternative, disobedience; but what price this, in the face of omnipotence and its threat of punishment? – but fatalism. An appearance of free will is kept up by saying that one has to pass a test, either of faith and works or faith alone; but it is a Hobson's choice.

Different faiths say different things about how to manage the relationship with the agency they believe is in charge of the universe. Ritual and observance are standard, praise and supplication too. Some religions, as noted, allow their followers to cherry-pick the easier bits of the scriptures and doctrines to follow – Christians indeed forgo stoning people who skip church on Sunday, though instructed to do so in Exodus 31.14 – while other religions infantilize their followers by refusing any deviation from belief or practice, and requiring a good deal of the latter on a frequent and regular basis; Muslims are required to pray five times a day. Failure to observe the ritual practices of a religion can be unsettling for devotees; failure to recite the required prayers, or to wear a kippa, or to go to confession every Saturday and Mass every Sunday becomes like missing one of the railings you are tapping with your stick as you walk along, or stepping on the join between paving stones; it feels unlucky.

There is, if one looks at it without preconceptions, something strange about religion, quite apart from miracles, contradictions, paradoxes and its morally repugnant aspects such as tolerance of natural evils. To see what it is, imagine yourself a rich, powerful, above-the-law slave owner to whom your slaves constantly come with praises and petitions. Let us suppose you enjoy being praised endlessly and begged for favours unremittingly. Have you solved the problem of the contradiction between mercy and justice? In requiring your slaves to do your will, justice is far more likely than mercy to achieve this end; indeed, mercy will sooner rather than later subvert this end. Imagine that you do not actually have to have slaves – you have a perpetual supply of all the food and drink, the clothing, housing, furniture, appurtenances, indeed absolutely everything you need; you can do any maintenance your mansion requires with a snap of the fingers; and so forth. So why have these slaves, other than to perform the observances of praising and begging? What is their purpose? On traditional definitions of deity as having neither needs nor lacks, we cannot say that creatures ('created things') are required for company or service or anything that scripture, tradition or claimed mystical experiences have offered in explanation. The answer theologians standardly give is – yet again – that the deity's purposes are beyond our powers of comprehension. Certainly, divine inscrutability is an infinite convenience.

The contradictions sit on the very face of the major faiths. In Christianity a central trope is 'love' – 'God is love', 'God loves you', 'love God', 'for the love of God'. Most people have direct experience of one of the various kinds of human love – romantic love, love of parents for their children, love of friends, all of them emotions with definite somatic and psychological manifestations either in their expression or loss. Apart from cases where simulacra of these can be willed into existence by a fervent believer, what is it to 'love' an ill-defined but, by such definition as there is, incomprehensible abstraction? Presumably many who (to take a Christian example) 'love Jesus' have in mind a particular image – one of those depictions of a bearded young man with wounded extremities and perhaps a crown of thorns, visual reminders of a physical suffering which in kind and duration has been greatly surpassed billions of times in torture cells and maternity wards the world over. (As to psychological suffering: presumably there was little or none of it, because Jesus knew that what was happening was all to the good.) But there is something forced about this, even if it is like the intense passion felt by a fan for a pop star only encountered in imagery. Similarly, the formula on the lips of every Muslim is that Allah is 'compassionate and merciful', which is the last thing some of his most fervent followers are; a stark and disturbing contradiction.

The view that religious faith requires suspension of rational judgment and a significant quantum of self-delusion is familiar. Yet more pertinent is the *self-alienation* that submission to an external will requires. This is why the philosophical act performed by an individual asking and answering the Socratic Question is so different from unreflectingly practising a religion or, in the minority case, performing the one-time autonomous act of choosing heteronomy – that is, of handing government of oneself to a supposed external will, *choosing not to be a chooser* any longer, submitting one's reason, judgment and direction to an outside agency, a supposed god (in reality, priests and mullahs); outsourcing oneself, one might say.

Doing this is regarded as a *virtue* by the faiths in question. That great sin, as Christianity sees it, of pride – thinking that you can stand on your own feet – is interesting when you consider that 'sin' means 'disobedience'. As Kant put it, religion requires no more of people than that they 'believe and obey'. The first sin of mankind was, according to the Bible, disobedience – and rather significantly, disobedience to a ban on acquiring knowledge. The tonsure – the little shaven patch on a monk's head – is a symbol borrowed from Roman times, when slaves were tonsured as a sign of their status; monks choose the tonsure to show that they are slaves of God. Faith – believing without having evidence; believing even in the face of contrary evidence – is celebrated as a cardinal virtue, as (to choose advocates of this view across two millennia of Christian history) St Paul, Tertullian and Kierkegaard all emphasized. A cynic might respond to these observations by pointing out that unquestioning obedience is a great boon to the human authorities in charge of religious organizations.

Defenders of religious commitment like to cite those who have responded to the foregoing kinds of challenge by making faith a hard thing to have, the invitation from the gods a tough call, the whole thing a great struggle. It is certainly so on an intellectual level for those emotionally desirous of believing – if they have powers of rational scrutiny at their command. It is instructive, in a field-anthropological sort of way, to observe this. A classic case is Miguel de Unamuno's *Tragic View of Life*, the first half of which is a brilliant demolition of the claims successively of religion, then of Christianity, then of Catholic Christianity; and the second half of which is a convoluted, vaporous and groping effort to justify believing in (Catholic) Christianity anyway, as a means of dealing with the fear of death, which was a particular bugbear for Unamuno. He was frightened that death is extinction, and wished to believe because religion offers the hope of continued post-mortem existence. Others – not least believers – fear death because of the judgment and torments they think await them; one of religion's crueller gifts.

Here we begin to trespass on the coming discussions, in Part II, of fear and angst, the existential torments, and the nature of death and its place in life. At this juncture let the case rest: that religion – religion in the sense of Judaism, Hinduism, Christianity, Islam; the religions of earlier times were never conceived of as philosophies of life – is not a viable option for what is under discussion in these pages.

One final point. It might be thought that religion provides a basis for morality – for good behaviour. Certain of the Ten Commandments – those that in sum say do not steal or lie – and injunctions to succour widows and orphans and to love your neighbour, are examples which would readily be cited. However, all moralities, not just religious ones, enjoin these things. But take a specific case: if you went to the Gospels and the letters of St Paul in the Christian part of the Bible – the New Testament – and enquired of them how best to live and behave, you would rather disconcertingly be told that the Kingdom belongs to those who give away everything they have, who make no plans for the morrow, who do not marry and have children, who turn their backs on their families if their families disagree with them, and who are blessed if they are humble, oppressed and depressed – a description of a life which some rather heroically tried to live by such means as fleeing to the desert. The unliveability of this ethic eventually (after several centuries) prompted the Church to adopt ideas from Greek philosophical ethics, not least Stoicism, and to co-opt the likes of Plato (in the *Timaeus*, the only book known by the time Christianity had become dominant) and Seneca to their cause. This paralleled the case of Christian views of death and the soul; because early Christians were Jews who believed that when you die you lie in your grave until the Messiah comes, at which point you are resurrected, St Paul said that saints and martyrs would 'see no corruption' in the grave (i.e. their corpses would not decay). When the Church became dominant and exhumed the bodies of saints and martyrs to place them as relics in their churches, they found that St Paul was wrong; the corpses had decayed. But here Plato's theory of the immortal soul, transmitted via Neoplatonism, came to the rescue, and was added to Christian doctrine; if we have souls they can go to heaven or hell, or to Purgatory (to be 'purged' of the stains of sin), and our bodies can decompose.

Examine the moral teachings of any religion, and ask whether those that stand up to scrutiny are particular to that or any religion, or whether they are shared by most moralities including non-religious ones. And ask also whether all of the moral teachings (all of them: do not hide from scriptural injunctions to e.g. kill homosexuals and adulterers, an injunction still obeyed in practice in some Muslim countries) of a given religion stand up to scrutiny. Perhaps these considerations alone might show that there is at least nothing distinctive, and at best little enticing, about a religious commitment as a philosophy of life.

And in any case: if your reason for being good, kind, generous and the rest is to earn merit points or to escape punishment, how is this moral, let alone ethical? It would be *prudent* to obey the dictates of an all-powerful agency, but not moral, and nor would it be even remotely ethical because it simply involves acting in exact conformity with all others existing in subjection to this agency, no differently from a coward – though, given that the prospect is something frightful and agonizing (once analogized as burning eternally in hellfire), the option of not being a coward is unrealistic. This thought makes a dismal end to all reasonings about the point and quality of religious ethics.

PART II

5.   *Happiness*, The Pursuit of –

Death, the great inevitable, *love*, the great desirable, *meaning*, the great mystery – and the great hope, *happiness*. What do these words mean – really mean? All of the first three – and others – get their own sections in what follows, but 'happiness' must be tackled straight away.

Is happiness the point? Of course it depends what is meant by 'happiness'. A standard current definition would describe it as a prevailing pleasurable emotional state of satisfaction, fulfilment and contentment. A person in such a state would typically feel and be relaxed, would smile and be nice to others, would regard life positively; a desirable situation. More intense emotions such as ecstasy, glee, joy, delight, exhilaration, elation, bliss – states which tend to be short-lived and triggered by particular events – are not the same thing, for they can be experienced even by an unhappy person. As this suggests, the original meaning of 'happiness' reflects its connection with the idea of a condition of life which is such that it generates the emotions of satisfaction and fulfilment at issue. This is made clear by the resonant phrase in the American Declaration of Independence's second paragraph: 'Life, Liberty and the pursuit of Happiness'. The third desideratum in this list is not the emotional state of *'feeling* happy' (in a smiley mood), but the circumstances that produce it: in this sense, you might just have quarrelled with your spouse and painfully stubbed your toe, but you will be happy (though not at that moment *'feeling* happy') because you have a roof over your head, food on the table, and secure prospects; you are 'happily placed', you are in 'happy circumstances'.

This is the sense of Aristotle's *eudaimonia*, earlier suggested as more accurately meaning 'well-being', which captures both the condition-of-life and emotional senses. Consider the literal meaning of the term: the *eu-* prefix means 'good', 'positive', and the *daimon* part means 'deity, genius' in the sense of 'spirit' – in fact, literally 'demon' but in a good sense, 'angel' not 'devil' – so to be eudaimonic is to be 'as if looked after by a good spirit'. If there were such things as good spirits that looked after people – as in those childhood representations of an angel stooping fondly over a sleeping infant's bed – then the lucky people in question would be provided with positives and protected from negatives in the general course of their affairs.

If, however, 'happiness' is restricted in meaning to the emotional state of being satisfied and content – which means: untroubled, unchallenged, at ease, at rest psychologically – is it 'the point of life'? I asked earlier: if it is, why not put Prozac in the public water supply? Many people achieve the same effect with physical drugs such as alcohol and heroin, or psychological ones such as religion. Accordingly a more interesting answer might be prompted by repeating the question 'Which would you rather be: a happy pig, or an unhappy Socrates?' The implication is that there are better things to do and be than to seek feelings of happiness for their own sake – that is, to be happy in the modern sense of being in a pleasant emotional state. For one thing, it has been well observed that the search for happiness, in this sense, is one of the main sources of unhappiness in the world; and for another thing, many of the activities that are right and profoundly worthwhile are not typically associated with pleasant feelings in the moment of doing them.

Yet large majorities of people, when asked, insist that happiness is what they most want for themselves and those they care about, though they have widely different views about what would make them happy.[1] Among people who are not, or not particularly, rich or famous or good-looking (and so on for other putative desirables) there are those who think that being one or more of these things would make them happy. That these are instrumental goals rather than ends in themselves is easily ascertained: ask anyone whether they would accept being rich if at the same time they would, in return, be horribly miserable, and almost all would answer 'No'. When people become famous and realize what constraints this places on them, how it limits them – even from walking to the corner shop for a carton of milk – and how it makes them targets of curiosity, prying, vilification, abuse, cloying adulation, even blackmail, they learn what bliss it is to be private and unknown.

Then there is the question of whether happiness is so important that it justifies whatever brings it about. Clearly, the answer is another 'No': that a serial killer is made happy by murdering people can never justify his doing it. By itself this implies that there are higher goals in life than 'feeling happy'. And there are persuasive arguments to show that this is so.[2]

First, though, one unpersuasive argument to the same conclusion needs to be mentioned in order to be set aside. This is the claim made by religions that those who observe their requirements, such as faith and obedience, are guaranteed happiness in an afterlife – all the more so if their current circumstances are unhappy. Inculcating such a belief is useful to those whose task or desire is to manage the unruly material of humanity. The nature of post-mortem felicity is very vaguely specified in all the religions except those that promise extinction. These latter, the Indian soteriologies sketched earlier, in effect define happiness as the total absence even of the risk of unhappiness; the state of nirvana is often characterized as 'the blowing out of a candle', with all illusion, self-awareness and desire extinguished. It is controversial quite what 'nirvana' means, but whatever it means it at least involves extinction of the ego and its attachments and desires, which in these philosophies are identified as the source of suffering.

The genuinely persuasive argument can be put most simply by considering again the Prozac option. If happiness really is the highest goal, then pouring Prozac into the world's water supplies would achieve it. As long as the supply were maintained in perpetuity, no one would mind or perhaps even notice if all other systems began to fail and disasters happened; we would keep smiling contentedly. The fact that this is an unpalatable idea shows that happiness merely as the *emotion* associated with being untroubled, unchallenged, at ease, at psychological rest – a negative condition – undermines things we value more, things that engage our striving and yearning, our improving, growing, inventing and discovering. Striving and inventing have often enough resulted in unhappiness, true; but they have produced knowledge and progress far more often than either has happened by luck.

Happiness often, though not invariably, accompanies the endeavours of striving, inventing and discovering, as smoke accompanies fire; but the endeavours themselves are the primary things, so that whatever happiness arises from them is an epiphenomenon – a side effect. But the observation that some people can be happy doing evil shows that the fact that happiness arises from a pursuit of goals is no guarantee that the goals are good in themselves. The point of debate both in ethics and in the narrower concern of morality is to identify which goals are good in themselves.

Even if one were to accept that happiness, just as such, is the supreme value, problems remain, for there is a Babel of conflicting voices on the subject of how it is to be attained, some from diametrically opposite sides. Aristotle and the Stoics clashed over both the ends and the means: Aristotle thought that happiness is achieved by increasing the satisfaction of appropriate desires, while the Stoics recommended limiting desires. Two thousand years later Bertrand Russell and Sigmund Freud adopted similar respective views – Russell thinking that a more expansive approach to life brings happiness, Freud doubting whether anything more than transitory happiness is ever possible.[3]

Russell was persuaded that being happy makes us good, and was equally persuaded that certain ideas about what is good make people unhappy. It is easy to agree with the second of these points while being far less sure about the first. Russell had puritanism in mind as regards the second point, and there can be little doubt that puritanism of all kinds has generated much misery. But there are no guarantees. The rigid practitioner of a self-denying morality might suffer in order to obey its strictures, but take pleasure in the suffering – indeed he might take great pleasure in imposing that suffering on others. Such questions are empirical rather than philosophical.

In the industry of 'Happiness Studies' that has grown up in psychology and economics departments at universities around the world, just such empirical questions are addressed. Take, for example, what the psychologists call 'resilience' as one proposed essential ingredient of happiness. To be resilient is to be able to cope with failure, loss, trauma — in general: stress. One implication is that those haunted by traumatic memories are being insufficiently resilient in dealing with them. William James, one of the founders of psychology — and also a philosopher of note — remarked: 'Happiness, like every other emotional state, has blindness and insensibility to opposing facts given it as its instinctive weapon for self-protection against disturbance.' A negative implication of this is that some degree of indifference, even callousness, is necessary to happiness. How can one be happy if too conscious of the deprivation and injustice rife in our world? If you cannot put that out of your mind, you cannot be totally happy — unless you actually like the thought that hundreds of millions of your fellow humans are suffering. This suggests that too much resilience is undesirable, morally speaking.

Is it acceptable to be happy on the basis of illusions — again, religious beliefs, or more generally any false information about one's situation? After all, it is not merely possible for people to be happy as a result of believing falsehoods; it is in fact a surer route to happiness than knowing the truth. Is truth so valuable that it should trump illusions that give people comfort? This is the very important question raised in the last chapter of Part I. A much-discussed example is Horace's story of a man called Lycas who laughed and applauded in an empty theatre, thoroughly enjoying himself because he imagined that a delightful play was being performed there. Alexander Pope, perhaps representing the poets' side of the matter, was on Lycas' side, but a formidable cohort of thinkers, including Confucius, Socrates, the Buddha, Montaigne, Voltaire, Diderot, Kant, and many others, were firmly of the view that because knowledge and self-knowledge are crucial to maturity, anyone doing as Lycas did should be put under medical care.

Here one is reminded of Robert Lynd's response to Epictetus, described in the Introduction. In theory, from the commanding heights of philosophical principle, one's commitment has to be that nothing can stand in the way of truth; among other things — and not least — because obeying the Delphic instruction to 'know thyself' is impossible otherwise. But in the tumult and confusions of practical life, the truth is too often damaging and painful, and most people resort to myth and self-delusion at least some of the time to help themselves get through. Here happiness or its substitutes trumps truth, and plenty of people – for Lynd's reasons – would understand why.

These thoughts open the way to a significant insight. We need to distinguish between the subjective point of view – how a life feels from the inner perspective of the person living it – and the objective point of view, in which a dispassionate observer watches that same person deluding himself to the effect that (say) he does not have cancer, that his wife is faithful, that his work colleagues like him. The observer might judge that insofar as the person's self-delusions are harmless or even have a positive effect – his cancer is incurable anyway, so why be burdened too soon by its implications; his home life remains stable for his children because he is blind to his wife's affair; he functions adequately at work because he thinks he is accepted there – then it is better that he believes them than that he knows the truth. Again, plenty of people – for Lynd's reasons – would agree.

But an interesting question now arises. What would the person himself think on at last discovering the truth – in his case that he is seriously ill, a cuckold, and his colleagues snigger about him behind his back. Is he glad he did not know? Others knew but did not tell him; what does he think about that? Suppose he is angry about being lied to, but is assured that the motives of those who withheld the truth were as benevolent as possible; would that excuse them, from his point of view? The truths are devastating and painful ones. Would he be right in saying that, yes, he would prefer to have known?

Parents lie to their children about the realities of life, only gradually exposing them to some of its unpalatable features as they grow old enough to cope with knowing about them. There is no question that there are right times and occasions for 'economy with the truth', as someone once evasively – or perhaps tactfully – put it. But parents' lies are, so to speak, temporary, and their purpose largely condonable. In the case of our dying unpopular cuckold, it seems that, on the face of it, the arbiter of whether knowing the truth is better than living a lie, or vice versa, is himself. Is this how matters should generally be – that it is for each to decide for himself or herself whether to live according to truth or falsehood? But then, how could you choose falsehood without knowing the truth first?

So, back to the contrast between the subjective and objective viewpoints. The nuanced answer is to say that, objectively, truth is the higher value, but that there are times when – temporarily; not as a fixture, not as a universal – telling a lie serves a better cause, in the moment when the cause needs serving, providing of course that the cause is worth serving. This rider is key. It is what saves parents from charges of mendacity in protecting their children from too much reality too early.

But in the business of thinking about one's philosophy of life, there is no room for falsehood and delusion. In this very serious matter there is room only for truth. That sounds tough and overly high-minded; but if one is to work out a philosophy of life for oneself, if one is to own one's life and truly choose its goals for oneself, things have to be seen straight and clear. It is often the case that truth is as liberating as it is painful, and either way profoundly worthwhile. If the truth about oneself and truths about life and society are too unpalatable to confront, and if the effort of seeking them is too much like hard work, one can always opt for normativity – the conventional life, or the comforting illusions of a religion.

This excursus has turned attention away from the question of happiness itself, but inevitably so. For as soon as one begins to dig into the question of happiness, it melts into other questions. 'What would make you happy?' is really a question about what other things are valuable in themselves, and when we look at them we see that there are some that carry no guarantee that having or doing them would be attended by '*feeling* happy'. 'Ah, but they might make you feel that you are doing something worthwhile or good, something that makes your life meaningful.' Yes – but this too is to acknowledge that happiness is not *the* point. Whatever personal rewards accrue from identifying and reaching for what one sees as intrinsically valuable, they might not include happiness as an indispensable part.

These thoughts in sum imply that questions about how we should live – and this includes questions about how we should treat one another – are not answered by considerations of happiness alone. For example: if one accepted the definition of happiness offered by the American novelist Willa Cather as the state of 'being dissolved into something complete and great', then terrorist mass murderers are happy in causing a huge amount of harm by doing what they think is 'great'. Not only is seeking happiness consistent with doing harm, it further implies that being happy is too often the result of error and illusion; Jonathan Swift's admittedly cynical view was that happiness indeed is nothing else, that it consists in 'being well deceived; the serene peaceful state of being a fool among knaves'.[4]

Yet despite the vagueness of the concept of 'happiness' beyond the feel-good emotion denoted by the word itself – indeed perhaps *because* of that vagueness – it obviously attracts a great deal of attention. It is a staple of popular magazines, which do not so much debate as prescribe happiness – the accompanying advertisements implying that the route to it lies through weight loss, skin creams, romance, sexual expertise, holidays in the sun and, in general, owning things. But it is also the subject of empirical research, in which social scientists investigate what percentage of given populations feel happy, and for what reasons.

A significant contribution in this regard is made by the World Values Survey, which periodically makes international comparisons of subjectively reported degrees of 'satisfaction'. Taking the results for a period of relative stability (despite the economic crash of 2008–9) in most regions of the world around 2010–12, surveys showed that Western Europe and the Americas were home to the 'most satisfied' people, while the 'least satisfied' were found in Eastern Europe. This kind of information interests politicians and policymakers, for obvious reasons, and consequently the study of happiness has, as noted above, become a serious academic enterprise, with the establishment of professorships in Happiness Studies, Quality of Life Institutes, and academic publications such as the *Journal of Happiness Studies*.[5]

A great crop of statistical information has accordingly been harvested in recent years. It ranges from the obvious (American high school students are less happy at school than on vacation, and less happy alone than with friends) through the confirming (the rising graph of income in Western countries since 1950 is accompanied by a straight line for subjective satisfaction, showing that more money does not mean more happiness) to the intriguing (Nigerians and Mexicans are the world's happiest people[6]).

Cultural differences are salient in these comparisons. For example: in Japan, life satisfaction comes from meeting the expectations of family and society, maintaining self-discipline, and presenting a friendly and cooperative attitude to the world. In the United States, satisfaction is gained by self-expression, a feeling of self-worth, and material success.

People who place emphasis on income and status are more dissatisfied than those who are less interested in these things, and as a result they are more prone to illness and depression, the products of stress. Their problem arises from invidious comparisons: people are made unhappy by feeling that they are doing less well in respect of income, image and standing than others in the social circles that matter to them. The obvious solution is to stop peering over the fence at the neighbours, and to choose better measures of success for one's doings.

What 'happiness studies' unequivocally show is that two of the most important factors in life satisfaction are *a sense of autonomy* – being in control of one's life – and being valued for what one is and does, *a sense of worth*. Neither of these factors depends on status or income. These points have a clear implication. It is, first, that public policy should aim at enabling national, local and workplace democracy – genuine democracy: proportionally representative so that every vote, every voice, counts equally – because this offers people an effective say in what is happening in their workplaces and communities. They thus participate in decisions about what happens in their lives. And second, employment and job security should be ensured – the latter on a reasonable basis of competent performance – because this would promote both the autonomy and respect desiderata. Alas, the opposite of this is the norm: many businesses seek to goad people into productivity by means of league tables, interdepartmental rivalry and performance-based criteria for pay and promotion, thus using *competitive dissatisfaction* as the motivating force – deliberately leveraging unhappiness. This is a recipe not only for discontent but, pushed too far, for social instability, primarily because of the inequalities that result. Inequality, social unrest and low subjective satisfaction form a toxic triangle: which is the cause and which the effects might be an open question, but their correlation is persistent and unsurprising.[7]

Out of all these considerations, the chief point to bear in mind is that happiness is an epiphenomenon, a condition that arises as a by-product of activities and circumstances that are independently and intrinsically worthwhile. As a by-product of such it comes unconsciously, often enough unexpectedly. It is worth remembering the observation reported above that pursuing happiness, reductively defined as the '*feeling* of happiness', is one of the best ways to be unhappy. Happiness is like the dot of light in a dark room which, if looked at directly, is invisible, but which comes into view when one directs one's gaze elsewhere. It is seen in the corner of the eye, as the accompaniment or result of activities that have value in their own right, independently of the different feelings they might prompt in different people.

It is of course true that there are – and right that there should be – familiar occasions for *feelings* of happiness, though they might more informatively be described as 'feelings of pleasure and fulfilment', such as leisure, friendship, beautiful things and places, success. In the moments of experiencing them one may not even realize one feels happy; the realization might come retrospectively, showing that it is a fact about happiness that one can have it without knowing it at the time. This once again demonstrates its epiphenomenal character, and helps to direct attention where it belongs: not to what one hopes will generate feelings of happiness, but to what is intrinsically worthwhile.

This conclusion immediately prompts the question: what is, or what things are, intrinsically worthwhile if 'being happy' is not it or them (or is only – and perhaps only sometimes – an epiphenomenon of their achievement)? An immediate difficulty with answering this is that doing so would be prescriptive, and by thus usurping individual autonomy goes directly against the premise that we must each identify and choose a life – and the goals that shape it – individually. For the person who dedicates herself to creating a beautiful garden, or weaving intricate tapestries, or teaching children to play the flute, or searching for vaccines against viruses, or raising a family, or exploring tropical forests, these are intrinsically worthwhile things, and doing them – especially doing them effectively, doing them well – will be satisfying, productive, rewarding. It is right to say that doing them will make the doer *happy*. But it is the *thing being done*, to which being made happy by doing it attaches, that is the worthwhile thing. The fact that its worthwhileness does not consist in its *point* being to make the doer of it happy is demonstrated by the fact that there are worthwhile things that might not bring feelings of happiness with them, particularly if (as is often the case) people think that 'satisfaction', 'reward' and 'contentment' are expected properties or at least concomitants of happiness. For example: scientific research which yields only negative results, archiving records, labelling spare parts, transporting foodstuffs from rural farms to urban markets, testing pH levels of water in public reservoirs, replacing library books on shelves – one could go on and on listing necessary and valuable endeavours at which people can acquire expertise and which some people might dislike doing or having to do, and that are intrinsically worthwhile in their context but are only accidentally connected, if at all, to happiness.

Some things regarded by their doers as having enormous intrinsic value even prove painful or costly to their doers. The researcher spending laborious decades in a laboratory or library on a speculative quest, the person running a small shop seven days a week to all hours to support a family, the impoverished mother making food stretch and clothes last for her children – they are doing things they believe or know are intrinsically worthwhile, and which might be exhausting, despairing and with doubtful chances of success. If there can be things intrinsically worth doing that have little or nothing to do with happiness, the case for separating the two notions is made. It is reinforced by observing that 'achieving happiness' can sometimes be an aim sought *at the expense* of something intrinsically worthwhile where this latter has the further character of being necessary in its context – saving a life, for example – and this seriously calls into question the idea that being happy trumps everything else.

But! – this last thought prompts the need for another distinction; a distinction between happiness in any present moment *versus* happiness as the supreme overall goal of life. If one had done onerous, painful, difficult but intrinsically worthwhile things that, in the doing, did not make you happy, would you not nevertheless feel – on looking back over your life as a whole – satisfaction (and hence happiness) at knowing you did what was intrinsically worthwhile despite the pains and difficulties? There is a subtler version of this thought: that even if you died before you had the opportunity to reflect on your life overall and thereby reach the judgment just described, you can know now that if you were in future in a position to make such a judgment, you would indeed make it, given the worthwhile character of what you are (in the moment, painfully and with difficulty) currently doing.

In this abstract way one can concede that 'happiness is the supreme goal' by accepting this as a principle: 'Doing what is worthwhile, whatever doing it feels like in the moment, will make you happy in at least the sense that if you were in a position to judge the overall quality of your life from a notional viewpoint beyond, outside or at the end of it, you would say: "I am happy that I did those things."' Fine; but it is crucial to note that in this sense of happiness, 'happiness' is not by a long chalk an occurrent emotional state; and it can also be observed that the *word* 'happiness' is here being pressed into service as a synonym for other terms that could equally be applied to a life in which intrinsically worthwhile ends are sought: for chief examples, 'a good life', 'an ethical life', 'a worthwhile life'.

Where does this leave the ethical schools of antiquity in their specification of the end or goal of life? Only Aristotle tries to make *eudaimonia* – as a positive state or condition of being – something not identified with what brings it about, regarding it as non-instrumentally sufficient in itself. But its achievement consists in living a life of 'reason in accordance with virtue', and thus is conditional on that continued practice. The other schools give 'naturalistic' answers, identifying the achievement of tranquillity with simplicity, being autonomous, and eschewing efforts to attain status and wealth. This was the aim of Cynics and Epicureans, though for Stoics, as noted in

Chapter 3, the conventional means to satisfaction are not dismissed but treated as 'indifferents' – that is, they are preferable to not having them, but possessing them or losing them does not interfere with living in agreement with nature and does not undermine the *ataraxia* and the 'smooth flow of life' which is the 'good for a rational being qua rational being'.

The ancients did not shrink from identifying happiness as the highest good, and happiness itself with those states and conditions that constitute it: pleasure, peace of mind, conformity with nature's ways, rational choosing. By transitivity of reasoning, this gives to the question 'What is good?' the answer 'pleasure, tranquillity' – *ataraxia* – and the associated notions. Many centuries later the philosopher G. E. Moore argued that this is a mistake, and he gave it the name 'the Naturalistic Fallacy', claiming that it is wrong to define 'the good' as any empirically identifiable natural property such as pleasure or happiness.[8] He argued instead that goodness is indefinable, and that any attempt to explain or define it is like attempting to explain or define a primary colour such as yellow, for you cannot, he said, define the colour yellow in words or in terms of other colours; you can only show an example of it to someone wishing to know what the word 'yellow' means. His argument for this view is known as the 'Open Question Argument' – if the good is defined as pleasure, the reply could be: 'Yes, this is pleasant, but it remains an open question whether it is (morally, ethically) good.' For any natural property put forward as what is good, said Moore, one can acknowledge that natural property's presence but still ask this question.

Moore's view is unpersuasive. First, the Naturalistic Fallacy is misnamed, for it is not a fallacy; even if it were wrong to identify what is good with some natural property like pleasure, it would not be a logical contradiction to do so. Nor is the 'fallacy' restricted to naturalistic candidates for defining what is good because, as Moore himself pointed out, it would on his view be a mistake, for the same reason, to identify the good with something transcendent such as 'what a god commands'. So it is neither a fallacy nor confined to what is naturalistic.

But the biggest problem with Moore's view is that identifying 'good' with 'pleasure' does not automatically leave open the question 'but is it good?' whenever one says 'it is pleasurable'. If the theory in question specifically aims to identify 'the good' with 'pleasure' and has a supporting case for doing so, asking 'but is it good?' of what is *offered* as defining 'good' either misses the theory's point or begs the question against it.

An interesting difficulty confronts Moore's view. Asked how we identify what is good if it cannot be defined, his answer was that we just 'intuit' it. Asked how we do that, he said we (he did not define who 'we' are in any of these occurrences, but doubtless had his Cambridge contemporaries in mind) have a 'faculty of moral intuition' which enables us to recognize the presence of goodness when we meet it. But this is implausible, given the ubiquitous and unfortunate evidence of moral disagreement within and across cultures. Moreover, if his view were true it would be decidedly unhelpful, because the claim that people 'just see' whether something is good or bad makes moral disagreements not only undecidable but undiscussable.

The point of mentioning Moore's view is that it shows, in its contrast with the approach of the ancient schools of ethics, how empirical and pragmatic these latter were. They based themselves on the actualities of life and human experience, and sought to offer strategies for avoiding life's bad aspects – if possible, completely; but enduring them if they came – and promoting those aspects which can rationally be regarded as preferable to their opposites or absence.

Recall Herodotus' account of the famous conversation between Solon and King Croesus, in which Solon is reported as saying, 'Call no man happy until he is dead.' One possible meaning of this is that you have to judge a whole life before you can tell whether it was happy. An alternative meaning is that happiness is not possible in life. There is an equivocation on 'happiness' here; in the first meaning 'happiness' is the quality of a life, taken as a whole – as eudaimonic – while in the second it is the emotional state of feeling satisfied and contented at most points, perhaps all points, during life. Solon's choice of the sons who pulled their mother's cart to the Temple of Hera, and who were rewarded by that goddess with the best thing any person could have – namely, an instant and easeful death – suggests the second

interpretation: that happiness is not possible in life.[9] But the first interpretation accords with the view expressed above that if happiness is
the point – if it is the end and goal, the highest good, the one thing
desirable for its own sake – then in light of the considerations there
advanced, it is as the property of a whole life that it is so, and results
from the consciousness, either at the end of life or in the summative
valuation one places on how one is living it, that one's endeavours are
intrinsically worthwhile however they make one feel at any particular
moment.

I think this is what the great essayist William Hazlitt meant when
he said, on his deathbed in September 1830 after a life of struggle, conflict, disappointment and much heartache, 'I've had a happy life.'[10]

Given the close association of the concept of *pleasure* with happiness
in discussions of the latter, it is necessary to look a little more circum-
stantially into it. It was noted earlier that Aristotle's idea of
eudaimonia as a sense of well-doing, well-being, flourishing and satisfaction, would be hard not to describe as pleasant, and the eudaimonic
life itself therefore as pleasurable, if in a gentlemanly 'megalopsychic'
way. The Epicurean idea that the pleasures of health, friendship and
conversation are far superior to indulgence in sensual gratifications of
the kind sought by Cyrenaics is not much different. But given that
the mere word 'pleasure' has immediate Cyrenaic connotations not
intended by philosophers of other schools, it merits examination.
After all, even in Epicurus' own day he was charged with Cyrenaicism because the 'pursue pleasure, avoid pain' slogan associated with
his school was as misunderstood then as it is now.

The kinds of things productive of pleasure are many, but the loca-
tions of pleasure in the human constitution are countably few: the
senses, and the psychological reaction to what the senses convey –
not just colours and sounds, tastes and tactile stimulations, but words
and pictures conveying their respective freights of ideas, stories and
information. One can even describe typical physiological responses
to pleasure; release of endogenous morphines, relaxation of muscle
tone, lowering of blood pressure (though not the two latter in the
arousal phase of certain somatic pleasures). Personal tastes differ

widely, so there are only imperfect generalizations to be made about
what causes pleasure; and it is here that a difficulty arises.

Epicurus' view requires upholding the claim that certain pleasures
are superior to others. John Stuart Mill, two millennia later, encountered much criticism for similarly arguing that there are 'higher' and
'lower' pleasures, an example being the contrast between, say, reading Sophocles and drinking a pint of beer.[11] Asked how one could tell
that reading Sophocles is a higher pleasure than drinking beer, he
said that someone who was in a position to do both would be in a
position to judge. The charge of intellectual snobbery is hard to
resist, given that someone capable of doing both might prefer beer,
and the case one would make in an effort to persuade him that he is
wrong would have to invoke considerations that have nothing to do
with pleasure itself.

For example, one might say that the depth, complexity and artistry of a Sophoclean tragedy, its uniqueness, and the profound effect
it can have – think of Oedipus at Colonus telling Antigone that he
can bear his woes because he is fortified by 'time, suffering, and the
nobility in the blood' – invites one back repeatedly to read and reflect
on it, new things coming to light on re-encounters; and it leads one
to read other things, so that it is the spring to a broadening river of
connections in myth, history and thought. Drinking beer is a transient and mundane pleasure, the same every time, with little intellectual
content – which no doubt is sometimes part of the kind of pleasure
it is – and even if drinking a beer proves to be the spring to a broadening river of interest in different beers, breweries and techniques of
brewing, and to encyclopedic knowledge of hops and barley and
everything else to be known (there is much; the brother of the writer
of these words is a brewer), still a Sophocles-reading beer enthusiast
might have to concede that though, if forced to give up one of the
two, he would give up Sophocles, Sophocles is nevertheless the *higher*
pleasure.

Note that the champion of Sophocles has had to reach outside
the effect that Sophocles has in the way of causing a reader pleasure,
and this introduces new challenges. Why is the 'depth, complexity
and artistry' of a Greek tragedy superior to the flavour, refreshment

and effect of drinking beer? But it is needless to enter that debate, since the fact that a person competent to imbibe both Sophocles and beer might rate the latter as the higher pleasure is enough by itself to close the case against Mill, who seems to have little available to rebut the intellectual snobbery charge.

Mill's critic might therefore appear to have a winning case in saying that what matters is not the kind or degree of pleasure but the simple fact that it produces happiness. Now, however, a different point comes into view. This is to say that it is not irrelevant whether someone's enjoying a pleasure involves doing harm. Mill's 'harm principle' says that if a person does harm to others we can legitimately violate his autonomy. (It is a contested point whether or not self-harm counts here too; certainly Mill had harm to others chiefly in mind.) In at least this case, therefore, the question of how a pleasure itself is procured, and what consequences follow for third parties from its enjoyment, matters to the question of its value. Generalizing the point further, one can say that what distinguishes the pleasures favoured by Epicurus and by Mill from those sought by the Cyrenaics and their ilk is this consequentialist dimension.

This discussion reminds us that all pleasure is ultimately mental, a matter of perception and reception, whether of abstractions conveyed by words heard and read, or by activation of sensory receptors on the body's internal and external surfaces. The same input might produce a reaction of pleasure in one person and pain or disgust in another. Of course the physiology of sensation makes up its own mind independently of consciousness most of the time — a very basic example is that the afferent and efferent neural pathways whose activation results in you jerking your finger away from a flame have looped to and back from the spinal column, not the brain, which only hears about the burnt finger later (in neural time). But we are talking of *pleasure* here, and one cannot experience pleasure without being aware of it even if in a swooning state of sensory bliss, any more than one can experience unfelt pain.

Pleasure as conscious enjoyment of our sensory endowment, enhanced by the capacity both to anticipate and to remember it, heightens enjoyment in the moment of listening to music, eating good food, engaging in sexual intimacy, dancing, swimming, sun-bathing, going on a country walk, and so variously on. Enjoyment 'in the moment' is the greater for not being subjected to intellectual analysis as it occurs; obviously, we do better to leave it to unfold as purely itself. But it is equally obvious that reflection on the nature and sources of pleasure is not irrelevant to their best enjoyment. The pleasure of a half-hour listening to music is the greater because the music was chosen, the quality of sound reproduction is good, antici-pation and expectation were engaged, and one prepared oneself to listen. Think of the informative contrast here, how pain or discom-fort is exacerbated by fearful anticipation; the tense dental patient who has been dreading the drill for days has a worse time than a relaxed patient. The key to seeing pleasure as a good is to see how it fits into an overall conception of the life worth living; this is how the ill consequences of certain types of pleasures-of-the-moment dis-count them as options.

One of the chief features of the renewed interest in art, literature and philosophy which constituted the Renaissance was its fostering of an intelligent interest in the pleasure of this life as against the puta-tive pleasures of an afterlife, gained if the pains of this life can be endured (ironically, these being pains you are almost guaranteed to experience if you flee pleasure as a snare set by the devil). One aspect of this was the appearance of treatises asserting the value of life in the here and now, for example the writings of Petrarch, Giannozzo Manetti's *On the Excellency and Dignity of Man* (a reply to Pope Inno-cent III's *On the Misery of Man*) and Pico della Mirandola's *Oration on the Dignity of Man*. As these titles suggest, a major theme was their challenge to the prevailing theological view that life is a dangerous passage of test and suffering, in which the devil is constantly at work to snatch away our immortal souls. By rigid adherence to duty and denial of the flesh, which is Satan's doorway into us, one can get into heaven at last. The intentionally minatory *contemptus mundi* religious literature of the time represented life as a site of tribulations; hunger, disease, injury, fear and anxiety, poverty and tyranny were depicted with macabre relish to alarm people into hope of a better future life, and thus into faith, and thus again into obedience to the Church.

The response of Renaissance humanism was to reject the claim that this is the invariable fate of humankind, and instead celebrate human powers of mind and the possibilities of beauty and pleasure, as productive of lives that are good to live. They pointed out that animals are enslaved by their instincts, whereas humans can make choices; their possession of language constitutes an infinite capacity to bring past and future into the present, and to embrace the universe within the power of imagination. The rediscovery of the writings, art and architecture of classical antiquity thereby brought a new sense of proportion. It revived the legitimacy of pleasure, and celebrated it in painting and poetry.

The point of mentioning this is that it illustrates in familiar terms, because the Renaissance's art and architecture is still vitally with us, what a rational Epicureanism meant in its day – more generally, what the Greek ideals of pleasure and beauty were as essentials, in association with reason, of lives worth living.

The discussion to this point accepts as uncontroversial the idea that pleasure and happiness are either the same thing, with the former constituting the latter, or that they are intimately causally linked, the former producing the latter. Some of the recent work in 'happiness studies' challenges this, citing the contrasting roles of the neurotransmitters dopamine and serotonin, the former associated with pleasure, the latter with happiness. Pleasurable activities, such as eating, shopping, sex, alcohol and other drug use, stimulate the secretion of dopamine. This substance has a bad press because it acts to prompt repetition of the rewardingly pleasurable activity, again and again to the point of addiction, whether to types of behaviour or substances. Serotonin, by contrast, is associated with emotional stability, calm, contentment and good sleep. Low serotonin levels are associated with depression, aggression, anxiety, memory dysfunction, impulsivity and insomnia – any one of which by itself undermines happiness. The idea is that engaging in activities that prompt serotonin secretion – enjoying relationships with family and friends, making a contribution to the community, eating healthily, exercising regularly, getting a good night's sleep – will lead to happiness.

Engaging in activities that stimulate dopamine secretion – partying hard and late, doing things that produce a high, or ingesting or injecting what produces a high and doing it in increasing quantity with increasing frequency because of dopamine's relentless repetition-addiction cycle – will be pleasurable in the moment but productive of unhappiness in the longer term. However one describes it, pleasure and happiness on this view are not only not the same but potentially antithetical.

Even without knowledge of the neuropsychological details, the Stoics and Epicureans clearly saw the contrast between what is pleasurable in the moment and what serves the longer-lasting state of *ataraxia*, peace of mind, which they both extolled as the goal. In the case of the Stoics, pleasurable activities were viewed as 'indifferents' – nice to have but not necessary to the ultimate good, and therefore not identifiable with it – while to the Epicureans the pleasure they had in mind was what serotonin produces, not what dopamine produces, as they would have put it if they had known. They unquestionably conflated the *mood* of 'feeling happy' with the state of being happy, as most do; but they get away with it by assuming, not entirely without justification, that the mood is a typical mark of the state, and the state is a very frequent maker of the mood.

This is consistent with the point made at the beginning of this chapter that happiness is not to be understood merely or only as an emotional state, but more accurately and fully as a condition of life. The search for happiness in the former sense can and often does undermine the attainment of happiness in the latter sense, as illustrated by the case of one who parties enthusiastically instead of giving enough attention to his studies or career – the irony being that anyone who thinks this is a killjoy point of view is failing to see how mistaking what dopamine produces for what serotonin produces can all too easily lead to happiness's very opposite.

6. The Great Concepts

At the centre of discussion in the ethical schools was the idea of *virtue*. To modern ears the word has a priggish ring, bringing to mind saccharine images of pious maidens and moralists wagging their fingers. But its meanings are as rich as they are important, for they involve the great concepts of ethical enquiry.

Consider the etymology of 'virtue'. In Latin *vir* means 'man', in the sense of masculine human being. *Virtus* means 'valour', 'strength', 'merit'. In Greek the word for 'fortitude, courage' is *andreia*, 'manly'. Look to a language yet closer to its Indo-European roots, Sanskrit, and you see *vir* there means 'to be powerful, valiant, heroic'; and it also means 'to split, tear open, break into pieces'.[1] Now you get the picture. In origin 'virtue' is a warrior concept. *Virtue* is *warrior virtue*: courage, strength, fortitude, endurance, ferocity in battle; preparedness to kill and die in defence of the tribe, the territory.

But note the rider: 'in origin'. Obviously enough, 'virtue' changed its meaning at some point to something much less military – to modesty, patience, mildness, restraint, honesty, kindness, probity. The claim might once – in a more sexist past – have been that the concept switched from a masculine to a feminine stereotype. Indeed the view taken by Nietzsche goes several steps further; he spoke of a complete inversion of outlooks, the heroic virtues being usurped by a 'slave morality' in which it is virtuous to be humble, downtrodden, poor, to suffer, to turn the other cheek. Recall the Christian beatitudes: blessed are the poor and the meek.[2]

But it would be less tendentious to say that the concept changed from having warrior connotations to having *civic* ones, the civic virtues being those that promote sociality – the desirable characteristics of cooperation, promise-keeping, truth-telling and mutual support which together make society possible.

One could say that there is a snapshot of the moment when the concept of virtue changed its meaning. It is Aeschylus' *Eumenides*, the third in his *Oresteia* trilogy, first staged in the mid-fifth century BCE in Athens, at the high moment and in the central location of classical antiquity.

Aeschylus' trilogy — *Agamemnon*, *Choephori* and *Eumenides* — tells of the return of Agamemnon, chief among Greek kings, from the Trojan War; his murder by his wife Clytemnestra; his avenging by his son Orestes; the pursuit of Orestes by the Furies in punishment for killing his mother; and the denouement of this bloody saga, recounted in the final play, where an immense shift of moral emphasis takes place. The importance of Aeschylus' trilogy as an observation — a portrayal, even in a sense a record — of this conceptual shift is in my view very great, coming as it does in the middle of the 'Axial Age', this being a term coined by Karl Jaspers to denote the period when philosophical reflection on questions of *values* — moral and social values — arose simultaneously in China, India and Greece, as exemplified in the iconic persons of those near-contemporaries, Confucius, the Buddha and Socrates — all philosophers, note; not priests or prophets, not announcers of divine messages, but thinkers who thought about life as people live it.[3]

The story Aeschylus tells is worth recounting. Remember that Agamemnon had been away at Troy for ten years. At the very beginning of the expedition he had been obliged to sacrifice his daughter Iphigenia to placate an angry deity who was preventing the Greek fleet from setting sail. The deity in question was Artemis, virgin goddess of the hunt, whom Agamemnon had deeply offended by killing a stag sacred to her. (Others say it was because after killing the stag he boasted that he was a better hunter than she.) In light of the immense commitment represented by the fleet of a thousand ships and the armies they carried, and in light of the oaths that the Greek kings had taken to rescue Helen, whose abduction by Paris of Troy was the cause of the war, Agamemnon had to accept the demand for Iphigenia's life. His killing of Iphigenia and long absence turned his wife Clytemnestra against him. She had taken a lover, Aegisthus, who wished to be king in Agamemnon's place. So when Agamemnon returned to Mycenae after the war, Clytemnestra and Aegisthus murdered him.

According to the code of warrior virtues, Orestes, the son of Agamemnon and Clytemnestra, had to avenge his father's death. Because his mother had killed his father, he had to kill his mother. So he did. This drew upon him the wrath of the Furies, the *Erinyes*, chthonic female divinities whose duty it was to punish those who broke sacred bonds such as the duty of a child to a parent. They chased Orestes across Greece; he managed to get to Delphi, home of the god Apollo, and there explained his plight: to be filial to his father he had perforce been unfilial to his mother. He was gripped in the vice of the remorseless Greek view that even if it was your fated destiny to do wrong, you would be punished for it. Apollo advised Orestes to seek help from his sister Athena at her city of Athens, because she was both clever and wise and would think of a way to solve his problem. Apollo put the *Erinyes* to sleep just long enough for Orestes to escape to Athens. There, after hearing his lament, Athena decided that she would do something novel: she would summon citizens of Athens to hear his case – a jury – and ask them to decide what to do.

A courtroom drama duly unfolds. Orestes had Apollo as his defence attorney, and Apollo told the jury that Orestes was not guilty of killing a parent because a mother is not a parent but merely a receptacle. Whether or not they accepted this argument, half the jury voted to set Orestes free. Athena added her casting vote to theirs. Just as she did so, the Furies arrived in Athens, and true to form they were furious, finding Athena, Apollo and the citizens of Athens engaged in the act of letting Orestes go.

And here is the great moment in human history recorded by Aeschylus: he has the *Erinyes* say to Athena, 'You young gods' – note that! 'you *young* gods' – 'You young gods have usurped our role! It was our duty to take revenge, but you have set up a talking-shop and after a lot of hot air you have let him off!' (I paraphrase.) To which Athena replies, 'Yes; for we live in a new world, where instead of seeking to restore justice by means of revenge, we must discuss what is best to do, and find solutions through consent and compromise.' (I paraphrase again.) *This* is the moment when the old dispensation is seen to give way to a new dispensation, an old way of justice to a new – an old order to a new morality.[4]

The virtues of courage and loyalty have always of course remained warrior virtues, needed in times of danger, but they have extended their meaning beyond the sphere of military striving, and have joined those specifically civic and personal virtues which constitute the traditional lists. In classical philosophy the four cardinal virtues are prudence, fortitude, temperance and justice; 'prudence' means practical wisdom or simply – if this is different – wisdom, and 'fortitude' means courage. There are of course many other virtues such as considerateness, generosity and industriousness, but most are parts of or subsumed by these chief virtues. As we saw in Part I, Aristotle solved the problem of how you identify a virtue by saying it is the 'mean' – the middle way – between opposing vices; courage is the mean between cowardice and rashness, generosity is the mean between meanness and profligacy. What counts as a virtue or a vice depends upon circumstances, and therefore has to be worked out on a case-by-case basis. For example, there is no single general thing which is 'cowardice'; running away from the enemy in battle and running away from a snake are both cases of running away, but in the second case it is prudence not cowardice, and in the first case it is cowardice if it is not prudence (and sometimes whether or not it is also prudence).

The Romans derived from their republican period a rich sense of virtues both civic and military and sometimes a fusion of both, as befitted a muscular, pragmatic, strong-willed and majestically self-observant, self-critical and aspirational society. To manliness, courage, fortitude, self-reliance, discipline, dutifulness, perseverance and tenacity – all of which would figure in a list of warrior virtues – they added mercy, justice, honesty, prudence, continence, dedication, generosity, selflessness, wisdom, humour, frugality, dignity, industriousness, wholesomeness, gravitas, courtesy, friendliness – and *humanitas*, meaning 'culture' and 'learning'. The Roman virtues were personal virtues, and these personal virtues made and upheld Rome. Mucius Scaevola – showing his captors, by putting his hand in a fire and holding it there, that torture would not compel him to divulge secrets – and Horatio on the bridge – single-handedly holding back Lars Porsena's Etruscan army while his comrades demolished the bridge behind him – are exemplars of everything that the defenders of republican Rome valued, and the loss of which they lamented when the imperial epoch began in the first century BCE. The likes of Caligula and Nero in subsequent imperial times are as remote from the Roman republican ideal of virtuous men as Pluto is from the sun.[5]

In Christianity three 'theological' virtues are added to the four cardinal virtues of the Greek philosophers, the theological virtues being – according to St Paul in 1 Corinthians 13 – faith, hope and charity. The first two might be viewed askance by a sceptic, first because they seem to be propagandistic excuses for the failure of a religion to deliver its promises,[6] and second because they are the opposite of virtues which have much to recommend them: faith is the opposite of the intellectual virtue of basing one's views on evidence and reason, and hope can too often be a substitute for the practical virtue of acting to put things right or making things happen rather than passively hoping that they will do so by themselves.

Later Christians added humility and love of God, and gave special emphasis to chastity, celibacy and pudor, this latter meaning that species of shame and even loathing for the body and its functions, especially sexual, which drove some devotees to extremes – an anchoritic existence in the desert, immurement in religious communities, 'mortification of the flesh' such as self-flagellation and even self-castration.[7] This was a far cry from the respective Epicurean and Stoic versions of 'nothing in excess', which those ethical outlooks regarded as both sane and practical – the self-advice of the mature mind. Nietzsche objected vehemently to the idea of making virtues out of humility, passivity, abasement, servitude, weakness and suffering, as the Sermon on the Mount in Matthew 5–7 does; it is this that he called 'slave morality' and to which he contrasted his ethic of the *Übermensch*, who exerts himself to be the opposite.[8]

But the names of the virtues – courage, mercy, fortitude, continence and the rest – denote generalities; and, as the practical-minded Aristotle notes, one must make them more specific. We need examples to anchor them to situations we meet in life as we live it. One thing that immediately becomes apparent is that there is a difference as well as a connection between the *exercise* of a virtue and the *possession* of a virtue: to be courageous on a given occasion and to be a courageous person generally are not the same, though the concept of 'being a courageous person' implies that, when courage is called for, more often than not the person thus described will display it. It thus denotes a disposition and a capacity. And that in turn leaves open the question whether a person can be described as courageous if never called upon to manifest courage.

The great concepts of virtue link and mutually inform each other, together providing a network of resources, when examined and understood, upon which an individual can draw in answering Socrates' question.

Start with *courage*. We typically still think of it as a warrior attribute, required for the dangers of battle, and by analogy extend it to all endeavours of risk and challenge, such as climbing mountains, descending to the abyssal depths of ocean, rocketing into space. But courage is a very various phenomenon, demonstrated even more often in ordinary life, where millions daily face and overcome pain, anxiety and heartache, all of them commonplaces of the human condition. The etymological root of 'courage' is Latin *cor*, 'heart', deriving from the view held by most ancients that the heart is the seat of emotion, and that a strong heart − a strong emotional centre − is required to bear with fear and adversity. This is a piece of folk wisdom that has survived the ages.

Courage can only be felt by those who can feel fear. Fearlessness is not courage. The observation in Plato's *Laches* that a lion is not courageous but fearless makes the point, though in fact lions are afraid of fire, loud bangs and packs of hyenas, among other things. The distinction explains what attitude one might take to the various characters in Homer's *Iliad* as regards who is courageous and who not. The most distinctive act of courage is recounted in *Iliad* Book 24, which tells of King Priam making his way through the enemy Greek encampment at night, to beg for the corpse of his son Hector from the brutal Achilles − who had been abusing Hector's body for days, dragging it behind his chariot round and round Patroclus' tomb in furious revenge for the death of his beloved friend.[9]

Achilles himself was not courageous but, like a lion, fearless, knowing that he was physically invulnerable except for a patch on his heel where his mother had held him while dipping him into the River Styx. Even without his invulnerability he would have been fearless, because for him – as typically for all Bronze Age warriors we learn of in legend – glory, achieved in battle whether or not one died in the process, was worth far more than life. Other examples of courage in the *Iliad* would be Ajax holding off the Trojan attack in Book 15, Menelaus defending Patroclus' body in a violent melee on the Trojan plain in Book 17, and Hector himself going nervously out to fight with Achilles in Book 22 – we know he is scared because he contemplates surrender, he runs away when on the plain alone with Achilles, and before venturing out to battle earlier he paid a tender farewell visit to his wife Andromache and his infant son Astyanax, the latter so frightened by the nodding plume on his father's helmet that Hector took it off to soothe him. But Hector guessed it was his last farewell, and his heart quailed. In the end he is tricked by the gods into standing and fighting alone with Achilles, a far superior warrior; and when he does, he exemplifies full courage to the end.

These high tales do not strike us with quite the same force as reports of more recent acts of bravery. An Australian soldier, Mark Donaldson, won the Victoria Cross in Afghanistan in 2008 for rescuing an interpreter from an exposed position during an ambush, and attracting hostile fire to himself so that wounded comrades could be carried away safely. As soldiers often do in the glare of publicity afterwards, Trooper Donaldson said he was just doing what he had been trained to do, and indeed the whole aim of military training for combat roles is to provide means for individuals in high-adrenaline situations of noise, tumult, confusion and extreme danger to act appropriately. But still: the far more natural reaction would be to freeze, run away or give up, and training designed to override these reactions is not invariably successful. Where proof of courage enters in Trooper Donaldson's case is that his actions showed appraisal of the situation and adjustment to achieve an effective response to it, in the process accepting high risk to protect others. If medals for bravery are ever merited, this is an example of when.[10]

In less convulsive situations, in ordinary life, courage is often required in proportionately if differently exceptional amounts. Getting out of bed in the morning under a weight of grief is a too-familiar one. There are many other kinds, not least the courage to face things new and different; Rilke rightly says in his *Letters to a Young Poet* that courage is needed 'for the most strange, the most singular and the most inexplicable that we may encounter'. That is a salutary point given that life has its unexpected turns, sometimes in an instant – because of an accident, a coincidence, the sudden irruption of sheer luck, good or bad. This even includes courage to accept things we do not normally regard as requiring courage: falling in or out of love, accepting the obligations of relationship or learning to live unsupported by them. The point about obligation applies, for a domestic example, when one has offspring; remember Tolstoy's Levin in *Anna Karenina*, whose reaction, on having his newborn son Dmitri first placed in his arms, is to feel his heart sink into his boots at the thought of the responsibilities thus incurred.[11]

One cannot contemplate the sundry kinds of courage, either in their adventurous or their daily forms, without also taking note of two associated though opposite phenomena: fear and cowardice.

Fear has, of course, a positive side; a capacity for fearing is evolutionarily advantageous because it makes us alert to dangers. We react aversively to a rustle in the bushes because in our species' past rustles might have signalled a predator. It has also been astutely remarked that a good scare is worth more to a person than good advice. But, in general, fear is itself more to be feared than most of the things people typically fear, not only because it can be inhibiting when action is required, but because it is a source of many wider social ills, such as racism and xenophobia, and hostility to things new or different, thus promoting bad kinds of conservatism. Fear is closely allied to ignorance; they feed off each other, as racism demonstrates. And it has its own inexorable logic, for what we fear comes to pass more often and more quickly than what we hope, mainly because the very act of fearing makes what is feared happen.

'Fear can never make virtue,' said Voltaire. He was thinking of the way the Church sought to control behaviour with threats of eternal punishment. But the point is more general, because one of the worst things fear does is to make cowards. A coward is one who flees when he should stand. Cowardice is a *warrior vice* in origin, condemned because, in addition to exposing the unworthiness of the coward himself, it lets comrades down. Admittedly, most people are cowardly to some extent even about commonplace things: not going to the dentist for fear of the shrieking drill, not going to the beach because loth to appear in a bathing suit. Dental treatment is now largely guaranteed to be painless in most countries that have or need it, but in living memory it was quite an ordeal, and anticipations of it wonderfully illustrated the truth that a coward dies a thousand deaths; those sleepless nights in anticipation of the dentist's chair were almost worse than being in it, and therefore multiplied the agony. Seneca's thirteenth letter to Lucilius addresses the issue in robust Stoic fashion: cowardice saps confidence, loses opportunities, wastes talent; the best course is to refuse to be afraid until fear is really required. 'More things are likely to frighten us than crush us,' he writes; 'we suffer more in imagination than in reality. Do not be unnerved before the crisis comes; it might never come, and anyway it is not here yet.'

Recognizing that the concept of courage sits among a cluster of implied or associated ideas about other virtues and vices, such as the two just mentioned, prompts one to pursue the links further. For example: for many kinds of courage – not the momentary kind exercised in an emergency or the heat of battle, but the enduring kind required in ordinary life – perseverance is a necessary accompaniment. This is particularly so in adverse circumstances – as Seneca also remarked, 'Even after a bad harvest there must be sowing' – and in such cases it is practically defining of courage itself. Perseverance is in fact a multiple virtue, in that it embraces determination and resolve, thereby importing both into courage's definition. It has to be distinguished from mere obstinacy, something it is not always easy to do. This is because both perseverance and obstinacy draw fuel from yet another virtue: a capacity for optimism, which therefore also has its place in an analysis of courage.

The words 'optimism' and 'pessimism' are of very recent origin, the first of them coined by the philosopher Leibniz in the course of expounding the idea (soon afterwards made famous by Voltaire's satirical attack on it in his novella *Candide*) that we live in 'the best of all possible worlds'.[12] Starting from the two premises that the world was created by God and God is wholly good, Leibniz argued that this world must therefore be the best world possible, even with all its imperfections of natural and moral evil, because evil must have been foreseen and planned by God, for whom a perfect world – one in which evil does not exist – would not be best, because it would not give the right opportunities to humanity to exercise faith, courage, charity, and the other virtues necessary for admission to heaven. This argument occurs in Leibniz's book *Theodicy*, a word that means (to use Milton's phrase) 'justification of the ways of God to man'. The word 'optimism' is coined from Latin *optimum*, 'best'. From 'optimist' it is easy to derive 'pessimist', which the French did under Voltaire's influence. A key point of Leibniz's argument is its distinction between what is best and what is perfect, and the case it makes for saying that what is perfect is not invariably what is best – which in turn leads to the observation that 'the best can be the enemy of the good' if futile striving for a putative best prevents achievement of what is good.

Though the *words* 'optimism' and 'pessimism' are new, the attitudes are of course not. This raises the interesting question of which outlook was most prevalent among our Stone Age ancestors, a question worth asking because the answer might suggest which is best as a general strategy, given that we, their descendants, are successfully here now. One cliché has it that pessimists are realists; is that how our ancestors survived among the sabre-toothed tigers? Another cliché says that optimism is essential to achievement, because (as William James observed) pessimism weakens us whereas optimism gives us strength. Our ancestors, and we their descendants, have in some respects done all right. So which were our ancestors – pessimist/realists, or optimists? The dilemma is reflected in the rich tradition of jokes about the matter. 'The optimist says this is the best of all possible worlds, the pessimist worries that he is right' is one such.

Perhaps Antonio Gramsci offers the best resolution: 'I am a realist because of intelligence, an optimist because of will.' There is in truth

little option to optimism in most respects, because if one were seriously pessimistic about life the solution is to jump off a cliff. This
thought brings us to an important point: given that jumping off a cliff
would probably take courage, we see that the connection between
optimism and courage is not a *necessary* one, for we here contemplate a
courageous pessimist. Then again: would it not be more courageous
for him not to jump, but to live on? If *this* question illustrates nothing
else, it shows the weakness of generalization and inspecificity, because
one cannot judge which would be the more courageous choice unless
one knew the putative jumper's circumstances. Still, one can say that
on the whole an optimistic approach to life is an adjunct to courage,
whether or not it is misguided or even a potentiator of folly, because
acting in the face of adverse circumstances indicates hope for what
lies on the other side of the act – and in this case 'hope' has a job to do,
as belonging to the essence of optimism.

Continuing to pursue links brings another of the cardinal virtues
into view: prudence. This is because if courage is, on Aristotle's
advice, to be distinguished from both the diametrically opposing
vices of rashness and cowardice, its connection with prudence is key.

Prudence is 'practical wisdom', *phronesis* in Greek. Indeed the adjec-
tive 'practical' is unnecessary, because wisdom – not the same as either
intelligence or learning – is about that most practical of things: life. Its
own immediate constellation of related concepts includes those of
common sense, maturity and judgment. These in turn presuppose
experience. If one were to describe a child as wise, and mean it literally, it would be because the child had seen enough to have acquired a
sound and proportionate grasp of the meaning of what is happening
around him in his world, and an understanding of what it is worth.
The old are credited with wisdom because, in many cases, they have
had enough experience not to place inappropriate value on things,
and to tell when it is better to wait than to act. It is a common feature
of the early and middle courses of life that what seems to matter most
are in fact inflated trivialities; either time or experience – and most
powerfully, both – tends to sort things into better proportions.

Most accounts of wisdom wrongly conflate it with intelligence

and learning, no doubt because being wise is the same thing as dealing with life intelligently, and because experience accrues knowledge.
The muddle consists in *identifying* 'being wise' with 'being intelligent', where the latter denotes intellectual capacities for handling
information and solving puzzles, or with being knowledgeable in the
'learned' sense of knowing lots of facts, dates and formulae. A mountain shepherd might be wise who has no head for mathematics and
has never learned a single fact from a book. Dealing with something
intelligently – by choosing the right means to deal with whatever it
is, and being effective as a result – can be done by someone who might
not count as 'intelligent', or as sufficiently well-informed, in the sense
required by, say, a university admissions tutor considering applicants.
Similarly, learning – book learning, theory – is not only not a guarantee of wisdom, but in some cases might undermine it. This is not
the same as the 'Einstellung effect' – trying to apply past solutions to
new problems even though simpler solutions exist – because this
effect can be displayed by both the learned and the unlearned. Rather,
it is that an overload of theory can obscure rather than clarify; George
Eliot's Mr Casaubon, the dry and futile scholar in *Middlemarch*, is an
example.

Most people think of themselves as both smart and wise, significantly overestimating their cognitive capabilities. This is known as
the 'Dunning-Kruger effect'.[13] The result of choices and actions based
on inflated self-worth are messy. Delphi's 'know thyself' bears on the
question of wisdom, therefore; rational self-estimation, neither over-
nor undervaluing one's capacities, is essential to it.

Prudence, practical wisdom, *phronesis*, was regarded by Aristotle as
a high intellectual virtue. As suggested by the use just made of the
word 'rational', another way to characterize wisdom is as 'practical
rationality'. What is *ratio*-nal is what is *proportional* : a rational belief is
one that is proportional to the evidence for accepting it; a rational act
is one that fits the circumstances. An interesting light is thrown by
considering what name we would use if the characteristics of wisdom were applied to malevolent or at least negative purposes. That
word would be 'cunning'. We do not think that a cunning person
has to be intelligent or learned to be cunning. 'Cunning' carries

connotations of deceit and evasion, of sneakiness – but of effective sneakiness, exploiting an accurate grasp of how things are and dealing with them appropriately for the ends in view. To be wise is to do the same, but for neutral or good ends.

Courage and wisdom are obvious candidates for nomination as cardinal virtues. To the modern eye, 'justice' might seem an odd companion to them, as something for which a society rather than an individual has responsibility. But as one of the cardinal virtues it means '*being* just'. For Aristotle, the virtue of justice, *dikaiosyne*, consists not only in according to others their due, but in everyone – including oneself – having the fair proportion of any distribution, this being the mean between selfishness (thus depriving others of their fair share) and selflessness (in the sense of 'disregarding oneself', neglecting what is reasonably owed to oneself).[14] So it relates to how we act towards others while not forgetting that we owe a fair share to ourselves too, remembering that ensuring our own welfare means that we are not a burden on others.

This last point relates to Aristotle's views about 'self-love'. Selfishness – by its nature a form of injustice to others – is familiar both as a phenomenon and a temptation, given how commonly we witness it in others and feel the temptation ourselves. But consider the fact that loving others means that we wish what is good for them, and therefore act accordingly. This acting includes being the kind of person who is a worthy friend to those we love – and this requires of us that we be good friends to ourselves in order to make ourselves worthy. So we must love ourselves in order to love others well – not selfishly and egoistically but, says Aristotle, maturely and virtuously. Part of being a good friend to oneself for the sake of others therefore includes being just, for justice means everyone (including oneself) is fairly treated.[15]

The etymology of *dikaiosyne* interestingly contains the idea of 'approval', suggesting an origin in what is agreed or approved in a sharing-out of (say) foodstuffs or burdens in a remoter historical past. The term *dike* has connotations of both 'custom' and 'approved judgment'. Personified as the goddess Dike (daughter of Zeus and

Themis, the goddess who rules judges and courtrooms) she stands for norms, rules, moral order, rightness. As a virtue, justice is a quality of acts; a just person is one who is fair, whose behaviour respects others, who helps maintain the arrangements that best serve everyone's interests.

At the individual level, the demand to be just and the desirability of being generous can sometimes conflict, just as the impulse to be selfish can militate against justice in the other direction. Matters are yet more serious when, taking justice in its sense of 'judicial justice', one thinks about the virtue of mercy. This is a good example of how the effort to exercise certain virtues creates dilemmas. For to be merciful is to remit a just recompense, to make a condign (fitting) punishment less severe, to accept less than is owed. To be merciful is to act in a more concessive way than one could act given what justice requires or allows in the case. In its sense of 'compassionate forgiveness' mercy is a lovely thing, and showing mercy from a position of power is noble – though cynics might point out that beneficiaries of mercy are not always exalted by the experience but merely relieved, and their being let off could be an encouragement to further bad behaviour – which is precisely where the dilemma lies, for justice exists to keep the social fabric firm, and mercy loosens it. Justice is not itself mercy; mercy is in fact justice denied; mercy and justice are therefore at odds in their different efforts at fostering the good society. Their conflict is a special problem for moral theologians: how does the deity reconcile them? In Exodus 34 God is described as compassionate and gracious, abounding in love, forgiving wickedness, rebellion and sin; but at the same time that he will not leave the guilty unpunished, indeed he will punish them and their children and their children's children 'to the third and fourth generation' – which is not only not merciful but not even just; and almost as bad, it is also the logical fallacy of *argumentum ad baculum*, the use of bullying or threats to coerce someone's compliance.

The conflict between mercy and justice has invited much philosophical reflection since Aristotle, not least because if the central concept in justice is 'giving each what is due', then mercy subverts it. Giving each what is due can be done in one of the three following ways: giving what is owed; giving or recognizing what is properly that person's right or property anyway; ensuring appropriate compensation or reward (and conversely, penalty or punishment) for what someone has done. Someone might argue that mercy is a component of justice, as when a judge imposes a lesser sentence than the standard 'tariff' for a given crime because there are mitigating circumstances. On this view, taking mitigating circumstances into account is *both* just and merciful. But is this really mercy, or is it in fact a finer application of justice? It is surely appropriate to justice that mitigating factors be considered. Perhaps – once again, as with what counts as courage – the point is that every situation is unique, so that to do proper justice, which the robotic application of an inflexible rule would fail to achieve, a judge must exercise her margin of discretion. If that is what 'making a judgment' means, then the concept of justice has to include it. But this is not the same as mercy. It is the different concept of *clemency*, discussed in relation to Seneca and his fellow Stoics in Nero's Rome in Appendix 1. To be merciful the judge must impose an even less appropriate penalty than all the mitigating circumstances already license.

Until 1822 in England, anyone convicted of stealing food faced hanging. Even the obviously guilty were acquitted by juries who felt that being hanged for stealing bread was excessive. You might think that the jurors were being merciful, but on the other hand you might think that the injustice of a law which condemned people to death whatever they did – for their choice was to starve to death or be hanged for not doing so – required the application of true justice. Here, therefore, is indeed a case of clemency, not mercy; clemency which is not unjust, but rather is both appropriate and just in countering the effect of injustice. Mercy can conflict with justice; clemency is a form of justice; with the latter the conceptual tension disappears.

Can it be argued that it is ever unjust to show mercy? Yes, if mercy is shown to one person who has earned a punishment but not to another who has earned the same punishment. Perhaps, more generally, mercy is unjust to society as a whole, which benefits more from consistently applied justice than from occasional and perhaps arbitrary acts of mercy. In Shakespeare's *Measure for Measure* the Duke of Vienna pretends to leave his city for a while, for its laws have grown lax and he wishes to see them restored by his deputy, Angelo, who has a reputation for strictness. Under the rigorous law against fornication one Claudio is arrested and condemned to death. His sister Isabella goes at his request to Angelo to plead for mercy. Angelo, smitten with Isabella, offers to let Claudio go if she will sleep with him. Isabella, horrified, refuses. (In Verdi's *Tosca* the heroine, similarly taxed, has a more robust solution; she pretends to agree to Scarpia's nasty request, and when they are tête-à-tête she stabs him to death.) Does Isabella show mercy to her brother, preferring Claudio's loss of life to her loss of chastity? Indeed, might she not be treating him unjustly? The cowardice of the Duke in leaving restoration of the laws to his deputy, and the hypocrisy of the deputy, are as unedifying as Isabella's judgment about the merits of her virginity compared to Claudio's life. Between them, however, they succeed in dramatizing the dilemmas at issue. Eventually justice is done in the form of Angelo's condemnation, and mercy is done to Claudio whose punishment is rescinded. (The chief injustice seems to be the Duke's peremptory decision to marry Isabella, who is given no say in the matter.)

Incidentally, Shakespeare's most famous treatment of mercy and justice, *The Merchant of Venice*, has an interesting outcome: Antonio, the merchant whose flesh is forfeit to Shylock as a surety for a loan, is saved not by mercy – Shylock refuses to show mercy to those who habitually treat him so mercilessly – but by the strictest application of justice: for as Portia in her disguise as the learned clerk Balthasar clinchingly points out, the contract specified a pound of flesh but no blood.

Mercy has always had its chief application more in the private than the public sphere of affairs. To forgive a child or an employee for some slip, to make allowances, to 'let it go this once', is contained within a small universe of expectations which, unlike 'letting it go this once' with murder or terrorism, would not damage the social fabric. Justice as a structural element of a functioning society might have space in it for clemency in the form of recognizing mitigating factors and offering opportunities for redemption and rehabilitation, but even this margin of discretion requires limits, lest the vital social purpose of justice be undermined.

Seneca understood the dangers of mercy in matters of justice, which is why he offered his interesting argument for clemency. Given that he was urging this concept on Nero when serving as the emperor's prime minister, his effort was a serious one. The key idea in his thesis is that clemency consists in acting on the perception that a guilty verdict would be unjust, despite what the bald facts suggest. This is not mercy, which is recognizing guilt but lessening the sentence – because, in saying that an imputation of guilt would be wrong in the circumstances, clemency is a legal judgment not an interference in a legal judgment.

One perhaps surprising thought that emerges from these reflections is that, whereas justice is a concept that required – as the *Eumenides* story shows – a major change from the warrior virtue's 'eye for an eye' idea of revenge to a civic-virtue idea of what society agrees is fair, the concept of mercy is in a different case. Mercy is in fact a warrior virtue rather than a civic virtue, for all that it seems to be the latter. It is a virtue whose origin lies in circumstances where an individual has total power over others but restrains his use of it sometimes for reasons which, on those occasions, seem good to him. The idea that the exercise of virtue haphazardly depends upon personal whim, as in this kind of case, is what drives all theoreticians of both ethics and morals to seek for something that *compels* virtue independently of personal whim. For religious folk, this is the commands and threats of a deity. For philosophers from Socrates to Kant and beyond, it is reason.

To be just towards others includes being honest. It is obvious that a society and its economy cannot function unless most people most of the time – indeed, nearly all the time – keep promises, honour contracts, are honest in their dealings, and are consistently responsible and reliable. That society on the whole functions adequately is evidence of a widespread, and generally successful, implicit agreement to keep to these terms. Even criminals require society to be generally honest, because they profit thereby, exploiting the trust of others.

Of course people take paper clips from the office and tell fibs to their spouses and in making excuses to people who invite them to dinner but whom they do not want to see – and so forth: a regular current of dishonesty, though within otherwise honest relationships, helps maintain society too, by keeping interpersonal peace and avoiding unnecessary offence. But this is the convenient or irenic evasion of hurtful or disruptive truth at a minor level, not untypically the domestic level. Dishonesty in business, politics, government, policing, manufacturing standards – in short anywhere that dishonesty causes serious harm – is a different matter. But a Stoic of the classical era is unlikely to think that minor dishonesties in the domestic sphere – of the 'no, that doesn't make you look fat' kind – are consistent with honesty in the public sphere. The chief reason is that being honest is not only about upholding social bonds, it is also about self-respect. One thinks of the story of the sculptor making a statue which is to be attached to a building, who is asked, on being seen to work carefully on the back of the statue, why he is doing this given that no one will see it; and who answers, 'But I can see it.'

Here, though, the question of *weighting* enters. Yes, truth-telling is a very high good. So is kindness. It is sometimes unkind to tell a person the truth. Indeed the Church of Scotland famously has a precept, 'It is a sin to tell an untimely truth.' Which value should trump the other? Again the answer is that it depends, of course, on cases. But *this* answer in turn immediately introduces another important consideration: that of *authenticity*. If one's judgment that such-and-such an occasion is one in which telling the truth would do more harm than good, and it is made authentically – not in a self-serving, pusillanimous, dishonest way – then one can claim justification. What is being invoked is the self-reflexive nature of ethical judgment: to be authentic is to be sincere in one's reasons for a decision, having a case that bears scrutiny, in the particular instance of these particular circumstances, that a better end is being served.

An illuminating example of authenticity would be provided by the person who is a vegetarian and is challenged as to why she is not a vegan. All things considered, veganism is both a more logical and a more moral stance than vegetarianism, since many of the harms caused by meat, fish and dairy consumption are not prevented by vegetarianism. So if the point is abatement of such harms, veganism is the appropriate course. A vegetarian might, when challenged, say that by being a vegetarian she is at least trying to play a part in minimizing some of the harms caused by industrial food production, but consistently with not diverting as many of her resources of time and energy as would be required by the demanding vegan lifestyle. She might put the point by saying she is 'doing her moral best'. Now, this phrase could be a real get-out-of-jail-free card. The murderer, caught with a smoking gun over the victim's body, might say he was 'doing his moral best' even though it wasn't enough to prevent his committing murder. But if a claim to be doing one's moral best were *authentically* made, then even if, generally speaking, only the person claiming this would know if it were true, it is a justification for the choice. Whether it is independently a good justification is another matter, and not irrelevant, but the agent herself is at least sincere in her endeavours.

Reference to authenticity will, for some, appropriately bring to mind the names of Heidegger and Sartre, for whom the concept played a significant role. The relevance of existentialism to discussion of the Socratic Question is great, and is explored later in these pages. For present purposes one might quote a remark by Sartre, made despite his view that authenticity is hard to achieve given the pervasiveness of 'bad faith': that authenticity 'consists in having a true and lucid consciousness of the situation, in assuming the responsibilities and risks it involves'.[16]

Authenticity is also required in the last of the four cardinal virtues, namely temperance, *sophrosyne*, which means 'continence, moderation and self-discipline'. In its guise of moderation it is a medical as well as an ethical virtue; both Stoics and Epicureans took the Delphic inscription *meden agan*, 'nothing in excess', as a principle that applies equally to health of body and health of soul.

Self-discipline – self-mastery – was a key notion for Stoics, not just because it is the hardest of the virtues to achieve but because it enables the others. They recognized that outright abstinence is easier than moderation, and therefore aimed at moderation. Yes: not abstinence but moderation. Their Cynic cousins – 'cousins' in terms of philosophical relatedness – chose to abstain from everything other than basic care of bodily needs, revealing one of the interesting differences between the two schools. Abstinence avoids the danger of things that begin insensibly and grow with time, such as an addiction or gaining weight, both of which get increasingly hard to reverse. If you abstain you do not start on that path. But if you tread the path moderately, you have to maintain vigilance. Stoics welcomed the challenge to maintain vigilance. In cases where the stern virtues of courage and determination are required, and the application of great willpower, the perpetual training in self-mastery would, in their view, amply prove itself. The abstainer, suddenly faced with a need to exert himself in such a way, would be at a disadvantage. Consider a Stoic and a Cynic captured by invaders of their city and subjected to torture; which would you place a bet on to hold out longer? One might say that the Stoics regarded abstinence as a form of *immoderate* behaviour – as excessive – because of such considerations.

It would seem that what Stoics and Epicureans respectively meant by moderation, on the other hand, involved a sharp contrast as regards degree. Moderation is a more austere notion in Stoicism, a more relaxed one in Epicureanism. One legend has it that on the principle 'moderation in all things including moderation itself' some Epicureans would have a tremendous annual party which, as they nursed their headaches the next day, would remind them of why moderation is a virtue.

The idea of continence (restraint, self-mastery), and its celebration as a virtue, is generally only possible in a state of affairs where resources are plentiful. In circumstances where finding water and food is hard, even risky, and often attended by failure, the idea of continence would seem irrelevant. But would it be? Imagine a group of our Stone Age ancestors coming across an abundance of food; would they emulate the lion, which gorges itself until too bloated to move for days, dozing in digestive stupor? Or would they ration the supply they found to make it last longer? The latter requires continence and involves forethought and planning, themselves early ingredients of the capacity for social organization to which they eventually led. This suggests another reason why *sophrosyne* is a cardinal virtue; it is required for the possibility of society. There is no surprise in this, because when one thinks of the need for general trust in social and economic relations, as described above, one sees that reliability and trustworthiness are more likely to be imputed to those – whether individuals or organizations – who manage themselves in a self-disciplined way, and that therefore we are more likely to deal with them than with their incontinent competitors.

All the virtues in the Roman list given above are easy to admire and enjoin, and the world would be a fine place if everyone cultivated them. This even includes 'frugality', which applies today because consumption – overconsumption – by the rich part of the world's population is destroying the world's environment, teaching at least that part of the world's population the value of judicious restraint. Of those listed, the virtues of generosity and tolerance stand out as essential for the creation and maintenance of social bonds; both are too often limited in supply. But some others mentioned by the Romans are not so obvious. They add 'manliness' and 'dutifulness' to the above list. Do these still impress? Certainly, some of their chief traditional manifestations have passed their sell-by dates. The toxic aspects of the first, and the implications of socially subordinating hierarchy in the second, are no longer palatable.

They also mention 'friendliness'. A claim repeatedly made across the tradition of ethical debate from Plato onwards is that friendship is one of life's great values, because it is the most achieved of all the kinds of relationships people can enter into. More on this important point in Chapter 8, on love. But to treat friendliness as a virtue is questionable, when courtesy and consideration more than cover the desirability of behaving constructively towards others without, unrealistically, bidding us to 'be friends with' all and sundry, given that we are not indiscriminate about whom we find genuinely companionable. To treat everyone as if they were actual friends rather than (as we normally do) just being polite to them, including those we find dull or disagreeable, is to ask too much.

That said, it is a crucial fact that we humans are social beings, and with very few exceptions we cannot flourish – cannot perhaps even survive – outside society. As Aristotle pointed out, the question of individual virtue and the question of how society thrives are closely linked. Individuals need society, and society needs the virtues of individuals because it needs mutualities, compromise, methods of adjusting and resolving tensions and overcoming problems. It therefore needs its members to cooperate through goodwill. It needs individuals to give respect where it is due and assistance where it is needed; it needs them to share an idea of a common good worth upholding. There therefore have to be practices and institutions which advance these desiderata, while at the same time preventing or at least managing what is disruptive, indeed destructive, of the social fabric – such as theft, violence, injustice and greed. In simpler times agreement was compelled and disruptive actions remedied by force; might was both the source and the arbiter of right. But when a certain level of complexity is reached in social development, this way of managing disruption itself becomes disruptive, and more peaceful and orderly methods are required – the very point made by Aeschylus in his *Eumenides*.

Nothing in human affairs can ever be perfect, given the diversity of interests and differences of opinion that arise even within small groups. Social living is a negotiation aimed at reaching compromises which – because most things are in constant flux – require perpetual renegotiation. This is done through politics, the public conversation in the media, formal and informal education, conversations over the dinner table. In monolithic societies, dominated by a leader or a religious or political ideology, there is considerably less negotiation. Such societies represent the more primitive arrangements of earlier times, where might was emphatically the arbiter of right. These cruder forms require coercive institutions like the Gestapo, KGB or Inquisition; more sophisticated is the grip over minds exercised by exceptionless religious beliefs, inculcated in childhood and reinforced by a demand for conformity. To get away from these primitive arrangements to a consensual society – one based on the mutually conscious desire of the members to form and maintain it for positive ends, not least among these ends the flourishing of the individual members themselves – is one potent reason why Aristotle said ethics is part of a theory of the polis, why Marcus Aurelius counted 'making a positive contribution to society' among the Stoic goods, and why, many hundreds of years later, in the eighteenth-century Enlightenment, the Earl of Shaftesbury could explicitly make the same Stoic idea of 'a common good' central to his *Inquiry Concerning Virtue or Merit* (1711).[17]

A final point, by way of reminder, is that to talk of virtues is very specifically to talk of ethics, not morals. As already made clear, *ethos* is character, *moralis* is about norms of behaviour in a given culture at a given point in its history. The Socratic Question asks each of us to consider what our individual *ethos* should be, which is the same thing as asking how we should live our lives. Moral codes, consisting of culturally determined norms governing interpersonal behaviour (although they also often have things to say about solitary behaviour), fluctuate between being more or less puritanical or liberal through the course of history. As noted in Part I, what is accepted at one time is not accepted at another – slavery, discriminatory treatment of women, homosexuality, cruel treatment of animals are major examples – and liberalizing tendencies can be reversed, just as puritanical dispensations can be overthrown. The ethical challenge remains throughout changes of moral fashion, even though ethical and moral considerations often exert mutual influence given that moral norms in the prevailing culture will either reinforce or challenge one's ethical sentiments, which in turn will influence one's attitudes to those moral norms, either endorsing them or being at odds with them. Changes in *moral* outlook often, if not indeed always, result from *ethical* disagreement with them.

A big difference between ethical and moral considerations is that where the first revolve upon the question of 'What sort of person should I be?' the second revolve upon the question 'How should I act?' – most specifically 'How should I act in such and such a case?' Utilitarian ethics – most closely associated with Jeremy Bentham and John Stuart Mill in the nineteenth century, although of much older vintage in origin – is a classic example of a 'consequentialist' view, which says that the moral worth of an act is to be judged by its consequences; the act is good if the consequences are good, bad if the consequences are bad. What kind of consequences, in general, make the acts producing them good? Crudely put: those that bring the greatest happiness, benefit or utility to the greatest number. Considerations relating to the character of the person performing the act are not essential, indeed are even irrelevant. This is a practical rule-of-thumb designed to overcome the difficulties faced by thinkers in seventeenth- and eighteenth-century Europe – the period of the Enlightenment and the birth of the modern – who, because religion no longer exerted a monopoly over thinking about right and wrong, were again ('again': i.e. since antiquity) exploring the foundations of morality, asking, 'What is the basis of moral laws? Why is such-and-such right and so-and-so wrong?' While this debate unfolded the questions still pressed – 'How do I act? What should I do?' – and the utilitarian view was offered as an answer.

Now, there is indeed a consequentialist aspect to virtue concepts. If you ask why it is good to be prudent, just, courageous and the rest, the answer is that in addition to making an individual a better person living a better life than would be the case otherwise, these virtues also constructively enhance that individual's contribution to society. *This* aspect looks consequentialist, in evaluating the outcomes of the ethical individual's pattern of behaviour as having utility. But the big difference is that the virtue approach says, 'Be the kind of person who produces such outcomes,' whereas the utilitarian says, 'What is good or bad is measured by the outcomes themselves, forget the agent.' If a person's malevolent intention by accident produces a good outcome – say, by saving someone's life while trying to commit a murder – we would not discount the question of the agent's intentions even if we applaud the outcome. Similarly, a person whose attempt at kindness or assistance accidentally causes harm is not irrelevant to how we judge the case – good intentions in bad outcomes are mitigating factors. We see that, in practice, what a person is like *as a person* matters; we are far from indifferent to ethical considerations in weighing what is good or bad from a moral perspective.

The idea that moral worth is only to be judged by consequences, by maximizing benefit or utility for the greatest number, is severely challenged by Ursula Le Guin's story 'The Ones Who Walk Away from Omelas'. Omelas is a city, 'bright-towered by the sea', where life is very good; the citizens are comfortable, happy, indeed joyous: 'Joyous! How is one to tell about joy? How describe the citizens of Omelas?' The story opens with a description of a summer festival, encapsulating the life of the city and its people in the sunny pleasure of their existence. There are neither soldiers nor clergy, neither strife nor discord; there reigns a 'boundless and generous contentment, a magnanimous triumph felt not against some outer enemy but in communion with the finest and fairest in the souls of all men everywhere and in the splendour of the world's summer: this is what swells the hearts of the people of Omelas, and the victory they celebrate is that of life'.

But there is a condition on which 'their happiness, the beauty of their city, the tenderness of their friendships, the health of their children, the wisdom of their scholars, the skill of their makers, even the abundance of their harvest and the kindly weathers of their skies' depends. The citizens know this condition, and living in Omelas signifies conscious acceptance of it. This condition is that a child must be kept in a dungeon, suffering alone in fear and misery: 'The child used to scream for help at night, and cry a good deal, but now it only makes a kind of whining . . . and speaks less and less often. It is so thin there are no calves to its legs; its belly protrudes; it lives on a half-bowl of corn meal and grease a day. It is naked. Its buttocks and thighs are a mass of festered sores, as it sits in its own excrement continually.' The citizens of Omelas, on reaching a certain age, are taken to see this child through the bars of its prison. Whatever they feel on seeing it, they know that if the child were released, at that very moment 'all the prosperity and beauty and delight of Omelas would wither and be destroyed . . . To exchange all the goodness and grace of every life in Omelas for that single, small improvement: to throw away the happiness of thousands for the chance of the happiness of one: that would be to let guilt within the walls indeed.'

The shock of seeing on what condition Omelas possesses its

happiness might be great at first, but over time people reflect that if the child were released 'it would not get much good of its freedom' in the ordinary non-joyous version of Omelas that would result. It might get 'a little vague pleasure of warmth and food, no doubt, but little more. It is too degraded and imbecile to know any real joy.' And so the citizens reconcile themselves to the condition on which the whole population has its wonderful existence.

And then Le Guin writes, 'But there is one more thing to tell.' Every now and then one of those who are taken to see the child does not go home afterwards, but instead walks down the street from the prison, and keeps walking; walks through the city's beautiful gates, and into the countryside; and keeps walking. 'Each alone, they go west or north, towards the mountains. They go on. They leave Omelas, they walk ahead into the darkness, and they do not come back. The place they go towards is a place even less imaginable to most of us than the city of happiness. I cannot describe it at all. It is possible that it does not exist. But they seem to know where they are going, the ones who walk away from Omelas.'[18]

The other major theory that focuses on acts rather than character is deontology, the view that what is right is *doing one's duty*. This requires specification of the duties that should be obeyed, and a case justifying why they are so. The great figure associated with this outlook is Immanuel Kant.[19] The chief advantage of deontology is that it consists in clear rules for behaviour, following which endows one with merit. Religious morality is also deontological, a deity or deities laying down the rules; in Kant's case, identification of the rules is achieved by applying 'practical reason' to answering the question 'What should anyone placed in this situation do?' where the answer – 'A person so placed ought to do X' – is *categorical* not *hypothetical* (that is, is not of the form 'if you want X, do Y', but is just unequivocally 'do Y'). A hypothetical imperative says, '*If* you want to be healthier, *then* you should give up smoking.' But if you do not want to be healthier, you do not have to give up smoking. A categorical imperative says, 'Keep your promises' – no ifs and buts.

As with consequentialism, deontology does not reach into the character of the agent or concern itself with the agent's intentions and general outlook; so long as the agent acts in conformity with the rules, the agent is moral. This is self-evidently unsatisfactory, not only because, as noted, in evaluating matters of *morality* more inclusive questions about agents matter, but because the importance to each individual of how it feels to live his or her life, the sense of self and self-worth it contains, and the aims and meaning of his or her life-forming endeavours, is crucial, and is what ethical considerations address. Deontology and consequentialism, as moral systems, leave ethics aside. They are third-party views, leaving out of account the first-person perspective and therefore all the questions that arise in that perspective: about how to live and what to be.[20]

7. Death

This most sombre-seeming and depressing of all topics hardly looks relevant to developing a philosophy of life, but in fact, for several good reasons, it is. For one thing, death is not as sombre and depressing a subject as most assume it to be. For another, it is a tenet of some of the deepest philosophical approaches to life that 'to learn to philosophize is to learn to die' – a saying that originated with Socrates, as reported in Plato's dialogue *Phaedo*, was quoted by Cicero in his *Tusculan Disputations*, and later famously served as the title of an essay by Montaigne.[1] As it stands it is an obscure saying, obscure enough to be misunderstood with the pleasant result of prompting a witticism: 'You don't have to learn to die, the first time works well enough.' What it means is, however, important. It means that once you have lost your fear of death, you can live to the full, freely and fearlessly.

By the same token one cannot fully make sense of death until one has some clear ideas about life and the purposes it can serve. More precisely: one cannot fully make sense of the unavoidable and inevitable fact *that one is going to die* until this is factored into the question of living. Given that answers to the 'question of living' are individual ones – we each and separately have to ask and answer it for ourselves – how we make sense of our own inevitable dying and death is a personal matter. Thus Socrates' 'to philosophize is to learn how to die' means 'to philosophize is to learn how to live'; the fact that one is going to die focuses one's mind on the question of what one must do, can do, desires to do, in the life one has. It focuses one's mind on choices, and the choices are individual and personal, tailored to who and what one is – to what kind of person one is, wants to be, and can become.

But of course there are general considerations too. The most important one is that being dead is nothing at all to the dead. When you are dead you do not know it or feel it; there is no feeling of 'being dead', no experience of one's own state of being dead. What you experience is *dying*; and dying is an act of living. You experience dying, whether it is easy or painful, welcome or frightening, as part of your life, albeit the end of your life. But you do not experience being dead. Death is therefore entirely a matter of other people. You experience death as loss, grief, shock, sadness, or perhaps as relief and liberation. Death happens to others; dying happens both to others and to you.

Because *being dead* is identical to *being unborn*, nothing about 'being dead' itself makes it good or evil. It is what it takes away from us that makes it seem so. If it takes away intolerable physical or psychological pain that cannot be escaped by other means, then it is good; when we think of how it removes connections with the beloved, ends our plans, cuts short our interest in life and our commitments to it, it seems bad. But the philosophers argue that one's own death is never bad because one cannot be aware that these connections, plans and interests are lost. It is the *prospect* of loss which is the evil, not the fact of it; so once again death is a problem only for the living, and only if we let it be. The question of how we manage our attitude to that prospect is unignorable, for on it turns whether the fact of our mortality can be made a good thing for us, or something which, because of our fears and repinings, degrades our experience of life. The principal way of dealing with the fear of death is by accepting and then ignoring its inevitability, so avoiding the coward's fate of dying in imagination a thousand times over. This is why Spinoza wrote, magnificently and wisely, 'The meditation of the wise man is a meditation not on death, but on life.'

There are those who believe, or hope, that there is some form of posthumous existence – an afterlife, personal existence and awareness continued in some disembodied way. The evidence for this is nil apart from religious traditions and superstitions, the probative value of which is also nil, as discussed in Part I above. Those who subscribe to such views are in a discussion very different from the one in these pages, because what answers they give to the question of life are wholly shaped by what they believe about an afterlife. Typically, gaining access to posthumous pleasure as opposed to posthumous suffering (the former tends to be rather sketchily imagined, whereas the latter is usually graphically imagined, mainly for minatory reasons) means subordination and obedience to a set of dictates about how to live – dictates that can get down to quite fine detail: not only what to do and not do, but what to eat or not eat, who to marry or not marry, when and how often to pray, how to dress, which parts of the anatomy must not be visible, and so forth. For outlooks of this kind, being dead is the point of life because only then does 'true' existence begin. The constraints imposed on living by such a view look suspiciously like the invention of priests rather than the teachings of deities, not least because if there were any deities one would expect – assuming that they are not malign – rather more logic to their requirements. But in any case, as mentioned, this is not the human life that philosophy asks us to think about. Therefore it is to death and its role in life that we must address ourselves.[2]

Distinguish the death of a *person* from the death of a *body*. When you die, your personhood becomes a matter of what you leave behind in effects on the lives of others. It is a truth to be accepted with realism and courage that your personhood too will die in time; a stroll in a churchyard is a forceful reminder of how soon the memory of individuals fades away, as one looks at the scarcely legible inscriptions on gravestones leaning awry among the weeds. A small number of people leave aspects of their personhood printed on history itself; Sargon the Great, King of Akkad in Mesopotamia, who lived over four thousand years ago, reigning *c.* 2334–84 BCE, is remembered by name and by some of his deeds, and is perhaps the earliest major individual in history to be thus remembered. Names cluster more thickly as history grows to the present, from Homer to Plato to Julius Caesar to Charlemagne to Michelangelo to Shakespeare to Napoleon to Charles Darwin to Albert Einstein – it is their achievements, their role in the unfolding of history, which makes their names stick. There may be thousands of people whose names one recognizes for achievements of their kind, if not degree, but in comparison to the billions of human individuals who have lived and live now, they are a tiny crew.

In more parochial settings, both of place and history, there are local Homers and Darwins, who might not be remembered for so long or so distinctly but after whom streets or schools or bridges are named, who might have a statue in the town square, who might be cherished as a local hero or heroine in the archives of the town's library. Even more locally still, in a family, a parent or grandparent might be missed every day of the lives of those who survive them, or remembered for some other reason, even a negative one. In all these ways, from the grand to the very local and temporary, the thought of people, and the effects they had, can live on when they have died; which is a form of posthumous existence after all. What has ended is the continued creative activity of the person, doing things that have further effects on others and which might therefore be remembered by these others.

When a *person* dies, therefore, the immediate event is the cessation of effect-creation – beyond the act of dying itself – because of the cessation of bodily function. The death of a person is accordingly cessation and diminution of effect-creation, and a tail of effects follows, which in most cases fades almost wholly away after a couple of generations. So the death of a *person* is a fairly lengthy event, whereas the death of the *body* – the moment when vital function stops; cardiac and respiratory arrest, and very soon afterwards brain death – occupies a few minutes at most (consciousness will cease even sooner), even if the body's functions have been faltering and failing over a lengthy period beforehand.

The death of the body is *change*. While blood circulates, the body continues to maintain, by and large, its coherence as an entity, opposing the decay and disintegration of most of its material composition (though a lot of cells are dying and being sloughed away constantly, throughout life; about a million cells every second, or 1.2 kilograms of you a day – while you live most of the lost cells are replaced). When this activity ceases, the body begins to decompose – a word which has but should not have unpleasant connotations, for it simply means 'disassemble, rearrange, reorganize', because a dead human or animal body does not vanish, it just *becomes something else*. Nothing in nature ever disappears, it only takes other forms. The atoms constituting the molecules that constitute the cells of organic matter are released when that matter decomposes, very likely recombining with other atoms into other material forms. So, a human body when dead is, quite literally, recycled into nature. It is rearranged. It changes form, it becomes dispersed into many other things, or even just into the atmosphere (which is a gas consisting of nitrogen with some oxygen and a bit of argon). Given that nitrogen and oxygen (along with hydrogen and carbon) make up the human body, which exhales carbon dioxide in respiration and which is about 60 per cent water, the 'decomposition' of the body means the release of the constituents of water and the other elements mentioned, to be taken up by other things or to float free in the wind. Thus viewed, it is quite a pleasing thought.

The astonishing thing is that the watery construction of simple chemicals that make a human body produces consciousness, intelligence and emotions, and introduces novelty into the history of the universe – humans make things, invent things, create things; they make choices, and billions of choices every day combine to nudge history along a path that would have been hard if not impossible to predict, in its individual details, just one day before.[3] It is this fact of consciousness and activity, or more precisely the thought of its loss or ending, that makes death seem a calamity to most people most of the time. This is a key point, to which we return.

Death of the body, therefore, is a natural process: the cessation of physiological functions, including consciousness, immediately begins the body's dispersion into its physical elements. Cessation of function and the beginning of physical transformation occur together at the moment of death, but what exactly constitutes that moment is a matter of controversy, an important point because many bodily functions can now be artificially sustained. But there is some agreement that brain death is the boundary.

In the rest of nature, cessation of function and transformation of physical elements is integral to life's continuity. It is an important commonplace that death and decay are servants of life. Autumn's falling leaves feed the following spring's growth. Death is therefore a condition of life and part of its rhythm. Human death does, however, differ crucially from the death of other things. Most humans are not just conscious but self-aware, and most (at least if non-religious) regard death as a loss of these supreme possessions and the powers of agency that attend them. It is not that they would, if they thought about it, wish to live for ever, at least in this world; George Bernard Shaw's Methuselah suggests that endless existence would be intolerable. Rather, it is that death comes too soon for most of us, before our interest in those we care about, and in the world at large, is exhausted.

To repeat: we experience *death* only in losing others, so the experience of death is one of grief. Because our own deaths are no part of our personal experience – we are alive *as we die* even if unconscious for the final part – from our own subjective perspective we are immortal. This thought sits alongside another, which is that because we experience the world from our singular point of view, and thus as the centre of the world from that point of view, the world exists – for each of us individually – as 'my world'. In line with the remark above about our deaths *as persons*, 'my world' lasts as long as the fact of my presence in it has any effect on it. In this sense, Sargon's world still exists. This is a corrective to the view that the world exists for each of us individually just as long as we are conscious of it, and that it dies when we die. As we see, this is not so.

The point is significant, because among other things it controverts an idea advanced by Marcus Aurelius. In true Stoic fashion, he remarked that when we die we lose only the present moment, because the past has ceased to be and the future has not yet come, so to comfort ourselves as we die we have only to look around and ask, 'Is this present moment really worth keeping?' But Aurelius was wrong. We are each of us a compound of memories and hopes, and the present is where past and future meet; who we are is defined by what our attitude is to the relationship between our past and our plans and what we are doing about them. We are creatures of narrative; the next instalment of our story, which is the story of our relationships and our world, interests us crucially. It is this fact, of course, that makes death – either of those we love or as the prospect of our own absence from the story – seem an evil. This is why the focus that the fact of death invites us to place on life is so important: like the frame round a picture.

There are those who welcome death, as the ultimate palliation of agonies of body or mind. In Roman times suicide was regarded as an honourable option, and its availability as an escape from intolerable situations was a welcome and life-enhancing fact. Religious proscriptions against suicide are premised on the idea that one's life is not one's own but belongs to a deity who endowed one with it in the first place; to kill oneself is to reject that gift, and is thus a terrible act of *lèse-majesté*. A major consequence of this is that it has taken a long hard struggle, in modern times, to decriminalize both suicide and assistance to people wishing to end their lives. The point is sometimes bluntly made that we are kinder to our pet animals than to our fellow humans, in helping them to escape quickly and easefully from suffering when it befalls them.

Of course it goes without saying, or should, that most cases of suicide are tragic occurrences, especially for bereaved families and friends. It too often happens that it is prompted by kinds of emotional anguish – shame, despair – which might have abated in time, with help. That is why relatives and friends so often feel an extraordinary degree of guilt, blaming themselves for failing the suicidal person at the time of danger. They might also or alternatively feel anger, if they experience the act as one of rejection and selfishness. But it is hard to think of suicide as either of those things. Leaving aside cases where *actually* dying was not the intended outcome of the act because it was in fact a plea for help, a suicidal person's desperation has to be immense for the act to be carried through. In the face of that thought, the appropriate reaction is sorrow that life can reach such a pass for so many.

To repeat: suicide can be a welcome resource too. Someone hopelessly and helplessly ill, suffering indignities and agonies, might yearn for the easy release that medical science can give. People generally think of pain as the principal motivator for this, and some argue that analgesics are now so good that pain cannot be treated as a justification for ending life prematurely. This is only partially true; some types of pain are not controllable. But there are other equally if not more telling considerations. Imagine being doubly incontinent, having to be cleaned up by others constantly, and knowing that the situation is never going to improve. Helplessness and indignity are cruel conditions. Heavy medication removes one from oneself and from others one cares about; a person taking a long time to die and increasingly drugged has almost died to herself and those others already, and yet she might know it but be unable to rise out of the fog and dependency of the drugged state, to be who she is for herself and them. Requesting – and being granted – help to leave that situation, especially if it is unrelievable otherwise, is a final assertion of self-hood, a final act of dignity.

To deny a person who displays a rational, settled, autonomous desire for such a release is as unjust as it is cruel. Debates about this matter have been won by the forces of sympathetic reason in some jurisdictions, but in others they remain obstructed by beliefs about the 'sanctity of life', another example of the way inhumanity can masquerade as piety. It is a familiar paradox that those who invoke the 'sanctity of life' concept in the cases of euthanasia and abortion are not as invariably opposed to war, arms manufacture and capital punishment. Yet euthanasia and abortion are intended to help the living, while war and weapons exist to harm them.

Clear thinking about what makes death good or bad has to start from this premise: that the *quality* of life is the sacred thing, not its mere quantity. Although disease and the natural mechanisms of age-ing can often bring life to a gentle end, it also often enough happens that the process of dying is very uncomfortable. When this happens both the dying person and those who love her can suffer hugely. Contrast a person who chooses, and is given, the opportunity to leave life before dying becomes too hard; she is able to say farewell, and to depart easily. And to repeat: she has her autonomy, one of the core dignities of her personhood, to the last. It is a consummation devoutly to be wished.

Assisted suicide is the best form of euthanasia, for it is chosen by the subject – it is voluntary. When someone is unable to express a wish one way or the other, but is in such a terrible and irrecoverable state that ending life is the merciful option, then it constitutes *involuntary* euthanasia but is 'euthanasia' nonetheless, this word simply meaning 'a good death'. There are many cases where both forms of euthanasia are justified. In jurisdictions where, despite being justified on moral grounds, it is illegal – even if widely practised; which is almost everywhere, for human pity is stronger than laws – many are condemned to suffering by the chief anti-euthanasia argument: that murder might lurk under a false disguise of kindness. And indeed, so it might; but the occasional risk of abuse is not a good reason for letting *all* cases of unrelievable suffering continue. It is instead a reason for arranging matters so that the chance of abuse is minimized, even granting that everything is open to it at times, given human nature and the state of things. Opponents of euthanasia imagine that inconvenient people – ageing parents, patients lingering too long in a needed hospital bed – will be destroyed like unwanted kittens. Some argue that a sufferer might ask for a final injection just weeks before a spectacular medical breakthrough occurs which would save him. These anxieties cause the sum of human distress to mount and mount in hospitals and nursing homes everywhere. But it is not a matter of mere numbers; the fact is that there are cases where it is obviously both right and merciful that someone wishing to die should be helped. It is not beyond human ingenuity to devise ways of determining the merits of candidate cases. There will be difficult decisions, and mistakes, and abuses might occur. But this is the most outstanding example of where mercy will justify what we do.

Positively incorporating the meaning of mortality into one's own life is one of the two fundamental matters to be addressed. The other is how to deal with death itself – that is, others' deaths. When they happen we grieve the loss of a great part of what made life worthwhile. Grief is a wound, and an inescapable process of healing – 'healing' means 'recovering wholeness' – has consequently to be endured. In many societies formal periods of mourning, typically between one and three years long, acknowledge this, and make time for it. In most countries with advanced economies, mourning is a private enterprise and 'compassionate leave' is a grudging moiety of what the experience of ages offers by way of psychological insight. But even with intelligent acceptance of the need to grieve properly and, as it were, organically, we never quite get over loss. What time teaches is how to live with loss. And yet there should be a consolation in the conjunction of the following two facts: that the dead once lived, and that we loved them. These are ineradicable elements of our world's history as we view it from our place at its centre, meaning that those lost are never wholly gone while they live in us.

How many of us, though, are actually consoled by such thoughts? People in today's economically advanced countries are not good at coping with death. We would rather escape it, or at least escape thinking about it, than accept it and incorporate its life-shaping meanings into our choices. In the context of contemporary materialism, there is a conspiracy of pretence that we live indefinitely. We hide death behind jogging and vitamin supplements and anti-wrinkle creams, until the last moment: and even then we leave handling death to others, to professionals in hospitals and hospices, morgues and funeral homes. Unless we are religious, with the kind of primitive faith that Tolstoy's Levin admired in the peasants on his estate, the formalities of dealing with death are often too stiff and awkward to give real comfort – the funeral, the tearful obsequies, the clumsy efforts of acquaintances to be kind at the reception afterwards; and then the fact that so many people turn away from the bereaved so soon in the weeks and months afterwards, unable to deal with them because the grief of others is frightening, demanding, strange.

In short, we find death far harder to deal with, and more difficult to accept, than our forebears did.[4] It seems stranger to us than to them; indeed, to them it was all too familiar. For them death was ubiquitous, more present than life's pleasures. It gave religion a good press, as the only harbour in the treacherous seas of mortality. Observations of nature's autumn and spring cycles must have been an early source of hope for people, faced with the incomprehensibility of death. That is why resurrection stories abound in religion and mythology; it is no accident that Easter is a spring festival. But this is not the only explanation for such belief. A yearning for justice also plays its part, and a profound hope that there is rest and pleasure to be found somewhere at some time. We forget that for the vast majority of humankind now – as through all history – existence is a heavy labour, and to them the promise of posthumous felicity is a sweet one. The urbane voices that reach us from the past are those of the few who had opportunities to speak, which was at the expense of armies of nameless, faceless strugglers with little to hope other than that, in another dispensation of things, they might get a chance to rest in sunshine. Indeed if one reflects on the matter, hopes for an afterlife are a sad reflection on the facts of this life, and a condemnation of them. That should make us understand even better Spinoza's dictum that 'the meditation of the wise man is a meditation on life, not on death', for it should help us see that if life for so many makes them envy the dead, humanity has failed itself badly.

When someone you care about dies suddenly and unexpectedly, giving you no time for preparation such as you might have with an elderly person or someone long ill, one of the major difficulties is the lack of a leave-taking and the absence of closure. The grief that ensues is all the worse because too much is left unfinished and unsaid. But there are sources of consolation nevertheless. A powerful one is to think as follows: ask yourself what you would want for those you care about and whom you leave behind when you die. Would you want their grieving to be too painful, to go on too long, to derail their lives too much or even at all? Or would you wish them to remember the best of you and to treasure the happier memories, yet to accept, even as they miss you and suffer those recurring pangs that characterize the long tail of mourning, that the world has changed in this particular respect, and to continue living hopefully and positively? That is assuredly what almost all of us would wish for those who survive us. And now consider that this is what the person would wish for us too, if in a position to do so.

Scarcely any human life is free from sorrow; that is a fact intrinsic to the social nature of our species. To be related to others by friendship, love or family ties is to invite the very high probability, indeed the certainty, of experiencing loss and its pains. Recall what the Stoics say: that although sorrows are inflicted from outside us, how we

receive them is our own responsibility; we have to challenge ourselves first to bear them and then master them. That is right; but then
the Stoics proceed to advise us to possess only what we would not
mind losing, on the grounds that the less we desire – the less our
peace of mind depends on what is external to us – the less we will feel
our loss if it occurs. Against them we might reply that we should not
deny friendship or love in order to escape the danger of losing either,
and not just for the sake of these high values themselves, but because
we learn from them – even indeed from losing them – deeper insights
into the human condition and richer sympathies in response to it.

It is a happy fact of human psychology that we forget suffering.
We do not forget *that* we suffered, but we do not relive the actual
experience itself. Life would be unbearable if this were not so. One
thinks of Jorge Luis Borges' character Funes the Memorious, the
man who could forget nothing; if that included not just millions of
memories mostly trivial but an inability to forget the raw quality of
actual physical and psychological pain, his agonies would be enormous.[5] But we do not forget the deaths of those who were close,
because they reconfigure our world, obliging us to learn afresh how
to navigate it. Absence is a large presence; which is why bereavement
is the most stressful and distressing of experiences, followed not far
behind by relationship breakdowns, and after that the loss of things
constitutive of identity and security such as employment or a home.
Such losses generate other losses: loss of faith in the world, loss of
confidence in ourselves. Philosophy says that understanding the
nature and practical inevitability of loss is a necessary preparation,
however hard it is to accept that we enter a contract for the possibility of loss just by living, and certainly by loving and by trying to
achieve anything of value. And this above all applies to the loss caused
by death.

If we gave more careful thought to death and its implications we
would see it as a constitutive fact of life which makes life more
focused and vivid. When we confront the fact of it we see that death
is nothing to the dead, and therefore nothing to us individually; that
dying is what might concern us, as an act of living, for we accept that
dying is sometimes not easy. We see that death is about other people

and therefore we experience it as grief; and that grieving is almost never easy. In seeing these things, we place death in its proportion, and can turn our vision to what matters most: the creation of value in the lives we and others live, while there is life.

One cannot leave the question of death without reflecting on a matter so often associated with it: old age. In one way, the association between death and age is something of a distraction, because at any stage in life people are always a mere hair's breadth from death, as we know from the fact of accidents, conflicts and disease. Robust and greedy for life as the human body can be, often surviving severe injuries and (especially in youth) recovering remarkably, it is also a frail, soft thing, 'heir to a thousand natural shocks' as Hamlet remarked. Nevertheless, for most of life we are neither expecting nor dwelling too much on the great inevitability of death, whereas in old age the expectation of it, the sense of its imminence and the need for some preparation, are inescapable. Even more to the point: old age itself is a site of great challenge, and dealing with it requires philosophy.

From a philosophical point of view, there is no difference between ageing and living. People grow a day older every day, and are therefore constantly ageing, and are aware of having different powers and possibilities at different ages, losing some and gaining others; and if they are reflective, they evolve along with the effects of time and experience on them, minimizing deficits and optimizing benefits. But of course when people talk of ageing they standardly mean a limited and limiting phenomenon: entry into the last phase of life – 'old age'. Its starting point is different for different people. Some feel they enter it when they retire, if they do so in their sixties. Some feel that the term 'old age' should only properly apply from the mid-seventies. As this suggests, ageing is a state of mind even more than a state of body, though without question the body will at some point speak loudly enough of the years it has accumulated. But most of what matters in life has far more to do with things psychological than physical, and therefore states of mind are key. The values of courage, reflection and fellowship play their part here therefore.

This matters for another reason too. From the point of view of the deficits of ageing – failing powers, the marginalization suffered by the elderly – the saying 'old age is not for the faint-hearted' well applies. But once the inevitability of the deficits is accepted, and their importance given their proper due, a landscape of possibilities opens.

First, though, what is meant by giving ageing's deficits their due? Granted, the elderly have to make rational adjustments to how they manage the practicalities of their days, and that can be a trial. Joint pain, limited mobility, compromised hearing and vision, unfamiliarity with rapidly changing technologies, exclusion from large tracts of social life, and liability to ill health are commonplaces for the elderly. So too, for many, are loneliness and depression, a sense of superfluousness and being a burden. But whereas physical changes are mainly unavoidable, these are psychological. They are in significant part caused by those physical limitations, but even the alleviation of some of the latter can make the sense of what old age is – a rapidly narrowing corridor in which there is no possibility of turning round and going back – a great enemy to peace of mind. This is where the considerations of philosophy most profoundly apply.

There can be few things more tragic than the thought of an elderly person trapped in loneliness and a despair that seems to have no remedy. To break free of that imprisonment, to snap its chains and step out from the shadow whose darkness deepens relentlessly, takes courage. But it does not take anything other than courage. It does not take money, other people, miraculous recovery from illness, or anything else. The remarkable thing is that it lies in a person's own hands. That fact is the miracle, so to speak, of the philosophical attitude.

This is not to suggest that ignoring the deficits and challenges of ageing makes them go away or not count. The dictum that 'the meaning of things lies not in things themselves, but in our attitudes to them' is almost universally true – but only *almost*, for in some circumstances, such as being old and physically hampered, the meaning of things is obviously not unaffected by things themselves. In this case the great questions are these: 'To what degree am I going to allow the inevitable to weaken me further than it needs to?' 'How much of a victory will I accord to external factors over those things that are still my own to command?' 'What are the things I value and can do that cannot be diminished by these inevitabilities, unless I let them?' The voice of the Stoics echoes in these questions.

In *De Senectute* Cicero says, 'Those who argue that old age has no part to play in public affairs are talking nonsense. The great affairs of life are not performed by physical strength, or activity, or nimbleness of body, but by deliberation, character, and expression of opinion.' His picture of old age was of a busy time, not least in learning new things and taking a vivid interest in affairs. Like Epictetus he thought that 'it is never too late to be wise', even in the very last moments of life. He dismissed the idea that physical frailty somehow disqualifies a person from a full part in life, by pointing out that frailty is not the exclusive accompaniment of age, but of sickness even in the young; from which follows the obvious point that maintaining health and fitness into old age is as important as it is at any point in life, but it is not a necessity – in the sense that the absence of health is not a disqualification for life.

Cicero also thought that one can identify the gifts of old age, and benefit from them. 'I am grateful to old age, which has given me greater appetite for conversation with fellows, while removing the appetite for eating and drinking. What you do not miss does not make you uneasy.' In praising the revived enjoyment he experienced of the beauties of nature, he might have added enjoyment of human beauty unaccompanied by desire and the urge to possess.

And then he mentions something of the highest importance, and transformative of the experience of age if the elderly would only realize it. This is that age has power; the elderly are powerful. If they speak up, if they take a stand, they thereby abash politicians, inspire the young, and find that few people are prepared to be rude enough to shout them down or dismiss them. The saying current in Cicero's day, *seniores priores*, 'elders first', has long ceased to apply in at least Western society, but even there one notes a residuum of respect for the old which they could apply to effect if they chose. The power of elders was considerable in antiquity, where ideas of wisdom, respect and recognition of experience combined to give a place to their influence that society needed, not having too many other resources for recalling and applying the past's lessons. This is no longer so; and correlatively a position for old people in the hierarchy of social respect is not only no longer automatic, but its apparent absence is reinforced by the fact that many elders themselves withdraw, take a back seat, feel timid about venturing views in the face of the assertive younger generations currently running things. Those younger generations perceive the elders' withdrawal, and discount them accordingly; they estimate the elderly at their own diminished sense of worth. And there lies the key: if an elderly person announces his or her own redundancy, everyone else will agree. And that is to throw away the great power that the old can wield.

The twelfth letter of Seneca to Lucilius, 'On Old Age', is a classic on this matter. Seneca built himself a house in the country when he was young; he tells Lucilius that on a recent visit to it he 'protested to my bailiff about the money he was spending on the tumble-down building. He said, "I'm doing everything I can, but the house is old." Old! I had built it myself! What is my own future, if the stones of my house are crumbling? I then complained about the state of the trees – "They too are old," he said; but I myself had planted them! And there was a decrepit old man at the gate – and he had been one of the servants I hired when he was young!'

But then Seneca reflected, and realized that his old country place was teaching him a lesson. I paraphrase: 'I owe it to my country-place to see how to cherish and love old age; for it is full of pleasure if one knows how to use it. Fruits are most welcome when almost over; youth is most charming at its close; the last drink delights the toper; each pleasure reserves to the end the greatest delights it contains. Even the very fact of our not wanting pleasures has taken the place of the pleasures themselves. How comforting it is to have tired of one's appetites, and to have done with them!'

And he then confronts the great question that stands before the face of old age, and cannot be left unanswered:

But you will say: it is disturbing to look death in the face. I answer that death must be looked in the face by young and old alike. We do not die in the order of our birthdate. Moreover, no one is so old as it would be improper for him to hope for another day of existence. A day has its sunrise and its sunset, and as Heraclitus said, 'One day is equal to every day.' Some interpret this to mean that the very longest period of time possesses no element which cannot be found in a single day. Hence every day ought to be regulated as if it closed the series, as if it rounded out and completed our existence.

Let us therefore go to our sleep with joy and gladness, saying, 'I have lived; the course which I have run is finished; if another day is vouchsafed me, I shall welcome it with a glad heart.'

And remember: it is wrong to live under a constraint; but no one is constrained to live under constraint. On all sides lie many short and simple paths to freedom.

Seneca acknowledged that this last aperçu was taken from Epictetus, but pointed out that any truth is everyone's property, and therefore he was entitled to claim it as his own.

The remark Seneca took from Epictetus, that no one has to live under constraint, has a powerful meaning as applied to old age. It means that if or when old age becomes intolerable, one has the great gift of death either to welcome or to take. Among people who are unafraid of death because they see it as a natural part of the world's rhythms, dying when one chooses – committing suicide – in response to how one measures the quality of one's experience, of what one still has to offer, or still desires to do or know, is a civilized matter. It was so regarded by the Romans, and it was a source of courage to them that each felt ultimately free, the arbiter and determiner of his or her own final fate.

It is frequently said that one should grow old gracefully; however much of a cliché that is, it is true. Desperate efforts to cheat age typically make a mockery of it, as some of the worst disasters of plastic surgery and dress sense show. Old people are beautiful, without the aid of anything other than the years they have lived. The inscriptions of life on their faces and hands, in the slowness of their walk and the stillness with which they sit, tell and retell the story of human life, in its ordinariness, its glory, its pain, its struggle, its hopes and compromises. A younger person looking on with sympathy can see great things there, even in the most commonplace of lives, because of the sheer fact that it was a human life after all. Therefore, for the elderly, arriving at this point in experience might indeed have its problems, but it is not a defeat, and could be a victory.

For as the earlier remarks show, one can be realistic about growing old, and yet live without being old in mind. Arguably most people are unrealistic about old age in the wrong way: by giving up far too much far too early, and failing to recognize that they retain a power, an influence, which they could use for the good of others – if they do this generously, free of prejudices and biases, genuinely interested in the flourishing of those younger than themselves. This is all the more important because relatively few of the causes that the elderly could champion will be for their own benefit; it would be like planting a sapling that others, but not they, will see grow to a fine tall tree in future. It will be the purest form of altruism to use the experience of life to try to benefit those who are following them along its path. Such would be the greatest triumph of old age: to use itself as a weapon for the good.

8. Love

In most cultures a very high place – sometimes, the highest – is assigned to love among the values of a good and worthwhile life. In representations and thoughts of it, the love at issue is most frequently taken to be one particular kind: romantic sexual love, in which heights of tenderness, reciprocity, passion and ecstasy constitute a paradigm of what is most exquisite in the possibilities of experience.

Most of what is thought and believed about romantic love is, however, such as to raise significant questions even when not actually incorrect. For it is as much a source of agony as ecstasy, as much a deluder as the grail of our emotional ambitions and yearning. Yet in other senses of the word 'love', and in other ways, love is unquestionably part of what can confer value on life, and in some respects its greatest value.

The ancient Greeks knew better than we about love, at least in regard to distinguishing its varieties. They identified several such: the love of friends for each other, the bond among comrades, family love, charitable love for humanity, infatuation, erotic love, playful love; and to each they gave its own name and stories. *Pragma* is the bond among comrades; *eros* is erotic love; *philia*, the love of friends; *storge*, family love; *ludus*, playful love; *agape*, the love of humanity (in Latin this is *caritas*, from which we get 'charity' and 'care'). In the Greeks' view, *mania*, which we call 'infatuation', was a punishment inflicted by the gods, and they were grateful to old age (they claimed) for releasing them from it. They prized *philia*, the bond of friendship, above all other kinds.

The only kind of love they did not specifically name – the only kind that can be genuinely unconditional in asking nothing in return, and often getting nothing in return – is maternal love. Maternal attachment is one of nature's themes; almost everywhere among mammals and birds, and not infrequently among fish, mothers (and sometimes fathers) nurture and protect their young until the latter can survive unaided. The ubiquity of the practice, and the obvious necessity for it, owes itself to the biochemistry of evolution. In that sense, at least, something is returned for the care bestowed, namely the survival of the species, the onward progress of the genes involved.

Although mother-love is biological it is not guaranteed to manifest in every case; the endocrinal processes that activate maternal instincts during pregnancy and childbirth can fail. The way humans have detached themselves, in richer countries at least, from the significant bookends of life – giving birth and dying, which our ancestors witnessed frequently among both themselves and the farm animals they lived with – even makes some women disgusted by the thought (as they would see it) of painfully forcing a baby out of their bodies and feeding it from their breasts – as some think, to the detriment of the latter's appearance.[1] Elective caesarean sections and the formula bottle, both themselves now commonplaces in wealthier communities everywhere, introduce a sanitizing distance between the primordial and the cosmetic aspects of motherhood. But in normal circumstances nature floods a pregnant woman's body with clever hormonal mixtures that trigger a repertoire of behaviours that amount not merely to their loving, but to their being in love with, their babies. It has been well said, therefore, that 'babies give birth to mothers'.

Although maternal love is biochemical, it is no less valuable for being so. There is no contradiction between chemistry and poetry here. The point of observing this is that it applies to most of the other kinds of love people experience too. The biochemical chiefly responsible for this in mammals is oxytocin, identified as what promotes trust and bonding between individuals and within groups. Birds and fish have their own forms of the same hormone – respectively, mesotocin and isotocin. But the hormones of lust are different; these are testosterone and oestrogen, produced by the hypothalamus in the brain; and when the hypothalamus is busy doing this, most of the rest of the brain is not busy at all. Therein lies the comedy and tragedy of infatuation, romance and sex, and the reason why the Greeks saw these phenomena as madness.

Romance is what most people mean by 'love' most of the time. The bliss of falling in love, especially when reciprocated, is the object of millions of daily dreams and reveries, of novels, films, songs and poems. Some of the most exquisite representations of the emotional height of romantic love occur in opera, because music is supremely apt for doing this: examples are legion, but two of the best-known are Lauretta's impassioned plea to her father in *Gianni Schicchi*, 'O mio babbino caro', begging him to allow her to marry her beloved Rinuccio, and Butterfly's dream, 'Un bel di vedremo', of the return of her American 'husband' Benjamin Franklin Pinkerton, imagining him climbing the hill towards her from Nagasaki harbour and calling her name.[2] The 'will you marry me?' moment – or its different contemporary forms (perhaps 'shall we move in together?') – is traditionally viewed as the consummation of the finest, most delicious experience of our lives. From Mills and Boon novelettes to Jane Austen to every 'romcom' movie, the arc of the story – (a) meeting, (b) attraction, (c) some vicissitudes (doubts, or obstacles), (d) vicissitudes overcome (e) ecstatic acceptance/recognition! (f) wedding! (or equivalent!) – is the same. If contemporary cinema is to be believed, nowadays the very instant that mutual attraction is acknowledged, the parties to it tear off their clothes and have sex on tables and kitchen counters.

It seems sadly reductive to attribute all this fine fury to the trick that genes play to pass themselves along. But so it is. Infatuation is the alembic in which future generations are forged, and the servants of our genes – testosterone and oestrogen – are very tough guys in sharp suits and dark glasses who brook no interference from reason, caution, the risk of second thoughts, and (too often) contraception.

The romantic conspiracy of modern times – since the eighteenth century, mainly – is that everything is going to be rosy after the wedding (or equivalent). As a ship comes to harbour by crossing the bar into calmer waters, leaving behind the ocean where it tossed and beat its way among storms, so the loving couple reaches its berth and settles down. 'Oh! the tranquillity of the marriage bed after the hurly-burly of the chaise-longue!' as the actress Mrs Patrick Campbell put it long ago. Romantic novels and films are largely silent about the aftermath of stage (f) above, resting on the implied but alas not invariably true assumption that there will be continued, if quieter, bliss. The truth is that the post-infatuation marriage-like state is more akin to running a small business than it is like romance. Evenings sipping wine on a moonlit balcony might still occur, but the groceries, bills, school runs, laundry, vaccinations, more bills, more groceries, more laundry, in their settled cycles of repetition, are the main content of life after infatuation.

Stripped of its packaging, romantic love and the assumed sequel to its blissful initiation is therefore, at bottom, just evolution's mechanism for ensuring a new generation of beings and protecting their vulnerable early period. The process has different phases: a brief triggering phase of infatuation, and a lengthier following 'small business' phase of habit and compromise. The infatuation phase involves considerable exchanges of body fluids and gases – chiefly sperm, saliva and breath, with their respective burdens of viruses and bacteria – which (in the case of a heterosexual pair) prepare the female partner's immune system to tolerate the foreign DNA of a foetus if one forms, and promote a degree of addiction between the partners, helping to keep them together at least during the early part of the following stage; important if there are offspring.

If this account seems cynical, it can at least be acknowledged as true. But once again it can be asked whether the facts detract from the poetry – even if they do not detract from the pain, either, given that the emphatic laws of biochemistry so often result in infidelity and partnership breakdowns, when new attractions supervene and new things are knocked off new kitchen tables. Still, many relationships survive, broadly speaking taking one of two forms: those that are contented and affectionate, marked at their best by mutual regard, affection, respect and concern; and those that turn on compromises and abandoned dreams, on emotional endurance rather than emotional sustenance. Tolstoy was one hundred and eighty degrees wrong in saying, at the beginning of *Anna Karenina*, that all happy marriages are alike (he says 'happy families' but the marriages in them are, usually, the main point), for happy marriages are the result of individually found solutions to coexistence, unique to each arrangement, whereas unhappy marriages have the same small and generally tawdry menu of things wrong with them, in which the presence of one or more factors such as resentment, infidelity, alcohol, insufficient money, boredom, contempt and sometimes even brutality explains all.

These remarks apply, note, to romantic love and its expected trajectory. No doubt couples have felt mutual attraction and acted upon it since our forebears lived in trees, in some respects the happier for not having such a burden of expectations weighing them down and such institutional arrangements as formal marriage holding them up – bearing in mind that formal marriage is a tripartite contract between two people and the state with its divorce courts. The more organized and complex a society becomes, not least in its traditions and economic structure, the more pressure is exerted by considerations of property and dynasty. Arranged marriage is a feature of such societies or sections of them, among European aristocrats and American plutocrats just as much as among Hindus and Orthodox Jews. It was accordingly long accepted in aristocracies that marriage is one thing, romance and sex – after the production of a couple of heirs – another.

The phenomenon of enforcing a marriage contract when the parties to it no longer wish to be together, by making divorce difficult, expensive or socially disgraceful – this being how it was within living memory in many societies – is an acknowledgement of the degree to which society feels it has a stake in private relationships. From one perspective, the idea that what people choose to do in their private lives is anyone else's business – so long as all involved parties are genuinely consenting – is amazing. Even more so is the idea that sexual acts acceptable to the involved parties should be declared illegal and punishable as criminal offences.

But whether or not one agrees that efforts should be made to enforce morals by law, a key problem is that no society – society in general, all the way down to a society of just two members – is a level playing field. Someone is, or some people are, always more powerful in any relationship other than genuine friendship, where equality or balance is a constitutive feature. A reason to have a legal framework for marriage-type relationships is that a young woman with young children requires a remedy to being abandoned by the children's father without any support from him, if he is earning, for their maintenance. A woman – it is usually a woman – who has managed a home and family as wife and mother for two or three decades and whose partner leaves her, in her middle age or later, without a profession or career of her own, is likewise entitled to remedy.

These considerations would apply independently of the question of whether romance is coupled to family life as in the modern ideal of romantic-companionate love. But they have become more of an issue because the romantic-companionate model, the coupling of *romance* to *domesticity and family life* – treating love and marriage as 'go[ing] together like a horse and carriage', as the song has it – has forced them to become so. The emergence of the romantic-companionate model not just as the ideal but as the expectation, with all the attention and yearning falling on the initial romance part, almost guarantees that many of the resulting relationships will fail – the divorce rate hovers close to 50 per cent in developed economies, though rates of marriage have declined in favour of cohabitation, but cohabitations fail at an even higher rate; indeed it is claimed that 90 per cent of all relationships, including early dating relationships, fail. This statistic by itself should raise doubts about whether 'falling in love' (becoming infatuated, aka being maddened by the endocrine system) is a good basis for long-term domestic arrangements and family life.

An interesting reflection on the romantic-companionate model is provided by Richard Posner, an American appeal court judge whose books on social issues are informed, indeed prompted, by his courtroom experience. In *Sex and Reason* he notes that one can tell what kind of marital model obtains in a given society by looking at the forms of prostitution there, and vice versa; like the jagged edges of a piece of paper torn down the middle, the two models correspond and complement each other.[3] In societies with the now-common romantic-companionate model, where the parties are not too dissimilar in age and are close in education levels and social status, prostitution services are almost exclusively sexual and likely to offer practices not always available in marriage. In societies where marriages are functional and age and education differences are substantial, prostitution tends to be more courtesanly, offering social as well as sexual companionship; a paradigm would be Venice in its heyday, whose courtesans were accomplished musicians and poetesses, or Japan's geisha tradition (now largely usurped, as the Posner thesis would predict, by the more emphatically somatic 'soaplands' alternative – bathhouses which are conventional brothels).

When romance and marriage-type relationships were separate things – the latter basically economic and practical arrangements – and with the typical disparities in age and education making a companionate aspect rare, the absence of romance from the long years of domestic conjugality did not much matter and was not in itself a reason for the arrangement to fall apart. A husband might frequent courtesans or have a mistress, and (though less acceptably; the double standard has existed in full since at least the unedifying story of Judah and Tamar in *Genesis* 38) a wife might have lovers, either fact accompanied by a spouse's relief or resentment depending on circumstances. But in the romantic-companionate model the demise of romance, or its refocusing elsewhere, is very much a reason for the arrangement to fall apart. Put bluntly, the idea of marital fidelity – that each party has exclusive claims over the other party's sexual and emotional expression – is a hand grenade with the pin extracted and the lever held down by sustained effort. It has been claimed that consumer societies need a high divorce and separation rate, because when couples split up they standardly each buy a new set of 'white goods' (fridge, cooker, microwave), so divorce is good for the economy. This cynical view imputes too much consciousness to social trends, as with the generalization that women tend to cut their hair short after break-ups, and men tend to grow stubble or beards when having affairs. But what is certainly true is that the more economic autonomy women have, the more options they possess if they find themselves in a dysfunctional relationship.

As the foregoing suggests, from an objective point of view love in the sense of romantic love – *mania*, *eros*, and in the earliest stages *ludus* too – scarcely merits the overwhelming attention it receives in films, songs, poetry and much literature. It lays landmines in the forward path of life by raising hopes and expectations sky-high, and inviting the real dangers of pain and loss. And yet it gets that overwhelming attention anyway. Why?

A large part of the reason has to lie in the transcendences that romance provides, and in the intense subjectivity of what is experienced. To feel a passionate need for another person, and to believe that the other does or might feel the same way in return, is intoxicating. Being apart even for short periods is painful, and the void is filled with yearning and reveries. Togetherness – embracing and enjoying intimacies – is ecstatic. The Other is all perfection, handsome or beautiful, desirable and precious – as a projection from one's vision of him or her. The phenomenon at work is what Stendhal in *De l'amour* calls 'crystallization', an idea he took from the tradition of the 'Salzburg bough'. Smitten youths of that city would suspend twigs 'no bigger than a tom-tit's claw' down the shafts of the salt mine until they were covered in crystals, whereupon the youths presented them to their inamoratas as tokens of devotion. Stendhal uses this practice as a metaphor for 'falling in love'; what it is to fall in love, he says, is to cover the object of infatuation in crystals. Thus the infatuated one projects an idealization onto the other, wrapping him or her round in a glittering disguise that hides the ordinariness or imperfections underneath – until, of course, time has chipped the crystals away.[4]

What this suggests is that romance is all about oneself. One is in love with one's own dream, projected onto and wrapped round a passer-by, with whom one acts out a story. This is the source of the intense subjectivity of the experience. The beloved is one's own creation. No doubt most would think this idea absurd: there he or she is, in all the glory of good looks, charm and desirability; we are not *projecting onto*, but are being *attracted by* the other towards him or her. So we feel.

Interestingly, Stendhal developed these ideas as a result of reading an essay by William Hazlitt in which the latter advanced the view that 'love at first sight', as happens in *Romeo and Juliet*, is possible because many people have a prepared vision of the perfect beloved – an idealized image or concept with which they are already in love – so that when they encounter someone who seems to approximate to that ideal, they are immediately infatuated. Hazlitt, who was always falling in love, had this experience most markedly when he met his boarding-house keeper's daughter, Sarah Walker, an event that in the end proved destructive and tragic for him.[5]

If Hazlitt is right, the projection-crystallization theory that Stendhal shares with him is instructive. It explains the intense subjectivity of romance; the beloved is the occasion, not the object, of the experience; the object of the experience is the experience itself. But no one is blameable for folly here. This is nature's way of ensuring, as Benedick in *Much Ado* remarks, that 'the world must be peopled'. A Stoic who advocates 'following nature' would, even if apprised of the means by which endocrinology seduces people into procreative intimacy, accept that this is nature's way, and would bow to its decree. The fact that people who cannot between them start a pregnancy, for example people of the same sex, can be just as infatuated with each other is not a refutation of the theory, but proof of the generalized physiological endowment in play.

Another part of the reason for the world's infatuation with romantic love is the press it gets. The films, novels, plays, songs and poems that vaunt it, laud it, celebrate its occurrence and lament its loss, long for it, explore it, teach it and weep for it, together and by far constitute the greatest amount of discussion of any form of human relationship we are ever exposed to. A supplementary reason for this, in turn, is that the most acute forms of romantic love are those in which love is unrequited, or prevented by obstacles, persecuted, subjected to separation – in general, kept going by vicissitudes, often for long periods. Consider how many of the films and poems, operas and novels are about this phenomenon, from Dante's remote worship of Beatrice to Heathcliff's separation from Catherine in *Wuthering Heights*, from the impassioned longing of Heloise for Abelard to the decades-long epistolary romance of Honoré de Balzac and the Countess Ewelina Hańska of Kyiv – whom at long last he married after she was widowed, just five months before his own death.

In the story of Heloise and Abelard, this ordering of their names is appropriate, because it is Heloise who stands out in the tale of their passion; she had a truly eloquent heart, making her a paradigm of those whose love is so profound that it defies the whole world and even the wrath of God. Abelard was a brilliant young philosopher at the University of Paris, who on hearing about Heloise, the beautiful and highly intelligent niece of a canon of Notre Dame, offered himself as her tutor – with the aim of seducing her, as he himself later acknowledged. They quickly became lovers, Heloise requiring no encouragement. Their wildly erotic passion resulted in the birth of a son, whom they called Astrolabe in honour of science. They secretly married, but Heloise's uncle, furious about the affair, hired a gang of thugs to attack Abelard and castrate him. This brutal event and the attendant scandal forced Abelard into a monastery and Heloise into a convent (at Abelard's bidding; she obeyed with terrible reluctance). Fifteen years after this debacle, Heloise saw a letter Abelard had written to a friend in which he recounted their woeful tale. She wrote to him, initiating the now-celebrated correspondence on which their fame as lovers rests.

Heloise's letters are exquisite: full of passion and yearning, of undimmed erotic desire, of agonizing self-control, of beautiful sentiment; they are unbearably poignant. Abelard's replies are stuffy and pompous, advising her to control her still-ardent sexual desires and apply her energies to serving God. Where her letters are full of warmth and longing, his are cold and sententious. She wrote:

> You know, beloved, as the whole world knows, how much I have lost in you, how at one wretched stroke of fortune that supreme act of flagrant treachery robbed me of my very self in robbing me of you . . . At every stage of my life up to now, as God knows, I have feared to offend you rather than God, and tried to please you more than him. It was your command, not love of God, which made me take the veil . . . If Augustus himself, emperor of the whole world, thought fit to honour me with marriage and conferred all the earth on me for ever, it would be sweeter and more honourable to me to be, not his empress, but your whore.

These words were written, remember, after fifteen years of silence between them. 'The pleasures of lovers which we shared have been too sweet,' she continues; 'they can never displease me, and can scarcely be banished from my thoughts . . . Even during the celebration of the Mass, when our prayers should be purest, lewd visions of the pleasures we shared take such a hold on my unhappy soul that my thoughts are on their wantonness instead of on my prayers. Everything we did, and also the times and places, are stamped on my heart along with your image, so that I live through it all again with you.'

The poignancy of these reminiscences was enhanced in recent times by discovery of parts of the lovers' letters written during the actual course of their affair, fragments tantalizingly incomplete but powerful nevertheless, revealing not just the scorching intensity of their passion but the occasional quarrels and separations all too common in the unsmooth course of love. To be fair to him, Abelard does better in these early letters than in the later ones, but even so history has been too kind to him; it is Heloise who is the true heroine of the tale, her love and honesty surviving intact while Abelard's post-testicular thoughts rise no higher than pretentious apologia, self-vindication and self-advertisement.

Cases of enduring romantic love are rare in the record until recently in history. The Old Testament gives us Jonathan and David, Homer gives us Achilles and Patroclus, Virgil gives us Nisus and Euryalus. In Ovid and Plutarch there are records of sexual infatuation (in the latter, always destructive; the girls are literally torn in half by the men vying for possession of them), but they are not romances paving the way to lifelong blissful marriage. After the tender, painful but ultimately happy tale of Daphnis and Chloe, told by Longus in the second century CE, there is a stretch of over a thousand years to Petrarch's love for Laura and Dante's worship of Beatrice. Both these latter are rather too close to the bloodless idealizations of courtly infatuation as sung by the troubadours to be comparable to the fleshly reality of Heloise. Romeo and Juliet reprise Abelard and Heloise, but they are Ovidian infatuates, not Jane Austen characters carefully pondering the pros and cons, the income and character credentials, required for rational matrimony.

It was the revival of the letter as a published literary form, and the true beginning of the novel – both occurring in the eighteenth century – that took the three different phenomena of erotic infatuation, romance and marriage and spliced them together by making the first central to the second and the second the supposedly natural and proper route to the third. The special importance of erotic infatuation and romance as thus fashioned was the focus of Samuel Richardson's hugely successful novels *Pamela* and *Clarissa*, and a tsunami of literature on the same themes followed, concentrating on the period from the heart-stopping moment of first meeting to the happy day of marriage, as if all life, all meaning – the very point and pinnacle of existence – lay between these points alone.

Arguably, the new valorization of romantic love changed the character even of the pragmatic arrangements that had, for so long beforehand, kept the domestic project of marriage going after sexual interest and affection vacated it. The French way of these things is often cited, mainly because the French have produced the world's leading letter-writers and some of its chief novelists, who between them recorded these matters well. Think of the great Victor Hugo, who fell in love with sixteen-year-old Adèle Foucher and in the three years they had to wait before marrying wrote her two hundred love letters. Although she later had an affair with Charles Sainte-Beuve (he wrote a novel about it, *Volupté*) she remained with Hugo and wrote his biography after his death. Hugo, meanwhile, had a mistress for fifty years, Juliette Drouet, who wrote him two love letters every day during that entire time; which did not stop him having yet another mistress, Léonie Biard, wife of the painter François-Auguste Biard and the first French woman to venture inside the Arctic Circle. Much of the best information required by Hugo's biographers exists in the letters by and about this circle of participants.

The frankly confessional practice of *publishing* love letters followed the success of letter collections of less amorous type, such as those of Madame de Sévigné to her daughter in the seventeenth century, and in the following century the epistolary exchange of the Parisian *salonnière* Louise d'Épinay and the Neapolitan diplomat Abbé Ferdinando Galiani. Whereas in London the bourses of ideas were the coffee houses, in Paris they were the salons of celebrated bluestocking hostesses: Madame Geoffrin, Mademoiselle de Lespinasse, and the latter's aunt and one-time mentor, the blind and formidable

Marquise du Deffand (who famously and acidly remarked of St Denis' achievement in walking to Paris with his severed head under his arm, '*Il n'y a que le premier pas qui coûte*', best translated as 'It was only the first step that was difficult'[6]).

The epistolary tradition became a vehicle for accounts of romantic love, usually prolonged, sustained, obstructed, delayed or unrequited, both in fictional form — exemplified by Rousseau in his *New Heloise* — and in real life, exemplified by Julie de Lespinasse. Julie was a poor relation of the Marquise du Deffand, whose salon was not an intellectual but an aristocratic one, her apartment famous for its buttercup-yellow watered silk wallpaper, decorated with flame-coloured bows, which people came from all over Europe to see. When the marquise grew blind in middle age, she invited Julie to live with her to help with the entertaining. It soon became apparent that Julie was attracting more attention than the marquise herself, and moreover was having an affair with the mathematician and *Encyclopédie* editor Jean le Rond d'Alembert, which made the marquise jealous, so she sacked her. Julie therefore established her own highly successful salon.

Julie's significance for our theme turns on the account given in her published letters of the two tragic love affairs that overshadowed her life — letters of intense poignancy and feeling, compared by Sainte-Beuve to those of Heloise. The first affair was with Don José y Gonzaga, Marquis de Mora, the son of the Spanish ambassador to the French court. Mora attended her salon, and affection duly flowered between them. They were deeply in love, but were obliged to separate because Mora suffered from tuberculosis and had to leave wet foggy Paris for the warmth of Spain to salvage his health. They wrote to each other, her letters full of yearning, tenderness and anxiety; so much so that they fatally drew him into attempting to return to her — for he died on the way, at Bordeaux, aged just thirty.

There may be consolation in knowing one was loved in return if one loses one's beloved, but in the second of Julie's loves there was no consolation, even though her affections were returned this time too. She fell in love with a soldier, Jacques Antoine Hippolyte, Comte de Guibert, then a colonel and later a general; through his writings one of the chief influences on Napoleon as a tactician, and through his army reforms one of the chief architects of Napoleon's later successes (Guibert himself died in 1790).[7] He was a busy man, often away, involved in great affairs; the asymmetry in the relationships of the time, resulting in a disproportion between men and women in the degree to which their emotional horizons were occupied by thoughts of love, was paradigmatically at work in this case. Julie longed for Guibert, saw him too infrequently, and was cast into despair when for reasons of family and money he married another woman. She wrote:

> What afflicts me is the number of days that must pass before we see one another again. Ah heavens, if you knew what the days are like when they are denuded of the interest and pleasure of seeing you! My love, for your occupations and dissipations movement is sufficient, but as for me, my happiness is in you, only in you; I would not wish to live if I could not see you, love you, love you every moment of my life . . . I yield to the need of my heart, my love; I love you, I feel as much pleasure and as much torture as if it were the first and last time in my life that I pronounced these words. Ah, why have you condemned me? Why am I reduced to this? You will understand one day – alas, you understand now. It is frightful to me to be no longer free to suffer for you and through you. Is it enough to love you? . . . My love, I suffer, I love you and wait for you . . .[8]

It is sad to think that when he hastened to see her on her deathbed, she refused to let him in. Her last words are said to have been, 'Am I still alive?'

Julie's case reminds us of an important distinction implicit in what has so far been said: the distinction between infatuation and romance. Her story is one of romance, but the second of her romances verged on the obsessive phenomenon of one-sided infatuation. This latter phenomenon is yet another reason why love is such a consuming topic. Literature and history are full of examples. Somerset Maugham's *Of Human Bondage* is a classic of the genre: club-footed medical student Philip Carey falls for self-centred, irresponsible waitress Mildred, and although she breaks his heart by going off with another man who makes her pregnant then abandons her, Philip cannot overcome his feelings for her, and becomes entangled in the mess of her life – the bondage of the book's title.[9] When he finally recovers he settles for life's compromises, turning defeat into acceptance, into complete submission to normativity by completely embracing it, concluding that 'the simplest pattern – that in which a man was born, worked, married, had children, and died – was likewise the most perfect'.

Other examples of one-sided infatuation, prolonged by the frustration and pain it involves, abound in both fact and fiction. Josef von Sternberg's film *The Blue Angel* traces the fall of a professor into a cabaret clown, and eventually a lunatic, as a result of his obsession with Lola Lola, nightclub singer and 'shared woman'. Turgenev loved the unattainable opera singer Pauline Viardot for decades, and his experience informed his novella *First Love* and the mature novel *Spring Torrents*. At the age of seventy-three Goethe fell in love with seventeen-year-old Baroness Ulrike von Levetzow, and proposed to her; her rejection of him was the prompt for his great poem, the 'Marienbad Elegy'. Oscar Wilde was destroyed by his fatal obsession with 'Bosie' – Lord Alfred Douglas – and Hazlitt likewise by his unrequited passion for Sarah Walker, which prompted his *Liber Amoris*, a book that wrecked his reputation (when Robert Louis Stevenson finished reading it he threw it across the room in disgust, saying 'This man's name will never pass my lips again'). Wilde's *De Profundis*, a long letter to Bosie written in Reading Gaol, is heart-wrenching in its reflections on what Wilde's feelings and Bosie's selfishness had brought upon him.

Less dramatic, but no less painful, are the cases of emotional enslavements exemplified by the passion of French poet Paul Valéry for Jeanne Loviton, coolly returned, and Lytton Strachey's faithful companion Dora Carrington, who doted on him though he was homosexual and theirs was a platonic relationship (when she married another man, unsuccessfully, she wrote to Strachey from her honeymoon hotel: 'I cried last night Lytton, whilst he slept by my side sleeping happily – I cried to think of a savage cynical fate which had made it impossible for my love ever to be used by you'). She committed suicide after Strachey's death, unable to live without him.

These calamitous examples appear to do the opposite of warning people against yielding to desire and falling in love; instead they render the idea of love and high passion all the more – well, romantic. We forgive people for the excesses they commit in the name of love. Indeed we honour them for it. We think of the poet Percy Shelley, just after being expelled from Oxford for atheism, running off first with Harriet Westbrook and marrying her in Edinburgh – he later described this as 'a rash and heartless act' – and then abandoning her to run off to Italy with Mary Godwin, later of *Frankenstein* fame. The nineteenth century regarded this as a serious moral crime on Shelley's part; the twenty-first century regards it as forgivably romantic.[10]

Somerset Maugham gave his best novel the same title as the fourth part of Spinoza's *Ethics*: 'Of Human Bondage'. The fifth part of that great philosophical classic is entitled 'Of Human Freedom'. For Spinoza, bondage arises from unclarity and confusion in our ideas, imprisoning us; freedom is achieved when we come to a clear understanding of ourselves and the world. This encapsulates the underlying lesson of all the ancient ethical schools, of the Indian soteriologies, and of the idea basic to almost all modern psychotherapies: that wisdom and inner liberty are the gifts of clarity. Everything one learns about romance, infatuation and sexual passion is that they are artefacts of confusion and illusion, the very opposites of clarity. This is a sad truth, but perhaps it would be sadder still if it were not so universally ignored.

Grant all the noise and tumult involved in celebrated or notorious cases of love, romance, infatuation, desire and sex, both literary and actual, and then reflect on this fact: the amount of time that romantic love takes up in most people's lives, unless they are serially amorous, is very short relative to their overall lifespan. The delirious part of it, when nothing – not gods or riches, not one's career or the winning of prizes or the fighting of a world war – matters beyond the passion itself, might be a matter of weeks or months merely. Feeling that one loves as one loved when in the full flood of romance, and is loved in return in the same way, might last a while longer, and moments of romance might return, bringing back those moonlit nights on a balcony with a glass of wine. But we still enjoy the ending of the film or novel when the hero and heroine get engaged; *that's* the thing, we feel, as if that moment of consummation, that summit of experience, is the point.

Picture the period of intense passion as the entrance hall of a house. The next step in romance is to envisage – as we try to peer into the interior of the house – the living room and kitchen and bedrooms, where we imagine another but quieter romance of togetherness and shared life unfolding, from which loneliness has been banished and security attained. The celebrated Dr Johnson described second marriages as 'triumphs of hope over experience', but he might as well have described first marriages (or marriage-like relationships) as 'triumphs of hope' *simpliciter*, because the knowledge that nearly half of all marriages fail and well over half of non-formal living-together relationships fail, and therefore that people in advanced economies have accepted that serial polygamy – multiple partners over a lifetime – is a norm, might bring a note of realism into the expectations of the entrance hall. There is, after all, nowhere more lonely and sad on the planet than the interior of an unhappy marriage.

It was mentioned above that the other half of long-term relationships, the ones that last, do so for one of two broad and not mutually exclusive reasons. Consider them again. One is that one (or both) of the parties makes compromises, sometimes very large ones, giving up tracts of himself or herself or his or her hopes, plans, ambitions, in order to remove obstacles from the relationship's path. That is the more usual way. The other is that the parties become friends. They might still be lovers, still spouses, still co-parents of their children, but above and through all these things they are friends. Or they might be friends who cease to be lovers, who allow a lot of space and air into their relationship, in ways that do not attenuate but strengthen their bond. In any variant the key is *friendship*. The great significance of this is discussed shortly.

A surprising fact indicated by the foregoing discussion is that the history of *romantic* love as opposed to other kinds of love (conjugal, fraternal, parental, and the love between friends) is a surprisingly

short one, in the sense that accounts of people falling in love specifically to initiate a permanent bonding only really begin, as a genre with
this as the theme, in the eighteenth century. This merits further
exploration. From the story of Paris and Helen, through Ovid, to the
courtly tropes of medieval chivalry, to Dante's longing for Beatrice,
and to Romeo and Juliet, one looks largely in vain for evidence of
the kind of romantic love regarded as the start of something long-
term that is not just, in fact, either sexual infatuation – example:
Romeo and Juliet – or idealized and typically bloodless infatuation –
example: Dante for Beatrice ('for' not 'and' because it appears she did
not even know about his feelings). In Renaissance odes to 'fair Cecilia'
and the like, the same idealization is apparent, though in this case the
chance of a tryst is more palpable; but that is about sex, not lifelong
commitment.

The counter-examples are few. Longus' *Daphnis and Chloe*, already
mentioned, is a touching tale of a young couple who want to be
together for more reasons than sex. In mythology there is a great deal
of desire and lust and rather little long-term love, though we find the
latter in Orpheus and Eurydice, Odysseus and Penelope, Hector and
Andromache – these two later examples surprising because rare indi-
cations of marital satisfaction and companionship.

The most unusual mythological example is provided by the tale of
Cupid and Psyche, leaving aside its rich symbolic meanings. Cupid's
feelings for Psyche survive her betrayal, prompting him to help her
complete the impossible tasks set by his mother, Aphrodite, in punishment. (Psyche is being punished because her parents said she was
more beautiful than Aphrodite – another example of the gods' queer
sense of justice, as ever.) Few question the suicides of Pyramus and
Thisbe and of Romeo and Juliet – suicides committed on the basis of
absurdly limited acquaintance between the couples: the first had been
whispering to each other through a hole in a wall and in the event
never actually met; Romeo, who had been sighing over someone else
until seeing Juliet at a party, had one night with her and both killed
themselves within a few days of meeting. If nothing else, such examples recall the Greeks' classification of sexual infatuation as *mania*
which, like all forms of madness, they regarded as an affliction.

The kind of grand passion that outweighs even the demands of empire – Antony and Cleopatra constitute the paradigm – is rare in the record, but striking when it appears. Shah Jahan's love for Mumtaz Mahal was memorialized in an exquisite tomb for her, the Taj Mahal, that was to have been matched by his own on the other side of the river. The lustful beginnings of Abelard's romance with Heloise turned to long-lasting love, at least from her side; her letters to him are wonderful testaments to that fact. But, as indicated, it is in the flood of romantic 'boy meets girl' Mills-and-Boon-forerunner novels beginning in the eighteenth century that the shift occurs, and it has become a dominant trope, enhanced by opera and poetry and more recently still by Hollywood and popular music. Samuel Richardson, Jane Austen and the Brontë sisters are superior examples of the genre, though not uncontroversially so. Fielding wrote *Shamela* and *Joseph Andrews* to contest Richardson's Machiavellian message, as Fielding saw it, that if a young woman can inflame a man's desire for her but hold him in check until he can no longer bear it, he will marry her; a strategy of deliberate sexual teasing. A cynical view of *Jane Eyre*'s subtext is that Jane gets Rochester when he is blind and crippled – his masculinity broken, subdued, in her power – and that this is every woman's underlying aim: to put a halter on a stallion and hitch him between the shafts of her cart.

The evidence of high literature could of course be misleading; our 'rude forefathers', to quote Gray's *Elegy* to the unsung and unknown, might universally have fallen in love with a view to settling into domestic bliss surrounded by rosy-cheeked children and hens and pigs. But what social history more plausibly suggests, as already noted, is that however much endocrine activity our rude forefathers underwent, marriage or its cognates tended not to begin with it, but instead was generally a practical affair, involving considerations of property, dowry, contract, family. In a number of societies today, from India to communities of Orthodox Jews, marriages are arranged by parents and matchmakers. English aristocratic marriages were dynastic and financial, rarely the product of romance; the understanding that after a couple of heirs had been produced legitimately the parties were free to seek emotional and sexual satisfactions elsewhere, providing they were discreet, is evidence of the decoupling of the domestic 'family' project from the unruly chances associated with infatuation and sexual desire. More generally, as long as divorce was hard to get and anyway attended by social opprobrium, the kind of discretion required by this arrangement was the default.[11]

The claim here about romance and romantic love is, as with all generalizations, subject to qualification, and some qualifying instances have been mentioned. But it is at least an interesting claim. Consider the situation portrayed in Shakespeare's *Twelfth Night*. We think we are in familiar territory as today's attitudes make us see it; Duke Orsino's 'If music be the food of love' suggests he is in love with Olivia in the same way that Darcy is in love with *Pride and Prejudice*'s Elizabeth Bennet. But as we witness the sudden smittenness of Olivia for Viola in the latter's disguise as a boy, and of Viola for Orsino, and of Viola's twin brother, Sebastian, for Olivia as soon as he sees her – reciprocated when the cross-dressing and mistaken identities are unravelled at the end – what do we have? A fizz of instant infatuations, which all no doubt lead to marriage, but on the basis of little acquaintance and less knowledge. Perhaps the only deeply based affection in the tale is, perversely, Malvolio's for Olivia.

Citing Jane Austen's Darcy is pointful here. Recall that he did not think much of the Bennets at first, Elizabeth included; his interest in her, despite her vulgar mother and dreadful younger sisters, grew as his knowledge of her increased, and as he witnessed her superiority as a person over his cousin Anne de Bourgh, whom his family expected him to marry. This is the Austen philosophy; for her, love depends on character, on growing to know the real worth of character, and on mutual accord of principles. For her, it starts in friendship – and in fact remains, and grows, as friendship. Infatuation – romantic dizziness of the kind much deprecated in the pulp novels of Austen's era and since – is criticized through the subplot of the elopement of Elizabeth's sister Lydia with the scoundrel Wickham. We are supposed to expect that the enforced marriage of Lydia and Wickham will not be a contented one.

The same point is made by different means in Austen's *Emma*.

Emma Woodhouse's egoism causes a lot of hurt and harm before she learns her lesson and improves her character accordingly. Her reward for doing so is marriage to the speakingly named Mr Knightley, who has been waiting for her to grow up before acting on his affection for her. Mr Knightley, of course, is already at the mature, sound, steady stage of being perfectly marriageable on Austenian principles. There is nothing of Romeo about Mr Knightley, and Austen would not have Romeo approach within a million miles of Highbury or Meryton.

The foregoing addresses romantic love in particular. In his discussion of the history of ideas of love as such, but with romantic-conjugal love at the focus, Simon May also regards current ideas about it as recent, emerging in the last century and a half and now constituting what is practically a new religion – love as god, inverting the religious 'god as love' conceit.[12] The point is well made; people hope to get from love the enduring affirmation that unconditional acceptance and commitment provides, and which is offered by God to his most faithful followers. And then May points out how disastrously high this raises expectations; no imperfect mortal can provide what a divine lover offers. Being loved by God gives the beloved a home in the universe, a guarantee of existential safety, which May calls 'ontological rootedness'; human secular clay-footed love can provide no such guarantees, despite all the protestations to the contrary that are the soundtrack of the early days of almost all relationships.

For May the paradigm of love is parental love, the selfless, open-ended love of parents for their children. He points out that sexual desire, attraction and beauty – which latter, Plato says in the *Symposium*, is what prompts us to fall in love at first but then directs attention upwards to the Forms of Goodness and Truth, making love the better for being purely intellectual: 'Platonic love' – offer nothing to match the unconditional commitment manifested in a parent's love for her child.

This is true. At the same time, even though love for one's children has its delights, in most normal cases it is mixed with much anxiety and unthanked sacrifice, and is subject to rejection by the children in their teenage years and condescension when they reach adulthood.

Biology handles the matter (generalization coming) by making women want babies; even at certain periods in their lives aching, yearning, for one – desiring that warm cuddly dependent delicious cute exquisite miniature thing, so easy to love and so powerfully soliciting protectiveness and concern. But note that what is wanted is a *baby*, not a difficult teenager or a soldier who goes to war or an adult son or daughter who moves to the other side of the planet. If one could prevision the long-term outcome of 'having a baby' it would give at least some pause for thought.

Still: a mother's love for her children is, as May describes it, unquestionably a paradigmatic example of unconditional permanent love, and no matter how reductive the explanations given by evolutionary biology for this phenomenon, it is a lovely thing. Children love their mothers back, and often their fathers too, and it might be that parents find their love requited by the need their offspring feel for them – the need for comfort and reassurance when the offspring are little; the need for material support (money, mainly) when they are older. Is it *the* paradigm of love? This depends upon whether there is one thing, love, rather than lots of different kinds of attachments and affections we *call* 'love' for convenience or economy because they share some traits and invite or provoke overlapping types of feelings. There is extremely little similarity between the sexual infatuation that a woman might feel for someone by whom she falls pregnant, and the love she feels for the baby that results. If any similarities are to be found, perhaps the anxiety and effort involved in raising a child can be thought of as paralleled by the tensions and misunderstandings of romantic love, for these things make love in both cases complicated. The one kind of love that is *typically* free of any such alloy, and provides a large quantum of the good things that flow from relating positively to a fellow human, is friendship.[13]

Friendship is arguably the best kind of mature human relationship, because it is both the most positive and the least negative in its effects when things go respectively right or wrong. If we become friends with our parents as we grow up, if we become friends with our children as they grow up, if we become friends with our spouses as time and shared experience accumulate, if we become friends with our colleagues, and if – in the normal way of social interaction, travel, life in general – we become and remain friends with some of the people we meet, then even as we remain the offspring of our parents, the parent of our children, the spouse of our domestic partner, the colleague of our workmates, we add this higher dimension of mutual liking and interest. The relationship is well explained by illustrations: a friend is someone you would willingly get out of bed to go and see if they telephoned you in the small hours of night needing help. Oscar Wilde said that a true friend is one who will stab you in the front – that is, will tell you an unpalatable truth if it is required – and for symmetry might have added that he will also 'have your back'.

We describe a friend as someone you enjoy being with, whom you trust with confidences, who will help you when needed and will feel free to ask your help in return, who will stand by you in difficulties, and whose failings (provided they are not too gross) you tolerate. Of course there are toxic and one-sided friendships which – therefore – scarcely merit the name; reciprocity and equality are key components. Indeed the fact of 'toxic friendships' is illustrative of the nature of friendship proper; this contrast is more illuminating of friendship's nature than the opposition between friends and enemies.

These remarks about friendship are obvious enough. Yet such great value was attached to friendship by the philosophers that they identified it as one of the central pillars of the worthwhile life. Aristotle devoted two books to the subject in his *Nicomachean Ethics*, closely analysing its nature and concluding that a friend is 'another self' – the implication being that just as you would be careful of your own well-being and reputation, you would therefore take care of the well-being and reputation of your friend. This might involve discouraging him from doing foolish or bad things, and encouraging him in his successes. You would share your good fortune with him, as he would with you; if either of you did something dishonourable it would reflect on the other, and both would feel the fall from grace. Aristotle's discussion set going a long and rich tradition of debate about friendship, although he was not the first to raise the subject; Plato's *Lysis* is the earliest text we know that examines *philia*, friendship, as distinct from *eros*. The philosophers in the period after Aristotle who most emphasized the high value and importance of friendship were the Epicureans.

Among the essential features of friendship, when formed between people who are not family members or lovers beforehand, is that it is natural, spontaneous, freely given and freely reciprocated. What draws two people into friendship with each other is doubtless a complex and largely subconscious matter of their respective psychologies, though if asked why they are friends they would refer to shared interests, opinions, tastes, appreciation of one another's sense of humour, and the like – and would doubtless be right. Nevertheless subliminal cues must play a part, because although we give reasons when asked for them, the explanation lies properly in emotion, and the wellsprings of emotion are mainly obscure even to ourselves. But even more important features of friendship's essence are mutuality and respect, which latter includes honouring the other's margin of autonomy. Oliver Goldsmith's remark that 'friendship is a disinterested commerce between equals, love an abject intercourse between tyrants and slaves' says something true about nearly all friendships though true only of most loves, the comparison nevertheless highlighting friendship's voluntary nature and its freedom from the artificial hierarchies that all other relationships, however covertly and subtly, involve – through dependency, imbalance of psychological and material power, imposed social roles, the fact that one needs or desires the other more than vice versa, and the like.

Friendship is what the other things we call 'love' should aim to become or include, both in the case of families and in the case of lovers (conjugal or domestic partners, spouses – call them what you will; I mean people in elective intimate relationships). In the case of families, bearing in mind that offspring and siblings are adventitiously together, having not *chosen* each other freely, the relationships do well to mature into friendship as the culmination of 'growing up', indeed as a mark of the fulfilment of that process. In the case of lovers, attaining the condition of friends while also remaining lovers amounts to cementing mutuality – the reciprocities of aid and sharing of daily life's normal burdens – and even more importantly the trust and respect for autonomy that any individual needs in order to flourish. The conditions that militate against the latter – such as jealousy, over-dependence, excessive need, unrelieved demands for attention or affection, stifling the other by any of the means too common among couples – are not friendship but, to employ Goldsmith's term as apt for the case, a kind of tyranny.

The concept of friendship has a rich load of meaning. To have a friend is to be not alone in the universe; it is to have a connection with another life and its interests and aims; it is to have the good obligation of giving something of one's time and mind to another, and to be receiving the same in return, as gifts that are voluntary, valuable, affirming and constructive. Though a friend might suffer at times so that one feels much pain on her behalf, pleasure is the overall quality of the experience of friendship. Its loss is a matter of grief; what we grieve for, when anyone we care about departs, is chiefly what this aspect of our link with the departed meant.

The outcome of these thoughts, as they apply to answering Socrates' question, is that the aim of our closer interpersonal relationships should be friendship, as one of the highest and most valuable features of a life truly worth living. In whatever way our connections with others begin – infatuation, birth, a social encounter – if they develop into a relationship, the best and most achieved state of that relationship would be that it is, or is also, a friendship.

Epicurus' Garden was a society of friends, more relaxed – as one would expect – in its conception of this relationship than was Aristotle's view, for Aristotle held that friendships can only exist between truly virtuous people and should never contain anything transactional in them. Epicurus saw that people often enough become friends because they supply each other with things the other lacks; they complement each other, even complete each other. In this sense a friend is not 'another self' because that implies too close an identity between the two – and in any case ignores the diversities in human nature and the uniqueness of personality. So to proscribe any transactional element in friendship is to miss the significance of its core property of mutuality. One might therefore agree with Aristotle about friendship's high value, but choose Epicurus' more inclusive view about what it is.

Stoics valued friendship as one of the 'preferred' goods, but in line with their view that one's peace of mind should not depend on what one cannot control, friendship should count among the 'indifferents' because one cannot control either what happens to a friend or what a friend does. This very practical take on the matter is exemplified by Laelius regarding the loss of his beloved friend Scipio, as reported in Cicero's *De Amicitia*, 'On Friendship'. But the account Laelius there gives shows that treating friendship as an 'indifferent' from the point of view of what effect its loss should have on oneself is not the same as having a tepid view of friendship itself, or downgrading its import- ance; quite the contrary. Laelius' description of the importance to him and Scipio of their friendship – how they studied together, went to war together, worked in government together, from youth onwards through a lifetime – is a beautiful illustration of what friend- ship can be. But when Scipio died, Laelius continued with his duties in the Senate and mastered his sense of loss. Someone asked him, 'Your wisdom consists in this, that you look upon yourself as self- sufficing, and regard the accidents of life as powerless to affect your virtue; how do you cope with the loss of your dearest friend who was also a man of illustrious character?' Laelius' answer is in the ques- tion itself: self-sufficiency and the refusal to allow life's accidents to derail him provide him with the strength to continue; possessing that strength does not diminish his love for Scipio, or make his sense of the magnitude of his loss any the less.

Cicero has Laelius explain matters in these terms:

Therefore though I grieve for Scipio, I take comfort and strength in what our friendship was like, and both he and our friendship survive this mere change. We walked the earth together, and learned and shared much together; none of this can be taken away. I think what he would wish for me, could he wish it now, is that I would not allow my missing him to make me fail in my duties to myself, to others, and to his memory. I dwell with pleasure on the good of the past, and summon courage to bear his absence now, and turn outward to others who likewise grieve, to comfort them in their affliction; for there is comfort in what we share, and in the knowledge that others understand how we feel.

And then he concludes with the same consolatory truth mentioned in the previous chapter: 'Nothing can replace Scipio, as nothing can replace any of those we love. We do not cease to grieve, but we learn to live with grief.'[14]

We see again that, to understand a phenomenon such as love, we learn much by examining what we lose in losing it. Losing someone loved, losing another's love for oneself or losing one's own feelings of love for another teaches the meaning of love as eloquently as the experience of discovering it. In my view we find, on conducting that examination, that what we lose in losing love or a beloved is a friend. That is not invariably the case when an infatuation ends, or when a family relationship does not develop beyond the imbalances of age and state.

If one dispensed with the word 'love' in describing, in full, the emotional attitudes implicated in parent–child, sibling, romantic and friendship relationships, seeking paraphrases for the word in listing the positive and negative aspects of each, the relationship that would turn out to have fewest hooks for negatives to latch on to is friendship. In thinking about answers to the Socratic Question, that is a germane consideration. But it is not the chief reason for so valorizing friendship. To see this, use again the strategy of the negative: imagine a life wholly without friendship, without friends, at any point from infancy onwards – a life of perpetual emotional solitude, of inner silence where the voices and laughter of friends would sound if one had friends. It might not, contrary to what Aristotle and the Epicureans think, be impossible to have a life worth living in such a case – a Stoic might manage – but it would be unlikely, and anyway in one major respect exceedingly bare.

9. Luck and Evil

How, it might be and has been asked, is philosophizing about what makes life worth living, about 'good lives' and the meaning of life, possible in the face of all the suffering, evil and inhumanity that stains history and pollutes the world around us? How is it possible in the aftermath of Auschwitz, in the shadow of the Holocaust – and in face of the fact that, despite that particularly dreadful shadow, the same kind of inhumanity, the same kind of evil, has been repeated time and again in the decades since, in Cambodia and Indonesia, in Rwanda, at Srebrenica, in too many places?[1]

At the same time it might per contra be asked: how can we not philosophize about these things, in the hope of understanding them and, by doing so, helping to abate in future the evils that people do? A problem that faces this latter more optimistic project is what the fact of repeated atrocities tells us about human beings and therefore about the potential for good and evil in human nature. Both good and evil exist; that is a datum. But what does their expression depend upon? Individual personality? Circumstances? Luck?

Some of what is relevant to the discussion of these questions can be approached as follows.

Note first there are at least three different but not exclusive senses of the phrase 'a good life'. One denotes a life of pleasure and enjoyment; a second denotes a life of moral piety and uprightness; and the third denotes a life that is good to live because the person living it feels that it is worthwhile, perhaps even positively meaningful. The senses are not exclusive because a person living a good life in either of the first two senses will feel that she is therefore living a good life in the third sense; and a person living a good life in the second sense might therefore be living a good life in all three senses, because she could find being pious and upright both pleasurable and meaningful.

A person living a good life in the third sense might, as this shows, do so because she feels that it is good in one or both of the first two senses. But it is possible for a person to feel that her life is good in the third sense without it being good in either of the first two senses, for example if the achievement of a purpose that makes it meaningful to her is a painful struggle, and has nothing to do with piety and uprightness.

The philosophers' main target is the third sense, with one or both of the other two senses constituting or at least contributing to it, making a life worth living because it is tranquil, or because it is virtuous, or both. But the philosophers of antiquity – unlike, say, some existentialists in more recent philosophy – did not make the goodness of a life dependent on it being meaningful in the sense of serving a purpose whose value is extraordinary (in the literal sense of '*extra*ordinary', out of the ordinary). For the Epicureans a moderate interpretation of the first sense, and for the Aristotelians and Stoics their respective views of the second sense, constitute a good life in the third sense; none annex life's worth to the fulfilment of *high* purposes or *important* meanings or triumphs in one or another sphere.

It seems obvious that living a good life in any of the three senses is far easier to achieve in certain circumstances than in others. If you live in a war zone, in constant danger, deprived of the most basic necessities, beset from hour to hour by fear, hunger, thirst and grief, the very words 'a good life' will be empty. If you are born in a country of peace and plenty, have an education, access to healthcare, and a satisfying or at least tolerable job providing a regular income, the idea of 'a good life' is taken for granted; this is what is possible for the majority in such a society, where the resources for satisfactory lives lie ready to hand.

In an advanced economy in today's world – one should qualify this by saying 'an advanced economy that meets sufficient standards of democracy and the rule of law' – missing out on a good life, in *material* terms at least, would seem to require being either incapacitated in some way – not just literally disabled but socially disadvantaged in profound ways – or so ideologically opposed to its politics and the form of its economy that you reject what it offers. (Given that the economic and political mechanisms at work in advanced countries often generate injustices, not least in economic terms, the scope for both these factors is large enough.) But for the kinds of reasons discussed in Chapter 5, living in an advanced economy is no guarantee that life will feel good; indeed it turns out that economic conditions have relatively little to do with the matter, given that there are happy and contented people – by some measures happier and more contented – in places poor in terms of money but rich in other advantages, such as community relationships and leisure. And at the same time, advanced economies offer plenty of opportunities to be unhappy and to feel that life is bad. The reasons are obvious. Very few people ever have enough money to indulge all the temptations of a consumer society. The majority of employees in a company will never get to the boardroom – career pyramids from foot soldiers up to field marshals slope too sharply. Comparisons with the neighbours' possessions and lifestyle can be vexing; this is cited as one of the main reasons for dissatisfaction in rich societies. And the manner of life in rich societies brings its own ills – mental health problems and high rates of heart disease and cancer chief among them. Add to this mixture the common elevators of stress – working out a tax return, watching interest rates affect one's mortgage, coping with price rises, dealing with a crashed computer, balancing work and private lives, the enclosures of obligation that are the very structure of normativity; they are all generators of discontent. And these remarks leave aside the problems of family life, growing up, growing old, illness, heartbreak, failure, the uneven paths of typical life – among which moments either of joy or tranquillity can seem, to many, too few.

These remarks point to the thought that although the circumstances in which an individual finds herself have a bearing on how she feels about her life, they are not the only factors and most probably not the crucial ones. That they are not the crucial ones is implicit in the teachings of the ancient ethical schools, only one of which – the Aristotelian – gives material considerations any significance as a contribution to the quality of life. (So too, of course, does the unconscious philosophy embedded in normativity.) Pushed to the limit of detachment from external factors, which is what Stoics and Indian sannyasis aim to achieve, the implication is that a person in a war zone with danger all round and not enough to eat, or in a prison camp treated with violent cruelty, should still be able to conclude that hers is nevertheless a good life.

Is that credible? At very least it seems a tall order. This suggests the need for further distinctions: a Stoic might wish to decouple the concept of *ataraxia*, equilibrium of mind, from the idea of 'a good life' where the hint of an objective third-party comparison between life in a war zone and life in a peaceful advanced economy enters the definition of 'a good life'. The Stoic might say, 'I do not claim to be living a good life by that kind of standard. I claim to be proof against anxiety and psychological turmoil even though I am living in a war zone.'

This response is persuasive. But in being so it makes Stoicism far more demanding than either the Aristotelian or the Epicurean view. Epicurean *aponia* includes having enough to eat, and *ataraxia* is among other things not being afraid, so the Garden would not grow in a war zone. Aristotle, always a pragmatist, believed that a life worth living implies a certain degree of material security and social position, which led him to acknowledge that 'moral luck' plays its part in the constitution of a life worth living. Admitting the influence of moral luck entails that if you live in a war zone, even if you are a person of practical wisdom and the other virtues, your life cannot be as good as if you are such a person living in peaceful and flourishing conditions.

These thoughts require consideration of the idea of 'moral luck' itself, and of what can be learned from circumstances of moral *ill*-luck in regard to the possibility of a life worth living – for a telling and relevant example, of what can be learned from Auschwitz.

One learns from Primo Levi's chapter entitled 'The Drowned and the Saved' in *If This Is a Man* that there were three types of people in Auschwitz.[2] In the chapter itself he talks of two of the types. The men in the camp were, he writes, of many different backgrounds and languages, crammed together, 'crushed against the bottom' of existence. None of them had any rest from the struggle for survival 'because everyone is desperately and ferociously alone'; anything any of them found or learned that would help him in his own struggle he would keep to himself. In the camp there was a merciless operation of the Law that says those who have will get more and those without will be deprived further.

To the majority of the camp's inmates Levi applies the slang term *Muselmänner*, translated as 'musselmans' in the English version of his book. (In the translation of Viktor Frankl's account of Auschwitz the word is rendered as 'Moslems'; neither explains why this term was used.[3]) Coined by the camp's Jewish inmates, the word denotes those crushed by exhaustion and starvation, most of them expecting death and already resigned to it. The minority include those Levi calls *Prominenten*, men who through astuteness and energy were able to navigate the challenges of the camp, getting themselves a position such as Kapo or *Blockältester* (block leader), kitchen worker, pot scraper, hut sweeper, even *Scheissminister* (latrine cleaner), and therefore surviving better, if only temporarily, than the mass of inmates. Most 'Aryan' inmates were automatically given a role of some kind; a Jew seeking to become a *Prominenz* had to 'plot and struggle hard'. Levi reserves his harshest judgment for those of his fellow Jews who were successful in this. They were offered a little privilege in return for betraying their own, and the more power they were given the more hateful and hated they became. 'When he is given the command of a group of unfortunates, with the right of life or death over them,' Levi writes, 'he will be cruel and tyrannical, because he will understand that if he is not sufficiently so, someone else, judged more suitable, will take over his post. Moreover, his capacity for hatred, unfulfilled in the direction of the oppressors, will double back, beyond all reason, on the oppressed; and he will only be satisfied when he has unloaded onto his underlings the injury received from above.' The 'Aryan' prominents were no better, but they were in any case 'stolid and bestial' criminals selected from ordinary prisons because of their suitability for superintending musselmans.

Those in the second, minority, group were those capable of fighting the cold, hunger and exhaustion by applying every ounce of their intelligence and strength of will. Either that, or they were able to strangle their own consciences, renouncing their 'moral worlds' and becoming beasts pitting themselves against the beasts around them, no quarter given. Levi gives examples of the way inmates in the minority group survived – by betraying others, by worming their way into the confidence of camp officials, by being mad in a way perfectly suited to the hellish circumstances of the camp but which would require immurement in an asylum outside it.

As for the majority, the musselmans, who finished in the gas chambers: they all 'have the same story, or more exactly, no story; they followed the slope down to the bottom, like streams that run into the sea'. It was easy for them to do this; they had only to follow orders, and eat no more than the ration – which was not enough to keep them fit to work; finding more to eat required the skills of the would-be *Prominenz* – and within three months they were finished. They were overcome before they could adjust to camp life, to learn how to navigate the tangled rules, to master enough German or Polish to understand orders and threats. They staggered in confusion on the downward slope, their bodies 'already in decay, and nothing can save them from selections or from death by exhaustion. Their life is short, but their number is endless; they, the *Muselmänner*, the drowned, form the backbone of the camp, an anonymous mass, continually renewed and always identical, of non-men who march and labour in silence, the divine spark already dead within them, already too empty to really suffer. One hesitates to call them living; one hesitates to call their death death, in the face of which they have no fear, as they are too tired to understand.' For Levi the image that encapsulates the evil of that time is of a skeletally thin man, hunched, with drooping head and blank eyes.

The camp regime was designed to strip inmates of their humanity, to make them merely beasts of burden for as long as they lasted, docile and unable to resist, and then to dispose of them when their utility was over. When Levi arrived at Auschwitz after days in a crowded cattle-truck, the women, children and elderly were taken directly to the gas chambers and he and other men deemed fit for work were taken to the labour camp. There, in the cold, they were made to strip, and wait; had their heads shaved, were herded into showers, issued with striped camp clothing, and assigned a number.

Consider what it is like, Levi asks, to be wrenched from home, separated from family, deprived of every little thing that has meaning and association – a photograph, a handkerchief – turned into an item in a shivering mass of naked men, branded with a number (Levi's was 174517), subjected to blows, thrust with suddenness into an appalling and incomprehensible new world.

The point, Levi says, is 'the demolition of a man. In a moment, with almost prophetic intuition, the reality was revealed to us: we had reached the bottom. It is not possible to sink lower than this; no human condition is more miserable than this, nor could it conceivably be so. Nothing belongs to us any more; they have taken away our clothes, our shoes, even our hair; if we speak, they will not listen to us, and if they listen, they will not understand.' Each inmate thereby becomes 'a hollow man, reduced to suffering and needs, forgetful of dignity and restraint, for he who loses all often easily loses himself'.

So far Levi has described two types who emerged from the demolition process: the musselmans and the prominents. He says there was nothing in between, no middle class as in the outside world. The ferocious circumstances of camp life squeezed men to these extremes. But what of the third type, of whom he does not speak *directly* anywhere in his book? What of the SS guards, the men and women who ran the camps? In introducing the two types of inmates, he says – with inmates exclusively in mind – 'We do not believe in the most obvious and facile deduction: that man is fundamentally brutal, egoistic and stupid in his conduct once every civilized institution is taken away, and that the *Häftling* [prisoner] is consequently nothing but a man without inhibitions. We believe, rather, that the only conclusion to be drawn is that in the face of driving necessity and physical disabilities many social habits and instincts are reduced to silence.'

It can be asked if Levi is right about this. The SS in charge of the camps, and those prisoners they used as Kapos, most certainly displayed brutality and inhumanity, yet it was not the case that 'every civilized institution' had been denied them; they did not experience 'driving necessity and physical disabilities'. Their behaviour towards the inmates was licensed by allocating the latter to a non-human category which they were permitted to despise, but they almost certainly behaved in normal civilized ways off-duty, among friends. Senior SS officers had their families with them, and although it gives one a sharp frisson of something worse than dismay to think it, some of them listened to Beethoven and read Goethe in the evening after choosing whom to send to the gas chambers and witnessing – or enacting – brutal treatment of other human beings. The terrible mystery here is how divided their minds were, how apparently otherwise ordinary people could do what they did and live with it.

There is some difference between those in charge of camps and those occasionally involved in mass murder events of the kind that happened at Babi Yar and elsewhere.[4] It appears that, despite official policy against alcohol consumption among civilians and certainly among troops, Himmler – in charge of the SS and the Final Solution – ensured 'special rations' of alcohol to units engaged in activities behind the Eastern Front. His stated reason was that after carrying out actions against 'Jews and Bolsheviks' it was necessary to help the troops to cope with what they had seen and done. ' "A good meal, good beverages, and music" were intended to "take the men to the beautiful realm of German spirit and inner life". Not coincidentally, these get-togethers often took place in the wake of mass executions – a fact reflected in Himmler's comment that such "celebrations" helped to prevent these "difficult duties" from "harming the mind and character" of the participants.'[5] But drunkenness prompted atrocity – 'On the evening of April 28, 1942, Gestapo official Heinrich Hamann and his Security Police comrades in the Polish town of Neu-Sandez (Nowy Sącz) were celebrating the mass execution of 300 alleged "Jewish Communists"; an intoxicated Hamann, together with a group of policemen and local Nazi officials, decided to enter the town's ghetto to continue their killing spree.' In another example, 'a female Jewish survivor of the Międzyrzec Ghetto recalled that drunken Gestapo men came into the ghetto on New Year's Eve, 1942. She testified that "[the Gestapo men] invaded the ghetto and embarked upon a so-called 'killing spree' (*Gaudi*)".' And issues of alcohol were used both before and after atrocities to get the work done 'as a catalyst to violence and sexual predation'.[6]

Himmler's reference to 'difficult duties' and the need to protect against their 'harm to the mind and character' reflects the fact that on the very few occasions when he had himself witnessed such operations he had been unable to stand it, and had to hurry away feeling sick and dizzy.[7] Against the background of these facts, the question about those who operated the camps daily over long periods, combining brutal inhumanity with normal social existence, presses with extra force. For here it is not a question of 'social habits and instincts [being] reduced to silence', for they were not silenced except in the presence of the emaciated and exhausted victims. And in the case of Himmler himself, in charge of the industrial murder of millions and yet incapable of bearing the sight of its actuality – well, one marvels at the capacity of the human mind to divide itself, to build thick walls between certain facts and certain feelings, to self-deceive and self-justify. One recoils, in horror, at the thought of treating another sentient being – even a dog or cat – with vicious cruelty; with how much more horror does one contemplate people who sent women and their children, and the grandparents of the children, to their deaths, right then, as they shuffled past. Understanding this feels impossible to an observer distant in time and circumstance from the platform at Auschwitz-Birkenau where the 'selections' were made, selections between those who would die right then at that moment, and those who would be worked to death later. Yet it happened, and human beings did it – people whose culture had for several centuries been among the highest ever known.

There is much published examination of the enabling conditions of camp organization and its purposes. A number of factors, usually in combination, are cited. One is the ethos of Nazism and its relentless propaganda against all Jews, 'undesirables' and enemies of the Reich. Another is outright sadism; Frankl observes that Kapos were typically chosen from criminal prisons for their callousness and brutality. There are also the effects of habituation, and of the psychological defence mechanisms that made some turn their reaction to what they were doing into increased anger against the victims, as if blaming them for their own distress and dehumanization. And finally there is the psychology of experiencing power and lust in dominating helpless victims.[8] In discussing the daily organization of the camp at

Majdanek at Lublin in Poland, which had a number of uses but
between the summer of 1942 and the autumn of 1943 was an extermin-
ation camp, Elissa Mailänder Koslov writes:

> cruelty [is] a specific form of violence that is distinguished by its
> intensity and motivation. Violence causes different grades of pain,
> but cruelty has not only the explicit aim to inflict pain and suffering
> upon the victim, but also to bring degradation. It can only be imple-
> mented in the context of an asymmetrical power relation. By
> ill-treating and killing a concentration camp prisoner, by humiliation,
> camp guards, both female and male, experienced and expressed
> their *overwhelming* dominance. Considering Elias Canetti's theory of
> power, the cruel act can be seen to have provided the perpetrator with
> a vital and lustful exercise of power.[9]

Examination of the psychologies of the Final Solution's perpetrators at all levels, from the leaders of Nazi Germany to the guards and
Kapos in the camps themselves, is a dismaying task. Investigators seeking explanations from those tried for crimes against humanity in the
aftermath of the war were largely frustrated by the unwillingness or
inability of perpetrators to provide them. One of the best-known discussions of the phenomenon is Hannah Arendt's *Eichmann in Jerusalem:
A Report on the Banality of Evil*.[10] In a totalitarian setting, she wrote, evil
is not abnormal, the result of individual pathology or malice, but
instead is organized, lawful, requiring efficiency. Building camps,
arranging the logistics of their staffing and supply, scheduling trains,
systematic information-gathering about those to be rounded up and
transported, matching labour needs to crucial war industries (Primo
Levi had himself been assigned to the Buna synthetic rubber factory at
Auschwitz – which in the event never produced an ounce of rubber),
keeping records, collecting shoes, clothing, gold teeth, watches and
spectacles from victims; all this adds up to a mountain of evil through
completely ordinary everyday organization, but it did not look like –
or to most involved in carrying it out, feel like – evil. It was at the
interface between guards and victims in the camps themselves that
overt acts of dehumanization and violent cruelty were perpetrated,
deliberately in order to subdue the victims and maintain control of

them, aided by starvation and exhaustion, though also as a 'natural' consequence of the relative positions occupied by masters and victims, and the location of the latter outside the realm of moral regard. Those who went straight from the trains to the gas chambers were kept docile by lies; the officers told them they were going for a shower, for delousing, that they would be reunited with family members shortly; the mental control allied to the physical control is expressive of a *system* which is malicious, independently of whether any of those operating it were themselves actively so.

Eichmann's defence was that he himself had killed no one. He was on a rung in the organization, far from the scene of the crimes. He was an official, doing his job, like any bureaucrat. This insulation from the raw facts of what his paperwork meant was the result of totalitarianism's normalization of the evil in question. It turns off thought and moral imagination. It deals with numbers. In this context, 'normalization' is the key.

Arendt's analysis is persuasive, but its focus is narrow; it applies to large modern bureaucratic states with the institutions and practices ready to hand for adaptation to the processes of industrial murder. Footage from areas of conflict in West Africa or the Middle East showing ragged youths brandishing Kalashnikovs and careering around in the back of trucks – intoxicated with the situation they are in and the camaraderie that sustains them, oblivious to danger, in a state of hyper-arousal, extremely dangerous because of their hair-trigger emotions and sense of invulnerability – are a far cry from the office routine of Adolf Eichmann. But the evil done to a single non-combatant civilian on the grounds of a religious or ethnic categorization unpalatable to someone – whether an armed youth in a tribal militia or a Nazi official in a Berlin office – is the same. In the one case arousal and excitement, in the other the humdrum refusal to contemplate the meaning of what is being done, is what takes people across the line to evil. And these are not the only possible explanations. The ruthless despot who calmly orders a massacre, and those who carry it out for fear of their own lives but exist afterwards with desperate memories and unsatisfactory attempts at self-exculpation, are positioned along the same scale in the service of human evil.

It is said that if one wishes to know what a person is really like, give them power over something helpless, like a kitten. The inmates of Auschwitz were in an impotent state, and their treatment from the first moment they were rounded up for transportation to the camps was dehumanizing. Those given power over them were tested by being given that power, and very many failed the test. But not all of them did. And this is the key point for present purposes, because Levi's *If This Is a Man* is not just the 'Drowned and the Saved' chapter with its unforgiving binary portrait of the inmates. On the contrary, his book – and likewise Viktor Frankl's book; and others – is a testament to something more remarkable and hopeful: namely, the fact that even in the horrendous circumstances of Auschwitz, humanity could flourish.

Levi cites the 'admirable and terrible Jews of Salonica, tenacious, thieving, wise, ferocious and united, so determined to live', who did not succumb to the every-man-for-himself attitude, but strove to survive as a group. He relates how a Polish civilian working at the Buna site gave him bread. He reports a day when the sun shone with spring warmth on his *Kommando* as it marched to its worksite: 'Today is a good day. We look around like blind people who have recovered their sight, and we look at each other. We have never seen each other in sunlight: someone smiles. If it was not for the hunger!' One of their number, Templer, the *Kommando*'s 'organizer', finds a giant pot of soup abandoned by Polish workers because they thought it was rancid; for the members of the *Kommando* it is heaven-sent. 'Templer looks at us, triumphant; this "organization" is his work. Templer is the official organizer of the Kommando: he has an astonishing nose for the soup of civilians, like bees for flowers. Our Kapo, who is not a bad Kapo, leaves him a free hand, and with reason: Templer slinks off, following imperceptible tracks like a bloodhound, and returns with the priceless news that the Methanol Polish workers, one mile from here, have abandoned ten gallons of soup.' The spoils are shared; the Kapo 'is not a bad Kapo'. There are occasions in the camp's squalor, misery, hunger and abuse when 'we are all satiated, at least for a few hours, no quarrels arise, we feel good, the Kapo feels no urge to hit us, and we are able to think of our mothers and wives, which usually does not happen. For a few hours we can be unhappy in the manner of free men.'

In January 1945, as the Soviet army was approaching and sounds of battle could be heard in the vicinity of Auschwitz, Levi fell ill with scarlet fever and was sent to the camp hospital. Among the others in the room were two French political prisoners, also with scarlet fever. Levi and they were 'lucky' to be ill; they and other patients were left in the hospital when the camp was evacuated and its many thousands of inmates sent on a forced march westward, almost all dying in the freezing weather on the way. Levi and the Frenchmen worked together to set up a stove for warmth, to find food, to adapt a battery to provide light at night. They formed the nucleus of a mutual group of patients who survived, helping each other and dividing tasks among them, until the Russians arrived. And then the Russians took care of them.

In the account given by psychiatrist and psychotherapist Viktor Frankl of his experiences in Auschwitz and Dachau, we learn that acts of kindness and fraternity, even in the midst of those horrific conditions, were far from uncommon. 'There were enough examples, often of a heroic nature, which proved that apathy could be overcome, irritability suppressed,' he writes. 'Man can preserve a vestige of spiritual freedom, of independence of mind, even in such terrible conditions of psychic and physical stress. We who lived in concentration camps can remember the men who walked through the huts comforting others, giving away their last piece of bread. They may have been few in number, but they offer sufficient proof that everything can be taken from a man but one thing: the last of the human freedoms – to choose one's attitude in any given set of circumstances, to choose one's own way.'[11]

It was not just individuals, but occasionally the entire group which maintained solidarity; he recalls an occasion when one of their number stole some potatoes: 'The theft had been discovered and some prisoners had recognized the "burglar". When the camp authorities heard about it they ordered that the guilty man be given up to them or the whole camp would starve for a day. Naturally the 2,500 men preferred to fast.' *Naturally the 2,500 men preferred to fast.*

Frankl mentions also the humane acts of some of the guards. 'It must be stated that even among the guards there were some who took pity on us . . . Human kindness can be found in all groups, even those which as a whole it would be easy to condemn. The boundaries between groups overlapped and we must not try to simplify matters by saying that these men were angels and those were devils. Certainly, it was a considerable achievement for a guard or foreman to be kind to the prisoners in spite of all the camp's influences, and, on the other hand, the baseness of a prisoner who treated his own companions badly was exceptionally contemptible.' In fact Frankl claims that most of the guards did not engage in brutal acts, though they did nothing to stop them: 'The majority of the guards had been dulled by the number of years in which, in ever-increasing doses, they had witnessed the brutal methods of the camp. These morally and mentally hardened men at least refused to take active part in sadistic measures. But they did not prevent others from carrying them out.'

In the psychotherapeutic system Frankl developed, logotherapy — predicated on the idea that neuroses result from feelings of loss of direction and loss of a sense of personal value, replaced by a sense of uselessness and purposelessness — there is an empirical rejection of Freud's belief that extreme conditions will strip people to the most basic aspects of their nature:

> Freud once asserted, "Let one attempt to expose a number of the most diverse people uniformly to hunger. With the increase of the imperative urge of hunger all individual differences will blur, and in their stead will appear the uniform expression of the one unstilled urge." Thank heaven, Sigmund Freud was spared knowing the concentration camps from the inside. His subjects lay on a couch designed in the plush style of Victorian culture, not in the filth of Auschwitz. There, the "individual differences" did not "blur" but, on the contrary, people became more different; people unmasked themselves, both the swine and the saints.

In the interesting though almost certainly self-exculpating account by the pathologist of the infamous Dr Mengele in Auschwitz, Dr Miklós Nyiszli, a prisoner who survived by serving in the camp's 'dissecting room' (Nyiszli mentions no vivisections), there are numerous instances of humane feeling even among the *Sonderkommando* prisoners who moved the bodies from the gas chambers into the flames of the crematoria.[12] On one occasion they discovered among the heaped bodies a girl still alive. They anxiously brought her to Nyiszli, who revived her. There was discussion about what to do with her; the Kapo in charge concluded that there was nothing to be done with her, no way of rescuing her further, and shot her in the head. But the initial action of the *Sonderkommando* men had been the instinctive one of rescuing her.

In an essay appended to Nyiszli's book, Bruno Bettelheim – himself imprisoned in Buchenwald for a time after the Nazi *Anschluss* of Austria, before being released and escaping to America – comments on the phenomenon observed by almost all who wrote about people who gave up and people who survived in the camps: 'Those who seek to protect the body at all cost die many times over. Those who risk the body to survive as men have a good chance to live on.' Frankl says the same thing in a different way: 'Even the helpless victim of a hopeless situation, facing a fate he cannot change, may rise above himself, may grow beyond himself.' Thus it was that even in Auschwitz courage survived, and humane impulses survived – and because of them, some humans survived – even though the main story by far was the immense inhumanity engulfing them all.

None of this says there were 'good lives' in either of the first two senses described above for any but those in charge at Auschwitz and other camps. But it does say that there were good lives in the third sense – lives worth living, and meaningful lives, even among the inmates, the brutalized, and those who died there. This is a significant finding.

Without doubt, plain luck – good or bad – was implicated in the fates of those in Auschwitz. You might be in the camp hospital when a 'selection' was made in your hut to send some to the gas chambers, and back in your hut when a selection was made in the hospital. The idea of luck – chance – extends further. Were you genetically more robust physically, had your upbringing made you more determined, were you grouped with someone who encouraged and helped you, were you and your people among the last to be rounded up so that the war's end was approaching as you arrived at a camp? Even more to the point: were you born at a place and time, and in circumstances, which led to your becoming a camp guard and there being required to participate in the activities of the camp – controlling slave labourers, marshalling people into gas chambers? If you had been born in a different country or at a different time, you would not have been involved in that activity. Were you as blameable as someone who willed that there should be slave and death camps and volunteered to participate in the activities there?

There is a natural assumption that people should be accountable for what they do voluntarily, but should not be blamed for what they could not help doing. If someone trips up a waiter in a restaurant and the soup he is carrying falls over you, you do not blame the waiter; it was not his fault. But consider this: two men unintentionally fire their guns because, by mistake, each has left off the safety catch of his weapon. One kills a child who just happens to be crossing his path at that moment. The other's bullet goes harmlessly into the ground. The former is punished, the latter not. There is no difference between their acts – they each left off a safety catch, they each loosed off a bullet. But the unintended consequence of the first man's act is factored into the judgment of him, and he is held accountable for it. Certainly anyone who carries a gun should be regarded as responsible for doing so safely, and both men were at fault in that respect. But why is the second man treated more lightly than the first given that his carelessness *could have* had the same result? This privileges consequences over virtues by a long way.

The gun example illustrates the problem of 'moral luck'. Kant held that moral praise and blame apply only to what is under an agent's control, thus making a principle out of the natural assumption described above. But in an influential essay, Bernard Williams argued that luck is a frequent arbiter of a person's moral status, a fact acknowledged at law when 'mitigating circumstances' are taken into account in explaining why this or that person committed a crime – as, for example, in the case of a youth raised in a den of thieves and forced by the adults there to participate in their criminal activity.[13]

In the gun case, the moral status of the first man is determined by an unintended consequence. In the criminal youth case, his moral status is determined by his circumstances. There are even broader circumstances of relevance: factors such as genes and upbringing, over which an individual has no control at all, undoubtedly make their contribution. This has been described by Thomas Nagel as 'constitutive' moral luck, which differs from the 'circumstantial' case because in the latter the individual has at least some degree of choice – the youth could quit the circle of thieves he finds himself in once he realizes the implications of belonging to it; but he cannot alter the constitutive element of his genes or his upbringing in early life.

The 'moral luck' dilemma arises in cases where it is thought to be correct to hold someone accountable despite the fact that he had no control over what he did, as in the first gunman's case. There seems to be something both right and wrong about this. On the one hand, the very idea of *luck* is the idea of what an agent did not intend, did not bring about, had no influence over: 'luck' and 'chance' are concepts that go naturally together. On the other hand we feel justified in punishing a murderer more harshly than someone who attempted murder but failed. We can specify that everything the murderer and would-be murderer did was identical; they planned to kill someone, put the plan into action, took aim and fired; but in the second case the intended victim, unaware of her danger, moved at the last moment and the bullet flew past her. The would-be murderer's failure is his lucky chance as regards consequences.

The extreme case of scepticism about moral accountability arises in the 'free will' debate, for there a hard determinist position entails that no one is responsible for anything, and the very idea of morality – which depends on agency, responsibility, the validity of praise and blame – vanishes. Trying to make sense of our intuitions – that the first gunman should be held accountable for the death of the child; that the criminal youth should be granted some leniency given his circumstances – swings the pendulum way over in the opposite direction, making people *accountable for* what they are *not responsible for*. This is very like the iron Greek view that even if you are fated to commit a crime, you will be punished for doing it.

Having subjected the problem of moral luck to an exhaustive examination, Nagel concluded, 'I believe that in a sense the problem has no solution.' This is because the idea of agency is incompatible with treating human actions as mere events, or people as mere things. Yet as the factors prompting a person's actions are brought fully into the light, it looks more and more as if actions are indeed events and people are things. 'Eventually nothing remains which can be ascribed to the responsible self, and we are left with nothing but a portion of the larger sequence of events, which can be deplored or celebrated, but not blamed or praised.'[14]

Before agreeing with Nagel's pessimistic conclusion, consider further the fact that in practice both our ordinary moral judgments and our systems of justice base themselves on the inconsistent ideas that circumstances make a difference to culpability (you and your friend's guns go off accidentally but only your bullet kills someone, so only you go to prison), and at the same time that inequalities that arise from circumstances just have to be accepted (you are adopted by a poor family, and your twin by a rich family, with all that follows; but that's just 'luck of the draw').

It is when we dig into the examples used to illustrate how we treat cases of moral luck that significant distinctions appear. Consider the first gunman; suppose it transpires in court that he is a man of sterling character – a philanthropist, loved and admired by the community. Or suppose it transpires that he is a careless and inconsiderate layabout. It would be unsurprising to find the court meting out very different treatments accordingly. So his character, not just what he did, enters the reckoning; a consequentialist approach gets him into court, a 'virtue ethics' approach might get him out of it – or alternatively, further in. 'A good person who does a bad thing', 'a bad person who does something bad accidentally'; in reflecting on the difference in the way we treat these two cases, we are led to ask: can one be a good person accidentally – as a result of luck?

The biggest problem with the idea of moral luck is that it seems to threaten the idea of morality itself, in that judgments about the moral *status* of agents bring in considerations that the agents themselves have nothing to do with, and that seems unjust. But what in fact it does is to say that there are often bigger issues at stake than a particular act. The first gunman's carelessness resulted in a death; the victim's whole family was harmed by their loss; society has an interest in not tolerating carelessness with outcomes of such gravity, and therefore must put those consequences into the judgment about how to respond. This thought is a reiteration of the fact that *ethics* – relating to the character of a person and of a society – is a larger matter than *morals*, a narrower matter of what governs aspects of interpersonal relationships within society.

This is to acknowledge that ethical considerations trump moral ones when important questions are at stake; it is to acknowledge that a society's self-management requires, as a pragmatic matter, that sometimes individuals *have* to be held accountable for what they are not responsible for. And it is also to accept the fact – as implied by the twins example above – that the prospects of good and worthwhile lives to a significant extent lie in the laps of the gods. It is easier to be good when you are not beset by struggles; long ago Mencius wrote that the natural goodness of human beings is perverted by poverty and hunger, which makes them turn to crime or unkindness because difficulties 'sink and drown their hearts'. That is a point Aristotle also conceded, and it is why Martha Nussbaum called her book on the subject *The Fragility of Goodness*, to mark the idea that the possibility of having a good life is vulnerable to things outside an agent's control. And that is precisely why the Stoics argued that what is outside one's control should count among the 'indifferents' – to remove ourselves from the tyranny of moral luck.

All this said, it remains that good, worthwhile, even meaningful lives can be lived even in the direst of circumstances: Auschwitz proves it. Morally relevant luck plays its part here, but so also does *will*, though the thought of an individual's determination to survive in those circumstances cannot be divorced from *why* he or she wills to overcome them; as Nietzsche said, 'He who has a why to live can bear almost any how.'[15] Frankl took this as a motto for logotherapy, the psychotherapy premised on the idea that discovery of meaning is the cure for neurosis.

Literature offers examinations of responses to circumstances of moral ill-luck. Alexandre Dumas' novel *The Count of Monte Cristo* relates how Edmond Dantès, unjustly imprisoned in the island fortress of the Château d'If, is educated by – and after eight years escapes with the help of – the ingenious Abbé Faria. The Abbé, too frail to accompany Dantès, has revealed to him the whereabouts of a treasure trove on the island of Monte Cristo; with his education by Faria in literature, history, science and politics, and this wealth, Dantès reinvents himself as a count and takes revenge on those who had contrived his imprisonment and deprived him of his beloved Mercédès. The intelligence, will and ingenuity of Faria's life in the Château d'If is detailed in an extraordinary act of imagination by Dumas, who might have acquired some of the ideas from prisoners whose long incarceration had likewise taught them necessity's inventions. Perhaps, too, some of the inspiration came from Daniel Defoe's *Robinson Crusoe*, the eponymous castaway dependent on resourcefulness and will for survival on a desert island. The determination of Dantès and Crusoe is a contrast to the embittered railings of Shakespeare's Timon of Athens and King Lear, both characters who – the worse for having brought it on themselves – cannot rise above their misfortune.

Shakespeare's 'negative capability' – Keats' phrase for the ability to accept, in human nature, 'uncertainties, mysteries, doubts, without any irritable reaching after fact and reason' – allows him to present Edgar and Kent in *King Lear* as good men, Iago in *Othello* as malicious, Lear as weak, and their characters as catalysts for events around them. In some cases explanation is given: Claudius in *Hamlet* commits fratricide and Macbeth commits regicide, each to get a crown, but Iago has no obvious motivation for destroying Desdemona and Othello. Shakespeare relies on the fact that 'that is how things are' with some people. So, both in fiction in the Château d'If and in terrible reality in the concentration camps, facts about human character – incorporating at its centre moral luck, good and bad – enter the picture essentially.

*

From these considerations one can draw many thoughts about 'ordinary' life and its philosophy. Answers to questions about moral luck, will, reasons to live, and whether a life is worth living given its circumstances, can be enriched by learning from the devastating lessons of the concentration camps, and from imaginative evaluation of what is explored in literature – literature being one of our best resources for delving into the complexities and nuances of human experience. This is a paradigm of how reflection on Socrates' question benefits from assembling materials to inform one's answer. For everything taught by such reflection is as relevant to ordinary life as to extreme circumstances; indeed, the philosophers teach that without making that reflection relevant to ordinary life, it will not be available if needed in harder times.

Nothing in the laws of statistics tells us that there could not be a person who, born with intelligence, beauty, wealth and health, could live actively until the age of ninety in a peaceful and civilized country without so much as a toothache or a stubbed toe to trouble her days. Happy in her relationships, contented with the state of affairs in the world around her, feeling permanently satisfied with everything in her life, she would be the personification of *eudaimonia*. Something like this might have happened at times, statistically speaking. But if so we can be sure that it is exceedingly rare, because plain general knowledge of the human body and the human condition tells us so. Physically, we are born to age and die, and in the process are vulnerable to many insults from microbes and viruses, falling rocks, abuse of our own organs by alcohol, nicotine and other drugs, radiation from natural sources, accidents, and many other things besides. Psychologically, we are born to anxiety, conflict, desire and stress more than we are born to happiness. This is because we are social animals and life among others is, psychologically, to jostle in the crowd, to have to compete sometimes, to experience uncertainty, to suffer setbacks and injustices small and large. 'Life isn't fair' we say, and like almost all clichés this is true.

From these familiar observations we can conclude that the song is right: there is trouble ahead. There is always going to be trouble ahead. This stark fact, which most people spend most of their time ignoring, is what made the philosophers advise us to think about how to live, because to have a plan is to be prepared. Indeed there is a good sense in which philosophy *is* preparation – for the next minute, day, year; for life itself, because all our thought and action is directed at the future, which breaks over us from moment to moment like the waves of the sea.

Of course it is not wholly right to say that we do not prepare for life's exigencies. We take out insurance policies and sign on to a pension scheme, we go jogging, we unwind with a glass of wine but not too much, we have savings. We make plans: for a garden shed, a holiday by the sea, a baby. In this sense we are not living blind to the future, nor are we naively assuming that everything will always be all right. But this is not what the philosophers meant. They were thinking of the near-inevitability, if the 'near' is not redundant, that we will experience illness, worry, even despair and defeat; that we will suffer loss, grief and anguish; that we will probably have to compromise – at very least – over the hopes and ambitions we nourished at the outset of life. In many cases, lives are smashed apart by an accident, a moment of bad timing, a mistake. In a trice, circumstances can change: the fit young athlete whose neck is broken in a clash on the sports field and is left paralysed; the child who darts out into the traffic and is run over. In less than a second, entire lives can be lost, ruined or permanently distorted.

These are grim reflections. But now contrast the following pairs of questions: 'How would you react if such a thing happened? What do you think the consequences would be for what you are doing, or the plans you have?' and 'How *should* you react? What should you try to ensure about the effect of the consequences on your plans?' This is where, taking advantage of the opportunity to reflect against the vast backdrop of human experience distilled in history, literature and our own lives, we face the challenge to formulate our response.

'We': that pronoun obtrudes again. But it is not clear that the demand here is deflected by considerations of intersectionality, ethnicity, inequalities, social and economic injustice, historical pressures, culture, tradition, religion, inherent personal qualities, talents, endowments and disabilities, general health, or all the other circumstances and conditions whose webs cling round each human being in his or her particularity. On the contrary, these factors sharpen the demand. To think otherwise is to think one is a *victim* of these factors rather than the subject of them, this latter setting the terms in which the answers to Socrates' question have to be individually framed.

This point is succinctly made by saying that if Socrates' question could be answered in Auschwitz, it can be answered anywhere. Even if the answer does no more than encapsulate an aspiration, provided one authentically wishes to realize it and authentically tries to do so – for how many of us would have survived in Auschwitz, still less been one of its 'saints'? – it comes close to being enough for the life worth living.

10. Duties

It is a vexation to some to reflect that, having not asked to come into the world, nevertheless upon arrival in it – at least, upon arrival at the stage in life when they become aware of the following facts – they discover that they have obligations and duties, that there are expectations, that like a fly stuck in a spider's web they are entangled in the net of prevailing social sentiment, opinion, custom, tradition and expectation, not least relating to other people's rights and demands, and to what they themselves are obliged to do in order to get by. In Chapter 1 the word 'normativity' was introduced to describe this net. A significant aspect of the acculturation of children – their 'upbringing' – is to educate them in the behaviour and sentiments appropriate to inhabiting normativity's net. The conventional philosophy of life they are equipped with in this way is fitted to the net, even if the net is not reciprocally fitted to people; as is obvious enough, for practical reasons the net's nodes and interstices gather up the awkward diversity of human individuals into a small number of categories, and demand overall conformity from them.

But although the entanglement in normativity is a vexation to some, it is in fact a convenience, and even a relief, to others – perhaps most others. Many people like having normativity's obligations because they provide a sense of purpose, and endow life's standard activities with a sense of significance which, again to the satisfaction or relief of many, is shared with most others – for few like to be at odds with society, or to stand out as abnormal. Cleaving to normativity makes people feel that there is shape to their days and years – indeed, to their lives. What is asked of them by their place in the net constitutes the terms of life, and therefore the challenge to answer Socrates' question does not arise; the duties defined by normativity stand before them, generally quite simple and clear, giving instructions about what to do in the family, at work, in the street, among other people in shops, buses and bars. To the question 'What sort of person should I be?' normativity gives the answer: 'Someone who fits in and gets by.'

Although there are shades of difference in the meanings of 'duty' and 'obligation', they are, in the present connection, the same thing: if you have an obligation, you have a duty to fulfil it. The family of other concepts with which both are associated includes 'bond', 'agreement', 'promise', 'contract', 'commitment', 'requirement' and even 'liability', and all of them connote ideas about trust and accountability. They all also imply constraint, and sanction for failure, whether legal or in the form of social disapprobation.

The obligations of normativity come in two broad types, voluntary and involuntary. The former are those we self-impose by signing a contract, getting married or booking a holiday. The latter are those imposed by the mere fact of membership of society. The distinction does not align with the kinds of sanctions that failing in the relevant duties invites. You can be sued for breach of contract, imprisoned for breaking a law, disdained by family and friends for marital infidelity. In general, society expects us to observe the requirements of normativity, on the perfectly rational grounds that too much rebellion against them would make society – and all the many benefits it offers – impossible.

In fact, too much rebellion against normativity makes one's individual life nigh impossible too. In the quest for freedom, for example, a person might kick so hard against the constraints of normativity that as a result he ends up in prison, or socially ostracized, in a worse situation than the one he sought to escape. The prudent individual chooses his battles.

From a practical point of view, given these thoughts, normativity considerations seem to imply that an intervening question has to be answered before trying to answer – perhaps, before wasting time trying to answer – Socrates' question. It is: 'Is it realistic to think that I am in a position to answer Socrates' question for myself? Was it not already answered by the sheer fact of where and when I was born, and the tight limits to my options that this imposes?' Interestingly, in one stretch of the history of philosophy an assumption was widely made that where and when you were born indeed settles the question of how you should live, because it defines your duties, and duties must be carried out – this 'must' being part of the very definition of 'duty'. The assumption is embedded in the concept of 'my station and its duties', a concept which, following Hegel, was extensively discussed by the idealist philosophers T. H. Green, F. H. Bradley and Henry Sidgwick.[1] It is not surprising that in this nineteenth-century debate the idea of a *station* in life – a specific location in the net – might carry a set of obligations particular to that location, where the 'station' is not just an *office* as a policeman or schoolteacher, or a *role* as a husband or son, but by implication a *social position* as a peasant or a lord. Few in this version of the debate would deny that a peasant could rise to be a lord in exceptional circumstances, but such circumstances would indeed be exceptional, so it was taken for granted that people found themselves not only in a job or a role but in a social class which presumably had at least as much influence in shaping their prospects, and therefore the associated expectations, as their intelligence or talent and the range of choices permitted them.

This implication is not clearly enough drawn out in Bradley's version of this theory. In his view, an individual is nothing apart from society, which alone gives him his chance of self-realization – 'self-realization' being, in Bradley's opinion, the end and goal of life – by fulfilling his duties in the station he occupies: 'We have found self-realisation, duty and happiness in one – yes, we have found ourselves, when we have found our station and its duties, our function as an organ in the social organism.' In effect, since society prescribes what is moral, being moral consists in obeying society's demands. Doing so is what it is to acquire virtue. Echoing Aristotle's equation of 'virtue' and 'excellence', Bradley writes, 'To fulfil one's station in social life is doing one's duty, by which virtue or excellence is acquired.' The indirect reference to Aristotle reminds us that he – Aristotle – did not think virtue and excellence were appropriate ideals for peasants, on the grounds that they would be incapable of attaining them. (This might be true for the – unacceptable – reason that they were denied the opportunity to do so – for example by being denied education or the chance to compete for positions in society matched to their talents.) But there is no question of the women in Bradley's world – any more than in Aristotle's – having as wide a scope as men for stations, whether they are peasants or aristocratic ladies. The immediate implication of Bradley's view for women is that at any level of society their station is extremely limited, almost entirely to being all or some of consort, mother, nurse and housekeeper, or if banished or abandoned to the social shadows, as magdalens. The socially conservative implication of this view is that one would not expect peasants or women to strive for the excellences of the Aristotelian megalopsychos, not because they are incapable of it but because they can achieve excellence on their own account in their own station, finding the form of excellence appropriate to that station and achieved by fulfilling its duties. To each station, its duties; and therefore its excellences. This is not explicitly 'know your place', but is almost so.

Sidgwick's view is not haughty like Aristotle's, nor oblivious to socially conservative implications as Bradley's appears to be, because he is alive to the need to 'frame an ideal of a good life for all, and to show how a unity of moral spirit and principle may manifest itself through the diversity of actions and forbearances, efforts and endurances, which the diversity of social functions renders necessary'. But this does not stop him from acknowledging the degree to which normativity defines what is to count as 'right' in how we behave. Family relationships provide one example, while another is social class: 'what social classes owe to each other, according to our commonly accepted ideal of morality, depends on traditions which result from a gradual development'; the 'mass of traditional rules and sentiments . . . is the element in which our outward moral life is necessarily lived'. Sharing with Bradley the nineteenth-century idea of society as an organism, Sidgwick sees an individual's contribution to promoting the good of society as a major aspect of his moral worth. In this respect the 'my station' theorists were reprising Marcus Aurelius' view on the same subject.

Neither Bradley nor Sidgwick were fully satisfied with their own theories, acknowledging the force of objections urged against them. There is much scholarly debate about their views – and indeed about their source, which is Hegel's even more specific annexation of the individual to the social organism and the dependent 'situatedness' of individuality. The term used by Hegel in this connection is *Sittlichkeit*, sometimes translated as 'ethical order' and sometimes as 'morality', but significantly *Sitte* means 'custom or tradition'.[2] In all these thinkers normativity plays a more determining role than it does in today's pluralistic societies, because movement around and within the net was so much more restricted. In today's pluralistic societies – not in monolithic ones such as those dominated by a political or religious ideology – the effects of education and opportunities to migrate between socio-economic classes enable far greater mobility around the net, and hence a greater range of choices – more 'stations' to occupy – for people in it. That said, the net still exists, and it is still highly constraining.

Aristotle apart, it is striking that the philosophers of antiquity did not see *station*, role, class, or anything like them, as having any significance for ethics other than as a foil to the values they identify. A Cynic rejects normativity altogether; an Epicurean or Stoic is an Epicurean or Stoic by choice, and lives accordingly. The Stoics take normativity as they find it but treat its offerings and demands as 'indifferents' if irrelevant to their core principles. The Epicureans choose what avoids pain of body or mind, by focusing attention on what is most likely to produce neither – including moderation, friendship and intellectual pleasures. Key to both the Stoic and Epicurean views is a clear understanding of the material nature of reality and what that implies about fate and death – namely, that neither is to be feared, thus liberating us from them as major sources of angst. It is not that the ancients had no relevant conception of 'society'; on the contrary, the polis was a much more tightly knit entity than any populous, diverse state today, and the demands of its normativity were every bit as stringent as in any of today's strict monolithic cultures. To live as a Greek in a fifth-century polis was like living in one of today's Orthodox Jewish communities or a Muslim-majority country. Therefore, the practitioners of the philosophies stood at a conscious angle to the normativity of their day: the Cynics outside it; the Epicureans evading those aspects of it which invited the anxieties and pains that meeting its expectations involved; the Stoics cultivating indifference to those anxieties and pains but fulfilling their obligations anyway.

Other aspects of the condition of life in the ancient Hellenic and Roman worlds – the aspects of time and place; of the economy and the weather – made such stances to normativity less onerous than they are now. In our more populous, more complicated societies, with law, property and personal economic concerns constituting massive barriers to living at an angle to normativity, it is harder to do so. Harder but not impossible, especially with enough money; one can choose where, and to a great extent how, to live if one has financial independence. But this is a minority possibility. The sheer necessity of earning a living – to put a roof over one's head, clothes on one's back and food in one's mouth, at least of any reasonable quality and regularity – is a constraint, indeed a discipline, that keeps most people travelling on normativity's straight paths.

Yet again it has to be conceded that this is not wholly a bad thing. The benefits of society to social beings cannot be overrated. The degree of security and opportunity an organized society offers – think of schools and hospitals, the services that pooling resources (through taxation) provides, the enhanced amenities of leisure and communication, and much more – requires society to function at least adequately, which it does only if people will do the duties of the stations (here in the sense of chosen roles, not fixed or semi-fixed stations of social class and gender) they occupy. Think of society as constituted by a tacit agreement among us to do our bit, each of us, to ensure that it works; this is the same idea as seeing the legitimacy of many of normativity's demands.

Granting all this, what scope is there for giving the Socratic Question a worthwhile answer? The answer is: a great deal, at the level of practical life and especially in the inner universe of one's mind. At the level of practical life we constantly make choices – about what to study, which jobs to apply for, whom to go on a date with, and so on, and although the consequences of such choices are not fully predictable, and although it may turn out that we regret some of them and have to start over, nevertheless we make them. Life is not so limited in the range of options most people have, in advanced economies at least, nor is it invariably the case that every occupation is soul-destroying and every marriage a failure, though undoubtedly many of both are. When they are, the fact should be a stimulus for new choices to be made and actions taken. Admittedly, our options narrow with time; we get locked into some of the choices we make at the outset. And it takes effort to bring about significant changes in one's career, private life and social networks in mid- or later life. The catch is that at the time of making some of our more significant choices we are young and have not experienced much of what the choices mean; to that extent they are a gamble.

But it is never too late to make different choices, however much harder it gets with time. It might be a fairly rare occurrence that someone gives up a lucrative career in finance to raise chickens on a smallholding, but it happens, and on the principle 'from what is actual one sees what is possible', *ab esse ad posse*, one could do something analogous if one had the will. Recall that at the end of every day Epictetus asked those who came to hear him lecture, 'How long will you delay to be wise?' – and that he also said it is never too late to become wise; even in the last hour of a long life one can do it.

It does not take throwing up one's career and buying some chickens to become wise, in the sense of making and living the choices that genuinely reflect what one wishes to be. A Cynic, and to a less drastic extent an Epicurean, might advocate changes of practice; a Stoic will tell you that it is your attitudes that are key – 'the meaning of things lies not in things themselves but in our attitudes to them' – and that the things of ordinary life are 'indifferents' if neither their possession nor loss would affect your equilibrium of mind, which is yours to govern. Whichever of these routes you take, you will have chosen it as the driver of how you are living, and that fact – the fact of ownership – is by itself in equal parts liberating and empowering.

Still, all three routes remain vulnerable to the limitations, not to say frustrations, of living as if in the midst of a packed crowd of others, with a lot of jostling and frequent difficulties when trying to push a way through from some *A* to a desired *B*. The other alternative, which is to find scope for self-creating choices in the inner universe of one's mind, is limited only by the extent of one's imagination. Here there is freedom – 'My mind to me a kingdom is / Such perfect joy therein I find / That it excels all other bliss / That earth affords or grows by kind'[3] – and resort to it applies the insights of both the Stoics and the Epicureans, the first literally, the second somewhat more figuratively in consisting in the cultivation of a mental garden, but no less effectively for that.

The Stoic precept that no one is free who is not master of his attitudes lies at the base of this. But there are at least two ways one could apply this idea. In classical Stoic ethics, decoupling one's well-being from external factors by treating them as irrelevant to the world of the self would, if successful, indeed free one from contingency, but it prompts questions about the cost of treating relationships with others, and commitments in one's work whatever it is, as 'indifferents' because one has insufficient control over them. The fully realized Stoic, in this idealized version, is an internal solitary. This is the aim also of the Indian sannyasi, practising detachment and separation from the world, and the Buddhist shedding desires and attachments on the way to an escape from suffering. Here, though, arises a consideration that suggests a limit to this kind of strategy. Buddhism preaches compassion for all life because life consists in suffering, but this view introduces a tension, if not a contradiction, given that compassion and detachment are inconsistent with each other – to feel compassion is to be affected by the suffering witnessed. The logic of the idealized Stoic's position is that he would master the sentiment of compassion if it risked his peace of mind. To that extent, the humanism of Seneca and Marcus Aurelius appears to belie their Stoic commitment, in the recognition that the fact of being a social animal makes connections to surrounding society ultimately unseverable.

The solution for a consistent Stoic is to say that there are kinds and degrees of social relations that are not 'indifferents' because they do indeed speak to the core of one's well-being. Friendship is the prime candidate, not least in being such that, unlike love affairs and marriage, it does not have the potential to attack one's peace of mind nearly so violently, but instead is almost wholly constructive. At the same time, recognizing suffering where it occurs in the world around one, and being motivated thereby to do what one can to end or mitigate it, can be claimed as an intellectual act which does not *neces-sarily* involve feelings of compassion, even if generally it does involve them; and therefore *recognition* of others' suffering, and of the success or failure of one's efforts in regard to it, need have no effect on one's equilibrium. This view involves rejection of the idea, principally associated with David Hume, that reasons can never by themselves be motives for action; Hume argued that emotions are alone capable of moving us to act. Stoicism is a view that *in principle* is predicated on thinking otherwise.

As the examples of Seneca and Marcus Aurelius suggest – and indeed as Seneca's model, Cato the Younger, illustrates – the idea of Stoic indifference to externals is caricatured by the figure of a cold, impassive, bland individual, empty of everything within other than fortitude. This was not the Stoic life as any of them lived it, and nor was it the life of the movement's founder, Zeno of Citium. At the same time, life that closely approximates the Stoic ideal would certainly be one of great restraint and constantly exercised willpower, because it does not avoid what would cause any ordinary person pain and upset, but deals with it by controlling the response to it. It would justly be thought by most people that although the Stoic adjurations constitute good advice, life both offers and should have more than the unrelenting exercise of self-control alone. This is where some Epi-curean thoughts apply.

Although the Epicureans described pleasure in terms of the absence of pain, whether physical (*aponia*) or psychological (*ataraxia*), the im-plication of this is not that one should live a life of avoidance, shrinking from any form of contact that might cause either kind, but instead should involve actively seeking what displaces them. Habits of good health through exercise and moderate diet minimize the chances of illness, while cultivation of friendship, conversation and philosophy (understood in its inclusive sense to mean enquiry and learning) pro-vide great satisfactions of mind. Such was the life in Epicurus' Garden. What it premises is the idea that life worth living is characterized by riches and fulfilments – riches that have nothing to do with money; fulfilments that are as easy to get as plucking fruit from a tree. The familiar and profoundly true observations that health is wealth, that a person who has enough is rich, that bread and water are ambrosia and nectar to the hungry, that the delight taken in conversation with friends is independent of whether it takes place in an expensive restaurant or on a park bench, bear these observations out.

Above all, the conception of an inner universe, where one roams free and has access to anything that imagination and thought can provide, is the ultimate resource of the self. It is common enough for it to be so, but if it is only ever used for the escapist purposes of daydreaming and fantasizing – pleasant as these activities are – or for thinking about current practicalities, it would be sadly underutilized. Imagination is the power to create a world; accepting the Socratic challenge to *think*, examine, explore, seek to know more and to understand, populates that world with meaning.

The range of human imagination is wonderful to behold. Consider the stories and characters of the Greek myths, recall the detail and incident of Dante's *Inferno* and Cervantes' *Don Quixote*, think of Shakespeare's 'negative capability', consider Goethe's Romantic sentiment, and the capacity to reach into the springs of human motivation displayed by George Eliot in giving us the characters of Dorothea and Lydgate in *Middlemarch* and by Thomas Hardy in *Tess of the d'Urbervilles*. In the writings of Ursula Le Guin and Philip K. Dick, alternative worlds reflect insights about the real world; such science fiction writers as Jules Verne imagine futures that come to pass almost as they envisage them. Shakespeare could ask his audience to imagine the 'wooden O' of a theatre's stage as a battlefield in France, and Ovid could expect his readers to see Daphne sprout leaves and change into a laurel tree to escape Apollo; in both cases they draw on the imaginative resources that we ourselves provide; their imaginings live in our capacity for the same.

Imagination is not reserved to literature. Several of Einstein's insights in physics came from simple imaginings. From visualizing a train being hit by two bolts of lightning, one at the front and one at the back, he realized that time is not constant between two frames of reference. If you see the lightning strikes from outside the train just as its midpoint passes you, they will appear simultaneous; but if you are sitting on the roof of the train at its midpoint, you will see the

strike at the front before you see the strike at the back, because the
light from the back will take a fraction longer to reach you. Einstein
recognized the equivalence of acceleration and gravity by imagining
what it would be like to be in an elevator whose cable snaps so that
the elevator plunges down; as it fell you would not feel the effect of
gravity (until you hit the bottom).

In one of the boldest experiments in statecraft in history, requiring great political imagination, courage and patience, leading figures
in the combatant nations of Europe after the Second World War
decided that the continent must leave behind its centuries of blood-
shed and find a way to live with itself in peace, so they set to work to
imagine the means, and to turn imagining into reality. In the eighteenth century, Tom Paine had argued that intimate trading relations
between states would guarantee peace; in the mid-nineteenth century the high priests of Victorian free-trade ideals, Richard Cobden
and John Bright, argued the same. Those who proposed what would
eventually become the European Union included Konrad Adenauer,
Alcide De Gasperi, Winston Churchill, Jean Monnet and Robert
Schuman. The EU's founding fathers took the lesson taught by
Paine, Cobden and Bright and applied it, first in the form of the Coal
and Steel Community in 1952, then the Common Market instituted
by the Treaty of Rome in 1957, followed by the European Union created by the Maastricht Treaty of 1993. As a result, Europe achieved
the longest period of unbroken peace in its history since the days of
the Roman Empire.

Literature, science and history are the products of imagination and
enquiry. Roaming in those domains exercises one's own imagination
and power of thought. It might be commonplace enough to remark
that learning and debating expands the mind – which, to use Edward
Dyer's metaphor of 'my mind to me a kingdom is', is to expand the
territory of one's personal kingdom, furnishing it with cities and cultivating its landscapes. In this territory one is freest to create oneself
and a life worth living – perhaps indeed a meaningful life.

11. Living Among Others

The points discussed in the previous chapter concern the fact that, because we humans are social animals, our connections to surrounding society are unseverable, and those connections impose duties. Of course, there are rare cases of complete solitaries – the anchorites, recluses and hermits who shun or are shunned by society altogether, and exist in isolation. Even hesychasts – people whose private inner world never admits anyone from outside it – live and move among other people, in the street and the shop, in the workplace, at the hospital, in cafés and cinemas, where they have to interact civilly in ways that are reasonably productive of the ends that interactions serve.

The Cynics rejected society, but lived in it; the Epicureans withdrew from outer society in order to create their own. Consider an individualist like Henry Thoreau of *Walden* fame; however much he distanced himself from most others and disdained social convention, living at times almost but not quite as a latter-day Cynic, he did not repudiate social connections outright, because he and his fellow 'American Transcendentalists', proponents of the 'self-reliance' movement, recognized and accepted that existence within society and some degree of participation in it – on one's own terms albeit – was a condition of rational life. There are several significant reasons why this is so, all having to do with our occupancy of the social net and normativity. The chief of them is the psychological fact that what we are *as individuals* owes a great deal to our relations with others. Even the anchorites and hermits who live eccentrically outside the net did not begin that way, but had at least some of their formation in their childhood relationships.

The fact that we owe to others so much of how our personalities express themselves is obvious enough: parents, teachers, friends, and society at large unceasingly influence us from birth to the dawn of self-consciousness and beyond, the major influence transferring itself from parents and community to companions and our preferred social subset as we grow up, with certain individuals among them – a role model, an admired friend, a lover, a boss – exerting special power. Such influence can be positive or negative, but in any case it exemplifies the mutually constitutive function of interpersonal connections. In the traditional ethics of sub-Saharan Bantu peoples this factor is given a positive cast in the notion of *Ubuntu*, most succinctly explained as 'I am, because of you', meaning that relationships – even casual encounters such as those between a shopkeeper and a customer – should be premised on the fact of shared humanity, requiring that people treat each other as fellows, with kindness and generosity; a recognition of interdependence, conferring a freely claimed entitlement and, simultaneously, a willingly accepted obligation to reciprocate.[1]

The virtues of kindness and generosity are not unique to *Ubuntu*, of course; most moral theories extol and enjoin both in at least some degree. At the same time, the question naturally arises about the limits of one's obligations to others. An important element of Aristotle's point about being as good a friend to oneself as to others was that by respecting oneself one would not be a burden to others, but instead would be better placed to serve as a friend to them. Accordingly, in the mutualities of *Ubuntu* and even in the bonds of friendship there have to be limits. A friend who asks too much too often, who imposes undue costs on a friend in the name of friendship, is himself not a good friend. And if that applies to someone who is or claims to be a friend, what of the stranger in the street, and the rest of humanity? Does being human indeed entail a freely claimed entitlement and a willingly accepted obligation to reciprocate, in general?

The answer, arguably, is 'Yes' – if properly understood. To see why and how, consider morality. Recall that morality is not the same as ethics; morality deals with the question of how people behave, especially in their relations with one another; it does not, as ethics does, aspire to the great task of answering the Socratic Question, but instead more limitedly seeks to guide (more usually, to instruct and direct) how people should act, independently of what their personal character and predilections are. And one sharp if surprising way to see what morality therefore is, is to recognize it as fundamentally a matter of *good manners*.

Cynics would disagree with this, of course; Ambrose Bierce's *Devil's Dictionary* describes manners as merely 'the most acceptable form of hypocrisy'. (Evelyn Waugh was predictably of the view that only unattractive people need manners; 'the pretty can get away with anything', he said.) But such views are mistaken. A moment's reflection shows that without manners – politeness, common courtesy – society itself would be impossible. Manners facilitate interpersonal interactions and are a buffer to conflict. Complex pluralistic societies manage the stresses of diversity, disagreement and competition by putting civility at the forefront of interaction, because other expedients – the blunt instrument of law, the desperate resort to social apartheids – cannot work anywhere near as well. Importantly, one should not confuse manners with etiquette, this latter concerning itself with refined rituals about what cutlery to use at dinner or whether an earl takes precedence over a viscount in a procession. These are irrelevancies beside the true point of manners, which is simply, but profoundly, to treat others with consideration. And this extends beyond face-to-face encounters, for to treat others with consideration is to be honest, to respect truth, to keep promises, to be trustworthy, to refrain from acting in ways that are inconsiderate or harmful to others, *in general*.

Indeed the contrast between manners and etiquette is very revealing about the moral force of the former. Good manners might well be displayed in ignoring breaches of etiquette, given how often the latter is used as a means to snub and exclude. When Queen Victoria saw Jan Smuts drink the water in his finger-bowl at her dinner table, she did likewise to put him at ease. It has been well said that the weak man's imitation of strength is rudeness, and too often etiquette is an unmannerly – hence unkind – means of hurting others. This is not to say that etiquette has no place; it had its origin in efforts to ameliorate the conditions of communal life – as when, for example, behaviour at mealtimes was a chaos of every man for himself, tearing meat from carcasses by hand, tossing bones to the floor, spitting and urinating right there at the table as dinner proceeded – a mayhem predicated on the carelessness of hunger and greed. Castiglione, author of *The*

Courtier, was one of the subduers of such grossness, advising his contemporaries on how to behave more appropriately, for example by not scratching their lice in public. But he knew that, although etiquette can be an expression of good manners, it is not the same as them – neither necessary for them nor ever a substitute for them. For he saw that the point of manners is, fundamentally, considerateness: taking others' circumstances and points of view into account, and factoring them appropriately into one's own behaviour.

This idea was not original to Castiglione. He was in fact applying Aristotle's concept of the megalopsychos, the *magna anima* ('great soul'), hence 'magnanimous' individual central to Aristotelean ethics. English translations of *megalopsychos* render it as 'gentleman' – not to denote a person who has this social rank because of accidents of birth or wealth, but anyone meriting colloquial description as 'a real gent'; a civil, kind, considerate individual. It is a happy fact that many people are thus, and that therefore good manners are displayed countless times every day in the common intercourse of society, which is why society generally functions. It is the unmannerly, the uncivil few, including among them criminals and fanatics, who make the world seem otherwise.

But this still does not identify the boundaries of the mutual responsibilities that good manners impose. The point might therefore be put by asking, 'How far am I my brother's keeper?' – that is, how much must I consider others' interests? What is the degree of my responsibility in relation to them? To ask this is already to accept that there must be a limit; what Aristotle recognized as rational and appropriate self-interest weighs against our concern for others. But when self-interest turns into indifference or even callousness – a danger with the idealized Stoic view – it is not only intrinsically wrong but threatens our personal well-being too, for selfishness is self-defeating. To understand why, consider the classic 'prisoner's dilemma' example in game theory.

Two men arrested for a serious crime are interrogated separately. Each knows that if neither confesses, they will both get a light sentence; that if one confesses and the other does not, the confessor will be released but the other will get a life sentence; and that if both confess, both will get twenty years in prison. The best outcome for each individually is achieved by confessing, provided that the other does not confess; he gains maximally on condition that the other loses maximally. But the risk each individually runs is that both confess and both therefore get a twenty-year sentence. The overall best outcome for both is for neither to confess, so that both get light sentences. Unsurprisingly, therefore, the optimal result is achieved by cooperation. And such cooperation happens most of the time in daily life; people make compromises and reach agreements. Alas, in high-stakes situations — international negotiations, military stand-offs — history shows that the selfish option is chosen more often than the cooperative one, the parties gambling on getting the maximum for themselves at others' expense. War is the standout example of this. Since this is also the riskiest option for each, it is no surprise that the world can get into a mess. At the interpersonal level, however, the example shows that the answer to the question 'How much am I my brother's keeper?' is 'Almost as much as I am my own keeper', in the sense that our *joint* interests are enhanced by being socially cooperative, compromising to get what each of us will regard as an acceptable outcome.

The cynic — and maybe even the Cynic, among whose reasons for rejecting involvement in society are the compromises and trimming required as the price for participating in it — will support his suspicion of any such game-theoretic analysis by invoking the fact that people cheat. He would quote Pascal's claim that 'mutual cheating is the foundation of society'. Social scientific research shows that the cynic and Pascal are wrong: most people are more willing to help others than to cheat them, even when the cost to themselves is considerable, and they are quick to punish cheating when they see it, even when not themselves its victims.[2] This is a hopeful and pleasing fact. It confirms the existence of altruism — disinterested (not 'uninterested'!) concern for the welfare of others.

Altruism, it transpires, is commonplace; and — to the present point again — society could not get along without it. Society depends on a large measure of mutual trust and assistance, on cooperation with others who are not immediate kin, and on preparedness to share, to sympathize, to give and to protect. The self-sacrifice of soldiers and rescue workers, and of all those everywhere in history who went 'above and beyond' on others' behalf, is a defining mark of the social instinct in humankind. If this seems improbable, it is because news media everywhere hasten to report conflict and the harms people do; only rarely do they mention the far commoner presence of cooperation in ordinary life. Suppose someone shoots someone else; the many others who get involved in the incident far outnumber the perpetrator and victim. They include the ambulance personnel, the doctors and nurses in the emergency room at the hospital, the police, eventually the government and society at large – either helping the victim, or working to bring the perpetrator to justice and thus prevent harm to others, or uniting to condemn the harm already done. It might seem that sentiment is ineffectual in the face of cruelty and crime, but the fact is that most people and most places are peaceful most of the time because the reverse is true.

The finding by the altruism researchers – that large majorities of people in their samples became angry when they witnessed cheating, even when they were only uninvolved observers of it – is supported by anthropologists, who note that in hunter-gatherer societies fairness matters because survival depends upon it, and therefore cheating is harshly punished. The same impulse, if in more complex ways, continues to operate in advanced societies. In market-economy versions of such societies, much is made of law and regulatory frameworks because too much cheating would undermine them. Even when it is admitted that cheating often enough happens in economic life, the *degree* of it has to stay below a threshold, for even the cheaters need most people to be honest most of the time for cheating itself to succeed.

These claims about altruism and fairness will doubtless appear implausible because self-interest seems so central a fact of life. We think of it as an expression of our 'selfish genes' in their tireless competition for the overarching goals of survival and reproduction, which remain even when disguised in civilization's sophisticated and elaborate forms; the businessman in his suit hurrying with his briefcase to a meeting is, under it all, thus still competing to survive and reproduce. Does this suggest that the preceding observations paint too cosy a picture? At best, it would appear that *both* self-interest and altruism are persistent features of human behaviour. And yet, are they not irreconcilable opposites? Economists have long assumed that self-interest is the only rational form of agency, and cynics are quick to note that anyone martyring herself for others is, subconsciously or secretly, enjoying herself by doing it, and therefore again indulging her self-interest.

There are some who accept these latter points, but turn them into positives as a basis for morality. A notable example is J. L. Mackie in his classic *Ethics: Inventing Right and Wrong* (1977). On this view, apparently other-regarding actions are indeed self-interested ones, but acceptably so because they are 'enlightened'. Agents recognize that they themselves benefit in the longer run if at their own expense they benefit others in the shorter run. A more general version has it that general benefits to the community are perceived by its individual members as directly or indirectly benefiting themselves. This accords well with biological observation of the fact that many species are so organized that sterile siblings of fertile individuals sacrifice themselves in the interests of the latter's offspring, which they are happy (so to speak) to do because in this way their own genes survive. This is especially notable in social species like ants and bees. Here the unit of self-interest is the species, whose individual members appear to be paradigms of altruism but which are in fact serving the overall interests of its genes.[3]

In conventional morality, altruism is praised and self-interest condemned – or at least regarded askance. This is illustrated by the familiar fact that the concepts clustering around 'altruism' include those of kindness, concern and self-sacrifice, while the concepts clustering around 'self-interest' include selfishness, egoism and greed. But self-interest is not automatically or invariably the same as these more disagreeable attitudes and behaviours; we regard as responsible, not as selfish or greedy, a person who takes care of herself and her immediate circle before she takes care of others, if altruistic behaviour to those others would result in the neglect of duties to herself and her circle. If self-interest can be responsible, as this and Aristotle repeatedly show, then it is not always bad.

This suggests that curating one's own welfare can be considered a duty. One's welfare is promoted, on this view, by self-reliance, independence, paying one's way, not battening on others. If – to repeat – care of the self exists alongside consideration for others, it enhances the part one can play in society, even in the minimal sense of not being a negative presence in it. If one had an inclination to be something more than merely a neutral presence in society, it is obvious that being poor, ignorant and disempowered as a result of self-neglect is hardly a good ground for it, and most certainly not for effective altruism. The key is not to confuse self-respect with selfishness and callousness, or to allow it to degenerate into them.

The thought that altruism and self-interest are not invariably or even very often mutually exclusive is important for normativity, whose interests are well served by promoting both. To the cynic who still thinks that altruism is a disguise for Machiavellian motives, there is another, and highly interesting, consideration to adduce, which arises when we consider again the fact that humans are 'essentially' a social species. This is the fact of our natural capacity for *empathy*. Immediately the invocation of *natural* empathy – implying a supposed general fact about human nature which rises above the threshold of the biological into the social – raises questions about 'we' again: different societies, or different phases in the history of the same society, exemplify different moralities and different ethical values, so how can we permit such a generalization?

This objection is most clearly framed in terms of *relativism* – the idea that there are no absolutes and commonalities in social life, but that everything social life involves, not least in matters of morality, is culturally determined. Specifically, *moral* relativism is the view that there are no universal truths about right and wrong, but instead that what counts as such is determined by each society's own beliefs and traditions. Since societies can vary markedly in these, and manifest very different moral systems accordingly, the relativist's central claim bites: that there are no objective grounds for deciding between them. This view seems compelling when we consider the sharply contrasting attitudes different societies have about (say) polygamy and homosexuality.

Among the further motives for relativism is the commendable one of avoiding cultural imperialism as practised by dominant societies in the past, which in colonizing other peoples imposed their own moralities – indeed, their own normativity – on them. Relativists wish to assert the equal dignity and validity of other societies despite their differing in key ways from one another, not least in their moral outlooks.

Well: one can acknowledge the commendable motive, but still ask the question whether there really is no way of deciding that female genital mutilation, or the self-immolation by Hindu wives on their deceased husbands' funeral pyres (*suttee*), or torture and capital punishment, or child marriage, or the massacre of civilian populations in war, or the denial of education to girls, or enforced religious observance, or arrest and detention without due process of law, and so on, are to be condoned because they are regarded as acceptable or desirable in the societies which practise them. The counter to attempted relativist justifications of such practices is to point out that there is a deeper level of explanation of why opposition to such practices is justified, relating to facts – natural and hence universal facts – about what conduces to human suffering and its opposite.

The facts in question are *natural* facts (as we see in noting that they apply also to animals, and for the same reason) because they are *neurological* facts, relating to the way sentient creatures react to features of their physical and social environment. Put simply: very few people – very few sentient creatures generally – like to suffer pain, cold, hunger, fear, isolation, confinement and brutality. One could include injustice in this list; empirical evidence shows that even monkeys dislike being treated unfairly.[4] To see anyone suffering one or more such states evokes a natural response in most observers, as exemplified by the way we wince when we see someone injured.[5] The point can be put another and more pertinent way by saying that *empathy is hardwired*. There is abundant empirical evidence for this claim, suggested by some to involve 'mirror neurons', though their role in mediating our 'theory of mind' – our ability to interpret others' intentions and states – remains controversial.[6] Mirror neurons or no, to smile and laugh when others do, to yawn when others yawn, to feel concerned

when witnessing someone in distress, to have a physical response
such as sexual arousal on observing the same physical state in someone else (which is how pornography works), is to observe the
hard-wired nature of empathy in action.

Empathy, note; actual fellow feeling. *Sympathy* might not involve a
degree of mimicry in emotion or sensation while nevertheless constituting an alignment of sentiment with a sufferer. One sympathizes
with a bereaved person without feeling bereaved oneself, but when
one winces and recoils on witnessing a football player break a leg, one
is empathizing; as also when one is upset by seeing someone in grief
or despair, we say we are 'moved' in such cases. Sympathy is a fine
moral emotion, but it is empathy that more profoundly prompts acting appropriately on recognizing the condition of a sufferer.

Some neurologists, notable among them Vittorio Gallese, argue
that mirror neurons are indeed the basis of empathy, activating in
response to what their possessor perceives to be the experience of
others and thereby generating a model of the other's experience – a
model which is more than a merely descriptive insight into the other's
state of mind but, much more, is a response-invoking one. These interpretative capacities have ultimately to be neurologically based, and
mirror neurons are among the most plausible candidates for involvement in them.[7] Some researchers suggest that malfunction in mirror
neuron activity might be a factor in autism, one of whose major features is an inability to engage socially with others. The key point is that
whatever neuropsychological structures underwrite the interpretative
ability in question, they provide the ultimate basis for moral judgment –
and because the structures are hard-wired, they are universal.

But what about the differences apparent between the moral outlooks of different cultures? One thing to note is that they are, often,
merely apparent. In some cultures caring for aged parents takes the
form of buying them a retirement bungalow; in others – this is
alleged of some Papua New Guinean tribes, a repository for this kind
of claim – it takes the form of eating them (so that they can live on in
their offspring).[8] But some differences are genuine differences, and
involve a cultural decision, at least by those in control, to ignore – in
full consciousness of them – the neuropsychological facts of

suffering in the name of some claimed higher purpose, usually religious in origin: the treatment of girls and women is the most obvious
and widespread example, involving not only denial of the same rights
as males but such egregiously unacceptable things as forced marriage,
genital mutilation, immurement in the domestic sphere, 'honour
killings', and more. That human beings do things contrary to natural
inclinations is no surprise, for it is often necessary: controlling natural propensities of aggression, greed and lust is required for mature
membership in society, and bringing up children consists in teaching
them to manage such urges. The ability to switch off or subdue
empathy for certain kinds of suffering is no different from the ability
to switch off or subdue aggressive or acquisitive impulse, and such
switching off happens.

No doubt this sounds like having things both ways: the roots of
morality lie in natural facts, but the natural facts can be socially over-
ridden. But note that as with many if not all hard-wired *capacities*,
their activation, their improvement by experience, and their maturation by reflection on that experience, has to happen too; if we are
born with a capacity to empathize it does not follow that we are
automatically empathetic towards everyone we meet. On the contrary, the preference we give to kin and others in our close circle,
even when we sympathize or even empathize with those outside it,
brings the 'brother's keeper' considerations into play again. But it is
possible, indeed necessary, to widen those boundaries, and widening
them is itself made possible by knowledge. Moses Maimonides, the
twelfth-century Jewish philosopher, rightly observed that 'ignorance
is the root of all the evils people cause each other', meaning that not
understanding another's viewpoint, whether or not one agrees with
it, is the first barrier to empathizing with him when empathy would
be appropriate. All those clichés – 'see where someone is coming
from'; 'walk a mile in his shoes' – bear on Maimonides' point, for he
added that among the chief reasons for the harmful ignorance in
question are our own beliefs and desires, blinding us.[9]

The plausibility of the foregoing account is increased by widening its
focus. Doing this brings the philosophers of antiquity back into the

picture, because their starting point is the same as ours, namely that a human being is a social creature living among others, and they regarded this fact as the chief source of good and ill – and for them, mainly the latter. Among the chief concerns for all of them other than Aristotle was the thought that, so far as any individual's peace of mind is concerned, society is a more rather than less toxic domain, encouraging people in ambitions and postulating goals for which the effort required is painful at best and generally harmful – and the achievement of which, if it happens at all, turns out to be a hollow and very transient satisfaction.

Stoics and Epicureans appear to write, as did Aristotle, as if they think ambition by its nature has to be conceived in grand terms of wealth, honour and fame – of having a statue in the agora to keep memory alive in coming generations – rather than in more modest and prosaic terms such as a farmer's satisfaction with a well-tended crop or a mother's pleasure in seeing her children grow. In counselling avoidance of society's conventional ambitions, and teaching the techniques of attaining and maintaining *ataraxia*, they converged on a common message: that to be free of anxiety and stress one must reject society's version of what brings happiness, its one-size-fits-all set of metrics about success and failure, status and position, of what should make one proud or guilty. Success, failure, pride, shame and guilt – the three last being emotions of self-assessment derived from a socially imposed scale; the two first having a social meaning which, the philosophers were thus arguing, the wise should replace by a personal one – are the central concepts in question.[10]

Popular wisdom is full of sayings about how to treat success and failure, and how to calibrate what truly merits pride and shame. In the age of the internet, there is no shortage of pithy, witty, apposite and striking one-liners about each. Schoolchildren in Britain once learned by heart Kipling's poem 'If—' with its line about treating the 'imposters' of triumph and disaster both the same: namely, with disdain. And in fact popular wisdom and popular verse of that kind distil a great deal of good sense. Of all the nostrums and good advice, those that bear on how to treat failure are the most important. The general counsel is to use failure as a spur to trying harder, trying better, rising from defeat, carrying on; and except in cases of obvious incapacity (if you are not going to run a hundred metres in less than ten seconds, aspiration to be an Olympic sprinter would be better replaced by another ambition) such encouragement is right. Almost all the value in things is in the effort made for them: as we are often told and we all discover, it is not the arrival but the journey that is the thing.

Like a lot of very simple points, the idea that one should be one's own arbiter of what counts as success and failure, and one's own determiner of what should prompt pride or shame, is very hard to apply in practice. Yet being one's own judge of these things lies at the heart of a philosophy of life. The degree to which society's metrics for these things continue to direct and trouble one is the degree to which one is not living one's own philosophy – *unless*, of course, one has examined those values thoroughly and chosen to live by them; but then it is the thinking and choosing that is the key, because they are what make what one chooses consciously one's own.

But here a qualification must be mentioned, in the form of a reminder: that not all of society's values are arbitrary; not all are bad merely because they are or have become conventional. To kick at them for no better reason than their being conventional will not do. Wishing that everyone would mind their manners is a major example of a conventional view worth keeping, for the reasons given. But as the *Ecclesiastes* preacher observed, there is a time for everything, including setting manners aside when appropriate: interrupting a lying politician on the hustings, refusing to give way to bullies, kicking down the door of a burning house to rescue the inmates would be cases in point.

What all these considerations show is that formulating and living one's philosophy of life, given that one does so among others in society, involves judgment. Judging is a practice, because it is continual, as is living itself. To live philosophically, therefore, is to live judiciously.

Powerful aids to getting a conspectus view of living among others, to add to one's direct experience and enrich one's reflection on it, are provided by literature and history. It is an understatement to say that there is in both much matter for contemplation for thinking about duties, self-interest and altruism as they bear on the question, for all literature and history is about little else. Especially illuminating examples include George Eliot's *Middlemarch*, Thomas Mann's *Buddenbrooks*, James Joyce's *Ulysses*, and the epic sequences of Balzac's *Comédie humaine*, Zola's *Les Rougon-Macquart* and Proust's *Remembrance of Things Past*. Each describes a ballet of individuals circling and relating, variously colliding, melding, helping or harming each other; they are moving (in both senses) pictures of people among people, studies of the chemistry of social life.

From a very different angle, Kafka's *Metamorphosis* and *The Trial* in significant part speak of what happens when communication fails and no understanding is possible – the psychological equivalent of one's fingers going numb so that one cannot feel what one reaches for, or going unexpectedly deaf and hearing nothing though people's mouths move. In Beckett's plays, silences and laconicisms are given the task usually reserved for words – namely, to be bearers of meaning, but with emphasis on the multiplicities and ambiguities of meaning, which are more obvious in silences and pauses. The idea is that not speaking is not the same as not saying something, which is the point also of Wittgenstein's remark, 'Whereof one cannot speak, thereof one must be silent.'[11] Loquacious or mute, the actors in the human comedy still relate, and still move among one another; society is the element of humanity, as water is the element in which the fishes swim.

History teaches a further lesson, this time about the tenuous and fragile nature of human arrangements, ever liable to being shredded by war or social upheavals – whether caused by pandemics and other natural disasters, or accumulations of economic and political difficulty. There is an unspoken assumption in all such discussion as the foregoing: that as an individual thinks and acts in society, so the society around her continues in a more or less predictable way, holding steady as a background to her choices; that normativity endures, a reliable setting for the possibility of philosophical self-creation, and a counterpoint to it. Well: the philosophers of antiquity, like their peers in the Indian soteriologies, were alert to the risks attending such an assumption. Their advice was *not* to make this assumption, but instead to create a stable universe *internally*, within oneself, either by not living among others in any but a spatial sense (Cynics and, more moderately, Epicureans, for whom chosen others will do), or not allowing the conditions of normativity, otherwise unavoidable if engaging in life among others, to be the arbiter of one's peace of mind (Stoics). Then, whatever happens, one will be secure.

This brings us to a crucial question. In thinking about what response to give Socrates' challenge, the facts of normativity and the social element in which we swim have to be taken into account; that is inescapable unless we become hermits. Will we take the ancients' advice, and withdraw our inner selves behind walls of psychological immunity by disengaging wholly or partly? Or by arming ourselves with *apatheia* towards the 'indifferents' of life? We have heard from the ancients mainly what is negative about living among others; what about an argument encouraging engagement by *accepting* that relationships and ambitions bring pain but that it could be worth striving for them anyway – in short, a counter-argument to the view that the only kind of life worth living is one of *ataraxia*?

We need to inspect more closely the idea of 'a life worth living' and the possibly different idea of 'a meaningful life'. That, accordingly, is the theme of the next chapter.

12. 'The Meaning of Life' and 'A Life Worth Living'

The question 'What is the meaning of life?' is standardly treated either as a joke because unanswerable, or as no joke but unanswerable, both on the assumption that life's purpose is too great a mystery to admit of an answer. This is even so for many of those who have a religious commitment, to whom the ways of God are inscrutable; the problem of why we are 'put on this earth', and suffer even when innocent, is evaded by appeal to that inscrutability. Others with a religious commitment might answer 'To serve God' or 'To love God' or 'To act in accordance with God's wishes', but these answers do not help, because even if the wishes of God (which are what? – love your neighbour, pray five times a day, stone adulterers to death?) were known, there remain the puzzles of what ulterior purpose is being served by obeying the commands they embody, and by the evil in the world and the suffering of innocents.

The 'What is the meaning of life?' question itself rests on a highly questionable assumption: that life has a purpose, in the sense that the universe exists for a reason; that people come into existence in order to fulfil a plan of some kind. The use of the definite article 'the' in the phrase 'the meaning of life' implies uniqueness, a single purpose that all lives exist to serve and that all lives have served throughout history. Yet often people speak of a preordained destiny individual to them; 'I feel that I was put on this earth to . . .'

When I am asked the meaning-of-life question, which often happens when it transpires that I am a professor of philosophy, I reply, 'The answer is that the meaning of *your* life is what *you* make it.' This reply encapsulates one implication of the grand Socratic injunction to think for yourself, which is that the responsibility for meaning – for creating meaning – lies with each of us individually, in the context of our own individual lives. On this view 'the meaningful life' and 'the

life worth living' are the same thing; it is the latter because it is the former; and there is no one-size-fits-all answer to questions about what
such a life is. If there were, as repeatedly noted in these pages, there
would be no need for philosophy, just acceptance of that one answer.

However, it is not clear that the ancient philosophers thought that
'a life worth living' and 'a meaningful life' are the same thing; indeed
it is not clear that they thought *meaning* has anything to do with a life
worth living at all. On surveying the ancient theories one sees that
they specify a good life – a life worth living – in terms of attaining
peace of mind, *ataraxia*, through a correct understanding of what
causes pain and trouble in life, and acting in ways that at least avoid
them and in the ideal promote their opposites, typically by living
according to the virtues. As recommendations about the good life,
these ideas apply to everyone capable of understanding them and setting them to work, and in that sense themselves appear to be
one-size-fits-all theories, no different from religions in requiring
individuals to live them consciously. Likewise the Indian soteriologies are not in quest of meaning but are recipes for escape from
individual existence altogether, and also apply to anyone who can
understand and act upon them. The Socratic injunction to each individual to think for himself or herself about what kind of person to
be and what kind of life to live, and moreover about the content of
the virtue concepts as they apply individually, accordingly *appears* to
be sidelined in the teachings of the Stoics and Epicureans, once these
are accepted as a prescription to follow for a life worth living. No
such appearance attaches to Aristotle's view, which enjoins taking
individual responsibility in navigating the middle way in each situation one finds oneself in. But a little reflection shows that the Stoic
and to a lesser extent the Epicurean teachings do not much differ
from the *practice* of the Aristotelian view, in the sense that applying
their guidance requires the same individual endeavour; one's own
character, as one seeks to develop it, and the particular circumstances
of challenge and opportunity one meets with, between them make
living the ethical life one's own creative responsibility at each point.
Here there is a large divergence from a religious life, which by its
nature has to be deontological: an application more stringently of

the content of the rules, not – as with the philosophies – their general form whose content is a personal responsibility.

A thought prompted by these observations is that normativity also offers *ataraxia* if one is not in a state of rebellion against it, particularly if it is leavened with acceptance of normativity's realities. These realities are that almost all of us will find that life's practicalities blunt the ambitions nourished in our youth, which therefore means that we have to accept disappointments; that there will inevitably be some physical and psychological pain to endure; that getting through life with the key boxes ticked – mortgage paid off, pension plan in place, enough consolation from the thought that we did the best we could in our careers, and satisfaction about our offspring's graduations, marriages, job promotions, and so on – counts as life having been *worth living* as normativity measures this worth. Most people are content with this as an outcome – and contentment is *ataraxia*. One could almost regard normativity as Epicureanism for modern times, if it were not for one significant difference: that normativity requires acceptance (to some degree, even if modest) of the view that money, status and reputation are markers of achievement, that possessions are public signifiers of these things, and that the enjoyment of luxuries, at least occasionally but as often as possible, is a desideratum, whereas Epicureanism explicitly rejects the idea that accepting any part of this view and acting on it is the route to contentment, regarding it instead as the route to its opposite.

A compromise between the normative and Epicurean views of a contented life is provided by insights from the happiness studies discussed in Chapter 5. These – supported by understanding the effects of dopamine and serotonin on mood and neuronal activity, and what promotes their respective secretion – suggest a simple, practical and proven approach to achieving a life of *ataraxia*. This approach, in four clear and straightforward steps, is: have good relationships, make a contribution to family and community, eat healthily, take exercise. There is no question but that this is right; it works. (As already noted, so too does believing in comforting falsehoods and illusions, but this fourfold approach has the merit of requiring neither.) The next question, therefore, is whether *ataraxia* is enough. This is the 'happy pig' point again. If one were a cosseted pig like the Earl of Emsworth's 'Empress of Blandings' in P. G. Wodehouse's Blandings Castle books, one would live a tranquil life; is that a life worth living?[1] Some might answer in the affirmative. But then they have to answer Schopenhauer's challenge: a life worth living, he said, has to be obviously better than non-existence. Is it better from the Empress of Blandings' point of view that she lived at all? It happens that her life had value in that it gave great satisfaction to the Earl of Emsworth and his pigman Wellbeloved. But from her own point of view, what is the difference between existing tranquilly and not existing?

Indeed, Schopenhauer went further – perhaps too far – and argued that to be worth living, a life has to be worth living for ever.[2] One can sharpen the point yet further and demand that, to be worth living, a life has to be worth living over and over again eternally. Is normativity's life – the mortgage paid off, the pension plan in place, and so forth – such a life? Indeed, is an Epicurean's or a Stoic's life of *ataraxia*, or an Aristotelian life of choosing the middle path, worth living on either of these terms? It is at this point that the question of a distinction between *a life worth living* and *a meaningful life* becomes significant, because whereas the Schopenhauer dictum sets the bar too high for all three of normativity, Epicureanism and Stoicism, it does not close the question against the meaningful life – depending on what is meant by 'meaning'.

One way to see this is to note that the Empress of Blandings' life had meaning in that it gave satisfaction to the Earl of Emsworth, independently of whether her life was, from her own point of view, better than non-existence. So one can ask: would the world be more or less the same – not affected by; neither noticeably diminished nor improved by – the absence of Socrates, Buddha, Confucius, St Paul (the creator of Christianity), Mohammed (the creator of Islam), Cervantes, Shakespeare, Newton, Goethe, Pasteur, Darwin, Einstein? Of course in some of these cases – Newton, Pasteur, Darwin, Einstein – someone else would almost certainly have made the discoveries they made, for their discoveries were implicit in what came before them. It is not so clear that Socrates, St Paul or Shakespeare are dispensable in the same way. But in all these cases, including the scientists, what they did made a profound difference far beyond their individual lives. 'Making a difference' and impacting the world beyond oneself might not be *necessary* features of 'a meaningful life' but they will very likely be among the chief concepts that cluster around the idea of such a thing. Insofar as the impact is positive, or is the source of effects in which the positive outweighs the negative, the proposition that it is better that such people lived than that they did not live would command agreement. Their lives were *meaningful* in this straightforward sense, and from the point of view of the world in general their existence was correlatively worthwhile in a high or relatively high degree.[3]

That a life is worthwhile from a third-party objective point of view is not the same as its being 'good to live' or 'worth living' from the point of view of the individual living it. One might live a meaningful life which brought benefit to the world, and yet suffer and be wretched within oneself. The genius Alan Turing, whose work in breaking the Enigma code helped shorten the Second World War – and who is a major figure in the development of computer science – suffered cruelly from the persecution of homosexuality, and eventually committed suicide; yet his life was a very meaningful one from the world's point of view. Someone's suffering might indeed itself be the source of the benefit that accrues to others; the lives of some artists have been such – an example is Van Gogh. One might live a life that had meaning in this way, and not have known that one's life had such meaning, perhaps because its effects only became apparent after one's death and were not obvious to oneself; Marie Curie's life, ended by cancer which resulted from her experiments with radioactive materials, might be such a case.

We now therefore have three concepts in play: the meaningful life, the life worth living from the point of view of the person living it, and the life which is worthwhile from the world's point of view whatever it felt like to the person living it. The first and third look closely similar, but in fact only in one direction: if a life is worthwhile from the world's point of view it will *ipso facto* be meaningful; but a life meaningful to the person living it might not have much impact beyond itself.

The key undefined terms in this increasingly dense thicket of considerations are 'meaning' and 'worthwhileness' as applied to individual human lives. To make sense of these, another angle of approach might help, as follows.

Consider some of the implications of the idea of a 'meaning of life'. Bear in mind that we are not assuming that meaning is imposed antecedently from outside, as by a deity, but has to be found or made within the course of an individual life. One can point out that the idea of 'meaning' in this sense implies a task of some kind, involving some degree of effort, of aiming for goals – not untypically seeking for *prominent* achievement. There is thus a flavour of heightened significance about it which marks the effort as reaching towards something with value either intrinsic or beyond the ordinary. Is this quest for meaning a characteristic of some but perhaps not many individuals? Is it cultural, in the sense that some cultures have a tendency to promote an achievement-oriented idea of 'meaningful lives'? An observer might say, thinking of what R. H. Tawney and Max Weber separately wrote about 'Protestantism and the rise of capitalism',[4] or what is sometimes suggested by the accomplishments in numbers disproportionate to their global population of Jewish musicians, scientists and writers, that the idea that life must have a purpose, and that the pursuit of such a purpose – independently of whether one fulfils it at last – by itself makes life meaningful, is a culturally determined one, which aspects of Protestant and Jewish culture in their different ways promote. It is striking that the kinds of goals at which most ambitious people aim – in their various forms, power (including wealth) and reputation – were regarded by the ancient philosophers as at best instrumental merely, but at worst and more usually corrupting, in relation to what is truly good and what should really be sought. It is a surprising reflection that the ancient schools conceived of the purpose of our endeavours as recognizing the vanity of worldly ambition and finding success either in indifference to the goals of such ambition (Stoics), disavowal of them altogether (Cynics, Epicureans), or seeing them as merely instrumental (Aristotle).

In converging upon the idea that, insofar as life might be said to have a point, it is to get by in as self-possessed and tranquil a way as possible, the views of the ancient philosophers are a far cry from the assumption that behind the question 'What is the meaning of life?' is the concept of purpose, of there being a point to life beyond the fact of merely existing – and certainly beyond the point of existing with the least trouble possible. This latter might constitute 'a life worth living' but it does not rise to the level of 'a meaningful life', in the definition of which a sense of purpose – a summit to be climbed, a peak to conquer – is characteristic. The ideas in this definition commonly apply to people who are the subject of biographies, but because biographies are written about people who have made a significant mark of some kind – a minority group – it does little to tell us how widely the hunger for meaning is spread. We have to bear in mind Thomas Gray's poignant poem about a country churchyard filled with graves of the unknown, who might have been, if their circumstances had been different, great generals, artists and statesmen. We should therefore, as a corrective, ask: how many have striven to conquer a peak in some field of endeavour, impelled by a sense of purpose – even indeed a *burning* sense of purpose – about whom we hear nothing? The psychologists Carl Jung and Viktor Frankl assumed that meaning is fundamental to human beings; Jung repeatedly asserted his conviction that a sense of meaninglessness lies at the root of both the actuality and the appearance of neurosis: 'Among my patients from many countries, all of them educated persons, there is a considerable number who came to see me not because they were suffering from a neurosis but because they could find no meaning in their lives'[5]; 'A psychoneurosis must be understood, ultimately, as the suffering of a soul which has not discovered its meaning.'[6] Frankl's best-known work is *Man's Search for Meaning*. On such views, those buried in Gray's country churchyard must be accounted either as frustrated in their desire for meaning, or as having found it in modest and minor ways – in family life, in planting a garden, in their working careers or community contributions. In this low-key sense 'meaning' is a widely shared conception synonymous with normativity's 'worthwhile life'; those who accept normativity, even those who have thought about whether to accept it and then do so, can regard many relatively modest meanings as bringing satisfactions into life that make it worth living from their point of view, and therefore might regard getting through life with reasonable *aponia* and *ataraxia* as all that is needed to make a life worth living.

This is all the more so if one 'accepts existence', as most people do. Finding that you exist seems to carry with it the assumption that you will carry on and do what you believe is expected of you by normativity; after all, when you wake to the fact of your existence you are already committed, already on the path laid out by normativity; you have already unconsciously assumed (at least, most people have) that you are going to go on living and try to do certain things and get somewhere, even if the aims are modest – and the achievement of them would undoubtedly be a source of satisfaction.

Others – those in war zones or poverty-stricken failed states or living under brutal regimes; those whom ill luck, disease and misfortune strike – may well envy the dead, yet still they might hope, because there is a story or a dream about a better life that they might cling to and, as best they can, pursue. A 'merely' worthwhile life would be a wonderful thing for them. Yet even in places where normativity itself is hard to achieve, the strivers, the ambitious, who think in terms of a great goal, exist; but in the minority still.

All this shows that 'a life worth living' does not have to be a *meaningful* life in the ambitious sense described. A way of sharpening one's view of what 'a life worth living' means is to reflect again on the idea of living one's life over again repeatedly, or if one were going to live for ever. How would one like one's life to be if either were the case? These thought experiments are rather informative, not least in making us happier about the fact that we are guaranteed what, on reflection, turns out to be the salvation of death.

Recall that when Solon told Croesus to 'call no man happy until he is dead' after recounting the story of Kleobis and Biton, he appeared to imply that, in comparison to life, death is more desirable. This returns one to Schopenhauer's claim that if there is such a thing as a life worth living it has at least to pass the test of being better than non-existence. If you think this sets the bar rather low, recall that Schopenhauer, like the philosophers of India, thought that the essence of existence is suffering, and that the great aim is to escape it. To the obvious response such a view might prompt – namely, 'Why not instantly commit suicide?' – the pessimists about life have to adduce considerations about suicide being bad karma, or immoral in causing hurt and harm to others, and the like. Not all these reasons are bad ones. But in any case it turns out that the test does not set the bar low after all. 'From this conception of it,' Schopenhauer wrote, meaning the idea that if life is to be worth living it must be better than non-existence, 'we should be attached to it for its own sake and not merely from the fear of death; and again from this that we would like to see it last for ever.'[7]

Schopenhauer knew that most people would find it hard to accept his and the Indian sages' view that non-existence is preferable to life – he described the passion for living, for being alive at all costs, as an 'inborn error' and remarked that he had censured it 'in the forty-ninth chapter of the second volume of my principal work', meaning his great two-volume treatise *The World as Will and Representation* – but that since people are so wedded to life they should have some advice about it anyway. After much detailed examination, he concluded by agreeing with the ancient view, shared for not dissimilar reasons by Aristotle and the Epicureans, that 'the prudent person aims at painlessness' – a view which, put like that, seems only marginally less dour than the idea that one is better off dead. On the face of it, given that if the focus were exclusively on trying to avoid pain the result would in equal parts be fruitless and dispiriting, resulting in a grey sequence of negatives merely, it is hard to see how one can be attached to life for its own sake and wishing it to last for ever. Rather the contrary. But a 'grey sequence of negatives' is not quite what Schopenhauer, or before him the ancients, meant; Schopenhauer's passion for music as the closest thing to a means of escape from suffering short of death, and the Epicureans' pleasure in friendship and conversation, are neither of them grey.

Still, the idea that a life worth living is one that one would wish to live for ever, or repeat ad infinitum, is at least odd. Would one wish to live the same life for ever? Suppose that one were immortal, but everyone one knew and cared about were mortal. Existence would be the experience of inevitable and endlessly repeated grief. I suppose it would be acceptable to live the same life over and over if one did not know one were doing so. But given that even the happiest life would not be unalloyed, and that too much repetition even of the choicest moments – the greatest triumphs, the most delicious ecstasies – would become tiresome, it is perhaps a relief to reflect that the ideas both of perpetual existence and of recurrence are fantasies.

This is not what Nietzsche meant when he talked of 'eternal recurrence'.[8] Had he employed the idea to state that one should live *as if* one were going to live the same life repeatedly for ever, one would see the point; but he appears to have taken the idea literally. If so, on the grounds just given, existence would seem eventually to amount to an eternal torment. As an heuristic in thinking about what makes life worthwhile, the idea of having to repeat it – even just once – has its uses, not least in seeing that from this point of view the aim of avoiding too many pains is sensible. But the thought that even good things would come to be insupportable – like the pleasure of licking an ice cream on a hot day, then a second ice cream, then a tenth, then a hundredth, then a thousandth, with increasing nausea and disgust – changes the calculation.

To bring the discussion back to earth, one has only to recognize that one could think life is worth living without having to wish to live it over again. It has only to be a life which satisfies normativity's requirements, earns some of normativity's rewards, and is not overburdened by the expected difficulties – pain and grief – that normativity accepts as inevitable. And here religion enters the picture too. In structurally secular societies, which in effect means most of the 'West', religion has a supporting role – like the first-aid box kept somewhere in the office, to be opened in times of particular stress in search of the aspirin and bandages of consolation. In structurally religious societies, such as a fundamentalist Christian community, an ultra-Orthodox Jewish community and most Muslim-majority countries, life is lived in that box already – a cynic about religion would say 'drugged on the painkillers and swaddled in the bandages'. The contrast makes the interesting point that the distractions of consumer culture in economically advanced Western societies also in fact constitute a first-aid box, though containing different and many more analgesics and bandages, serving as 'distracting distractions' (to echo T. S. Eliot's line in *Burnt Norton* : we are 'distracted from distraction by distraction').

And this point brings us back to 'meaning' again. There are those who see themselves as seekers after, or makers of, meaning, and it is characteristic of them to regard distraction from truth, value and 'what really matters' as alienating us from ourselves, and by implication also from one another and the world. And those who think this see it as a duty to find or make value – the 'what matters' – therefore. By considering a paradigm case of a view (a family of views) that approaches life from the meaning-focused direction, we can see what this involves.

The view which has exerted a considerable influence on many, and has a lively interest for the concerns of this chapter, is *existentialism.*[9] Although existentialism became most salient in the period from before and for at least two decades following the Second World War, it has been a recognizable philosophical phenomenon for a long time, at least since early modern times – for example, in the thought of Blaise Pascal in the seventeenth century – and it is widely distributed among thinkers who never used the label, such as Kierkegaard and Husserl, and who explicitly repudiated the label, such as Heidegger and Camus. Yet there is a distinctive cluster of ideas which they share variants of, and which merit being labelled together as 'existentialism'. Sartre's version is a paradigm example of one of the two strands into which existentialism falls, these two strands being, respectively, theistic existentialism and atheistic existentialism. Sartre's and Camus' versions of existentialism – Camus called his 'absurdism' – belong to the atheistic strand. In the case of Heidegger's existentialism, it has to be assigned to the borderlands between the two strands, because its chief doctrines are indistinguishable from a theistic version of existentialism if certain of its chief concepts are recognized for what they arguably are – namely, de-divinized versions of theological concepts. Heidegger was not an epigone of Kierkegaard and a former Jesuit seminarian for nothing.

Indeed, existentialism can be seen as having arisen from a religious dilemma in the first place. A reconstruction, simplified for brevity, goes as follows.

In the Reformation movements of the sixteenth century, some parts of Europe adopted one or another Protestant form of Christianity while the rest remained loyal to the Church of Rome. In the Protestant parts of Europe – Lutheran, Zwinglian, Anglican, and to a lesser extent Calvinist, which, like the Roman confession, sought to keep a grip on the orthodoxy of its adherents by coercive means – religious authorities had insufficient power to control the spread of ideas which the new technology of printing was making increasingly available and diverse. In Roman Catholic Europe, trials and burnings at the stake continued into the first decades of the seventeenth century (culminating most famously in the conviction of Galileo in 1633 for saying that the earth moves), in a vain endeavour to stop the spread of heterodox ideas of science and philosophy.[10]

This new thinking was at odds with long-established dogma about the nature and origins of the universe, and more generally – by implication though rarely explicitly; explicit opposition came later, from the eighteenth-century Enlightenment onwards – at odds with churches and scriptures as sources of authority and truth. Now, imagine being a person who earnestly desires the comforts of faith but is faced with these dogma-undermining new theories. Without God, without the assurance of an afterlife in the face of either 'annihilation or eternal torments', will the following not accurately describe such a person: 'He then feels his nothingness, his forlornness, his insufficiency, his dependence, his weakness, his emptiness. There will immediately arise from the depth of his heart weariness, gloom, sadness, fretfulness, vexation, despair.'[11] This is Pascal in his *Pensées*, in effect describing existential *angst*. It is why he clung to the idea that even if there is only the smallest possibility that there is a god, one should believe it, because the value of doing so is so great. It rescues us from the 'dreadful necessity' of contemplating something 'than which there is nothing more terrible': the choiceless choice between misery and annihilation.

We do not require great education to understand that here is no real and lasting satisfaction; that our pleasures are only vanity; that our evils are infinite; and, lastly, that death, which threatens us every moment, must infallibly place us within a few years under the dreadful necessity of being for ever either annihilated or unhappy. There is nothing more real than this, nothing more terrible. Be we as heroic as we like, that is the end which awaits the noblest life in the world. Let us reflect on this, and then say whether it is not beyond doubt that there is no good in this life but in the hope of another; that we are happy only in proportion as we draw near it; and that, as there are no more woes for those who have complete assurance of eternity, so there is no more happiness for those who have no insight into it.[12]

The dilemma is that people in this state of mind retain the fears but have lost — by losing their faith — the hope of being rescued from them. They were raised in an ideology which tells them they are born sick (with sin) and therefore in need of cure (by the church's salvation offered in return for faith), for otherwise they will be annihilated or condemned to unending torments when they die; but then they begin to doubt that there is any such salvation, and yet are still afraid that they are indeed sick with inherited faults and frailties (not only 'original sin' but, inevitably, supplemented by acquired sins also), and therefore are destined either to eternal torture, perhaps for entertaining these very doubts, or alternatively for annihilation, every bit as bad for those who have been made to fear the idea and to yearn to exist for ever. So, burdened with these thoughts and semibeliefs, and at the same time these doubts and terrors, their suffering from existential angst is inevitable.

There are several famous theistic existentialists after Pascal, notably Kierkegaard, Karl Jaspers, Gabriel Marcel, Paul Tillich, Martin Buber and Jacques Maritain. A highly reductive but not inaccurate summary of their varied positions is that existential angst is to be overcome by believing in the existence of a god and conforming to what that god desires. In some of them — but I will leave them to speak in more detail for themselves — wrestling with the deity is itself the source of existential angst, as much if not more than the angst that arises from doubt or from contemplation of a universe devoid of deity. But whether or not a deity is part of the problem, in their thought deity is always part of the solution. And for the reasons given in Chapter 4, if this is so – if we are under the government of supernatural agencies with firm ideas about how we should think and live – then any further philosophizing is pointless.

As this suggests, and as mentioned already, there is no question but that religious faith – and most of all what Tolstoy extolled as 'peasant faith', simple unquestioning faith – is a sure way of avoiding any form of angst and achieving *ataraxia*. In light of this it is a wonder to contemplate the number and complexity of tomes that have been written to arrive at this shared and uncomplicated conclusion. That religion gives comfort is of piece with the fact – for fact it is – that anything that gives comfort, whether true or false, will by definition give comfort if implicitly believed. The big questions are, first, whether it matters if the beliefs at issue are true or false and, second, if they are false, whether comfort is more important than truth.

For atheist existentialists the starting point in angst is a given. Where the theist existentialists begin with a hypothetical – *if* there were no god what a terrible place the universe would be; *if* you are not a believer you are faced with the terror of existence and its meaninglessness, because there is nothing to give you comfort and significance – the atheist existentialists take the godlessness and antecedent meaninglessness of the universe for granted. You wake up, as it were, when you reach the point in life where you are capable of thinking about such things, to find yourself in a universe which is not here for any reason, and neither are you: that is just how things are. This realization might fill you with existential angst, typically in the form of dread, emptiness, objectless anxiety. The philosophy of existentialism in its atheist version is a response to such angst. This – collecting the chief ideas from the various articulations of the view, keeping in mind that it is not a uniform school with a fixed set of doctrines – is the version I now discuss.

Confronted by the inherent meaninglessness of the universe and the accident of one's presence in it, existentialism enjoins recognizing the radical freedom this entails, which can be a burden because it forces us to make choices. We come without a ready-made blueprint as to who we are or what we should do, so we have to choose who to be and what to do; we have to create ourselves. Recognizing that there are emotionally and intellectually honest and dishonest ways of doing this, we have to make these choices honestly – we must strive to be authentic. That demand might not seem immediately obvious, until we contemplate what we would feel about ourselves if we said, 'I choose a dishonest way of creating myself.' We have to infuse value into our lives by choosing what to do and be; there is no other source of value than the unfolding, continuous process of self-creation and the relationships between our evolving selves, on the one hand, and on the other hand the people we encounter and the world at large. The fact that self-creation is a continuing process means that we are always in a state of tension between the facts of the situations we find ourselves in – the historical setting, society, our own physical natures; 'facticity' – and our efforts to transcend the constraints imposed by facticity in the effort to make ourselves what we seek to be. Our radical freedom makes us responsible for what we do; no one else is accountable for our choices and their effects. Being human is a subjective condition, expressed through attitudes, moods and responses, and there are certain emotional states that are particularly revealing about our existence as subjects: anxiety; a sense of the antecedent absurdity (meaninglessness) of the world; a feeling of guilt and responsibility. Our values emerge from the work of creating ourselves by rising above the limitations of facticity, and by doing so authentically.

In this epitome of existentialism the key concepts are radical freedom, choice, self-creation, authenticity, responsibility, facticity and the effort to transcend it, and the subjective perspective and its moods in which our existential condition is revealed. The pivot of the view is: we are radically free in a world which offers no antecedent meaning; we have come into the world without a blueprint; we ourselves have to create ourselves. We exist before we become who we are: *existence precedes essence.*

It is important to be clear about what 'radical freedom' and the absence of a blueprint mean. The latter does not mean that we have no genetic endowment or family circumstances or social pressures – no normativity – but rather that whatever effect these factors have, in the end it is what people *do* that makes them what they are. In *Existentialism is a Humanism* Sartre writes:

> Suppose that, like Zola, we showed that the behaviour of these [base, weak, cowardly and sometimes even frankly evil] characters was caused by their heredity, or by the action of their environment upon them, or by determining factors, psychic or organic. People would be reassured, they would say, 'You see, that is what we are like, no one can do anything about it.' But the existentialist, when he portrays a coward, shows him as responsible for his cowardice. He is not like that on account of a cowardly heart or lungs or cerebrum, he has not become like that through his physiological organism; he is like that because he has made himself into a coward by actions.[13]

At the same time, 'freedom' is not 'the ability to do whatever one wants' or merely 'freedom from external constraints imposed by law or society' – these notions relate to the trivial matter of indulging one's wishes as these wishes have themselves been shaped by facticity (of which normativity is a part). The idea of political liberty typically defines itself in these terms – not that we do not wish it for its own sake, but it is not the sense of freedom at stake existentially. *This* sense is the sense in which we are always at a decision point, and nothing determines what we ought to do at it other than our own choice of what to do; we are radically free at each such point. Everything is a choice – even not choosing, not acting, not deciding, is a choice – and since we are responsible for our choices and their effects, the fact of that responsibility, by its very nature as responsibility, shows that we are *radically* free – free at the root of our existence – to choose. And choosing is self-creating.

One of the best accounts of a subject's infusing meaning into existence by decision is Camus' *Myth of Sisyphus*.[14] The myth of Sisyphus itself is a dark and complex one whose most memorable, and for present purposes most relevant, aspect is that Sisyphus is condemned to an eternal punishment for his various crimes, the punishment being that he is to roll a boulder to the top of a hill but can never get it there because the boulder rolls down again every time he nears the summit – again and again and again for ever. Camus uses the story to illustrate the essential pointlessness – 'absurdity' – of life, the 'unreasonable silence' of the world, its emptiness of value. But even in such circumstances we have a choice: to continue existing, which means continuing to struggle against absurdity, or to commit suicide. The essay begins with the assertion 'There is only one truly serious philosophical problem, and that is suicide. Judging whether life is or is not worth living amounts to answering the fundamental question of philosophy.' If we choose not to commit suicide, how are we to bear with the absurdity of our condition? Camus says: by rebelling against absurdity, by accepting the challenge of it, even joyfully so, thereby defining oneself in opposition to it and making oneself superior to one's fate. Camus imagines Sisyphus recalling the amazing words of Oedipus at Colonus about how to bear one's condition: by applying the lessons of 'experience, suffering and the nobility in one's blood'.

The key point is that Sisyphus' fate 'belongs to him'. In a remarkable peroration, Camus ends the essay thus: 'I leave Sisyphus at the foot of the mountain! One always finds one's burden again. But Sisyphus teaches the higher fidelity that negates the gods and raises rocks. He too concludes that all is well. This universe henceforth without a master seems to him neither sterile nor futile. Each atom of that stone, each mineral flake of that night-filled mountain, in itself forms a world. The struggle itself toward the heights is enough to fill a man's heart. One must imagine Sisyphus happy.' Note that the essay was first published in 1942, in the darkest days of the Second World War; the occasion adds a sharp poignancy to the closing sentiment.

The fact that existentialism was 'fashionable' in the period before, during and after the Second World War is easily explained by the fact that it directly addresses the circumstances in which people face uncertainty, wartime's catastrophes, sudden death, cruelty, oppression, stress, all stripping away the padding of normativity that offers – illusorily, given how easily and quickly normativity fails in such circumstances – a sense of security. What the catastrophe of war showed was that normativity prevents people from confronting life and understanding their responsibility to choose. And indeed it is right to say that the civilizational earthquake that began in August 1914 and lasted until 1945 (it could be said: lasted longer, indeed until the end of the Cold War at least) very rudely abolished illusions for those not in a hurry to re-embrace them as a comfort blanket. But the existential crisis had been apparent to sharpened sensibilities for much longer, as the example of Pascal shows. They took full form in the nineteenth-century reactions to the end of religious hegemony over thought, itself an achievement of the Enlightenment in the preceding two centuries; afterwards recorded in Matthew Arnold's line in 'Dover Beach' about the 'melancholy, long, withdrawing roar' of the Sea of Faith from the shores of the (Eurocentric) world. We see it in the thought of Hegel, Marx, Kierkegaard and Nietzsche, in reactions to Darwin, and in the replacement of the comforts of religion by the comforts of material consumption and the associated dream of being rich – money-rich, necessary for buying things, which in turn is the driver of the wheels of commerce and capitalism and is therefore encouraged by a society increasingly dependent on this form of a production-consumption cycle as what gives life (the illusion of) meaning, or at least as what makes it feel as if it is worth living.

Both Marx and Kierkegaard viewed industrial society as alienating people from themselves and from each other, though their diagnoses and ensuing prescriptions for cure are very different. As a secular humanist, Marx saw the relationships that people have with themselves and others in material terms. When the value of things is equal to the value of the labour that produced them, when the institution of private property has been abolished so that resources are not appropriated by some and thereby denied to others, when people interact on an equal footing, the alienation induced by economic conditions will, he argued, be overcome. Marx's prescription is to change social and economic relations in order to free individuals from their oppressive and alienating effects. He did not envisage individually owned private property being replaced by the entire state itself becoming Party-owned private property, which in effect is what the Soviet and Maoist appropriations of Marxist thought amount to. But the direction of movement in his solution is from economic organization to individual life.

For Kierkegaard the prospects for reforming society depend first on the reformation of individual life – the direction of movement is the reverse of Marx's. His diagnosis is that people have forgotten what being an individual means; man in industrial society is 'fractional (fragmented) man', 'lost' in the crowd, anonymous out of a timid desire to conform. The task is to recall people to themselves, and make them fulfil the potential within them to be 'uncommon'. The move from the aesthetic (sensory) life to the ethical and finally the religious life, the three arenas described by Kierkegaard in which the last is where he thinks we should be, will be provoked by the boredom, dread, frustration and alienation of the merely sensory life. Confrontation with this boredom, and then with the dread of having to make choices about how to escape it, precipitates a plunge into despair if one tries to find the solution within oneself alone. This despair is the 'sickness unto death', for which the cure is the leap of faith to theism. The paradox implicit in this lies in the free giving of oneself to submission to God – the free donation of oneself to bondage. For the theistic mind, that is redolent of virtue. For the philosopher, it is the ultimate in self-alienation and the abandonment of the possibility of truth in exchange for fantasy.

Kierkegaard, like most others, repudiated Hegel and the latter's claim to have achieved philosophy's final and definitive statement. But there is in Hegel a prefiguring of existentialist insight; as Marcuse summarizes it, Hegel's view is that: 'The world is an estranged and untrue world so long as man does not . . . recognize himself and his own life "behind" the fixed form of things and laws. When he finally wins this self-consciousness, he is on his way not only to the truth of himself, but also of his world.'[15] For Hegel the recognition of contradiction and the impulse to pass beyond it to a new synthesis in thought occupies the place taken by Marx's alienation and Kierkegaard's boredom and dread. What few of Hegel's successors agreed with was his solution to the contradiction he described, which was to 'take action and make the world what it essentially is, namely, the fulfilment of man's self-consciousness'. For those existentialists who did not follow Kierkegaard, Jaspers, Tillich, and others in finding the solution in religious commitment, the solution is crucially different: it is *to take action and create oneself.*

This is the result of a more potent influence than that exercised by Kierkegaard. This is the influence of Nietzsche.

Nietzsche's whole concern was to answer the Socratic Question, 'What sort of person should I be? How should I live?' even though he regarded Socrates' own response, predicated on reason, as partly responsible for the perversion of values he saw everywhere in Western civilization – in privileging only Apollonian intellect and excluding Dionysian feeling. The main responsibility, however, he attributed to Christianity. His announcement in *The Gay Science* that 'God is dead' was a declaration that everything built on the foundations of Judaeo-Christian thinking is rotten. If the civilization founded on Christianity no longer has any legitimate basis, then a 'revaluation of all values' is necessary. The confusion and anxiety of life among the ruins of the collapsed order are made worse by realizing that not only does that order have no foundation, but it is in fact positively harmful: it undermines what human beings can and should be.

The first step to remedying this situation is to understand it. Nietzsche provides his diagnosis in *The Genealogy of Morals* as follows. What is 'good' was in the past determined by the self-evaluation of natural aristocrats, the noble-minded, while what was 'bad' was exemplified by the 'low-minded, the vulgar, and the plebeian'. This order was upended by 'a slave revolt' inspired by resentment, and the 'good-bad' contrast was replaced by a different contrast – this time between 'good' and 'evil'. Pride, a property of the noble-minded outlook, has become a sin, while those who are humble, poor and meek are good. Humility and meekness are precisely the characteristics of those subjected to enslavement and exile. On this latter view, it is virtuous to be compassionate, and both self-denial and self-sacrifice are extolled; Nietzsche labels these the 'unegoistic' virtues and thereby marks their difference from the noble virtue of self-assertion. His description in *The Antichrist* of the value system he opposes to Christian 'slave morality' is given in his answers to the questions 'What is good? What is happiness?' thus: 'What is good? Everything that heightens the feeling of power in man, the will to power, power itself. What is bad? Everything that is born from weakness. What is happiness? The feeling that power is growing, that resistance is overcome. Not contentedness but more power; not peace but war; not virtue but fitness.'

When Nietzsche became irrecoverably mad in 1890 his sister Elisabeth Förster-Nietzsche took control of his literary estate and gave a sinister interpretation to such passages, which the Nazis invoked as inspiration.[16] There is a photograph of Hitler gazing at a bust of Nietzsche in the Nietzsche-Archiv in Weimar. But when these remarks are put alongside Schopenhauer's views, one sees what Nietzsche intended. In Schopenhauer's view the *will to exist* constitutes the underlying reality of the world, but because the will is forever doomed to frustration – it is too weak to overcome the many obstacles it has to encounter – it is therefore the source of the world's suffering. Nietzsche's point is that the *will to overcome* this frustration, to conquer it and therefore live and flourish, is what is ethical. To strive and thereby overcome is to be an *Übermensch* – 'Superman', meaning 'superior man' – and thus to be truly moral. One does this, Nietzsche says, by the affirmation of life, by being a 'Yes-sayer', by living as positively and nobly as possible. But this is not to live under illusions: as he points out variously in *The Gay Science* and *Ecce Homo*, embracing life involves pain and grief also, and therefore needs courage.

But the affirmative life is not all struggle and pain; there are sources of consolation in art and music. 'We possess art', Nietzsche writes, 'lest we perish of the truth.' Art teaches us 'how to make things beautiful', it makes us 'poets of our lives', enabling us to treat our own lives as a creative work with an aesthetic value which is part of its ethical value. This requires that we be autonomous, self-creating, rejecting the constraints and false values that society and its conventional morality – normativity – everywhere seeks to impose.

Nietzsche did not give a systematic statement of his views, but expressed them polemically, and through invoking the contrast between what Apollo and Dionysus allegorically represent. In his *Birth of Tragedy* (an early book which he came to regard as unsatisfactory) Nietzsche argues that *both* Apollonian order and rationality *and* Dionysian instinct, ecstasy and (often) chaos are essential for drama; that the tension between them is indeed the source of all art.

Nietzsche's view, in consequence, is that Aeschylus and Sophocles represent the highest achievement of that fruitful tension, whereas Euripides and Socrates, in preferring the Apollonian to the Dionysian – reason over feeling – brought Greece's great age of culture to an end.

Nietzsche was not a nihilist; he attacked both nihilism and pessimism as the consequence of the loss of faith in religious morality when nothing is put in its place. In *The Will to Power* he writes, 'The higher species is lacking, i.e., those whose inexhaustible fertility and power keep up the faith in man . . . the lower species ("herd", "mass", "society") unlearns modesty and blows up its needs into cosmic and metaphysical values. In this way the whole of existence is vulgarized: insofar as the mass is dominant it bullies the exceptions, so they lose their faith in themselves and become nihilists.' His recognition of the problem that results from rejecting traditional values is what makes thinkers like Heidegger misread him as a nihilist, which entirely misses his point: he did not 'devalue all values' but 'revalued' them.

An interesting contrast between Kierkegaard and Nietzsche is that whereas the former regarded everyone as capable of escaping the condition of existential angst – by leaping into faith; thus, by overcoming the agony of self by losing or at least subsuming the self – the latter did not think that everyone is capable of magnifying the self's potential and thereby achieving the status of Superman. His Zarathustra – which is to say, Nietzsche himself – accordingly arrived at the conclusion that many who started with high hopes of educating humanity into better versions of themselves eventually reached: that the message is for a few not the many. The thought is not an exclusionist or elitist one, but a regretful one. The invitation always remains open to all; the few incessantly call to the many to join them.

The proximate influence on existentialism is Heidegger's *Being and Time*.[17] It is a book Heidegger wrote in a hurry in order to qualify for the post of professor at Freiburg University in succession to his former mentor Edmund Husserl, and never fully finished. It starts as a study of the concept of 'being', the topic of Aristotle's *Metaphysics* which explores the concept of 'being qua being', *ousia*, asking what it is for anything to exist, what the different levels of existence are, and what the most fundamental form of being is. This enquiry is called 'ontology'. This is a heavyweight topic, its difficulty increased by the fact that it is analogous to an eyeball trying to see itself, since the enquirer into existence is himself an existing thing possessed of the fundamental attribute he is trying to understand. To Husserl's dissatisfaction but to subsequent 'Continental' philosophy's enrichment, Heidegger's enquiry rapidly withdrew from the general question of being as such, to the question of the being who asks the question about being – namely, the being who is a human being already fully existing in the world, engaged with the world, part of the world, experiencing his own existence in and through belonging to the world. For the being-in-the-world thus identified as the primary target of understanding 'being', Heidegger used the term *Dasein*, which literally means 'being there' and as a noun means 'a being-there'.

Heidegger's starting point is the idea that an answer to the question of 'being' has to be derived from considering the way the question poses itself, and to what or whom it poses itself; the being who asks. Investigating *this* being, he says, might help us to understand 'being' in general. But the investigation is not to proceed as psychology or standard philosophy would proceed, but must be conducted *phenomenologically* – a concept developed by Husserl to denote a focus on pre-theoretical awareness of being-in-the-world, hyphenated in this way to show that the being in question is not separate from the world in a subject-object relationship with it, but is *in* and *of* it.

Dasein possesses *logos*, by which Heidegger does not mean reason or language – the usual meanings – but the ability to gather and remember the things encountered in the world. When we use a tool, for example a garden fork, the network of meanings of which the fork is part – what it is used for, why there is a need for such uses, and so on – together with all other things with their networks of meanings, constitute 'the world'. In this way, Dasein is a collection-point where – as Heidegger puts it – beings 'come out of concealment' and thereby 'make themselves present'. These two notions are key to his theory.

The aspect of Heidegger's view which a number of his contemporaries put to work in adumbrating an existentialist philosophy is the idea of Dasein as 'stretched' between birth and death, having been 'thrown into the world' at an arbitrary point in time, faced with a number of possibilities from among which she has to choose, her choice determining whether she will exist 'authentically'. Especially relevant to achieving authenticity is confrontation with the inevitability of death, the inescapable fact of which emphasizes Dasein's individuality and causes her dread, anxiety, *angst*. Dasein's 'having to do with something, producing something, attending to something and looking after it, making use of something, giving something up and letting it go, undertaking, accomplishing, evincing, interrogating, considering, discussing, determining' is the 'care' (*Sorge*) or concern that constitutes relationships with objects and other people, and it constitutes the 'structure of Dasein itself', a relationship Heidegger also calls 'handiness' and 'equipmentality' to emphasize the fact that to be is to be in and part of the world, not an abstract observer separate from the world. The idea he borrows from Parmenides, of truth as 'coming out of concealment' or 'disclosure', plays its part here: disclosure is brought about by anxiety and care. Note that anxiety is not *fear*; fear is always fear of something particular, whereas anxiety is an indefinite general *mood* of dread or anguish, and it alters the way Dasein sees the world. Disclosure is like 'a clearing in the forest', an opening in which Dasein achieves self-understanding of what 'care' is; what Dasein thus comes to understand is that 'care' has three components: *thrownness* – we are thrown into the world without knowing why, still less why here and why now; *projection* – seeking among things around us to find ways of escaping our anxiety; and *fallenness* – Dasein's tendency to fail itself, to distract itself from achieving authenticity. Yet it is only by achieving authenticity that the anguish of existence can be overcome.

From these various sources a classic statement of existentialism – Sartre's existentialism – came to be distilled, the distillate contained in the published version of Sartre's lecture 'Existentialism is a Humanism', delivered in 1946. Sartre himself, for reasons chiefly to do with his political evolution in the 1950s and 1960s, came to distance himself from some of the essay's ideas, but for those same decades they were the chief existential inspiration for a generation, as I can

personally attest; the ideas both caught and encouraged the intellectual mood of the post-war world. Whatever its shortcomings as a
philosophical treatise, embedded in it are key existentialist themes.

Sartre described the essay's purpose as being to defend existentialism against criticism. One criticism is that existentialism counsels
'the quietism of despair'. Another is that it focuses too much on all
that is mean and sordid in the human condition, neglecting what
brings beauty and charm into life. A third is that it considers human
beings in their individual isolation, not as social beings in solidarity
with one another; and that this starting point locks the existentialist
inside the Cartesian ego from which there is no successful route out
again to connections with others. And finally, Christians complain
that without the eternal values embodied in the commandments of
God, 'everyone can do what he likes and will be incapable, from such
a point of view, of condemning either the point of view or the action
of anyone else'.

To the charge of existentialism being a pessimistic and gloomy
outlook, Sartre responds by saying that it is not gloom and pessimism
that annoy critics, given that most people – as common proverbs and
the sorts of things people typically say about life, politics, the weather, and so on, show – are gloomier and more pessimistic still, but
instead that what annoys its critics is existentialism's optimism. For
existentialism 'confronts man with a possibility of choice', on the
basis of recognizing that *'existence* comes before *essence* – or, if you
will, that we must begin from the subjective'. To say this is to say that
a human being exists before she can be defined, because her
definition – what and who she is as an individual – follows from
'encountering herself, surging up in the world', discovering what she
can be if she chooses. She is nothing to begin with, and becomes
something through her choices; she makes herself. 'Man is nothing
else but what he makes of himself; that is the first principle of existentialism.' To denounce this as over-concentration on 'subjectivity'
is to miss the point; the existentialist emphasizes the subjective in
order to register the dignity of human beings, who, unlike stones and
plants, are things that 'propel themselves towards a future and are
aware that they are doing so'. And 'before that projection of the self

nothing exists . . . man will only attain existence when he is what he purposes to be'.

Because existence is prior to essence, it follows that people are responsible for who they are, because what they are is the product of the choices they make. 'Thus, the first effect of existentialism is that it puts every man in possession of himself as he is, and places the entire responsibility for his existence squarely upon his own shoulders.' But this is not a kind of ethical solipsism. For 'when we say that man is responsible for himself, we do not mean that he is responsible only for his own individuality, but that he is responsible for all men'. This is a corollary of the two facts that when we make a choice, we always choose what we see as the better alternative, and at the same time think that this is how it should be for everyone. This is a Kantian thought, which Sartre adapts by remarking that a person who makes a choice knowing that, if everyone made that choice, things would be bad, but who consoles himself by saying, 'Oh well, not everyone will do it,' is deceiving himself: 'The man who lies in self-excuse must be ill at ease in his conscience, for the act of lying implies the universal value which it denies. By its very disguise his anguish reveals itself' – an anguish Sartre says is so named by Kierkegaard in his comments on the story of Abraham and Isaac (see Appendix 1). From the question 'Who says it is God who is speaking' in giving this horrible command to Abraham, one derives the question 'Who says that I am the proper person to impose by my own choice, my conception of man upon mankind?' In choosing what I take to be the better option, and thinking that this is the choice all should make who are similarly placed, I appear to be arrogating to myself the position of exemplar for all. But, says Sartre, 'If a man does not say this, he is dissembling his anguish. Clearly, the anguish with which we are concerned here is not one that could lead to quietism or inaction. It is anguish pure and simple, of the kind well known to all those who have borne responsibilities.'

All leaders know the anguish of responsibility, and the anguish is the very condition of their action, because the action 'presupposes that there is a plurality of possibilities'. This anguish is the greater because without a deity or a set of absolute a priori moral principles to justify or guide, people have to find on their own responsibility the answer to the question 'What shall I do?' But existentialism is not without resource even here. The universalization point has already been made; another is the related conception of the 'dignity of man', revealed through the discovery of the intersubjectivity of subjects: 'Thus the man who discovers himself directly in the *cogito* [i.e. Descartes' 'I think therefore I am'] also discovers all the others, and discovers them as the condition of his own existence. He recognises that he cannot be anything (in the sense in which one says one is spiritual, or that one is wicked or jealous) unless others recognise him as such. I cannot obtain any truth whatsoever about myself, except through the mediation of another. The other is indispensable to my existence, and equally so to any knowledge I can have of myself.'[18] So 'the human kingdom' is 'a pattern of values', and even if we cannot specify a *human nature* as such, we can recognize and describe a *human condition*. This is why it matters how we choose; even not choosing is a choice. In my choices I implicate the whole of humanity, so the choices cannot be a product of mere caprice. In taking into consideration the effect of alternative choices, man is recognizing that he is 'in an organised situation in which he is himself involved'.

But this does not deterministically, in an a priori fashion, settle what is right, for there might be alternative right choices. Sartre cites examples from George Eliot's *The Mill on the Floss* and Stendhal's *Charterhouse of Parma*. In the first, Maggie Tulliver loves Stephen, who is engaged to an 'insignificant young woman', but sacrifices her own happiness so that Stephen can honour his engagement to the 'little goose'. By contrast, in Stendhal the character Gina, Duchess Sanseverina, 'believing that it is passion which endows man with his real value, would have declared that a grand passion justifies its sacrifices, and must be preferred to the banality of such conjugal love as would unite Stephen to the little goose he was engaged to marry'. Both Maggie and Gina choose on principle, not out of careless self-interest and greed – though very differently. 'One can choose anything, but only if it is upon the plane of free commitment.' It is in this sense that existentialism 'is optimistic, is a doctrine of action', for:

Man is all the time outside of himself: it is in projecting and losing himself beyond himself that he makes man to exist; and, on the other hand, it is by pursuing transcendent aims that he himself is able to exist. Since man is thus self-surpassing, and can grasp objects only in relation to his self-surpassing, he is himself the heart and centre of his transcendence. There is no other universe except the human universe . . . What is at the very heart and centre of existentialism, is the absolute character of the free commitment, by which every man realises himself in realising a type of humanity.

Commentators on existentialism are apt to cite sociological considerations to explain its motivations: the moral rudderlessness following the 'death of God' in the nineteenth century, and the horrors and destruction of the world wars in the first half of the twentieth century, giving rise to a mood of despair and emptiness to which existentialism offered itself both as diagnosis and remedy. Sartre's essay is sociologically interesting in its portrayal of existentialism – or at least, the word 'existentialism' – as already highly fashionable and much discussed in the Paris of the mid-forties after the Liberation. He reports a newspaper columnist anonymously signing himself 'the Existentialist' and a lady who let slip a swear word saying, 'Oh dear! I'm becoming an existentialist.' But the fact that one can push the roots of existentialism back to Pascal – and why stop there; are not the Cynics and Sceptics of antiquity in their way choosing a life predicated on a rejection of normativity and therefore the absence of its values, which entails the radical freedom of their choice? – shows that the underlying ideas are not as historically dependent as this implies. For a little reflection shows that there is a profound insight in the idea that subjective awareness and the inescapability of choice, if not already pre-empted by a too-successful immersion in the values and expectations of normativity, is a datum of intelligent human life. In fact, subjective awareness and the inescapability of choice are assumptions of the Socratic challenge itself, and they are therefore not an innovation of modernity. Matters are the other way round: the Socratic challenge, and the efforts of the ethical schools to meet it, constitutes a form of existentialism which was displaced by the dominance of Christianity – which was a new kind of religion, postulating a personal responsibility to a 'loving' but in fact demanding, potentially dangerous and apparently capricious, all-powerful patriarchal-monarchical figure, and requiring a very particular way of thinking and believing to the exclusion of critical challenges to both.[19] In the eighteenth century Enlightenment questions about the foundations of ethics again became a subject of debate, and it is no surprise that in the following two centuries questions of ethics and the basis of morality should become increasingly contested though the residual effect of religious ethics remained – as demonstrated by the limerick 'There was a young man from Moldavia / Who could not believe in the Saviour / So he erected instead / With himself as the head / The Religion of Decorous Behaviour'. Against this background, the thinking of Marx, Nietzsche, Freud (in his psychoanalysis of Western civilization in *Civilization and Its Discontents*) and Sartre, all interpreted as addressing the Socratic Question, is to be understood.

The same sociologists, in speaking of a 'cultural mood' – giving the impression that the entire population of the Western world is plunged into hand-wringing anxiety over the lost condition of humanity, while in fact being 'distracted by distractions' into sensing the emptiness beneath their feet only occasionally and momentarily – are really talking about the articulate and self-conscious minority from whom the literature, art and thought of the culture emanate. And what is being generalized is the common experience especially of young adults in going through a phase of existential crisis in the transition from dependency and tutelage, under authority in family and educational settings, to the vertiginous and sometimes risky freedom of circumstances in which a lack of experience, judgment and defined aims coincides with unaccustomed degrees of autonomy. A reading of biographies, and an accumulation of personal observation, teaches how common and painful the transition can be; it is especially noticeable in undergraduate communities, where intelligence and ambition meet with a relatively sudden increase in the degree of autonomy. The months and years of the biggest impact of this are like crossing a stretch of icy road.

The point has been well made that in the rapid modernization of Russia in the nineteenth century, the self-awareness of writers was particularly fruitful in expressions of the existential dilemmas forced upon them, as evidenced by Turgenev, Dostoevsky and Tolstoy. The two latter found their solutions in fideistic ('just believe, don't question') versions of theism, though Dostoevsky acutely remarked of the character Levin in Tolstoy's *Anna Karenina*, who at the novel's end decides to give up his search for answers in philosophy and instead to embrace the simple unquestioning Christian faith of the peasantry, that 'two weeks after the novel's end he will snag his soul on a rusty nail'.

And yet what is exposed in these moments of personal crisis is precisely the set of questions about what one should do, what one should be, how one should see life and live it. In the confusions of the crisis itself it is hard to formulate, and still harder to answer, the questions, but once they have been asked the task of answering them is set – though how often they are hidden away, suppressed, and left to the next moment of crisis: the midlife crisis, the death of parents, the divorce, the realization that one is not going higher in one's career, the diagnosis in the doctor's surgery!

Sartre tells an anecdote about a young man who visited him during the war in search of advice. His dilemma was that he felt two burning desires in competition with each other: one was to escape to England to join the Free French forces to fight the Nazis; the other was to stay and look after his beloved ageing mother, who would otherwise be alone and bereft. Which should he do? Sartre's answer was that no one could decide for him, and that he must do what he *felt* was more right in the circumstances. Although it is obvious that the good this young man could do would be greater if he stayed with his mother – a small fly caught in the vast cobweb of war is an impotent thing, except perhaps in a tiny way for a moment or two, whereas the net effect of caring for another person over an extended period is manifestly greater – Sartre's answer was right in principle, though unhelpful in practice; for when a person asks for advice, it is often helpful for the advisor to give it by her best lights, because the advisee is still free to choose and might make up his mind (to the opposite

of the advice, perhaps) as a result. But the principle is that the ultimate responsibility for a choice is an individual's own, in full cognizance
of the 'existing arrangements' of things and how the choice will
affect them.

This was Socrates' assumption in challenging his Athenian contemporaries to think about how they would answer his questions
'What sort of person should I be? How should I live? And by what
values?' – namely, that it is for each to answer it on his or her own.
And one question which has to be answered alongside answering
them is: 'Do I seek a life worth living because it is meaningful,
whether or not it feels good to live it, or do I seek a life worth living
because, whether or not it is meaningful by whatever standard would
define a life as such, it is better than not existing?'

But there is something compelling, perhaps inescapable, about the
insight that the existentialist analysis offers, if you accept the two
ideas that we possess ultimate freedom of choice and that there is no
antecedent blueprint other than normativity – itself an outcome of
the vagrant processes of history and chance. This is that we must
choose, and that our choices create us. This is a deep and important
point. And one of the first steps in choosing – as if one were tracing
the very first branches of a flow chart – is whether we are going to
live or die, and if to live, whether to pursue a life worthwhile because
meaningful, or just worthwhile.

It is obvious that the range of human experience is wide; it stretches
from lives of terrible suffering and waste, of misery, despair and subjection, to lives that are satisfying, fulfilling, successful, and in some
cases noble and great. On which side of the balance do most lives
lie? One can tentatively venture a guess that whereas all lives have
some degree of suffering in them, the worst of human experience –
the agonies of disaster, disease, oppression and struggle – are features
mainly of parts of lives, and at their worst of a minority of lives,
however large the numbers in absolute terms; for observation suggests that most people find some good in most of the circumstances
they are placed in, and that in average lives there are aspects that those
living them can regard as achievements and as things worth doing

and having. This suggests further that for many such people their judgment that they live worthwhile lives might be construed by them, each from his or her own subjective standpoint, as amounting to the claim that their lives are not merely worthwhile but meaningful, whatever a more demanding third-party judge of 'meaningfulness' might say. Think of a person who, as a child, conceived the ambition to be – say – a policewoman, and in due course became one, and had a successful career, during which she justifiably felt that she was helping her community, putting bad people behind bars and making society better. This is a worthwhile life which she would find meaningful, and that is one sense of the term for which she can make a case that a third-party judge would understand.

Nevertheless, suppose we settle for a picture in which it is only a minority in humanity who have a sense of great purpose, a need for meaning, and who therefore strive to achieve it – some successfully – while the majority of people everywhere and at all times are content with the widely shared more prosaic purpose of getting by satisfactorily. Accepting such a picture might seem to be a rather low-key result, but I can offer an argument to the conclusion that 'getting by satisfactorily' is enough for it to be worthwhile, even in normativity's terms, that humanity exists – and by entailment that the lives of at least most humans have been, and that most current lives are, worthwhile. I call this, for reasons that will become obvious, the Universal Argument.

The argument is this. Suppose (as is indeed something like the case) that the universe comes into existence from the 'nothing' of the quantum vacuum and its play of virtual entities, simply as a function of the laws of physics, not 'created' or 'designed' by some agency with a plan. Suppose, having adventitiously come into existence, the universe continues to exist for billions of years, evolving throughout this time according to the same physical laws and then dying by one or another means such as contraction to a singularity under the force of gravity, or fizzling out in a 'cold death' long after it has expanded beyond the capacity of photons to reach from any one source of their emission to any other. In the course of this history, on a small planet in a commonplace solar system orbiting an ordinary star in an outer arm of an ordinary spiral galaxy, there briefly flickers – perhaps for a couple of million years or so – self-conscious awareness and intelligence: human beings (and to a lesser extent a few other intelligent mammalian and avian species). And then self-conscious awareness and intelligence flicker out again, because of climate change, pandemic disease or devastating war; all three far too likely for comfort given that intelligence and wisdom are, very sadly, not the same thing. Well: if the sum of things positive – happiness, satisfaction, *eudaimonia*, *aponia*, *ataraxia* – outweighs things negative – pain, sorrow, fear, injustice, hunger, frustration – then that fact makes it *good that the universe existed*. But if the negative outweighs the positive, then it makes it *bad that the universe existed*. How things are for self-conscious beings therefore affects the ethical quality of the entire universe and its entire history. This consideration by itself justifies the modest achievements of what normativity specifies as the aims of life – the job, the mortgage, the family, the pension – when these are productive of satisfactions appreciated by those enjoying them. And it gives a reason to people to seek, at very least, happiness, satisfaction, *eudaimonia*, *aponia*, *ataraxia*, because they thereby help to make it a good thing that the entire universe exists. And that is a majestic goal.

However: for those with a more urgent desire for a sense of meaning, this impersonal result is not enough. They regard seeking the satisfactions of normativity as a process which alienates people from themselves. In their view, the standard tropes of normative life are either blinkers or distractions – the blinkers of work, earning a living, paying the bills, keeping within the guidelines of acceptable behaviour; and blinkered too by the distractions of TV, alcohol, beach holidays, news about celebrity divorces and the semi-farce of politics. Most are unaware of being distracted from themselves in this way; these are Eliot's 'distractions from distraction'. As a result of being blinkered and distracted, people allow themselves to be marshalled into a great congested crowd, shuffling along a corridor at the end of which is an abrupt drop into oblivion. They are not marshalled by a single agency, a single conspiracy, but by the joint effect of the many agencies and the many intentional and unintentional impulses that together constitute normativity, a semi-blind concatenation of forces.

Struggling in this crowd whose density and solidity carries the majority perforce along, those who seek – or seek to make – meaning often find themselves at odds with those around them, because they jostle them, trip them up, impede them. Perhaps they inspire some of them, among whom a few follow them while others, though they admire them, continue to be carried along in the crush towards the corridor's end.

Of course the seekers and makers of meaning also reach the precipice at the end of the corridor. But it might be said that when they do so, they do not fall over the edge, they fly from it. Why? Precisely because in the journey along the corridor they saw the possibility of something more. They saw things to do and be that are more fulfilling, more consequential, more impactful, more interesting and stimulating, than satisfying the requirements and achieving the benchmarks of normativity. And they reached for those things accordingly; they tried. They saw that human capacities are generally underutilized; they saw that the majority of people slip into habit, into a rut – a good metaphor, despite being a cliché; a wheel running in a well-worn rut keeps its direction and has fewer bumps – and cleave to what is familiar and easy, within their level of competence. This is true even of the kinds of ambition met with in the workplace: to get a promotion, a rise, achieve higher rank, become the boss; this ladder is normativity's ladder. To aim to become the manager of a bank and to aim to write the Great American Novel are both ambitions, but they are not the same *kind* of ambition (as one can see by noticing that they are not alternatives, nor incompatible) and they make very different demands. Normativity has its own creative folk: business entrepreneurs, social entrepreneurs, some politicians assuredly fall into this category. In being so, some of these are seekers and makers of meaning too. One might say of those entrepreneurs who are not such that their aims are internal to normativity's world. Their aim to change things is to change the position of the chairs on the ship's deck; the most ambitious of the seekers and makers of meaning change, or try to change, the ship's course across the ocean.

That said, one thing ought to be asked, and another thing remarked, that adds to the thoughts we might have about the foregoing.

The question is: if the search for meaning were to reduce the amount of overall *aponia* and *ataraxia* in the universe, even if the meaning were made or found, so that the universe is a place where bad experience outweighs good in the long term, but with more meaningfulness to it, would the search for meaning still be justified? This invites us to ask whether 'meaning' and 'what is good' are or can be different things. For if meaning is a good in itself, then any increase in meaning, even if it involves suffering, would either balance or outweigh the suffering. One aspect of this question renews another: which has more importance – what is found or done, or how things ultimately feel?

The thought is that even within the context of normativity, setting goals and working to achieve them – however modest; making a garden, learning a language – and having principles of helping not harming, of respecting others, of promoting mutuality and amity, quite clearly makes a life thus lived worth living, both for itself and others, because such endeavours themselves have something admirable in them and add a dimension of quality. This meliorist view is the ultimate justification of the goods specified by normativity. But in light of the question in the preceding paragraph, another question asks itself: is this enough?

As repeatedly noted, 'the meaningful life' and 'the worthwhile life' are not automatically the same thing, but nor are they mutually exclusive; and neither are either the same as the life that feels good to live – which, if it were a life premised on selfishness and indulgence at the expense of others might well not be a worthwhile life. So the big question now is 'What *kind* of life are you living? And why?' And finally: 'Is it enough, or is it not enough? And if the latter – what will you do?'

PART III

13. Philosophy as a Way of Life

Answering Socrates' question requires thought and choice. Putting the choice to work is a process, because the choice is about a way of being and living which might be different from, or a modification of, the way of being and living that conforms to normativity as the almost certainly unconscious philosophy that has so far guided one. It is not like consulting a map which is folded away after a route has been picked. It is more like a travel guide that accompanies one along the route – but a travel guide internalized, and consulted constantly. For antiquity's ethical schools, philosophy was a practice – a conscious application of their principles to daily life, as Martha Nussbaum and especially Pierre Hadot have shown.[1] This gives weight to the philosophers' views; they meant what they said, and lived what they meant.[2]

The large difference between deliberately choosing and applying one's views about how to live, on the one hand, and the unreflective acceptance of some current normativity on the other hand, is that the latter generally comes down to *hoping* that things will turn out all right if one goes along with normativity's prescriptions, whereas the former consists in working to *make* them turn out all right. Normativity indicates a general direction for everyone to follow – and even if the map is not folded up, the fact that it is for everyone means that it purposely has to avoid detail. But to answer Socrates' question for oneself is to pick a personal direction, a specific route. For a prosaic example: normativity is like telling someone to 'get a job' after their formal education is over, without considering both the person and her education to decide what kind of job, where to look for openings, how to apply, and how to do one's best in getting it and after getting it.

Nussbaum begins her *Therapy of Desire* with the words 'The idea of a practical and compassionate philosophy – a philosophy that exists for the sake of human beings, in order to address their deepest needs, confront their most urgent perplexities, and bring them from misery to some greater measure of flourishing – this idea makes the study of Hellenistic philosophy riveting for a philosopher who wonders what philosophy has to do with the world.'[3] This is true, and it immediately establishes the practical nature of the philosophical views in question. The discussions of them in Nussbaum's book are rich and detailed. She identifies, and by the end finds unresolved, a tension between the ethical schools' variously prescribed focus on *ataraxia* and the possibility of realizing other goods, other commitments, that make life worthwhile and even meaningful. For her, the practice of the schools eliminates too much of the emotional dimension that in the end determines the quality of life – in particular passion, love, *eros*, loyalty, mercy, all of which involve taking the risks implicit in human relationships – seeking by application of 'narrative understanding' to fathom the complexities of one's own and others' motivations.

This is a compelling and sympathetic observation, and it is certain that most people would agree. But there is a point that has to be pressed: is Nussbaum begging the question against the philosophical schools? After all, they are expressly aiming to avoid the messiness of human life that comes from passion, *eros*, and risks in relationships, having concluded from wide and constant observation that these – either in their very nature, as Stoics say; or at least the wrong ones in too great a degree, as Aristotle and Epicureans say – are the very sources of perplexity and misery that a more considered life aims to avoid. Nussbaum has begun her enquiry into the schools' endeavours with an assumption in place: that the quest upon which the schools are embarked is for 'a practical *and compassionate* philosophy' – my emphasis. It is immediately obvious that Stoicism is not a quest for a compassionate philosophy, given that compassion involves being moved by what happens to others – hence, being affected by things over which one has little or no influence; and the Stoic prescription is precisely to avoid making oneself hostage to such responses because they undermine one's *ataraxia*. Likewise the Epicurean valorization of friendship and conversation, avoiding Cyrenaic excesses of the flesh, is very milk-and-water by comparison to anything describable as a *passionate* life. The importance attached to friendship by the Epicureans entails the values of fellow feeling – hence of pity and compassion – but in accord with the doctrine of moderation, not to the extent of succumbing to wild grief or any self-losing excess of emotion, which would be the very opposite of *aponia* and *ataraxia*.

The Greek and Hellenistic attitude to passion can be read from the etymology of the word itself. We now think of passions – anger, love, desire, hatred – not as 'passive' but as *active* things. But the words 'passion', 'passive' and 'patient' have a common root in Greek *pascho* and Latin *patior*, 'to suffer, to be acted upon'. 'Agent', 'actor', 'action', 'act' derive from the third conjugation Latin verb *agere*, 'to set in motion' (*ago, agere, egi, actum*; linked to Greek *agein*, 'to lead or carry'). The philosophers regarded erotic desire as an infliction, a madness visited upon them by the gods: a *theia mania*. This was not a feature of the good life; it was disruptive, a disturbance at best and destructive at worst of peace of mind. And they knew that upset and stress not only interfere with the rational conduct of life's business, but are a threat to bodily health. So they would challenge Nussbaum's view as it stands. That view constitutes a disagreement if it rests on an articulated alternative case to the effect that a life worth living must have passionate dimensions, but it misses the ancient philosophers' point if it merely assumes that passion is a necessary feature of a life worth living.

These thoughts bear on the question of a philosophy of life as a practice, because it is evidently the case that the passions come very naturally to human beings – we love and hate, grieve and exult, pity, care, despair, desire, hope, feel shame and guilt; and one of the main points of a philosophy of life is to make one capable of dealing with these states. We are so often wracked by them that interludes of calm reflection seem rare by comparison. The impression that life is a series of passionate disruptions is reinforced by every novel, film and television drama series; the essence of most stories is problems and upsets, tensions and conflicts, through which characters must travel an arc from one emotional state to another through various intervening and associated such states. We forget that stories, which we human beings love and need, basically consist in gossip about what goes on in the many corners of life, through which most of us are groping our way with larger or lesser degrees of uncertainty. The ethical schools' objective was to escape the messiness of a life driven hither and thither by passions, and to pitch camp on more rational and equanimous ground.

And this in turn means that, as a practice, a philosophy of life is a discipline, because the fact that passions come naturally to us means that guiding ourselves through them requires application. When we see the tenets of the ethical schools as intended to be practical and action-guiding in this way, we get their point more fully.

Before turning in detail to the question of philosophy as a practice, two remarks are in order. The first is that the point just made about the ethical schools' view of the passions should not of course be taken to imply that all the schools share the Stoic ideal of maximum *apatheia*, dispassion, which a critic would see as coldness and selfishness. Not just Cyrenaics but Cynics might counsel indulgence of whatever passions come naturally – sexual arousal, for example, as in the case of Diogenes – while Epicureans see the practicable route not as extirpation but moderation of the passions. Aristotle, who thought that the passions have their appropriate place ('It is right to be angry for the right reasons in the right way at the right time') would argue for reflection on the best course of action in circumstances where passions are roused, superinducing reason on the situation as one might pour oil on troubled water. But all except the first of these views are agreed on the danger that the passions can represent – even the ordinary everyday passions – and counsel ways of handling them (which means: managing oneself) accordingly.

The second remark is that the schools' teachings can look beguilingly like a package, at least in summary accounts of them, so that in accepting one or other package outright, treating it as a rule book rather than a guidebook, you become 'a Stoic' or 'an Epicurean' in a paid-up sense. The point has been repeatedly made in these pages that a key assumption of the Socratic challenge is that one must think for oneself, and not adopt wholesale someone else's ideas, which would either be tailored to their originator's individuality or be generally applicable to many. Instead the task is to take what persuades from all or any of the schools, and use it as part of the materials for living one's own choice of 'considered life', under government of the demand that it bear scrutiny – which means: that a case can be made for it, not least in regard to how it might affect others. At the same time, it is quite likely that the general tenor of one or another way of thinking about life will attract; describing Walter Pater or Oscar Wilde as 'Epicureans' does not pigeon-hole them exactly as such, but indicates where most of the dots would cluster if you drew a scatter graph of what they agreed with in views about how to live.

A selection from the insights of the schools has obviously to be principled, not haphazard or motivated by convenience merely; again, one has to have a case for one's choices. In reflecting on her growing interest in Stoicism, Nussbaum commented on this challenge, noting that the Stoic's commitment to treating emotional responses to things outside their control as, in effect, embodying false judgments about those things – and therefore as threatening their *ataraxia* – is inconsistent with her view that the emotions are necessary for a good life. Yet at the same time she concedes that the Stoics have 'a lot to offer us in the area of unwise attachments' to things such as money, honour and status, for the emotions of 'unwise attachment' – such as desire and possessiveness – can undermine the possibility of a good life.[4] We therefore need a criterion for distinguishing attachments and emotions into wise and unwise categories, something not as easy to do as one might hope, because the same emotion might be wise in some situations and unwise in others, and the same circumstances can prompt contrasting emotions in different people – as when something a person does prompts pity in one onlooker and contempt in another. Given that emotions typically embody beliefs – a person is angry because she believes she has been treated unjustly; another is sorrowful because he regards a friend's situation as tragic – the question of the respect in which certain kinds of emotions add to the good of a life depends on their truth-value. Can we regard a life as good when it is coloured by positive emotions induced by false beliefs? Note that if we asked, 'Would we regard as bad a life coloured by negative emotions induced by false beliefs?' we would certainly answer 'Yes'. To give the same answer to the earlier question requires a great deal of justification.

A point made in Chapter 9 on 'circumstances' is that the target of the schools' teaching is psychological states, not – except as a dependent outcome – the conditions of social and material life. This is what underwrites the effort to decouple psychology from circumstances (as Cynics and Stoics advise) or to constrain or channel the latter's effect on the former (as Aristotle and Epicureans advise). So any focus on the role – let alone the value – of the passions will necessarily involve the large question of their management. In significant part, this is what 'philosophy as practice' is about. *Philosophy as practice* – as a way of life – is the theme of this chapter.

Pierre Hadot is the historian of philosophy who did most to show how the ancient schools taught a way of life – a *manière de vivre* or *bios* – as a practice, complete with the equivalent of 'spiritual exercises' to structure and fortify them. Indeed he saw the Christian conception of 'spiritual exercises' – for a chief example, those developed by the founder of the Jesuit Order, Ignatius Loyola – as a borrowing from the Hellenistic schools. Hadot had himself been ordained in the Roman Catholic Church as a young man, though he left the priesthood within a few years, and this gave him insight into the parallels. It was not merely a matter of noticing similarities; for a number of years he lectured on the Latin Fathers of the Church, including Ambrose and Augustine, and became an expert on Plotinus and Porphyry, the Neoplatonist thinkers who had a great influence on the development of Christian thought in the patristic period. Hadot's study of Marcus Aurelius demonstrates how the text of the *Meditations* consists in Aurelius' exhortations and reminders to himself of the principles on which he lived; the equivalent Christian practice would be confession and prayer. The exercises in the *Meditations* are, Hadot writes, 'as rigorous, as codified, as systematic as the famous *Spiritual Exercises* of Saint Ignatius'.[5] They belong to a standard genre in antiquity: *hypomnemata*, daily jottings addressed privately to oneself, just like a private journal today.

In Hadot's view the influence of the ethical schools is not confined to its conscious presence in the thought of later philosophers or to its adoption into Christian thought, but through both of these into

Western culture in general, whose 'problems, themes and symbols' have come 'for the most part in the form that was given to them either by Hellenistic thought, or by the adaptation of this thought to the Roman world, or by the encounter between Hellenism and Christianity'.[6] The transitions between Greek and Roman – and between Hellenistic and Christian – ways of thinking were not without mistranslations, reinterpretations and straightforward misunderstandings. Hadot demonstrates how a number of key ideas in the Church Fathers resulted from these factors.[7] Language, translation and interpretation can mislead as well as communicate and inform, and this was the case in the first half of the Common Era's first millennium. Similar misunderstandings happen with the texts of the ancient philosophers today; Aurelius' *Meditations* are read as offering advice formulated by Aurelius himself, rather than as rehearsal of advice he was admonishing himself to take and apply.

The struggle between 'paganism' – Hellenistic and Roman thought – and Christianity, occurring chiefly in the fourth and fifth centuries CE, ended in public terms in victory for Christianity (Theodosius I's Decree of 380 CE was a decisive moment), at the price to Christianity of having to adopt many pagan ideas – especially in ethics, because of the thinness of its own resources in this respect.[8] But an earlier historical transition had already affected the character of the Hellenistic schools themselves. This was that, in the course of the century following Greece's absorption into the Roman world,[9] the schools of Athens dispersed to other centres of culture around the Mediterranean and Middle East. The tradition of oral instruction in the schools during their first centuries of existence was superseded, in this diaspora, by a reliance on texts and therefore, increasingly, textual exegesis. Hadot points out that: 'In order to affirm their fidelity to the founder, the four philosophical schools [Platonist, Aristotelian, Stoic, Epicurean], scattered to different cities of the Orient and Occident, can no longer depend on the institution that he had created, nor on the oral tradition internal to the school, but solely on the texts of the founder. The classes of philosophy will therefore consist above all in commentaries on the text.'[10]

Two significant consequences flow from this. One is that as texts receive comment and interpretation, so interpretations of them multiply – even to the point of generating schisms among followers – and concepts change; 'being', as a present participle denoting something that an existing thing does, becomes 'a being' – a noun denoting a thing – and even 'Being' with a capital 'B', denoting an *important* such thing. The second is that the original doctrine evolves, and grows, until it would be unrecognizable to the originator of its earliest form. In itself that is not a bad thing; ideas inspire further ideas, philosophical creativity can be prompted by alternative under-standings of previous formulations. Perhaps the only person inconvenienced by this process is the scholar attempting to recon-struct the original inspiration for a line of thought.

A virtue of Hadot's work is his situating the thought of the Hel-lenistic schools in its various historical contexts, taking into account the problems, necessities and constraints imposed by the times in question. He is also alert to the literary genres used to expound ideas – Plato's dialogues, Aristotle's treatises, Epicurus' letters, Epic-tetus' discourses, Lucretius' poetry. A grasp of these considerations is a powerful help to understanding the philosophers' intentions.

In the case of Aurelius' *Meditations* Hadot saw that they consisted in exercises of discipline over the three functions of the mind described by Epictetus: judgment, desire and will. Unlike the acci-dents and contingencies of the world around us, these can be brought fully under our own control. Individual meditations in Aurelius accordingly correspond to these three topics, but not in a casual way; there is a strict order to them, so structured that one can discern 'an extremely rigorous conceptual system' underlying them.[11] The sys-tem reflects the way Epictetus himself characterized the three *topoi* – judgment belonging to logic, desire belonging to physics (in the sense of 'the philosophy of nature'; hence, our bodily and natural appetites), and will belonging to ethics. Astutely, Hadot observed that the fact that Aurelius was meditating regularly and systematic-ally on these matters does not allow us to infer much about what he was actually like as a person; someone might fill his private journal with adjurations to himself about sobriety and responsibility *because* he is an alcoholic who is letting everyone down and desperately wishes he were not doing so. As Paul Valéry similarly observed, many of us write not to teach but to 'make our own minds'. This latter is what Aurelius was doing.

In fact, Hadot says, far from being the spontaneous personal reflections of Aurelius, the *Meditations* conform to a model of how *hypomnemata* should be written and what themes should occur in them. 'Often he only says certain things because he *must* say them in virtue of models and precepts that impose themselves on him.'[12] Given that modern commentators have attributed depression, despair, pessimism, resignation, disgust at the world – even signs of gastric ulcers and opium addiction – to Aurelius from their reading of his *Meditations*, as well as courage, nobility and aspiration to the good, this is a salutary corrective. Someone who wrote, as Aurelius did, that sex is nothing but 'the rubbing together of two pieces of gut to produce the spasmodic secretion of a little bit of slime' might be a person who, wracked by sexual desire and delight in sexual activity, wished to pour cold water on both, and did it by writing thus. It would be easy to interpret the words as evidence of asceticism, puritanism, celibacy, revulsion at the idea of intimacy; and perhaps be wrong. In short: a sense of context is essential, and Hadot's reading of the ancients par excellence exemplifies it, thereby guarding against the 'dangers of historical psychology applied to ancient texts'.[13]

But the hermeneutical (interpretative) value Hadot finds in exploring the Hellenistic ethical schools with context in mind applies just as much to Augustine's *Confessions*, which he analyses as a carefully constructed theological treatise rather than a factual autobiography, and to Wittgenstein's philosophical intentions, although in this case Wittgenstein was explicit about them, seeing his philosophy as a form of therapy curing other philosophers of the philosophical disease – perplexity – that needlessly arises from misunderstanding the way language works. Hadot's insight relates to the manner of Wittgenstein's writing: his 'mission to bring a radical and definitive peace to metaphysical worry' itself imposes 'a certain literary genre: the work cannot be the exposition of a system, a doctrine, a philosophy in the traditional sense' but rather seeks 'to act little by little on our spirit, like a cure, a medical treatment'.[14]

To think in terms of 'spiritual exercises' when reading the Hellenistic philosophers, Hadot argues, is to perform a gestalt. This is because one no longer interprets them as setting out systematic philosophical views, and therefore the puzzling and sometimes contradictory things they say become explicable. When historians of philosophy assume that the ancients are 'doing philosophy' as it is done today, they invite misunderstanding. In Hadot's view, writing was, for the ancients, a far second best to oral exchanges, by which the chief work of philosophical exploration and teaching was done. The living word, debate, question and answer, challenge and explanation have greater power both probatively and suasively than words fixed on a page, which Hadot describes as no more than an 'echo' of oral exchanges. Moreover, he says, writing philosophical ideas down turns them into formulae, fixed propositions which eventually become dogmas, and when a reader has questions about them, perhaps centuries later, the answers come from herself or other readers, not from the mind that produced the idea and which in oral encounter can be prompted to rephrase or explain the intended meaning.

Hadot has a great deal of support for this theory in the texts of the philosophers themselves. It is clear that Aristotle, the Stoics and the Epicureans were principally engaged in teaching an art of living. The precepts they taught were intended to form the character, and in consequence to structure the actions and responses, of their followers daily throughout life. This was to be a conscious endeavour – thus, a *practice*. Aristotle encouraged the formation of habits embodying the principles, by training oneself in their application; the same can be said of the other schools. There is a world of difference between merely assenting to a proposition and living what it says every day, and what the ancients taught was explicitly aimed at achieving the latter.

There is, however, a risk of throwing the baby out with the bathwater in Hadot's otherwise highly instructive thesis. This is that the philosophers did not produce mere nostrums about what to do and think; they backed their teachings with a case about why one should do those things and think that way. They offered argument-supported theories about how the world is, and how people are, and how both these 'hows' entail the actions and attitudes they enjoin. In fact there is no serious *ethical* theory (consequentialist and deontological *moralities* are different) which does not rest on a basis of theories about the world and human nature, or at the very least about human nature.[15]

A good example is Epicurus on death. He identifies the source of the fear of death as incorrect beliefs about the nature of things – 'The Nature of Things', recall, is the title of Lucretius' poem setting out the Epicurean view: *De Rerum Natura*. Elucidating the nature of things is the work of 'physics', the part of philosophy that deals with the world, requiring a view of epistemology – how we know what we say about the world – and the application of logic in reasoning about it and drawing the relevant inferences to the ethical view which is the enquiry's principal target. On the basis of observation Epicurus takes the world to manifest itself as a wholly material realm in which everything is made of atoms and in which change consists in their rearrangements. There is no ghostly otherworld, no afterlife; if there are gods they are material too and have no interest in or power over the world of human beings. The question of how to live is answered within this framework, and the nature of things is directly relevant to our attitudes and practices within them.

The Epicurean metaphysics is straightforward, though ingenious in the way it overcomes problems for atomism such as those identified by Aristotle.[16] Much more elaborate is the metaphysics of the early Stoics, also materialist but with the added concept of reality as a rational order ('reality is rational' is an assumption of any enquiry; if one did not assume this, there would be little point in investigating it except perhaps to describe some appearances of it, however temporary or pointless, that one happened to observe).

Stoic physics turns on the view that the signature of reality is causality, the capacity to act or be acted upon, and that therefore the only things that exist are material bodies. Matter is the fundamental stuff of the universe, and is indestructible and eternal. Also indestructible and eternal is the rational order of the universe, which the Stoics called *logos*, a word rich in meanings for Greek thought; literally it means 'word' but also 'reason', 'order', 'principle'. *Logos* pervades and organizes the universe, making it go through its regular cycles of change. The Stoics also called the *logos* 'fate' and 'god'. The Roman

Stoics dispensed with detailed metaphysical theories, and transformed the idea of the *logos* into that of 'providence'. This feature of late Stoicism made aspects of it congenial to Christianity. But even Roman Stoics did not think 'providence' was something they could talk to or request favours from, or that would come to their rescue or support them in times of trouble; for this every individual is on his own, and this fact – viz. that we are each responsible for our own ethical fate, for whether we live a life of *ataraxia* or are the playthings of appetite and chance is up to us alone – follows from the nature of the universe as an ordered material realm, with whose rhythms and pulses we are exhorted to align ourselves ('first follow nature') in acquiring the disciplines of self-mastery and *apatheia*.

It is hard to see discussion of the physics, theory of knowledge and logic of the schools as components of a spiritual exercise, whereas it is persuasive to see the ethics underpinned by these views as being so. Hadot thought that the metaphysical and logical aspects were indeed part of the spiritual exercises also, in encouraging a sense of 'membership of the cosmos' that informs one's relationship with all existence. This is unpersuasive because the similarities among the schools' views about the desirability of *ataraxia* are not matched by similarities among the underpinning theories. The Epicureans did not claim that oceanic feelings are part of the aim of companionship in the Garden, and the Stoics' cosmopolitanism was about the equality of human beings, not metaphysical oneness with the universe. There is a nice exegetical point at issue here. The Stoics thought that physics and logic were enquiries separate from philosophy in the sense that philosophy, which is about wisdom (recall that the word literally means 'love of wisdom'), is very particularly wisdom about *how to live*, so these other enquiries were separate though necessary adjuncts to this matter. When they said that studying physics is to study the *logos*, that studying reason is to study the *logos*, and that studying how to live is to study the *logos*, they did not mean to imply that the methods and outcomes would be the same in each case, but rather that rational order is present in the way appropriate to – respectively – material phenomena, reason, and ethical principles, and is discoverable in each case.

By contrast, it is reasonable to surmise that once a disciple has grasped why certain ethical teachings are the right ones for achieving *ataraxia*, the next important stage is rehearsing and practising them and putting them to work consistently, not just summoning them up in situations of challenge but meditating on them daily; in this way educating one's attitudes and responses and forming habits out of them, thereby making them constitutive of oneself. What Hadot identifies as 'exercise' in the teaching of the schools is assuredly this aspect. Contrary to his inclusion of *all* aspects of the schools' thinking under this heading, examination of their theoretical underpinnings was, as the early Stoics themselves claimed, the legitimate province of critical reason; and this has remained true of almost all philosophical thinking at all times.

Another thought relates to the texts containing the teachings of the schools. Hadot's argument that oral dissemination of views was the philosophers' own chief and favoured method is strongly supported by what Plato and others say about this matter. In the *Phaedrus* Plato has Socrates remark, 'You know, Phaedrus, that is the strange thing about writing, which makes it truly correspond to painting. The painter's products stand before us as though they were alive. But if you question them, they maintain a most majestic silence. It is the same with written words. They seem to talk to you as though they were intelligent, but if you ask them anything about what they say from a desire to be instructed they go on telling just the same thing for ever.' Indeed there was a long tradition that Plato's 'real but secret' philosophy was something imparted to disciples in oral discourses only, and never committed to writing, precisely because only the former could genuinely convey truth.

But there is an irony in Plato's *Phaedrus* view, beyond the obvious one that the stricture on writing occurs in a written text. It is that, whereas Plato's form, the dialogue, is intended to capture the back-and-forth of oral debate and development of ideas, in most cases it fails of this purpose; too often Socrates' interlocutors meekly reply 'Yes Socrates' and 'No Socrates' at intervals in what is in fact a treatise disguised as a dialogue. Moreover the point of writing down the arguments – to preserve them, to provide a resource for carrying on discussion of them later and elsewhere – would be defeated if the writing were not carefully enough done to be as clear and full as the author could make them. This suggests that written philosophical texts in antiquity are not a second-best merely, like hasty notes jotted down to record bullet-point ideas. Perhaps the outstanding examples of philosophical texts which cannot, because of the careful art with which they are written, by any stretch be described as second-best statements are the letters of Seneca and Cicero, and Lucretius' *De Rerum Natura*.

There is also the fact that Epictetus himself advised writing one's thoughts down, keeping them nearby, and rereading them frequently as a source both of strength and comfort. The same would apply to the written record of Epictetus' discourses themselves; one can image his disciple Arrian, who kept that record and published it, taking his cue from this remark.

Moreover, Plato is wrong in making his Socrates say that writing says the same thing every time it is read, for meaning is a relationship between text and reader, and different readers may read different things in the same text – or the same reader may find further, deeper, other things in the same text on revisiting it; or a text might set in train a sequence of thoughts for any reader, different trains for different readers. Texts are living things under eyes with responsive life in them.[17]

All this said, Hadot is unquestionably right that the Hellenistic schools were in the business of teaching a way of life – more richly: an art of living – and that adoption of the prescribed way of life demands application. There is a particular reason for this, which is that the required exercises are not just a matter of memorizing ethical prescriptions, but of *becoming a person whose whole being consists in attitudes and responses that accord with them*. It is in this sense that the exercises are 'spiritual'; they are about the person's 'spirit' or character, her existence as a person. The ethical outlook is not an add-on, not one component among others such as mathematical ability, interest in sports or enjoyment of music. Rather it *is* the person. 'In antiquity,' Hadot observes, 'the philosopher regards himself as a philosopher not because he develops a philosophical discourse, but because he lives philosophically.'[18]

A theme which has echoed through the history of reflective minds is captured in this last remark. In the sixteenth century Montaigne's essays, although not written to a formula in order to exercise his ethical commitments, were nevertheless exercises in living philosophically by means of self-examination. In the eighteenth century Lord Chesterfield, writing to his illegitimate son Philip Stanhope, whom he hoped to make a gentleman, in the first of a series of letters that spanned twenty-five years, wrote:

> Your distresses in your journey from Heidelberg to Schaffhausen, your lying upon straw, your black bread, and your broken *berline* [coach], are proper seasonings for the greater fatigues and distresses which you must expect in the course of your travels; and, if one had a mind to moralize, one might call them the samples of the accidents, rubs, and difficulties, which every man meets with in his journey through life. In this journey, the understanding is the *voiture* that must carry you through; and in proportion as that is stronger or weaker, more or less in repair, your journey will be better or worse; though at best you will now and then find some bad roads, and some bad inns. Take care, therefore, to keep that necessary *voiture* in perfect good repair; examine, improve, and strengthen it every day: it is in the power, and ought to be the care, of every man to do it; he that neglects it, deserves to feel, and certainly will feel, the fatal effects of that negligence.[19]

A major example of the Hellenistic schools' influence, and one which bears out Hadot's thesis, is Lord Shaftesbury's *Askemata* (Exercises), private introspective reflections on the Stoic model.[20] In two notebooks discovered after his death in 1713, Shaftesbury transcribed passages from Epictetus and Marcus Aurelius and wrote comments on them. He described the project as 'care of self'. It is of special interest to note the relation between the meditations of the *Askemata* and the theme of his published *Characteristics of Men, Manners, Opinions, Times* (1711) which collect his essays, the chief among them written in the form of letters after the ancient model. In these latter he promoted a sane, moderate outlook of good humour and tolerance, opposing 'enthusiasm' – which meant religious zeal – and defending the use of satire and wit in his criticism of the age's morals.

His outlook is Epicurean in the *Characteristics*. In the *Askemata* he is more of a Stoic, making notes on the affections, nature, providence, ideas about simplicity and the emotions, and the nature of philosophy itself. There is no inconsistency between the public and private thoughts, however; rather, one sees how the enterprise of reflection underwrites the advocacy of a way individuals, and society in general, can comport themselves in the interests of meliorism, taking materials from the best of different schools of thought.

We now reach a point of crucial significance relating to the practices advocated by the Hellenistic schools. In particular, one sees Hadot's Stoics working hard to control, indeed to extirpate, feelings about matters over which they have no control, not least among them things that happen to other people, or that other people do, which plunge those people into misfortune. The discipline to be achieved by a literalist Stoic practice – dispassion, *apatheia* – includes attitudes to others' joys and sorrows. The Stoics steel themselves against the passions as gates through which powerful disturbances of *ataraxia* come, so a successful Stoic would be as proof against sympathy, concern and compassion as he is against love, hate and grief. But this austere indifference is not what either Shaftesbury or Nussbaum regard as making life good, and as noted it presents a problem for the latter in that she recognizes that some of the Stoics' 'apathies' – those relating to such conventional desirables as money and status – are right. So, once again, the task is to distinguish between those externals which can disturb and upset us but which are so valuable that we regard the disturbance as a price worth paying, and those for which we should develop Stoic indifference. This is a question not just for Stoics. Is a principled, generally applicable way of drawing the line between positive and negative externals necessary, or is a subjectively drawn line good enough if the subject can make a case? The latter is the easier task. A general case about the value of the passions requires much more work against what is, figuratively speaking, a brick wall of an observation: that for all the delight and happiness that comes from the emotional dimensions of life – love for one's children, response to natural beauty, pleasure in music – they are also the source of sometimes devastating pain.

A chief problem here relates to the point made in Chapter 9 about the vulnerability of human beings to circumstances and chance, and to the way human nature's innate and acquired propensities (acquired from beginning where almost everyone does, in the midst of normativity) govern them in mainly unconscious ways. The ethical schools urge us to make them conscious and master them. The mastering might take the form of preventing their expression, as with aggression and selfishness, or channelling them in socially acceptable ways, as with appetites for food and sex. Even those like Nussbaum who take it for granted that passionate attachments are central to a good life would agree that mastery is required, not least through education of the sentiments.

The way this enterprise is framed owes much to the way ethical debate started in the Western tradition, as recorded in the writings of Plato and Aristotle. The idea of virtue as an *excellence*, as intimately connected with truth and reason, immediately introduced a restriction in regard to its possibility. Unlike the Stoics who asserted the equality of humankind and the equal citizenship of all in the world – cosmopolitanism – Aristotle's views apply to a particular class in a small community, the polis, and indeed to a sex- and age-restricted segment of that class: mature males who are full citizens. The maturity point relates to the fact that he did not think ethical reflection would make much sense to youths and young men because their experience of life would be insufficient. The charge of 'middle-aged' added to 'middle-class and middle-brow' levelled at Aristotle's thinking, though unfair (and incorrect: his view is not middle-class but aristocratic, not in the lords-and-ladies sense but in the sense of 'best', *aristos*; the class aspect of his view relates to citizenship not social hierarchy), is at least correct in this regard. If that were a correct interpretation of his view, would it be a fault? Consider the Indian schools, who reserve to later stages of life the opportunity to become a sannyasi. But in fact Aristotle did not mean that achievement of *eudaimonia* is an age-dependent ambition, for he recommended youths and young men to emulate those who had acquired habits of practical wisdom and who lived accordingly, thus themselves acquiring those habits and becoming exemplars in their turn. Living according to the dictates of practical wisdom, seeking the middle path, whether by imitation or reflection – though the latter is the aim – generates *eudaimonia* at any age.

Still, the ideal of 'excellence' sets a high bar, and it is notable that Epicureans and Stoics alike place emphasis on the causes of disturbance to *ataraxia* and treat the defences against them as sufficiencies rather than excellences. Recall that the Epicureans classify desires into three groups: 'natural and necessary', 'natural but not necessary' and 'both unnatural and unnecessary'. The third group includes wealth, power and status, and the observation that the quest for them causes anxiety is enough to divert interest away from them if the premise of one's thinking is to avoid or minimize anxiety. The second group, which includes sex and an interest in tasty foodstuffs, is such that indulgence of them is fine if it does not disturb *aponia* and *ataraxia*, which they are less likely to do if moderate. The first group of desires, which includes the basic needs for companionship and healthy sustenance, is easily satisfied. To achieve the sufficiency for *ataraxia* that observance of this implies, withdrawal from public affairs to an actual or figurative garden is advised. It was this withdrawal that provoked some of the chief criticisms from Stoics, who by contrast regarded engagement in affairs of state and society as a duty.

The Stoic conception is accordingly more strenuous. For Stoics, control of the appetites and emotions – and exercise of the virtues of courage, honesty, justice and wisdom – provides the structure to a full engagement in life, including the acquisition of status and wealth, though as 'indifferents' their possession or loss is to have no effect on one's equilibrium. The idea of a life of reason – in the Stoics' case characterized as living according to the *logos* of the universe – is very close to Aristotle's view, but the large difference is that Aristotle's more pragmatic outlook made him recognize the importance of external goods as necessary, alongside internal virtues, for *eudaimonia*.

Stoicism's founder, Zeno, spoke of attaining 'a good flow of life', a harmonious and untroubled existence, and with this the Epicureans and Aristotle agree. By contrast, views to the effect that the passions are important constituents of a good life concede that times of turbulence and pain will occur, but regard them as an acceptable price for what the passions themselves bring – in the way of rich experience, education of the emotions, contribution to others, fulfilment of aspects of oneself. This is Nussbaum's view.

These recapitulations of the schools' chief tenets point to a set of achievements that underlie them. A major one is that they represent the outcome of explicit psychological analysis. The point has often been made that the stories of the Greek myths are rich in psychological insight (as indeed are all mythologies), in symbolically representing archetypes, fears and conflicts, and the obstructions and disappointments faced in life's uneven journey – myths are full of journeys with monsters and mysteries in the way. But the Hellenistic philosophers undertake an explicit examination of human needs and desires and the motivations associated with them. Seeing themselves as therapists for the pain in lives tossed about by chance, uncertainty and the frustrations prompted by false desires, they propose practical solutions, and therefore need to be clear about the problem they seek to solve. This clarity is the work of philosophical analysis, which they provide; it is always worth repeating that they do not offer mere nostrums, but evidence and arguments. A large part of their evidence is derived from scrutiny both of emotions and of the social construction of the desires which inflame or frustrate emotions. This represented a new departure in human thought.

A problem enters, however, with the idea of 'therapy', the medical metaphor used by Epicurus himself in characterizing what he – what in effect all the ethical schools – sought to do. We might well think that the ideal of an ethical education should be to produce intelligent autonomous ethical beings, which entails that responsible ethical teaching cannot be about producing automata. There is a risk in the conception of *habits*, the nature of which is to supersede fresh thought prompted by circumstances in any present moment. The idea of a *training* in a manner of life, and its continual practice, is as explicit in Aristotle as it is implicit in all the schools, as Hadot demonstrates. The process consists in the development of habits of self-management and therefore response. But an objection to this is well expressed in Pater's remark, edited lightly: 'Our *failure* is to form habits: for habit is relative to a stereotyped world, and it is only the roughness of the eye that makes two persons, things, situations, seem alike.'[21] In his introduction to Shaftesbury's *Characteristics*, Lawrence Klein writes, 'The challenge for the adviser, for the philosopher and, indeed, for all who would teach and edify, was how to create and encourage, and not undermine, the autonomy of the subject: philosophy had to create moral agents. (The magisterial approach, by contrast, induced passivity before authority.) The form of *Characteristics* was meant to meet this challenge, to make philosophers of readers and to ensure that, as philosophers, they would be morally intelligent agents in the world.'[22]

A training aimed at enhancing autonomy is a matter different from inculcating habits and responses aligned with fixed rules. Nevertheless it appears evident that, given their principles, the Stoics had to have enhancement of autonomy in view. Nussbaum finds the Epicureans somewhat more culpable in this regard: 'Epicureans place emphasis, here, on the role of the wise teacher who demands the pupil's trust and "confession", and sometimes uses techniques (such as memorisation and repetition) that do not require the pupil's own critical activity.'[23] Epicurus even demanded that pupils come into residence in the Garden and support themselves on their own resources while there. The problem is that an education, still more a training, in the art of life offered by a school 'might *subordinate truth and good reasoning to therapeutic efficacy*' (Nussbaum's emphasis).[24] If so, that would defeat the objective of producing intelligent autonomous ethical agents, and substitute for this a different – and controlling – outlook for the one identified as the source of anxiety.

There is of course an argument available on behalf of the ancient schools: that the substituted outlook, since it produces *ataraxia*, is preferable even on these terms. But this revives yet again the Prozac-in-the-water-supply question. And this in turn adds force to Nussbaum's challenge about making truth less important than the cure. Indeed, that this is a crucial matter is complicated for Nussbaum because of the role she assigns to the passions in the good life, in which truth is already implicated in the emotions requiring therapy. She writes, 'it is not unreasonable to define ethical truth (to some extent at least) in terms of the deepest needs and desires of human beings'.[25] Although she is right to say, immediately afterwards, that 'all ethical theories make the connection between truth and desire', the major theories do so by identifying the connection as one to be cut or limited precisely because *desires* are the source of trouble: the therapy that the ancient philosophers advise is surgery.

This remark does not apply to Aristotle, whose practice was always to begin an enquiry by surveying ordinary opinions (the *doxa*) about the matter in hand, and then to proceed by examination and refinement of them. At no point does he condemn desires for such things as wealth, honour and power; his argument is that they are not ends in themselves but instrumental to the thing which alone is desired for its own sake, *eudaimonia*, and for which none of the instrumental desirables is by itself necessary and certainly not sufficient for the achievement of it. But in this respect he is alone.

One absence from discussion of the Hellenistic schools is a parallel and a contrast between the teachers of ethics and the tradition of the sophists, whose heyday occurred earlier in the period of Greece's independent city states, before the city states became part first of the Macedonian and then the Roman empire. In the term's original meaning, 'sophist' meant an expert in some field (*sophos* means 'skilful', 'clever', 'wise'). By the high classical epoch of the fifth century BCE the word had come to denote something more specific: a professional teacher of the arts of oratory and rhetoric. Public oratory was a prized skill in that period; the culture was still largely oral, and individual reputations turned on performance in public debates. Sophists accordingly made a good living. Socrates and his circle, including Plato, were hostile to the sophists, because in exchange for money they taught the ability to argue for any point of view irrespective of its merits. Their techniques were designed to win arguments, not to discover truth; this was anathema to the philosophers. Plato attacks them in the *Euthydemus*, adding to the pejorative connotation that the word 'sophist' acquired.

But this view of the sophists is not wholly fair. In addition to teaching rhetoric they also taught what an effective public speaker should know, given that eloquence is of no account if one has nothing to be eloquent about. Therefore the sophists also taught history, literature and ideas, much as they might be taught in a school today, as information. The wealth and sophistication of Greek society had led in the fifth century BCE to greater literacy, and there was a desire for education beyond the traditional basics – and a wider interest in philosophical topics and debates. Accordingly the sophists were teachers of more than just rhetoric, and part of what each of them offered was a 'philosophy of life'. This was what drew Socrates' attention, and it was principally the sophists whom he challenged with his questions about what they meant by the concepts they used in ethical debate. As a point of historical interest, Cynicism and Cyrenaicism originated among contemporaries of Socrates; famous sophists like Protagoras, Gorgias and Hippias were his contemporaries also, but unlike Antisthenes and Aristippus they did not leave schools behind them. It is the example of these latter, and of Plato and Aristotle, that is reflected in the development of self-conscious schools of philosophy, formalizing the project of teaching what the sophists in less systematic ways had offered – namely, an art of living.

A thought prompted by these remarks concerns the idea of an art of living just as such, independently of what it is living *for*. Aristotle and the Stoics just assumed that people would live and act in society in external respects as if they were not informed by a philosophy, but with the big difference that they were indeed so informed and therefore living better and more successfully – as measured by their set of values – as a result. Therefore the purposes of their lives in social terms related to the jobs they did and the positions they held. Cynics and Epicureans, however, advocated dropping out of society, radically in the former case and considerably more genteelly in the latter case. The question one might ask a Cynic is: 'What is the point of living at all? Does existing in this minimalist fashion have a point beyond the negative one of repudiating the artificialities and vexations of living the normative life?' One can imagine answers – enjoyment of the simple things, the sunshine, and so forth – but the question always nags as to whether an intelligent being can bear the repetition of a few simple things for an entire life without having to close down or numb many of the points of cognitive entry and exit that make a typical human being.

The Epicureans spoke of conversation and friendship, and these are attractive features of the Garden life. But here too the essentially negative or escapist underpinning of the enterprise raises similar questions. Will the conversations lead to something – discovery, enlightenment, new ideas? This suggests the possibility of ambition, and ambition is one of the 'unnecessary natural' things that in turn constitutes a possible source of anxiety. What about the emotions of friendship? To be a friend is to be concerned about your friend, and this implies taking action when the necessity arises. Sometimes such concerns can be grave, and such actions strenuous and difficult. The ideal immunization of the Garden life from *ataraxia*-disturbing eventualities would have been difficult enough in the good weather of Greece and the relative economic and social simplicities of Hellenistic times, but they would be even harder now without a scaffolding of the right conditions: enough money, a secure place of retirement, an easy regime of responsibilities as a citizen in a world of bills, forms, documents and requirements.

An implication of these remarks is once again that learning from the schools involves a principled degree of modification (and you might say, cherry-picking) of the tenets – or the spirit of the tenets – at issue. One could describe the internal 'garden' of Walter Pater as an attitude, but also as a mental space to which he could resort; at any rate it would provide justification for choices, and a form of unity both to them and the ensuing behaviour, which made sense to him and constituted – at least at times – the elixir of *ataraxia*.

Still, there is one major consideration left out of this chapter's discussion altogether. It is that whichever school one belonged to, it would matter that one's attitudes and actions in respect of *other people* would have to conform to a requirement implicit in the idea of living philosophically – which means, to repeat: living thoughtfully, and therefore living a life good to live; not just for oneself, but in its effects – which is that one could not respect oneself if one's behaviour to others fell below a standard that at least respected their humanity. Racism, sexism and other discriminatory attitudes and practices are predicated on varying degrees of blindness to the humanity in others, and to denial of their right to fair treatment and to be respected – unless they forfeit respect by their actions. For negative attitudes and practices not to take possession of one, one needs to *know* things about others; one needs a capacity to see things from points of view not blinkeredly and monotonically one's own; one needs to have an effectively inclusive sense of the world and the variety it contains.

The idea of a 'care of the self' accordingly refers not just to one's self-regarding duty as an individual to think, to educate oneself, to master oneself, but also one's other-regarding duty as a social being whose choices inevitably affect others. The two considerations are linked, obviously, because one's social responsibilities require enough information about the varieties of human points of view to be able to take them into account. It also requires what Daniel Kahneman calls 'slow thinking', by which he means careful thinking – digging into things, asking questions, not leaping to conclusions or accepting the first bit of putative information that flashes up on some social media platform.[26] Educating one's sensibilities and overcoming ignorance are key aspects in the view taken by Plutarch of how one should form oneself ethically – by modelling oneself on the example of the 'good guest'. In his essay 'The Dinner of the Seven Wise Men' he describes two of the sages on their way to a dinner party discussing the respective duties of a host and a guest.[27] They conclude that a host's duty is to provide food, drink and entertainment, while a guest's duty is to be 'a good conversationalist', that is, someone who is informed, knowledgeable, has intelligent views that he can expound and explain, but who is also a good listener, who is attentive and really hears what his interlocutor says – he does not merely think he understands; not listening properly is a common cause of difficulty in the world, not least in domestic matters – and as a good listener he is able to draw out his interlocutor and discuss, debate, exchange ideas with him, educating and being educated in the process. That is what it is to be a good guest at a dinner party; it is Plutarch's implication that this is what it is to be a good guest at the dinner of life.

In the present state of the world some find it hard to see how anyone could contemplate withdrawing from society in the Cynic way or in a comparable version of the Epicurean way, given that the conditions of anxiety – the threat of environmental disaster, rapid accumulation of new technologies (some of them dangerous), a crowded and contentious world – makes such withdrawal look like a form of surrender and an abnegation of responsibility.[28] For such, 'concern means action'; to know what is at stake and to do nothing is to be worse than a failure as a human being. To live philosophically today, on this view, is to be engaged; it is to be an activist. This is a compelling point of view. It is one that would find formidable resources for the resolve and commitment it needs in Stoicism, although not – by definition – Stoicism's *apatheia*. But even this does not rule out an eclectic borrowing from the Epicurean view about amenity too; a life relentless and grim is likely to be less effective than one which from time to time refreshes itself and keeps its responses of mind and emotion flexible. Periodic retreats to the Garden *of the mind* is one that someone committed to a rational ground for life could applaud consistently with a strenuous view of obligations.

It remains that on the straightforward teaching of Stoicism and Epicureanism, one would either act but take care not to care, or neither act nor care, respectively: that is the logical consequence of any view which says that the goal of ethical endeavour is the internal state of *ataraxia*, and the means to it is detachment from external contingencies or the danger of being stirred emotionally by them. An opposed view would say that concern for the good of the world must be a feature of one's own good – accepting the cost to one's peace of mind.[29]

14. A Life and Its Philosophy

There is legitimate interest in knowing how a dietician eats, how a doctor medicates herself, how a teacher learns. How does a philosopher live? Obviously, individual dieticians, doctors and teachers will have their own theories about how best to act upon what each sees as the dictates of the specialism in question. One dietician might favour a low-carbohydrate diet; another a diet rich in vegetables, fruit, dairy and wholegrains; a third a 'paleo' diet concentrating on the meats, nuts and fruits that a hunter-gatherer lifestyle would yield. Vegetables, fruit and grains are high in carbohydrates, so would not suit the dietician of the first type; dairy and grains require agriculture, so they and most of today's vegetables would not have been available to hunter-gatherers; the diet of these latter would not suit the low-carbohydrate dietician because nuts and fruits are high in carbohydrates; and each of these diets might not suit the vegetarian or vegan because of the presence variously of meat, fish and dairy products. The dizzying array of theory on the subject of what to eat and not eat makes philosophy look in comparison like – so to say – a piece of cake.

In the schools of antiquity there was a marked contrast between those which advocated principles for living fully in society – the Aristotelian and the Stoic – and those which advocated some degree of withdrawal from society – the Cynic and the Epicurean. In the case of Epicureanism the withdrawal is not complete, as with the Cynics, but what they would not do is seek status and wealth given the pains that attend worldly aspiration with its suite of likely disappointments and stresses and its great dependency on external factors. The Stoics, in treating the things shunned by Epicureans as 'indifferents' and not allowing the absence of them – or any success or failure caused by contingencies outside their control – to disturb their *ataraxia*, were thereby justified in seeking and attaining office, and in not disdaining wealth or power when it came their way. An Epicurean would, by choice, always withdraw to a garden; Pater and Wilde in the nineteenth century, as noted in Chapter 5, made a garden of the mind (Pater) or of mind and lifestyle (Wilde).[1]

A striking example of the garden idea is offered by Voltaire in the conclusion to his *Candide*. The eponymous hero and his entourage of Cunégonde, Dr Pangloss and the others end their tumultuous adventures by settling in Constantinople and cultivating a vegetable garden together, still disputing with one another but finding a common solution in the labour of tending their plants. One principal aim Voltaire had in writing *Candide* was to demonstrate the superiority of meliorism over perfectibilism – 'meliorism' is the view that one's aim should be to make things better, and indeed that this is the most practicable aim for human beings given the realities of life, while 'perfectibilism' assumes that perfection is attainable and urges us to strive for it. Voltaire himself made his own Epicurean garden at Château Ferney on the French-Swiss border (chosen so that he could escape to Switzerland if in trouble again with the French authorities), where he spent the last seventeen years of his life, though he died in Paris after returning there to see the staging of his drama *Irène*.[2]

There are attractive elements in the teachings of all the ethical schools, and different elements will attract different people. Most people would therefore rightly do as Cicero and most later thinkers did, namely, be eclectic, even if they have a primary philosophical inclination – as indeed Cicero had; he adhered to the teachings of Plato's Academy in his theory of knowledge, but respected Stoic ethics and agreed with some of its principles. Likewise Seneca, a Stoic, discussed and often approved of Epicurean views in his letters to Lucilius. Thinkers of every stamp in the Renaissance, the Enlightenment and secular modernity have typically followed suit. There is every reason to be eclectic, choosing aspects of different views to construct an outlook for oneself, on two conditions: that one can authentically justify the choices, and that the result is internally consistent. Eclecticism is legitimate because the diversity of individuals makes it unlikely that any one ethical view will, taken in its raw state, suit everyone in the same way, or will speak to everything in an individual's life.

In any case, wisdom (to repeat the point, for it must endlessly be repeated) belongs to everyone, and should be appropriated and put to work wherever one finds it. No single school has a monopoly of wisdom. For this reason one does well to shy away from putting oneself under a label and allowing the '–ism' in question to do one's thinking for one. Accepting an '–ism' label is like donning spectacles that make the world look a particular way, magnifying some things and blocking out others. The Socratic challenge, on the interpretation given here, is to strive to avoid this and instead adopt the stance of intellectual freedom, trying to see clearly, without prejudices, and from different points of view. This is a desideratum which, it is true, is hard to attain; we all come with baggage, and however careful we are in self-examination and in scrutinizing our beliefs, not a few of our prejudices will remain hidden to us, and will influence our choices. But critical self-awareness is part of the duty imposed by addressing Socrates' question; it is among the chief aims of doing so that one seeks liberation from the hidden prisons of prejudice.

In my view the practice of discipleship, of being an epigone of an individual or a devotee of a school, is contrary to the fundamental challenge of philosophy, which is to think for oneself, to examine ideas critically, to see how well the claims of various philosophers stand up to scrutiny, to approach theories and thinkers alike in a spirit of constructive scepticism, and – in taking a position of one's own, learning from and thinking about as much as one can gather of life and ideas as one goes along – to strive to ensure that one's position is as cogent as one can make it, all the while being prepared to modify or abandon it if better arguments and evidence come along. It is distressing to see how many think this or that philosopher has all the answers and that philosophy is basically a matter of applying that philosopher's views. When I was an undergraduate in the 1960s this was the case among a large swathe of philosophy professors who had fallen under the spell of Ludwig Wittgenstein, and spent all their time expounding and interpreting his texts and addressing all philosophical problems in his manner.[3] His texts, with the vatic and oracular air they possess because they consist of short, unsystematic (apart from the *Tractatus Logico-Philosophicus*) observations, edited into their present form by his followers, have just the right degree of

obscurity to make possible an entire industry of speculation, interpretation and adumbration.[4] The same is true of Heidegger, who like
Wittgenstein is too frequently introduced to students as 'the greatest
philosopher of the twentieth century' and his chief work as 'the
greatest philosophical work of the twentieth century' and so on. (If
there is more than one 'greatest' of anything at one and the same
time, the problem is hyperbole.) Remarks like these suggest an obei-
sance of thought, a surrender of critical capacity in favour of
acceptance of the 'greatest' philosopher's principles and assumptions
and a subordinate role as expounder of them.

To say this is not to deny the interest, genius, insight and power of
the ideas that one meets with in the work of great philosophers –
which is why they are *great* philosophers; they open new spaces
within which to think, new perspectives from which to see things.
This applies to practically all the big names of philosophy from the
earliest times. But to be mesmerized by any one of them is to be like
one of the children led away by the Pied Piper of Hamelin. To honour the contribution of interesting philosophers, one should
appropriate the compelling aspects of their thought and make use of
them: for to repeat yet again, wisdom and insight belong to everyone
and should be freely taken and applied – though their originators,
and the influence they have had on one's own thought, must always
be acknowledged.

Obviously enough, not just thinkers but other people generally
influence who we are. When it comes to the tenets of normativity it
is parents, friends, the collective society around us who are the principle conduits through which the great majority of us learn
normativity's desiderata and practices, mostly without being aware
that we are doing so. Teachers can be especially influential, whether
for good or ill. A bad teacher can destroy confidence and direct a
pupil's gaze away from choices that might have been productive for
her. A good teacher is one who inspires a pupil to teach herself – for
that, in the end, is what education is: inspiring pupils and students
to teach themselves, which is what 'learning' really means. Although
there is a quantum of information that has to be downloaded from
a teacher's neck-top computer to the neck-top computers of his

pupils – formulae, dates, techniques for solving equations, mixing chemicals safely, distinguishing pentameter from hexameter verse, and so forth – the real substance of education is what people teach themselves; and to be inspired to do this, and to be shown fruitful ways of doing it, is the gift that a good teacher bestows.[5]

I can name six teachers who inspired me, two at school and four at university. (Here, with due diffidence, I begin a potted 'my life in philosophy' excursus in response to the point that people have a justified curiosity in knowing how a dietician eats, how a doctor medicates herself – and how at least one philosopher has lived qua philosopher.) As regards the schoolteachers it is first relevant to remark that because of my father's work we lived abroad in Africa, mainly in the countries now called Zambia and Malawi, so I had a rather fragmented experience at a variety of schools in various parts of that continent – seven in all – some of them reached and left at the beginnings and ends of school terms after several days' train journey each way, and later by air, crossing the mighty Zambezi River southward to school, northward back to where we lived. The African interior occasionally served as a sump for unsuccessful expatriates in those days, 'those days' being the two decades after the end of the Second World War as the sun was fast setting on the British Empire. As a result some of the people who secured jobs in schools were either not trained teachers or were teachers some of whom, for a variety of more or less entertaining and eyebrow-raising reasons, had ceased to be employable at home in Britain.[6]

No names need be mentioned of the numerous ineffective, or worse, teachers encountered in the course of these adventures. They either taught nothing beyond what was in textbooks we could have read ourselves, or they terrified some youngsters into not asking questions, not challenging, not daring to be curious and sceptical, but instead being conformist and subservient. What a crime. These latter teachers made me bristle, much to the cost of my rear end.[7] Somewhere between being willing to learn and eager to question – though closer to the second – is a healthy place for a learner to be; and we are all learners, always. But it helps also to listen and learn from someone who can show the way.[8]

One of the good schoolmasters was a man called Jim Marshall, who taught English. He was an enthusiast for poetry and Shakespeare, and his delight in both – and the pleasure he took in the possibilities of language – was stirring. Because literature offers many windows into human life, flung open by stories for us to gaze through at experiences, personalities and situations which we might never personally encounter, his classes were the vestibule to revelations; the brilliant sense of possibility felt as one opens a book to its first page has been a lifelong legacy of his classes. Mention of his name makes me see again his curiously shaped head with a tuft of hair protruding backwards from the crown, like the feathers atop a hoopoe.

The other schoolmaster was Peter Williams, a large (*sensu* both tall and fat) man with one arm withered by polio, and a lisp. He had an odorous mongrel dog called Nietzsche and drove an old Mercedes with the gear shift on the steering column, which meant – since he drove one-handed – that he had to change gear by letting go of the steering wheel. Since the gear shift was on the left, and his left arm was the withered one, this involved perilously reaching across and around as fast as possible with his right hand, navigating the obstructions of stomach and steering wheel as he did so. In consequence his trajectory along the roads of the town – where traffic was mercifully light, in those early African days – was a series of violent swerves.

But Peter Williams was a prodigy. He was one of the school's maths masters who had been dragooned into teaching Latin, because he had in fact read classics as an undergraduate but had long before been translated into a maths master by the schools he had escaped to in Africa (he was gay in an era when this was a criminal condition); in schools for indigenous pupils Latin was not on the curriculum. This chance to teach his first love reignited the flames. He was a marvel; with Virgil or Ovid – even Livy – in hand, reading it aloud, his lisp turned the ancient tongue into a magical incantation. As one might expect, he took special relish in texts like Book IX of the *Aeneid*, in which the lovers Nisus and Euryalus die passionately together in their effort to cross the Rutulian lines at night. But he could not and did not resist the need to put it all in context; the history of classical antiquity, the range of its literature, its philosophers and philosophies were spread before us like Yeats' embroidered cloths enwrought with light.

Now, this was heaven to me, because several years before encountering Peter Williams I had already fallen in love with two things here conjoining: philosophy, and the ancient world.

The ancient history and mythology part came about as the result of an incident at my prep school when I was aged eight. One day, while at the cricket nets, an older boy told me to run up to the school to get something for him from his locker. It happened that there had recently been some thieving among the boys at the school, and the headmaster had placed a strict prohibition on any boy looking into any other boy's locker, the crime now to be punishable by expulsion. I reminded the older boy of this serious matter, and he replied that I would get a punch in the head if I didn't do as he asked. This was not my first encounter with the *argumentum ad baculum* – the logical fallacy of enforcing agreement by threats of violence – which in any case was a stock piece of equipment in the parental toolkit of those days; but as he was considerably older, very considerably larger, and possessed of a mean reputation, prudence urged my young legs towards the school house. I was in the very act of rummaging in his locker when a stern voice called my name. Horrors! – caught in the act. Fortunately it was my brother, five years older than I, a great man in the school: a prefect, and Head of Boarders. He had under his arm a book. When I'd explained why I was looking in another boy's locker, he gave me the book, saying, 'This is a present for you from our grandmother. As your punishment you're to memorize the first two pages by tomorrow morning. If you do that successfully I won't report you.'

It was a book about Greek mythology, and by the following morning I could have repeated the entire text by heart, enraptured. It was already a habit, formed early, to find out as much as possible about anything that gripped the interest; later, when first set Shakespeare to read at school (*Henry IV Part I* and *As You Like It*) I was impelled to read *all* the plays, sonnets and long poems, and did so over the course of the following school holiday. The same trigger was pulled by my grandmother's present. Devouring everything discoverable about

Greek mythology and history led to encounters with the names of the philosophers, and the desire to find out about them too.

In our big old colonial bungalow in Ndola on the Copperbelt in Zambia, just a couple of miles from the Congo border and the site of the air crash that killed Dag Hammerskjöld during the Katangese War that raged near us, we had a ten-volume encyclopedia in dimpled red faux-leather which I spent many hours paging through, lying on my stomach on the cool flags of the veranda during school holidays. Many were the discoveries and sensations provided by those volumes. One example is the photograph, like all the other illustrations a blurry picture in sepia tint, of a little corrugated *camion* on the streets of Paris. I was alarmed by the thought that perhaps each country had its own type of motor vehicle which looked strange and out of proportion compared to those I knew, suggesting that other parts of the world might be very different in unexpected ways. Then I remembered that my father (then) drove an Opel and my mother a Volkswagen and her friend Madge a sophisticatedly curvaceous Citroën C7. This was reassuring.

Intriguing, however, were the pictures of handsome busts of Plato and Aristotle, and of the mischievous snub-nosed bust of Socrates. I tried to understand the articles about them in the encyclopedia, and the others mentioned in the course of the articles – Parmenides, Heraclitus, Zeno of Elea, Plotinus, and more. The articles were short and summary, deeply dissatisfying. I wondered what it would be like to read Plato's own words, and longed to try doing so. When I was twelve my mother got me a ticket to the adult section of the library in Ndola, usually a privilege attained at the age of sixteen. The library was an exhilarating melange of books bequeathed by colonial officers who had gone out to Africa to run the empire but promptly died of tropical diseases. They had taken their undergraduate books with them (for an educated person a library is a mezuzah), and their relatives had not wished to ship them back. So there, in astonishing splendour, was the complete works of Plato in the translation by Benjamin Jowett. In delight I took down the first volume, and opened it at the first page of the dialogue called *Charmides*.

The *Charmides* – which is about continence, restraint – starts by recounting Socrates' return from the battle of Potidaea, wanting to know which boy has become the apple of everyone's eye since his departure. He is told that Charmides is the current favourite. He says he wants to see this boy, and he and his friends go to the gymnasium. Socrates is much taken with Charmides' beauty, and asks to have him called over, saying, 'I wish to see whether he has the thing that is greater than physical beauty, and that is: a noble soul.'

Before being aware of doing so I had read the dialogue through, absorbed. If it was accessible to a twelve-year-old it is accessible to anyone. As is characteristic of the early dialogues, the discussion does not reach a conclusion – it is aporetic – but it is illuminating never-theless, and (as people say without fully grasping the significance) it 'makes one think'. I said to myself, on that long-ago afternoon in the depths of Africa, that if these great iconic figures of our culture had dedicated their lives to this endeavour, I would do likewise.

The Jowett Plato was the only philosophical classic available to me at that stage. I read at random in it, being baffled by the *Parmenides* and *Theaetetus*, affected by the argument in the *Phaedo* and *Symposium*, but like the ball in a pinball machine pinging about among the vol-umes without an overall sense of Plato's thinking and its development. This began to be put right by the next bit of good fortune. Not long before encountering Peter Williams I bought, for sixpence at a vil-lage fête one Saturday afternoon, a battered copy of G. H. Lewes' *Biographical History of Philosophy*.[9]

I read this book over and over, until it quite literally fell apart. I have it still, taped up and glued together unusably. Not long afterwards I got hold of a copy of Bertrand Russell's *History of Western Philosophy* and devoured that too, interested in the differences and similarities between Russell and Lewes. These were sometimes considerable; Lewes regarded Auguste Comte, the nineteenth-century French soci-ologist, as a great figure who had brought philosophy to an end with the introduction of 'positive knowledge', at last (in Lewes' view) end-ing the tennis match of competing philosophical views. Russell does not even mention Comte. In Russell the medieval theologians get a lot of space, and Byron is accounted a philosopher of sorts, while Lewes, who regarded the expression 'Christian philosophy' as a contradiction in terms because a religion rests on faith and philosophy on reason, ignored the medievals entirely.

A quantum of good luck attaches to the fact that, apart from Jowett, I had only *histories* of philosophy to slake my interest until I was back in England, where I had access to proper libraries and then the university study of philosophy. This is because I read about philosophy as a great conversation, a tradition of debate, a development of ideas and theories; not in a neat dialectical fashion, though sometimes so, but as a growing, proliferating attempt to make sense of the world and humanity in it, multifaceted in being an interweaving collection of efforts to answer questions about reality, knowledge, truth, reason, concepts of the good, society, and above all – for me as it had been for Socrates and the ancients – how to live. So I did not fall under the spell of any individual thinker. In these histories of philosophy practically the only philosophers mentioned who lived into the twentieth century other than Russell himself were F. H. Bradley and G. E. Moore.

This is where Peter Williams proved so useful. For in addition to enriching and enlivening an existing interest in things classical, I first heard the names of Wittgenstein, Heidegger, Sartre, A. J. Ayer and Gilbert Ryle on his lips. Williams was not especially informative about them – he had not read Ayer's *Language, Truth and Logic*, Sartre's *Nausea*, Ryle's *Concept of Mind* or Wittgenstein's *Philosophical Investigations*, all of them quite recently published (this, remember, was the early 1960s; the respective publication dates of these books were Ayer 1936, Sartre 1938 but in English 1949, Ryle 1949, Wittgenstein 1953), but he had heard of them, and mentioned them as books that had stirred much discussion and were exemplars of current philosophical controversy. I was bursting with curiosity as a result. I found and read *Nausea* and was immediately an existentialist, on the strength both of the novel and the introduction to it, later at first hand on more acquaintance with Kierkegaard, Nietzsche, Sartre, Camus, and writers influenced by these latter. I had read all the others within a few months of beginning undergraduate study. Wittgenstein did not persuade me that the great questions of philosophy were merely misunderstandings about language, and the relentless focus on Wittgenstein of most of the philosophy students and dons I first met was rebarbative.

This focus on Wittgenstein might have had the effect of putting me off philosophy – a result Wittgenstein himself would have approved, since he vigorously discouraged students from continuing with the study of philosophy. But it did not have this effect; the attachment was already too strong. In any case a corrective to what seemed the sterility of the caressing adoration of Wittgenstein's texts was provided by one of the four philosophers I count as *Lebensmenschen* in this regard: T. L. S. Sprigge.

Timothy Sprigge is the only person I know, apart from Peter Singer, who *lived* his philosophical commitments with complete sincerity and intent. He was an Idealist whose views had developed in response to reading Green, Bradley, Royce and McTaggart – the Idealist philosophers, sometimes somewhat inaccurately described as 'British Hegelians' – and also Spinoza and Santayana. He had a large nineteenth-century beard, and was physically rather frail, which gave him the air of a retiring, self-deprecating Old Testament prophet, if such an oxymoron makes sense. The fact that he wore sandals with socks and a small much-used and therefore floppy fedora made him reminiscent of a 1930s alternative-lifestyle Englishman – which is what indeed he was. A vegetarian, irenic in his attitudes, he was relentless in his philosophical questioning, a paradigm of the eternally puzzled, lost but determined enquirer. He had begun his academic career after Cambridge as an editor of the Bentham papers at University College London, in part being driven to the philosophers of *Geist* by what to him seemed the sordidly prosaic and banal worldliness of Bentham's views.

I was never able to sympathize with Sprigge's philosophical commitments, though I greatly admired the sincerity with which he explored them and tried to make a case for them. Frankly, his project was to find a justification for his metaphysical intuitions – for that, in truth, is what he was undogmatically and often rather anxiously trying to do. He was a panpsychist who believed that the universe consists of parcels of experience which between them make a whole, existing in an eternal present; and that this connectedness among all things directs our ethics, of which vegetarianism was for him a

component.[10] Once, when he was visiting me in Oxford, we had dinner with Peter Singer, visiting from Australia on research leave, and
the conversation at that table was part of the prompt for my
becoming – and for several decades remaining – a vegetarian also.

My two main teachers at Oxford were A. J. Ayer and P. F. Strawson, both famous in philosophy, but very different men as personalities
and as philosophers. After I ceased being a student my relationships
with them continued, with Freddie Ayer in friendship, and with
Peter Strawson in the 'former student' role of colleague, for example
when we went together to China to lecture there. On landing in Bei-
jing we were given an enormous welcoming banquet of dozens of
dishes and many long speeches in Mandarin, after which Strawson, as
the senior member of our little party, was called upon to make a
speech in reply. Although unprepared and jet-lagged, he rose and did
so – very gracefully, as was his wont. When he sat down I leaned
across and said, 'That was an exceptionally good speech.' He whis-
pered back, 'Do you mean I usually make bad ones?'

I visited Strawson fortnightly in his rooms in the New Buildings at
Magdalen, my college at Oxford, having sent him an essay in advance
each time. His response to my essays was, on the first several occasions, to say through a cloud of cigarette smoke, 'I find nothing to
disagree with in this.' Frustrated by not getting a fuller response, I
wrote increasingly long and detailed essays, still eliciting the same
response, though now with the occasional alert to the presence of a
typo on (as it might be) page thirty-eight. I reported my frustration
to a fellow student who had worked with Strawson for much longer:
'All he ever says is, "I find nothing to disagree with in this." It's mad-
dening!' My fellow student was amazed. 'Good heavens!' he said.
'That's his highest term of praise!' This is a somewhat self-regarding
anecdote, to be sure, but it has the merit of being true. Heartened by
this, I decided to write about something that bothered me in a key
argument in Strawson's *Individuals*. It is a technical argument which
need not detain us here (for the interested, see this footnote[11]). It elec-
trified Strawson; he was on the edge of his seat, and we talked for
hours, examining the argument and its implications from every
angle. I came away in the darkness of evening exhilarated.

Whereas Peter Strawson was like a precise little bird, pecking carefully at ideas with great courtesy, Freddie Ayer was a different creature. In the seminars he gave in the New College Undercroft he would stalk up and down, smoking furiously and talking very fast, always keen to see where the ideas offered by that day's student presenter might lead us. This indeed was an aspect of his teaching that was especially valuable. I worked with him for several years, regularly meeting him in his rooms in New College and then, when he retired from the Wykeham Chair of Logic and became a Research Fellow at Wolfson College, in his rooms there. He would listen to the exposition of an idea I was developing and say, 'I'm not sure I agree with that, but let's see where it will go!' The conversations were always lively – and, it must be said, nearly always aporetic – but that did not matter; I came away from them full of enthusiasm.

I dined often with Freddie at New College, each occasion a source of anecdote. On one such, another guest was the Bishop of Oxford, with whom Freddie, a vigorous atheist, had a row in the Senior Common Room after dinner, fuelled by the abundant circulation of port and brandy. When I was helping Freddie down the stairs afterwards he stopped, raised his fist to the heavens and shook it, saying, 'And if you do exist, you have a bloody lot to answer for!' On another occasion he said to me (what I am sure he said to others too; it has the polish of a well-rehearsed remark), 'I am a very vain man, but not a conceited one. I am not in the first rank of philosophers, but I am in the very first rank of the second-rate.' If one considers that the first rank of philosophers consists of Plato, Aristotle, Kant and rather few others, this is in fact quite a claim.

To Freddie's biographer Ben Rogers I recounted a striking thing Freddie said to me, which Rogers records in his *A. J. Ayer: A Life*.[12] Freddie said (in more or less these very words; certainly the last nine words of the last sentence are verbatim): 'If you look at my life, it seems as if I have had a glittering career. A scholar at Eton, a scholar at Christ Church and then a Research Student there, a Fellow of Wadham, Grote Professor of the Philosophy of Mind at University College London, Wykeham Professor of Logic at Oxford, given a knighthood, elected a Fellow of the British Academy. But all this time I have expected to feel a tap on my shoulder and hear someone say, "What are you doing here, you dirty little Jew?"'

This shocking remark is revelatory. How few people know that scholars at Eton – known as Collegers or 'tugs', the clever boys there on the foundation – were once looked down upon with contempt by the Oppidans – the boys whose parents pay for them to be there. I do not know what Freddie's sentiments were when at Christ Church and Wadham, though at the former place he once dined with Einstein, who said of him, within his hearing, 'That's a very clever young man', a remark Freddie treasured. But later at New College he had the uneasy feeling that his appointment to the Wykeham Chair was regarded by some in philosophical circles – especially among the Young Turks who were moving philosophy away from traditional concerns in epistemology, to which Freddie had devoted so much attention – as a mistake on the grounds that he was a has-been. The Young Turks were travelling towards the philosophy of language; a picture of Freddie on the front cover of his book *The Problem of Knowledge* (1957) sitting with a terrier on his knee has him looking directly into the camera and the terrier looking off to one side. The joke was that the dog knew where philosophy had gone but Freddie did not.

This was the result of a sustained attack on Freddie's views by the formidable J. L. Austin, who in annual lectures at Oxford – subsequently published as *Sense and Sensibilia*, a typical Oxford joke[13] – tore into Freddie's views on perception and knowledge, using an early book by Freddie which Freddie himself had already come to think inadequate, *The Foundations of Empirical Knowledge* (1940, written in army barracks as he was training to be a Guards officer[14]). Austin died in 1960, and Freddie's reply did not appear until 1967, by which time most people no longer cared much about the argument, which is a pity because Freddie's reply is good.[15]

Because the debate about knowledge – that is: about what we can know, and how we know it, challenged by sceptical considerations about the unreliability of perceptual experience and the fallibility of our reasoning powers – had been made central by Descartes and the subsequent tradition in which Locke, Berkeley, Hume, Russell, Price,

Ayer and others were leading figures, my own major interest in philosophy at that early stage related to this question and the desire to resolve it. I took it that the way the project was framed – that the central task is to answer, indeed if possible to refute, scepticism about our knowledge claims about the world – was right, and devoted my attention to the task in that form. An intensification of this interest resulted from the experience of reading Berkeley as an undergraduate.

The trigger moment was so specific and consequential that I remember it still, vividly. It was a Saturday evening in April 1969, in the spring vacation. I had been in Paris for the earlier part of the vacation, where I had run out of money despite staying in a very cheap hotel near the Pont Neuf on the Left Bank, a steep narrow decrepit building in the rue de Nesle which later became a brothel – as I discovered on trying to book in there again a year or so later. I only succeeded in getting back to England by borrowing from some helpful Sorbonne students who had told me in great detail about their part in the *événements* of the previous year. I was reading Berkeley's *Principles of Human Knowledge* very carefully for a second time, having gone through the text earlier that day. Suddenly I looked up – the ugly orange curtains of the windows of my room were drawn; I gazed unseeingly at them. *My god*, I thought, *he's right!* Fifteen years later I published a book about Berkeley analysing his argument in detail – a much misunderstood and maligned argument, by the way; for although he is wrong overall he is wrong in an interesting way, while at the same time partly right in a respect that is similar to what, in their different ways, Hume, Kant and today's neuropsychologists conclude (in effect, that the world of perceptual experience is a virtual reality). I recognized this part of how he was right on that April evening, though how I framed it is incorrect, thinking that he had shown that the external world – the putative materially real world existing independently of my or any other finite experience of it – does not exist.

I *really* felt the force of this view at that moment, and it precipitated what in colloquial parlance was once known as a 'nervous breakdown' but much more fashionably as an existential *crise*. In truth, it was the occasion rather than the substance of the *crise*, properly speaking, for it is not uncommon at that age – either side of twenty – for people moving from youth into adulthood to find themselves in turbulent waters, and to be tipped into them by something adventitious – the break-up of a relationship, leaving home for university, getting into trouble of some kind, reading philosophy. Except for those struggling with genuine psychosis, a sense of fearing that the world might be unreal is not a belief but a mood – it is not practically possible to *believe* it given the necessity for catching buses and eating breakfast – and the mood, whatever prompts it, is doubtlessly a common experience for many in early adulthood: a mood of disassociation, of being behind a membrane. Anyway, for reasons partly to do with this state of anxiety and partly to do with external events, the next few years were difficult, sunk in a state well-characterized as *angst*. But I found great solace in the study of philosophy, both from the process – the unconsciousness of self that comes from deep absorption in exploring ideas, researching, writing, following lines of enquiry – and then, as I worked at formulating philosophical views and they took more definite shape, a sense of progress. In particular I began to work out some ways of addressing the metaphysical questions that pressed, and of how experience relates to the targets of thought, reference and theory, and to come too to some conclusions about the ethical dimension of being in the world. With these advances a degree of equilibrium returned.[16] Though anecdotal, this account lends support to the thesis that working out a philosophy of life has great benefits for whoever accepts the invitation to do so.

A reading of Dewey and Heidegger, and a grasp of the implications of Wittgenstein's 'private language argument' for the Cartesian tradition in epistemology, are healthy correctives when one is tempted to wonder if a subjectively idealist epistemological solipsism might be true. All three of these thinkers in their different ways rejected the idea assumed by Descartes (and the epistemological tradition of the following three centuries) that the knowledge journey begins with the private data of consciousness – experiences – from which we must work outwards to a world beyond our heads, therefore needing something to guarantee that the *connection* between the contents of consciousness and what putatively lies outside and independently of them is reliable enough, despite what the sceptic says about the vulnerability to challenge of that connection. Descartes invoked the idea of a *good* god whose goodness – entailing that it would not wish us to be deceived – ensures that the connection between our ideas and the external world is safe. Descartes' successors did not accept this solution, and sought, equally unsuccessfully, for a better way. But to start from private inner data to move to certainties about an outer public world proved to be hopelessly difficult. Russell tried repeatedly to achieve the task, from *Our Knowledge of the External World* in 1914 to *Human Knowledge: Its Scope and Limits* in 1948. Dewey with his idea of the participant perspective (pointing out that we are Darwinian organisms in environments, and that this is the objective setting of our getting and applying knowledge), Heidegger with his being-in-the-world (with the world 'ready-to-hand' and 'present-at-hand'), and Wittgenstein's view of private language (which entails that one can only speak of private experiences in a language that is *essentially* public, and which therefore can only be learned and spoken in a public context), all reversed the order: from thinking that we move from inner to outer, they variously assert that the outer is primary.

This is a positive change, and is an effective remedy for any solipsistic anxieties. But it left still unsettled the question both of first-person knowledge and of testimony ('testimony' being *others'* first-person claims), because it left unanswered the sceptical challenge: 'How can you personally be sure, now, on the basis of your current sensory experience and the inferences you are drawing from it, that what you claim to be the case is indeed so?' In challenging someone else's testimony the same question applies as in challenging one's own belief-formation. The point generalizes to memory, to shared bodies of empirically based knowledge, and to the reliability of the various forms of induction that are the standard ways of reasoning about contingent matters past, elsewhere and future. In short, discussion of empiricism in epistemology – whose defence by Russell, Logical Positivists, Ayer and others in the first half of the twentieth century had been vigorous though unsuccessful because of the Cartesian starting point they shared – was still not over for me. My doctoral thesis and my second and third books arose from this problematic.

'Second and third books': there is a brief tale to be told, in passing, about the first book, *An Introduction to Philosophical Logic*, the first edition of which appeared in 1982, almost simultaneously with the completion of my doctorate. This juxtaposition is explained by the fact that while working on the doctorate I found myself in need of a book that conveniently and clearly discussed key concepts that arise in practically all philosophical arenas: truth and truth-bearers, necessity and possibility, analyticity and syntheticity, the a priori and a posteriori, meaning and reference, modality, possible worlds, existence and identity. There appeared to be no such book available. So I set my thesis aside and wrote it. It was an educative process in its own right, and proved successful; right into its third edition it was a resource for students – at Oxford proving especially useful to those taking the 'Logic' (which meant 'general philosophy') paper in Final Schools.[17]

Taking a couple of years out to write this book deferred – helpfully, because deferral meant maturation – the task of completing my thesis. I therefore ran beyond the time limits of the postgraduate grant I had, and began part-time tutoring and part-time journalism to make ends meet. One day Freddie Ayer asked me how I was getting on for money, and I told him. He said nothing, but a couple of days later I had a note from the President of Magdalen asking me to see him. Rather anxiously, not knowing what if anything I might have done wrong, I presented myself to him in the Lodgings. He said – this is again verbatim – 'Professor Ayer thinks we should give you some money. So we will.' That was an Oxford that has, I think, since changed considerably; formal applications and committee debates would now be the least of the requirements for such a thing to be decided. The resources of the Mackinnon Scholarship were diverted to my needs and I was able to finish my thesis without much further delay.

I have a great love for Magdalen. It is a beautiful place. Its handsome cloister, exquisite bell tower ('the most absolute building in Oxford' said King James I), deer park, Addison's Walk, and the water meadows decked with fritillaries in springtime, make it a majestic version of an Epicurean garden. The antiquarian Anthony à Wood called it 'the most noble and rich structure in the learned world . . . as delectable as the banks of Eurotas, shaded with bay-trees, where Apollo himself was wont to walk, and sing his lays'. In James Ingram's *Memorials of the Colleges and Halls of Oxford* Wood is described as praising 'in the highest terms the lofty pinnacles and turrets, the stately towers, the tuneable and melodious bells, the antique buttresses of the cloister, the chapel, the library, the grove and gardens enclosed with an embattled wall'. Existential angst could be left outside those walls, and philosophy found within them.

Afterwards I taught for a decade at St Anne's College, Oxford, of which I still have the honour to be a Supernumerary Fellow, and formed as great an attachment to it, which remains. As is properly the case, I had excellent teachers at St Anne's – namely, my colleagues and even more so my students; for it is a great truth that *docendo disco*, 'I learn by teaching'. Later I taught at Birkbeck College in the University of London, with very different students – mature students, most of whom came to study philosophy in the evenings after a day's work; different, but equally educative and stimulating. Between them my Oxford and Birkbeck students, and more latterly my students at the New College of the Humanities, were great sources of inspiration and instruction, not least for the reason that philosophy is an enterprise of debate, clarification, questioning, exploring, making sense, exchanging ideas, seeing things from different perspectives, being forced to think, to justify one's replies, and to listen. These activities, which lend support to Hadot's point about the primacy of oral exchange as a prime medium of philosophy, are a significant aspect of philosophical study for student and don alike, and they are very good things – for our minds, for the content of our thoughts, and therefore for who we are.

The fourth philosopher with whom a personal encounter made a difference was Michael Dummett. I attended his lectures and seminars, and got to know him personally while serving as a lecturer at New College in Oxford, filling in for Jonathan Glover who was on research leave. Dummett was a Frege scholar who, as a result of his engagement with Frege's philosophy of language, had developed an 'anti-realist' theory of truth and meaning with which I found myself largely in sympathy, though with some significant twists.[18] We got on well, to the extent of my being something of a go-between for him and Colin Haycraft of the publishing house Duckworth, who had been Dummett's publisher until the two of them had a bitter falling-out. Since Colin was a personal friend of mine and my own first major publisher, I was well placed to serve as a conduit, to good effect. Finally, however, my attitude to religion caused a rupture with Dummett, a staunch Catholic, who read something by me on the subject, exploded in rage and wrote a letter in that mood. Dummett's exploding in rage was a fairly frequent occurrence in the experience of colleagues and friends alike, and he typically forgot about it very soon afterwards; but in this case our acquaintance proceeded no further. His powerful mind, which ground away at questions in the philosophies of language and mathematics like one of those massive earth-moving machines in open-cast mines, was impressive, as was its contrast to his childlike, unselfconscious, irritable persona, which could be charming one minute and black as thunder the next.

Other substantial figures in philosophy whom I came to know and like were John Mackie, an Australian philosopher at University College, Oxford, who was full of kindness and helpfulness to students; Hilary Putnam, with whom I spent time in China as well as Europe; Patricia Churchland, whom I first met when she was my guest on a programme I hosted for the BBC World Service on science;[19] Alex Orenstein, a long-standing City University of New York friend; Simon Blackburn, who taught in his distinguished career at both Oxford and Cambridge as well as in the United States; and Dan Dennett, who became a visiting professor at my New College of the Humanities along with Simon Blackburn, Steven Pinker, Rebecca Goldstein, Peter Singer and Richard Dawkins. In the course of my career I shared platforms with W. V. Quine, Donald Davidson and John Searle among others, met Richard Rorty and Martha Nussbaum among others, and encountered much brilliance and talent on the way. One of the most intensely brilliant *scholarly* philosophical minds I ever encountered belonged to Sebastian Gardner, who was for a short time a colleague at Birkbeck. This institution had a number of noted philosophers teaching at it at different times, not least among them Christopher Janaway, David Wiggins and Martin Davies.

A deep interest in physics and cosmology resulted in several important friendships, including Lawrence Krauss of the Origins Institute and Tejinder Virdee of Imperial College and CERN, who hosted me on visits to the Large Hadron Collider. Both also lectured at the New College.

No doubt this list reads like the kind of thing authors put in their Acknowledgements section, and in a significant sense it is. But it is also an indication of interests, of the ideas and thinkers compelling attention, and of those in conversation with whom, whether agreeing or disagreeing with their views, much was learned.

Two enterprises dominated this career. One was – is still – some central problems in epistemology and metaphysics (thus: knowledge and reality). The other was – still is – the exploration of answers to Socrates' question. They are connected, in that the first exploration addresses the nature of inclusive reality, what it is and how we know it; while the second addresses the question of individual life and social reality – this latter being that part of inclusive reality, a narrow sliver of it, which matters most to most people – and how we inhabit and navigate it best, for ourselves and others.

I briefly sketch the main themes of the first enterprise in Appendix 2. They are chiefly of relevance to debates in technical philosophy. The second enterprise – exploring answers, and resources for answers, to Socrates' question – has been carried out in essays and books for a more general readership. The aim in them is to display the many materials available for us as individuals to use in choosing our lives and infusing them with meaning, or at very least making them genuinely worthwhile to live; and to suggest the wide connectedness of ideas, an overall context for thinking and living. The ambition is the same as motivated Shaftesbury; recall the description of the aim of his *Characteristics*, which was 'to make philosophers of readers and to ensure that, as philosophers, they would be morally intelligent agents in the world'. I might take that as an epigraph, save that I would substitute 'ethically' for 'morally'. There is therefore an exhortatory undercurrent; as the words 'at least genuinely worthwhile' imply, the idea that existing merely to pass through the standard hoops of normativity with as little trouble as possible betrays the large potential almost every human being possesses to be and to do much more. This undercurrent itself is prompted by a belief in the meliorability of humankind through education (especially self-education) and reflection; and the urgent need for both education and reflection, given the way that normativity, often unthinkingly, allows abuses – to the planet, to individual rights, and to human possibilities by blunting and wasting them.

The samplings I have thus undertaken of ideas, society, culture, the sciences, arts and humanities, these arenas of human creativity constituting a rich treasury from which anyone can take resources for making good lives, are collected in eight volumes of essays,[20] two volumes on the history of ideas,[21] and an encyclopedia of ideas.[22] They were written in the belief that a palpable difference to how we see and respond to others and the world results not just from *knowing* things – obviously enough – but in taking the step that is beyond and higher than knowing, which is *understanding*, something that happens when, following E. M. Forster's injunction 'Only connect', we make ramifying acquaintance with the landscapes of thought and culture, and reflect on them. Some will discern, in the patterns of things said and experiences reported in the great conversation that humanity has with itself about life and what matters in life, something that will especially catch their attention, triggering an insight, or a hope, or initiating a quest, or posing a question they feel impelled to answer. This is how meanings call out to us, if we are attuned to hearing the call.

Socrates' question comes to have a special significance when one looks up from a work of literature, a volume of philosophical essays, a survey of advances in the natural sciences, a history book; or steps out of a theatre into the night after being transported into intensive witness to other lives and circumstances. In my case the study of philosophy – not just the technical curriculum of logic, metaphysics and epistemology but the other half of philosophy little taught in universities, namely the ethical schools discussed in these pages – was richly supplemented by miscellaneous browsing in second-hand bookshops, for hours on end over years on end, and in spending every available penny on theatre tickets. In those bookshops one of the chief attractions was the essayists, now too neglected: Montaigne, Cowley, Dryden, Addison, Johnson, Hazlitt, Lamb, Leigh Hunt, Thomas De Quincey, Isaac Disraeli, R. L. Stevenson, Augustine Birrell, G. K. Chesterton, and more. Admiration for Hazlitt's writings began early and remains, and prompted a biography of him, *The Quarrel of the Age* (2000), as an illustration of a life not itself normative but full of unblinking observation of normativity.

Fine essayists of more recent times such as George Orwell, Gore Vidal and Joan Didion emerge from this great tradition. It was once the case that the two principal forms of literature were poetry (which included drama) and the essay, with the novel being regarded as an inferior form until the works of Richardson and Fielding made it both more popular and better regarded in the eighteenth century. Periodical fiction in the nineteenth century – Dickens, Trollope, Thackeray – was to that age what the cinema and television later became. But in all cases the opportunity provided readers, as it still does today to audiences in theatres and gazing at screens, to expand their experience vicariously, to witness the human comedy and its drama, and to reflect on it in potentially life-enhancing ways.

But as Aristotle remarked, important as knowledge and understanding are, they are insufficient if never applied: the fruit of *gnosis* must be *praxis*. He also said that the ethical and political are seamlessly connected, because good individual lives for social beings require a setting in a good society. One of the key spheres relating to the possibility of societies in which individuals can make lives for themselves that are their own, is that of human rights and civil liberties. And one of the key elements in ensuring that rights and liberties exist is ensuring that everyone has a voice in the choices made about how society is to be organized, and that the variety of voices and their opinions should be represented and reflected in the consequent arrangements for ensuring that society governs itself in the interests of all. These are matters that require everyone's participation and contribution – 'the price of liberty is eternal vigilance'. Given that the nature of politics even in 'advanced' democracies requires this, the participation in question is not optional if one cares about the possibility of making a life that is one's own, while recognizing both the instrumental and intrinsic value of playing one's part in society's collective endeavours. As Plato remarked, 'Those who take no interest in politics are doomed to live under the rule of unworthy people.' For this reason some philosophers are *engagé*, engaged with the social and political questions of their times. In my case, along with participation in human rights and civil liberties campaigns, the result has been the writing of four books on the issues involved.[23] Those on the principles of democracy have a key theme: that government must transcend politics as far as possible, which it can do on two conditions – that the system of representation for electing representatives to legislatures is genuinely proportional, and that constitutional arrangements are in place to specify the duties and limits on powers of elected and appointed officials. Polities that approximate this tend to be more stable and economically successful than those where government is an extension of highly adversarial politics in which factions compete to get their hands on the levers of power in order thereafter to rule as a one-party government – the situation that obtains in almost all countries with unrepresentative 'first past the post' electoral systems.

To say that government must 'transcend politics' is to insist that government is for all the people, acting in their collective interests, not just for the supporters of one side of a political divide. Politics – political debate and argument, as exploration and discussion of a state's economic management, foreign affairs, social provision and general direction of travel – is important, and has continually to be among the most central features of the public conversation; but once a government is formed, its duty is not to continue politicking but to serve all on the basis of the negotiation – arising from the public political conversation – on which it is formed. In the tenth of the *Federalist Papers* James Madison warned eloquently against 'factionalism' – party politics – and the harm it does to responsible government; he has been proved right a thousandfold in the direction that democracies have taken in places like the US and the UK (and most

'Westminster Model' polities), with their decreasing sensitivity to the diversity and complexity in the popular will.

All the considerations mentioned in these preceding paragraphs bear on the question of meaning and the life worth living. In this connection my own governing impulse could be described as a collage of the principle tenets of the ethical schools and the lessons – some hard-won, not least through folly, as is the human norm – of life itself, in the following way. From Aristotle I take the insistence that we employ the distinguishing feature of being human, namely the possession of reason, with its implication that to enquire, learn and reflect are among the best expressions of what we can be; and that because we are such creatures and have these capacities, we accordingly have a duty to them and to the world upon which and in which we can bring them to bear. From the Epicureans I take the naturalism, the meliorism, the focus on intellectual and social pleasures, above all friendship, and the idea that one can – figuratively – make a garden of one's choices in order to live a life rationally coordinated with one's self-understanding. From the Stoics I take what is needed to confront the more challenging occurrences of loss, grief and disappointment, this being the determination to master oneself as effectively as possible, and to bear as bravely as possible with the inevitabilities and uncontrollable accidents that come at one from without. I admire also the Stoics' sense of commitment and dedication to the tasks they set themselves, and the discipline of their approach to life.

Taken together in this summary way, these commitments doubtless paint a cerebral and somewhat ascetic picture, but the Epicurean aspect leaves wide a gate to affective and aesthetic dimensions whose enjoyment brings colour and stimulation into life. There are few people who can dispense with music, the arts, affection, amusement and the things of nature – sea, countryside, mountains – in the course of life; for those denied them, life is drear. As emotional beings we wither and diminish without them, and as social beings we wither and diminish without personal relationships of value to us. Even the most austerely rational person, if indeed *rational*, would not ignore these dimensions of what makes a life worth living.

But there is more. I respect anyone who, upon *reflection*, accepts normativity's prescriptions for a worthwhile life and *chooses* to live accordingly, the reflection and consequent act of choice being the chief prompts for the respect. But anyone particularly aspirational and ambitious, who would like to contribute, to make a difference, to build or create, to feel that he or she has left a mark, who does not wish to slide through the world semi-anonymously but in some sphere to be *present* by what he or she could do, will say those words: 'But there is more.' This more is the *meaning* of the life of the person in question. For me, the *more* is the desire to make sense of life and the world, and to articulate, with as much clarity and insight as possible, the outcome of the endeavour as a contribution to the conversation humanity has with itself about what that sense is. Pursuing this aim has been the principal desire, and it is what makes life richly meaningful to me. In all the ways of trying to understand the world and ourselves in it – ranging from the sciences to the arts, from the teachings of history to lived experience in the present, all of them component parts of philosophy – the two great connected tasks are: making sense of things, and finding and furthering the good.

When I first encountered the Uzbek philosopher known to the Eurocentric world as Avicenna I liked his remark – on being advised that because he was ill he should not accompany the army of his patron, Rustam Dushmanziyar, on a campaign – 'I prefer a short life with width to a narrow life with length', for he would not stay closeted at home when there was a world to see and learn about. The desire to know, like the urge to create or the philanthropic impulse to help, is profoundly meaningful. Seeking truth yields knowledge of things; seeking the good yields knowledge of what is to be done. They go together, because they aspire to tell us what the universe is, and what matters in it; and because each one of us is the centre of a universe, what matters in our universe – and in the great universe that is the overlapping of all such universes – *really* matters therefore.

Not only does this personal philosophy directly accept the assumptions of the Socratic challenge – that one has to think, and think for oneself – but it captures also the Socratic character of accepting the responsibility to choose. For it turns out that to think is to grasp the implicit choices in seeing things a certain way, and that the very act of existing – existing consciously, as one exists when engaged in deliberate thought – embodies the responsibility to choose, a responsibility all the greater for the absence of anything definitive in the nature of things to push the choice one way rather than another. A surface reading of the dramatic generalizations of existentialism is often met by the thought, so powerfully framed by genetics and neuropsychology, that forms of determinism are at work in our living and choosing, so that there is in fact no such thing as the 'radical freedom' that makes the circumstances of choice purely contingent. But even if this were true, it would be wrong – it would be a surrender – to say, 'Oh well! I'm the creature of forces that will take me where they are going, despite giving me the illusion of being able to do anything about it.' The struggle with or against one's own nature is on the same footing as one's struggle with the world in creating meaning; the struggle, the purpose, the aim, are all constituents of the meaning. Success is not the essence of this as long as the endeavour to attain it is authentic; as the well-known trope has it, it is the journey that counts.

In my own writing and teaching, as one committed by vocation and profession to reflection on the topics discussed in these pages, I have sought to throw windows open onto landscapes of thought and literature, inviting others to wander there, to find in them as much and more as I encountered there – and I encountered bliss there, despite the presence of bitter herbs also, which mortality and the sufferings of humanity, together with one's own losses and mistakes, bring in as seeds on the wind. Shadows might fall across that landscape, and thorns stab the reaching hand, but nevertheless: this is where the good is to be found, and where it might be made to prevail.

Consider Nietzsche's answer to the Schopenhauerian question of why we should live, given the suffering that afflicts life and the inevitability of annihilation at its end, the immorality of all human affairs, and the illusions which trap us in so many ways on all fronts. His answer is: to affirm – to enact – the Dionysian, aesthetic 'YES'.

It is interesting how Schopenhauer, Nietzsche, Kafka and others found a form of pessimism to be either the answer or the starting point for something better than pessimism. None of them starts from optimism. They would say that it must be frustrating for a thinker of a different stamp – a Confucian, say – who is convinced that humans are essentially good and nature essentially beautiful, to look at the degrading evidence all round us. But a starting point in pessimism – even if one never leaves it; and truth be told, Schopenhauer *did* leave it, when he heard music – means that the only way is up. Kafka tried and rejected (in his fiction at least) art, religion and love, the three nostrums one of which is meant to save us; even the endlessly winding corridors of a castle without exits would present, as Sisyphus' rock did, a challenge that Camus argued need not be without meaning. For both Schopenhauer and Nietzsche salvation lies in art, and most specifically in music. Yet there are qualifications to be placed even on the truth they stated. Art – the arts – is indeed a salvation. But so is the tireless work of intellect, discovery, insight and understanding. Aesthetic experience and acts of understanding combine at the point that stands still in the eye of the turning world; in the eye of all its hurricanes.

Stendhal wrote that 'beauty promises happiness'. Those for whom happiness is an emotion rather than a condition of life are apt to think that happiness makes things beautiful. If beauty only *promises* happiness it might fail to keep its promise: thus with a beautiful face, the beauty of the dawn on the day one dies – unless death is welcome. Yet there is healing magic in beauty, all beauty – not just a face, a work of art, a landscape, but a proof in mathematics, an insight in philosophy, a truth however devastating. Some of our problems arise from being too restrictive in our definitions.

What can we know of others, or the past, asks the relativist? I direct her to the passage in Homer where Achilles grieves his Patroclus, walking on the seashore; to the passage in Virgil where Nisus sees Euryalus surrounded by Rutulians, and cries out to offer himself in his place. Who has not felt emotions like these? When Ovid asks '*cetera quis nescit*' ('who does not know the rest?') of what followed when Corinna came to him that sultry afternoon immortalized in his poetry, who does not know the answer? The human theme is by definition common to humanity; across time and culture, age and experience, it is always the foundation from which we can build a shared house. But in it each must have his or her own room in his or her own time – a room with a view: a philosophy of life.

Such is at least one example of a life in philosophy in our times. Some philosophers, especially in the 'Analytic' tradition, specializing in a technical area of the philosophies of language and mind, or the philosophy of science, or logic – even those who specialize in ethics, which in Analytic philosophy is almost wholly restricted to examination of concepts and reasoning used in ethical thought ('meta-ethics') – treat their vocation on a nine-to-five basis, life being largely normative outside office hours.[24] Leading figures among 'Continental' philosophers have a greater tendency to live self-consciously as intellectuals. Between these two ways in which professed philosophers treat the influence of philosophy on their lives there is a large gap all the way to those who produce the popularizing books of cod-philosophical nostrums – which do a disservice because if someone is seeking materials for philosophical reflection, the 'rules for life' and 'what you can learn from (insert famous name)' genres will prove so thin a gruel that it will make them think: 'If this is philosophy then it is useless to me.' A philosophy of life other than the unconsciously imbibed normativity version is not something one can take off a shelf. To take your philosophy off a shelf is to be as passive a recipient as one who unreflectively accepts the values of normativity. Instead, a philosophy of life has to be a product of one's own agency, a philosophy that is one's own so that one's life is one's own: something to be chosen and lived.

15.   Envoi: Preparation

What message is to be taken from this book?

One of the wonders of the human species is how its progress has been the work of a minority, how its normal arrangements depend so much on lack of questioning by so many, so that both the good and the bad achieved in human affairs have been the inspiration of a few in any generation. Likewise with the best products of human genius: all that is salvaged of them, and carried like flickering candles across the floodwaters of time and indifference, is owed to a small band. Like the elect of the Calvinists, the candle-carriers know who they are. Unlike the Calvinists, the candle-carriers always hope to bring others with them to the further side. A truly important rider to these comments is that the invitation to be a candle-carrier is open to everyone – and therein lies the significance of the Socratic Question.

The message derived from discussions of Socrates' question has been carried like candles across those floods, to provide illumination for any who wish to see. It is the simple but deep insistence that the philosophy by which one lives has to be individually and consciously chosen, for to repeat: everyone lives a philosophy, yet the vast majority live a philosophy they are unaware of, which they did not choose for themselves, which was insensibly instilled in them by those they live among and the time and circumstances they live in – an unconscious philosophy which is in control of them rather than the other way round.

If it is conscious and chosen, the philosophy we live by is individual to each of us. We might find ourselves agreeing with many others in our choices and values, and therefore in our way of life, not because we copied those choices but because they have intrinsic merit which we see for ourselves and upon which rational reflection converges, thus generating agreement.

Everything in this book is intended as materials from which each reader can take what is helpful – accepting or rejecting, agreeing or disagreeing, modifying and adapting, but in all cases reflecting before doing any of these things.

A corollary of this message is that philosophy is preparation, and philosophy is living. It is both a preparation for living and living itself, because living is always about the future: the next moment, the next day, the next month, year, decade. It is about the long carpet you unroll ahead of you, consisting of the effects and consequences of every step taken, every choice made. Even 'the present' is the future; it consists of the seconds and minutes, the hour and the day, immediately ahead. To philosophize is to prepare – and to be ever prepared for – this unfolding present and future.

If living is about the future you might ask: 'What use is the past?' The answer is: a great use. It is the reservoir of experiences, lessons, models, to be used in living. The future is created moment by moment by our choices and actions, and these are informed by what we have seen and done; by what we have tried, and practised, and not least by the mistakes we and all others have made if we have learned from them.

But if the past hampers us because it has entangled or damaged us in some way, philosophy is all the more needful. From Spinoza to Freud – indeed, from Socrates to today – bringing thought into clarity has always been recognized as an act of liberation, especially when the thought is confused or obscurely disturbing, like having a sharp stone in one's shoe when one has to run and cannot stop running – which is rather what life is like.

Of course, some of what happens is the unavoidable outcome of choices already made, working through us into the future from the past. Some of the future might already be written into our genes and the way our experiences have shaped us. But some of what is on track to happen because of past choices can be redirected, changed, even avoided, by what we do now; any tomorrow can turn out differently depending on what happens and what we choose in the next minutes or hours of today. But much of the future, the greater part of it, lies open to the real possibility of being chosen by us, different from and better than the futures that a blind unrolling of those carpets would create – blind because in this case our philosophy is not our own, it is others' philosophy that we are trying uncomfortably to live; which makes us insufficiently aware of ourselves, unthinking, often unwilling to make the effort to think and work at identifying the best choices, leading us passively to accept conventional outcomes as inevitabilities, hoping that they will turn out all right.

'Hoping that they will turn out all right' is not philosophy; seeking to make them turn out all right is philosophy.

One's best efforts at self-direction might fail. What is never a failure is the sincere attempt itself. In truth, given that we work with the material we have, which includes our own individual personality and the luggage it carries, extremely few if any of us will get anywhere near perfection. But that is not the point. The greatest failure is to say that because perfection of life and self is unattainable, we should not even try.

One can have a life 'worth living' because the balance of positives in it outweighs the negatives. It will seem particularly worth living if the positives outweigh the negatives by a satisfying margin. The best judge there can be of how satisfying the margin is, is the person living that life. Such a person might have modest requirements when it comes to positives; the positives might be 'the absence of too many pains, vexations or demands' – an Epicurean life. A critic might say that living too minimalist a life is like eating soup with a fork. It sets aside the possibilities inherent in any creature with intelligence to do something more than exist along lines of least resistance merely. So many people fall victim to habits and routines, to circling the same familiar patch of territory because it is safe and undemanding. For such people many days are repetitions of other days, because they want them to be so; they like it that way. All repeated days amount to a single day; add them up, and such people live less than a lifespan, because each repeated day is subtracted from the total. A person who lives creatively – each day bringing new activities, ideas, discoveries, an expansion of the self – lives more than his or her lifetime, because the days of that life have been multiplied, expanded; such a person might live many lifetimes in one. Such a life is more than worthwhile; it is meaningful.

The meaning of a meaningful life is what the person living it – this might be you, the reader of these words – honestly and authentically want it to be, can make it to be, and can make a case for it to be in the face of sceptics who might challenge it on the grounds of how it affects others. The life of normativity belongs in great degree to a large consortium of others; the meaningful life belongs to the person living it. But one thing that belongs absolutely and inalienably to all individuals is the *choice* about who their lives belong to: those others, or themselves. If the latter, it is because they have, or are seeking, their own answers to Socrates' question.

Appendix 1

Three Instances: Stoic Justice, Epicurean Experience, Athens versus Jerusalem

The discussion in Chapters 3 and 4 is about systems of ideas. It enriches our understanding of them to look at examples of how they have been applied in practice. The examples I choose are Stoicism in first-century Rome; Epicureanism in the nineteenth century; and an 'Athens versus Jerusalem' contrast between Enlightenment and Romantic thinking in the views respectively taken by Immanuel Kant and Søren Kierkegaard of the story of Abraham and Isaac in Genesis. As these examples show, '–ism' concepts have an internal complexity that repays closer examination.

Recall that Seneca was the tutor of Nero and then, effectively, prime minister in the first five years of Nero's reign. In the latter role he made extensive efforts to get Nero to adhere to a policy of *clementia*, clemency, in the exercise of justice – not just as a matter of morality but as a principle of positive law. His argument was that clemency should have the status of a verdict, based on the detail of individual cases, showing that a verdict of guilty would be unjust despite what a statement of the bald facts implies. In particular, he argued, clemency should not be equated to a pardon, *venia*, because a pardon implies that a wrong has indeed been done but is being forgiven; neither should it be confused with mercy, *misericordia*, which likewise implies that a wrong has been done, but in remitting the appropriate punishment conflicts with the point of justice.[1]

Seneca represents a tradition in Stoicism, found in Marcus Aurelius likewise, predicated on the idea of the oneness of humanity, of everyone being a citizen of the 'cosmopolis', the world-community, requiring of us that we recognize our kinship with one another and therefore that we treat one another with kindness and compassion – a 'fatherly attitude', as Aurelius put it – and never with anger. The cosmopolitanism of Stoicism stands in sharp contrast to the socially local and hierarchical view of Aristotle.

Another strand in Stoicism is sterner in its adherence to principle. 'Hardline Stoics', as Bauman calls them in his study of crime and punishment in ancient Rome, did not agree with Seneca about justice.[2] They argued that, in the interests of clarity and consistency, the punishment prescribed for a given offence should be imposed just as the law stipulates, with no room for discretion and therefore no place for 'clemency'. Their primary reason was that firmness in the application of laws was in the public interest, *utilitas publica*; all would know what the law required, and none would be treated differently from anyone else. The views of strict Stoics in the senatorial class prevailed until Nero and his successors found that they could no longer tolerate the opposition to their own laxities that this represented.

An instance of this tougher Stoic view is the 'Pedanius case'. Pedanius Secundus was a Roman official who was murdered by one of his domestic slaves.[3] Under a law designed to protect slave-owners, if a slave murdered his or her owner all the slaves in the household at the time of the murder had to be questioned under torture and then put to death, the assumption being that they were all complicit. The only defence a slave could offer was that he had done everything possible to avert the mischief. Pedanius' slaves, numbering around four hundred men, women and children, were therefore collectively put on trial by the Senate. The central question debated was whether the penalty prescribed by the law – torture and death – should be applied, reduced or remitted. The blind Stoic senator Cassius Longinus argued that the prescribed penalty should be applied in full. His principal argument was the *utilitas publica* one – made the more significant in his view by the fact that, whereas family slaves had been more loyal in the past, the enlarged empire had brought a mixture of slaves of diverse backgrounds into Roman homes, and to keep control of them the law must be condign, and seen to be so. 'No doubt innocent people will die,' he said. 'But when a defeated army flogs every tenth man to death, the brave must take their chance with the rest. There is an element of injustice in every major precedent, but the public interest outweighs that of individuals.'[4]

A majority of the Senate voted for Cassius' proposal, and despite mass protests – Nero had to post troops along the route to the place of execution – the sentence was carried out, in all but one respect; there were freedmen among the four hundred, whom the Senate had proposed should be punished along with the rest, but by exile rather than execution (both are forms of capital punishment, but obviously different in severity). Nero vetoed the decree that they should be punished at all, but he did not exercise either *clementia* towards the rest, nor of course *misericordia* – mercy.[5]

In Bauman's view, Nero's clemency to the freedmen but not to the slaves reflects the lingering influence of Seneca's tutorship, in two ways. The first is that he exercised even a modest degree of clemency; the second is that he prudently did not (at this stage of his rule) go against the Senate majority on a matter that touched them nearly – they were, after all, Rome's wealthy and powerful slave-owning class. In the later stages of his career, as the historians Suetonius and Tacitus tell us, Nero manifested no Senecan influence; Suetonius claims that Nero wanted to have some people executed by being thrown to crocodiles.

In his writings on justice Seneca argued as follows:

> The wise man [i.e. the Stoic] should not grant pardon, for it is the remission of a deserved punishment. The wise man does not remit a punishment that he ought to impose. But he may give the same advantages as a pardon in a more honourable way: he may spare, show consideration, rectify. One he will merely reprimand, not inflicting punishment if the wrongdoer's age holds out hopes of reform. Another whose guilt is manifest will be absolved if he was misled or influenced by wine. All this is the work of clemency, not of pardon. Clemency means a free discretion which does not judge according to a formula but according to what is right and fair . . . But it does not fall below the level of what is just, for it assumes that it is doing the most just thing possible.

He also argued that it is better to cure than punish, if one can; and that judges must never act in anger, but always slowly and thoughtfully, taking a long time to reach a decision.[6]

These are wise thoughts. Also wise, but with a markedly different tendency, is the pragmatic and socially oriented view of Cassius Longinus. But this sterner and more consistent Stoicism led, predictably, to a serious rupture between the Stoic senators and Nero, as the latter's behaviour became more erratic and less consistent either with law or the Roman and Stoic sense of virtue. It culminated in the final years of Nero's reign in the trials of a number of Stoic senators charged with involvement in a plot to overthrow him – the 'Pisonian plot'. Seneca and Cassius Longinus were among those sentenced to death, and notably with them Plautius Lateranus, cited by Epictetus as a model Stoic for the following reason. Condemned to death by Nero but not allowed his patrician's right to bid his family farewell and then commit suicide, Plautius was immediately dragged to the place reserved for the execution of slaves and killed there by a man called Statius Proxumus – who was another of the Pisonian conspirators, but Plautius did not expose him. Proxumus was unnerved by having to kill a comrade in these circumstances, and his blow to Plautius' neck was feeble; Epictetus tells us that Plautius flinched only momentarily, and then extended his neck further to ensure that the next blow would be effective, exemplifying Stoic fortitude and the correct attitude to death.

Bauman writes: 'The confrontation with the Stoics came to a head in 66, when Thrasea Paetus [and, it should be added, Rubellius Plautus and Barea Soranus, these with Thrasea being the three "Stoic martyrs" who had all been students of the eminent Stoic teacher Musonius Rufus] and others were tried by the senate. Nero was now attacking the sect itself, not merely individuals whose crimes may have been linked to Stoicism. As Tacitus says, "After butchering so many eminent men, Nero finally planned to extinguish Virtue itself." '[7]

The foregoing shows that, as the outlook widely shared among educated people in the Roman period, Stoicism was not monolithic, but admitted of variations in emphasis. The contrast between the views on justice of Seneca and Cassius demonstrates this well. At the same time, both Seneca and Cassius are manifestly Stoics. The difference between them is not nearly so great as between those who professed the label of Stoic and those who self-described as Epicurean.

No Stoics admired what they saw as the soft and self-indulgent lifestyle of the Epicureans, though some – like Seneca himself – appreciated the wisdom in their teachings.

To turn from this account of Roman Stoicism to modern Epicureanism is to experience what is well described as 'culture shock'. A classic statement of modern Epicureanism, and therefore worth quoting at length, is the concluding essay of Walter Pater's *The Renaissance: Studies in Art and Poetry*, published in 1873. Pater writes:

The service of philosophy, of speculative culture, towards the human spirit is to rouse, to startle it into sharp and eager observation. Every moment some form grows perfect in hand or face; some tone on the hills or the sea is choicer than the rest; some mood of passion or insight or intellectual excitement is irresistibly real and attractive for us – for that moment only. Not the fruit of experience, but experience itself, is the end. A counted number of pulses only is given to us of a variegated, dramatic life. How may we see in them all that is to be seen in them by the finest senses? How shall we pass most swiftly from point to point, and be present always at the focus where the greatest number of vital forces unite in their purest energy?

To burn always with this hard, gemlike flame, to maintain this ecstasy, is success in life. In a sense it might even be said that our failure is to form habits: for, after all, habit is relative to a stereotyped world, and meantime it is only the roughness of the eye that makes any two persons, things, situations, seem alike. While all melts under our feet, we may well catch at any exquisite passion, or any contribution to knowledge that seems by a lifted horizon to set the spirit free for a moment, or any stirring of the senses, strange dyes, strange colours, and curious odours, or work of the artist's hands, or the face of one's friend. Not to discriminate every moment some passionate attitude in those about us, and in the brilliancy of their gifts some tragic dividing of forces on their ways, is, on this short day of frost and sun, to sleep before evening. With this sense of the splendour of our experience and of its awful brevity, gathering all we are into one desperate effort to see and touch, we shall hardly have time to make theories about the things we see and touch . . .

Well! we are all condamnés, as Victor Hugo says: we are all under sentence of death but with a sort of indefinite reprieve – *les hommes sont tous condamnés à mort avec des sursis indéfinis*: we have an interval, and then our place knows us no more. Some spend this interval in listlessness, some in high passions, the wisest, at least among 'the children of the world', in art and song. For our one chance lies in expanding that interval, in getting as many pulsations as possible into a given time. Great passions may give us this quickened sense of life, ecstasy and sorrow of love, the various forms of enthusiastic activity, disinterested or otherwise, which come naturally to many of us. Only be sure that it is passion – that it does yield you this fruit of a quickened, multiplied consciousness. Of this wisdom, the poetic passion, the desire of beauty, the love of art for art's sake, has most: for art comes to you professing frankly to give you nothing but the highest quality to your moments as they pass, and simply for those moments' sake.[8]

This passage provoked great controversy on publication. It served for some – among them Oscar Wilde – as a manifesto of 'aestheticism'; while to others in that high Victorian moment it gave off a putrid smell of decadence, moral corruption, dissolution.[9] Wilde and his lover, 'Bosie' – Lord Alfred Douglas – and their imitators seemed to bear this out. Bosie was certainly one such, but in fact Wilde himself was far more serious than the stereotyping made him out to be. He was a man of genius; and although it is true that he was a performer of aestheticism, he was no mere poseur. He meant it. Nevertheless his *Picture of Dorian Gray* was interpreted as proof of decadence, as was the behaviour of the louche *jeunesse dorée* of the epoch in general.[10]

Pater did not like being associated with 'aestheticism' in this guise, and disliked Wilde accordingly. As a corrective he wrote a novel, *Marius the Epicurean*, to depict someone whose life had moral nobility while nevertheless exemplifying the philosophical impulse that lay at its heart.[11] The novel is set in the Roman Empire in the second century CE, and has Marius serving Marcus Aurelius at one point, though ultimately he decides that even in Aurelius' version there is a coldness about Stoicism, arising from a lack of emotional commitment to what is beautiful in the possibilities of things, including friendship. In the last part of the novel Marius falls in with some Christians, and although he does not himself become a Christian he finds much to like in their sense of fellowship and the security they repose in their beliefs. Commentators on the novel have tried various ways of making sense of this episode, which they find ambiguous; they ask, 'Would Marius have converted to Christianity if he had lived long enough?' It is, however, obvious that by representing Marius as appreciating the behaviour of the Christians he meets, Pater thereby shows that his own Epicurean principles equally admit of moral rectitude. It was his defence against being regarded as a prophet of decadence.

It is also, therefore, a chapter in the long story of efforts to distinguish Epicureanism from the Cyrenaicism its critics identified it with, either through misunderstanding or malice. But Pater and Wilde were far from the only nineteenth-century figures impressed by the life-affirming invitation of Epicureanism, even if they interpreted it differently in their moral outlooks. (Notice the 'ethics-morals' contrast once again at work: ethics relating to character, morals to behaviour.) Marx and Nietzsche are two others; the former described Epicurus as 'the greatest representative of the Greek enlightenment' in rejecting Hegel's dismissive view of him, and the latter admired him for his 'heroic-idyllic' philosophical practice, writing to his friend Peter Gast, 'Where do we want to renew the Garden of Epicurus?'[12]

Nietzsche's attraction to Epicurean ideals of friendship among free spirits in a place apart, the Garden – understood as where one 'lives unnoticed' a modest and retired existence of self-cultivation – was chiefly attractive to him in his middle period. But increasing disaffection with the society around him drove him in his later period to the more outward and activist *Zarathustra* role of prophet: summoning hearers, or at least those capable of understanding his message, to be creators of value, *Übermenschen*, rather than dwelling in bondage to the devalued 'slave-morality' that he saw as the 'enemy of human culture'.[13]

Nietzsche is one kind of philosophical Romantic. Another, but of a very different stamp, is Kierkegaard, who labelled as 'aestheticism' (from its literal meaning, 'of the senses') the condition in which most people linger: egotistical, unsatisfiably engrossed in sensuality, professing an incoherent melange of scepticism and irony, and suffering from boredom to the point of its being an existential affliction. A higher stage of existence than this is the ethical stage, which consists in acceptance of conventional morality applied to all things prudent and right in ordinary affairs. But there is, Kierkegaard says, something higher even than the requirements of ethics, something that might indeed fly in the face of conventional ethical norms. This 'something' is exemplified by Abraham in the Genesis story of God's instruction to Abraham to sacrifice his son Isaac.

The story, located in Genesis 22, begins, 'God did tempt Abraham, and said unto him, Abraham; and he said, Behold, here I am. And he said, Take now thy son, thine only son Isaac, whom thou lovest, and get thee into the land of Moriah, and offer him there for a burnt offering upon one of the mountains which I will tell thee of.' One must remember that Abraham's wife Sarah had been barren, and the couple did not have offspring until Isaac arrived extremely late in their lives. Hagar, one of Sarah's maids, had borne Abraham's son Ishmael, but when God 'opened Sarah's womb' when she was aged ninety and Abraham ninety-nine, they at last had the great blessing they longed for. So God's demand that Abraham sacrifice Isaac was to demand an especially heavy sacrifice indeed – if it is possible for such a sacrifice to admit of degrees in any circumstance.

Abraham cut firewood, saddled his asses, and journeyed three days to Moriah with Isaac and two servants. When they reached the appointed place he left the asses with the servants and he and Isaac, onto whom he loaded the firewood, set off up the mountain. Isaac asked him, 'Where is the lamb for the burnt offering?' and Abraham said, 'My son, God will provide himself a lamb.' When they reached the appointed place Abraham built an altar and laid the firewood, then bound Isaac and placed him on it. 'And Abraham stretched forth his hand, and took the knife to slay his son.' At that moment an angel of the Lord called out to stop him, saying, 'Lay not thine hand upon the lad, neither do thou any thing unto him: for now I know that thou fearest God, seeing thou hast not withheld thy son, thine only son from me.' Abraham then notices a ram caught in a nearby thicket, and sacrifices it instead. God again speaks to Abraham through the angel, saying, 'For because thou hast done this thing, and hast not withheld thy son, thine only son: that in blessing I will bless thee, and in multiplying I will multiply thy seed as the stars of the heaven, and as the sand which is upon the sea shore; and thy seed shall possess the gate of his enemies; and in thy seed shall all the nations of the earth be blessed; because thou has obeyed my voice.'[14]

Consider the sharply contrasting views of Kant and Kierkegaard on this story.

Kant is one of the great figures of the Enlightenment; indeed, he is the source of its definition – in his essay 'What is Enlightenment?' – as enlighten*ment*, the *process* of minds becoming enlightened by freeing themselves from superstition and bondage to absolutist authorities, whether secular or religious, and doing so by the use of reason. Applying reason to the story of Abraham and Isaac, Kant points out that whereas one can be certain that killing one's son is wrong, one cannot be certain that the apparition instructing one to do so is God. He writes: 'It is quite impossible for man to apprehend the infinite by his senses, distinguish it from sensible beings, and *recognize* it as such. But in some cases man can be sure that the voice he hears is *not* God's; for if the voice commands him to do something contrary to the moral law, then no matter how majestic the apparition may be, and no matter how it may seem to surpass the whole of nature, he must consider it an illusion.' In a footnote he adds: 'We can use, as an example, the myth of the sacrifice that Abraham was going to make by butchering and burning his only son at God's command (the poor child, without knowing it, even carried the wood for the fire). Abraham should have replied to this supposedly divine voice: "That I ought not kill my good son is quite certain. But that you, this apparition, are God – of that I am not certain, and never can be, not even if this voice rings down to me from heaven."'[15] What Kant is saying one should say to the voice from the sky would, in our far less polite age, be expressed in two words of one syllable each.

Behind this argument is Kant's conception of the moral law, expressed by the 'categorical imperative' that 'one ought never to act in any way other than according to a maxim which one can at the same time will should become a universal law'. The 'determining ground of the moral will' is the purely formal concept of *lawfulness* as such, which is a concept of reason; independently of the content of the law, it is the formal property of being such that everyone similarly placed recognizes that everyone else must, rationally, obey it. Kant's argument is therefore this: it is wrong to kill one's son. Any rational being can recognize this. If a god existed it would be perfectly rational. Therefore it would not enjoin anyone to kill his son.

Kierkegaard's take on the story is of course completely different.[16] He sees it as an exemplary case of absolute and unquestioning faith in God and obedience to him, which is the 'higher something' that trumps even the ethical rule that you must not kill your son, or indeed anyone. In *Fear and Trembling* Kierkegaard offers different ways of interpreting the story, in one of which Isaac loses his faith in God because of the profoundly unnatural and wicked thing God demanded his father do. But the conclusions Kierkegaard draws from the story are not consistent with each other. One, in line with the idea that there is a duty imposed by faith that is higher than morality, is that 'faith makes it a sacred thing to wish to sacrifice one's son'. But then he also claims that Abraham was completely certain that God would not, in the end, let him sacrifice Isaac: 'All the while he had faith, believing that God would not demand Isaac of him, though ready all the while to sacrifice him, should it be demanded of him. He believed this on the strength of the absurd; for there was no question of human calculation any longer ... Abraham ascended the mountain and whilst the knife already gleamed in his hand he believed – that God would not demand Isaac of him.' And Kierkegaard was emphatic in arguing that this was not *resignation* on Abraham's part, but faith, the genuine article; for resignation is merely a kind of 'wretched lukewarm sloth' whereas faith licenses you to sacrifice your son on God's command.[17]

Kierkegaard dwells at length on the three days' journey to Mount Moriah; on the accumulation of details such as collecting the firewood, saddling the asses, whetting the knife, but especially the three days – nay, three *and a half* days, Kierkegaard insists – so that we can see that Abraham has plenty of time to contemplate the horror of what he is being asked to do. Kierkegaard dramatizes this because he wants faith to be a confrontation with, and the answer to, existential horror, even though the latter is continuous, requiring a constant iteration of one's commitment of faith. The despair, emptiness and boredom to which he says the aesthetic life is doomed is anatomized in the *Either* part of his two-volume *Either/Or* and his *Sickness unto Death*; to it he opposes the idea of a 'leap of faith' (not actually his phrase) as transcending the 'bondage of logic and tyranny of science' by embracing the faith exemplified by Abraham. As one commentator writes, 'By means of the dialectic of "the leap", he attempted to transcend both the aesthetic and the ethical stages. Completely alone, cut off from his fellow-men, the individual realizes his own nothingness as the preliminary condition for embracing the truth of God. Only when man becomes aware of his own non-entity – an experience that is purely subjective and incommunicable – does he recover his real self and stand in the presence of God.'[18]

There is another inconsistency here. Fundamental to the existential dread we face is that there is no criterion by which to choose what to do, Kierkegaard says. And yet the 'horrors' – the emptiness and boredom resultant upon the *Either* life of aestheticism, as Kierkegaard sees it – would seem to indicate that an alternative is rationally motivated thereby. Yet he wants to extol the *irrationality* of the act of faith, 'the leap' – this is the underlying Romantic impulse in his view, because central to Romanticism is the assertion of the superiority of feeling over reason, conceding authority to emotion, intuition and desire. In politics, Romanticism appeals to the tribe, the race, blood, the fatherland, patriotism; we know where that has led. We would not be without Romantic music, art and poetry, certainly; but Romanticism in philosophy raises questions in turning fundamentally on a rejection of the 'bondage of logic', and justifies what by reason's standards is unethical by the claim that 'something higher' justifies it – 'something' vague and mysterious, something expressed by an undefined word. No doubt those who flew aeroplanes into New

York's Twin Towers in 2001 had no less conviction than Abraham on that exact same score. The ultimate problem is that abandoning the *handrail* of logic gives one no better ground for any choice than what one happens to feel like choosing; Kierkegaard could as well have leapt to belief in the existence of pixies and gnomes or Chinese ancestors as to belief in the doctrines of Christianity. Choice without reason is arbitrary, and is therefore not choice at all.

These examples illustrate what happens when one gets down to a more granular level of what is implied by a philosophical outlook, and how it works in practice. The Roman Stoics were consistent Stoics, but unsurprisingly disagreed about some of the practical applications of their principles. That does not impugn Stoicism, but shows how a set of attitudes and doctrines inevitably relates to practical affairs – in effect, as a map stands to a territory. Pater's Epicureanism richly elaborates what can – in his view should – furnish the Garden in the way of experience and its objects; *that* is what pleasure consists in: the best quality of the moments of that experience. This would be Cyrenaicism if the assumption is ignored that the highest enjoyment of art and thought requires knowledge, the acquisition of which is, along with its possession and application, a component of pleasure; and Pater's pleasures are supremely intellectual. One can see how the case extends from the enjoyment to what produces it, and from both to the conclusion about the life worth living: pain and anxiety are excluded because the pleasure created and enjoyed displaces them and gives them no foothold.

The contrast between the commitment that lies at the base of all the Hellenistic schools – namely, that life should have a rational ground – and the abandonment of any pretence to such a ground in the absoluteness of faith, could not be more sharply drawn than in the Kant and Kierkegaard attitudes to the Isaac story. It is an especially interesting contrast because in Kant's case it turns on an idea of the majesty of reason so unassailable that even the most convincing display of deity must be subordinate to it. It offers an answer to one version of the question 'What can provide a handhold, a bannister, something to grip on to, as I try to make sense of things and work things out?' – for *reason* at work is scrutiny, reflection, evidence, consistency, constructive scepticism, and a refusal to accept any proposition which lacks adequate grounds. In debates about the 'ethics of belief' the principle at stake is expressed in the words of the nineteenth-century Cambridge mathematician and philosopher William Clifford: 'It is wrong always, everywhere, and for anyone to believe anything on insufficient evidence.'[19] The other side of the contrast consists in making a virtue not just of believing on insufficient evidence, but in the very face of contrary evidence; for that is the definition of 'faith'.

Appendix 2

A Technical Aside to Chapter 14

In epistemology I reached what seemed to me a satisfactory way of rebutting sceptical challenges to ordinary knowledge-claims made about the world of perceptual experience, by showing how their justification-conditions include general 'covering law' assumptions about the nature and properties of entities and events in that world, assumptions which are also constitutive of shared conditions of meaning for language; and the theory includes an account of the defeasibility of such claims (that is, an explanation of why they fail if they do).[1] Together with an argument to the effect that the justificatory scheme as a whole is coterminous with any putatively alternative scheme which we can recognize *as* a scheme – this because the schemes have at the minimum to be inter-interpretable to be mutually recognizable – the sceptic is met both at the level of individual claims and the level of relativism about schemes.[2]

But this theory is only a beginning, because it shows that the world of ordinary empirical experience is a construct, and leaves the question of its metaphysical underpinnings open. Kant and the contemporary science of neuropsychology are at one in identifying the world of phenomena (the world of ordinary experience) as a projection, a virtual reality. In this respect Berkeley was right too, though his way of putting matters – that things are made of ideas, which only exist in mind, and that therefore things exist only in mind – is rudimentary and limited in comparison to later articulations of the insight, as to both the mechanisms involved and the implications for our conception of reality – indeed especially as regards this latter. Considerable progress has been made in philosophy and psychology on the question of the relevant mechanisms when these are couched in terms of the phenomenal world, where we can talk of the structure and operations of brains, undertaking lesion studies of them and recording real-time blood flow in them by functional magnetic resonance imaging (fMRI), ignoring for fruitful purposes that brains and their structures are phenomena too.

As these remarks suggest, the implications for thinking about reality are a different and larger matter than is involved in the parochial matter of perceptual experience alone. The problem can be put most simply by observing that enquiry into the structure and properties of the physical universe proceeds by investigating the phenomena with ever-increasing sophistication, extending human powers of observation with microscopes (including electron microscopes), telescopes (including radio, X-ray and infrared telescopes), and particle accelerators like the Large Hadron Collider at CERN. Chemistry, biochemistry and biology proceed likewise at more familiar and accessible scales. Mathematics is a powerful tool of description and further inference, especially in fundamental physics and cosmology. The further science reaches beyond the familiar domain of ordinary objects, the more remarkable nature seems. Classical Newtonian science is competent to describe most phenomena at the human and larger scales, but at the quantum level of subatomic phenomena many of the standard intuitions of the classical – the ordinary – scale of experience fail, and the reality described at that level appears strange.

Among the reasons why the quantum realm seems strange might be that theories about it are wrong or have not yet gone quite far enough, or that our classical, ordinary intuitions about things are an artefact of the kind of creature we are – contingent on the scale we occupy in the universe, and in no way even remotely representative of how reality is at its deepest levels, which our fundamental physics more accurately describes. But we and our experience are nevertheless part of the universe, and therefore part of that reality, even if just a sliver of it; so *our* reality is indeed 'real', though not metaphysically fundamental. This point should in fact be uncontroversial, but it raises – more accurately: keeps very much in play – questions about the assumptions and methods employed in trying to get *from* how human cognition organizes experience of a reality tractable to its own scale *to* an understanding of the fundamental nature of reality as such. One way of dramatizing the point (accepting important disanalogies) is to ask: if you were wearing a virtual-reality headset giving you the experience of walking through a forest, could you infer from that experience (seeing trees and bushes, hearing birds chirping) the nature of the wiring, microchip and battery inside the headset? *In a sense* that is the task on which science is embarked. That it is doing so with great success in terms of its applications via technology – aeroplanes, computers, antibiotics – suggests that it is getting a lot right. But questions (such as: is it invariably the case that the successful application of a theory proves the theory right?) remain, prompting further thought about the epistemology and metaphysics involved. I give an informal account of these matters in my *Frontiers of Knowledge* (2021), and a more philosophically technical treatment in *The Metaphysics of Experience*.[3]

Acknowledgements

Though generations of students, colleagues, editors, publishers and friends are too numerous to mention individually – they will know who they are – I should like to single out Joe Palumbo, David Mitchell, Naomi Goulder, Adam Zeman, Simon May, Patrick Markwick-Smith, Mick Gordon, Jane O'Grady, Bill Swainson, Daniel Crewe, Catherine Clarke and John Grayling for special mention. They will know why they are.

Bibliography

Aeschylus, *Oresteia*, trans. E. D. A. Morshead (Project Gutenberg eBook, 2007), http://gutenberg.net.au/ebooks07/0700021h.html.

Aho, Kevin, *Existentialism* (Cambridge: Polity Press, 2020).

Algra, Keimpe, Jonathan Barnes, Jaap Mansfeld and Malcolm Schofield (eds.), *The Cambridge History of Hellenistic Philosophy* (Cambridge: Cambridge University Press, 1999).

Annas, Julia, *The Morality of Happiness* (Oxford: Oxford University Press, 1993).

Arendt, Hannah, *Eichmann in Jerusalem: A Report on the Banality of Evil* (New York: Viking, 1963).

Aristotle, *Nicomachean Ethics*, trans. W. D. Ross (Internet Classic Archive, 2000), http://classics.mit.edu/Aristotle/nicomachaen.html.

Aurelius, Marcus, *Meditations* (Project Gutenberg eBook, 2001), https://www.gutenberg.org/ebooks/2680.

Bailey, Cyril, *Epicurus: The Extant Remains* (Oxford: Clarendon Press, 1926).

Bauman, Richard, *Crime and Punishment in Ancient Rome* (London: Routledge, 1996).

Borges, Jorge Luis, *Collected Fictions* (London: Penguin, 2000).

Bradley, F. H., *Ethical Studies* (Oxford: Oxford University Press, 2nd edn, 1927).

Branham, R. Bracht, and Marie-Odile Goulet-Cazét (eds.), *The Cynics: The Cynic Movement in Antiquity and its Legacy* (Berkeley: University of California Press, 1996).

Brown, Peter, *The Body and Society: Men, Women and Sexual Renunciation in Early Christianity* (New York: Columbia University Press, 1968).

Budin, S. L., and J. M. Turfa (eds.), *Women in Antiquity: Real Women across the Ancient World* (London: Routledge, 2021).

Buss, David (ed.), *The Evolutionary Psychology Handbook* (Hoboken, NJ: Wiley, 2005).

Camus, Albert, *The Myth of Sisyphus* (1942; London: Penguin, 2013).

Chesterfield, Philip Dormer Stanhope, *Letters to His Son* (1774; Project Gutenberg eBook, 2004), https://www.gutenberg.org/ebooks/3361.

Chomsky, Noam, *Knowledge of Language: Its Nature, Origin and Use* (New York: Praeger, 1986).

Cicero, Marcus Tullius, *Tusculan Disputations* (Project Gutenberg eBook, 2005), https://www.gutenberg.org/files/14988/14988-h/14988-h.htm.

———, *De Amicitia*, in *Ethical Writings of Cicero*, trans. Andrew P. Peabody (Boston: Little, Brown and Company, 1887), https://oll.libertyfund.org/title/cicero-on-friendship-de-amicitia.

Clifford, William K., 'The Ethics of Belief', *Contemporary Review* (1877), https://people.brandeis.edu/~teuber/Clifford_ethics.pdf.

Conradi, Peter, *Iris: The Life of Iris Murdoch* (New York: W. W. Norton, 2001).

Cook, David, *Apostasy from Islam: A Historic Perspective* (2006), https://core.ac.uk/download/pdf/10180565.pdf.

Cooper, Anthony Ashley, Third Earl of Shaftesbury, *Characteristics of Men, Manners, Opinions, Times*, ed. Lawrence E. Klein (Cambridge University Press, 2003), http://library.mibckerala.org/lms_frame/eBook/Shaftesbury%20-%20Characteristics%20of%20Men,%20Manners,%20Opinions,%20Times%20(CUP).pdf.

———, *Inquiry Concerning Virtue or Merit* (1711; Early Modern Texts eBook, 2017), https://www.earlymoderntexts.com/assets/pdfs/shaftesbury1711book1.pdf.

Cooper, D. E., *Existentialism: A Reconstruction* (Oxford: Blackwell, 1990).

Cooper, John, *Reason and Emotion: Essays on Ancient Moral Psychology and Ethical Theory* (Princeton: Princeton University Press, 1999).

Cosmides, Leda, and John Tooby, *Evolutionary Psychology: A Primer* (Center for Evolutionary Psychology, University of California Santa Barbara, 1997), https://www.cep.ucsb.edu/primer.html.

Crisp, Roger (ed.), *The Oxford Handbook of the History of Ethics* (Oxford: Oxford University Press, 2013).

Dawkins, Richard, *The Selfish Gene* (Oxford: Oxford University Press, 1976).

Dobbin, Robert (trans.), *The Cynic Philosophers: From Diogenes to Julian* (London: Penguin, 2013).

Dudley, D. R., *A History of Cynicism: From Diogenes to the Sixth Century AD* (Chicago: Ares, 1990).

Eliot, George, *Middlemarch* (1874; London: Penguin Classics, 2003).

Epictetus, *Discourses* (Internet Classics Archive, n.d.), http://classics.mit.edu/Epictetus/discourses.html.

Erasmus, Desiderius, 'Convivium Religiosum' ('The Godly Feast'), in *The Colloquies of Erasmus*, trans. N. Bailey (London: Reeves and Turner, 1878), https://files.libertyfund.org/files/549/0046-01_Bk_SM.pdf.

——, *Ciceronianus* ('The Ciceronian') (1528), trans. Izora Scott (New York: Teachers College, Columbia University, 1908), https://archive.org/details/cu31924027221443.

Flintoff, Everard, 'Pyrrho and India', *Phronesis*, vol. 25, no. 1 (1980).

Foot, Philippa, *Natural Goodness* (Oxford: Oxford University Press, 2001).

Foucault, Michel, *History of Sexuality*, Vol. 1: *An Introduction* (London: Penguin, 1981).

Frankl, Viktor, *Man's Search for Meaning* (1946; London: Rider, 2008).

Frazer, James George, *The Golden Bough* (London: Macmillan, 1906–15).

Freud, Sigmund, *Civilisation and Its Discontents* (London: Penguin Classics, 2002) [originally *Das Unbehagen in der Kultur* (Vienna: Internationaler Psychoanalytischer Verlag Wien, 1930)]

Ganeri, J. (ed.), *The Oxford Handbook of Indian Philosophy* (Oxford: Oxford University Press, 2017).

Giddens, Anthony, *The Constitution of Society: Outline of the Theory of Structuration* (Cambridge: Polity Press, 1984).

Gilbert, Martin, *The Holocaust: A History of the Jews of Europe During the Second World War* (New York: Holt, 1985).

Gilson, Étienne, *History of Christian Philosophy in the Middle Ages* (New York: Random House, 1955).

Glicksburg, Charles I., *Literature and Religion: A Study in Conflict* (Dallas, TX: Southern Methodist University Press, 1960).

Gould, Steven Jay, and Richard Lewontin, 'The Spandrels of San Marco and the Panglossian Paradigm: A Critique of the Adaptationist Programme', *Proceedings of the Royal Society of London B.*, vol. 205 (1979).

Grayling, A. C., *Wittgenstein* (Oxford: Oxford University Press, 1992).

——, *The Quarrel of the Age: The Life and Times of William Hazlitt* (London: Weidenfeld and Nicolson, 2001).

——, *Scepticism and the Possibility of Knowledge* (2007).

——, *Towards the Light* (2007).

——, *Truth, Meaning and Realism* (London: Continuum, 2008).

——, *The Good Book* (London: Bloomsbury, 2011).

——, *The Age of Genius* (London: Bloomsbury, 2016).

——, *Democracy and Its Crisis* (2017), *The Good State* (2020).

——, *The History of Philosophy* (London: Viking, 2019); and see also references in note 4 of the Preface of this book.

——, *The Frontiers of Knowledge* (London: Viking, 2021).

——, *For the Good of the World* (London: Oneworld, 2022).

Hadot, Pierre, *Philosophy as a Way of Life*, trs. Michael Chase, ed. Arnold Davidson (Oxford: Wiley-Blackwell, 1995).

——, *The Inner Citadel: The Meditations of Marcus Aurelius*, trans. Michael Chase (Cambridge, MA: Harvard University Press, 1998).

——, *What Is Ancient Philosophy?*, trans. Michael Chase (Cambridge, MA: Harvard University Press, 2004).

Hagen, Edward H., 'Controversies surrounding Evolutionary Psychology', in David Buss (ed.), *Handbook of Evolutionary Psychology* (Hoboken, NJ: Wiley, 2005).

Hall, David L., and Roger T. Ames, *Thinking Through Confucius* (Albany, NY: State University of New York Press, 1987).

G. W. F. Hegel, *Science of Logic* (1812–16), Vol. 1 (London: Musaicum, 2020).

Heidegger, Martin, *Being and Time* (1927; Oxford: Blackwell, 1962).

Helms, Randel, *Gospel Fictions* (New York: Prometheus Books, 1988).

Herodotus, *Histories*, trans. G. C. Macaulay (Project Gutenberg eBook, 2008), https://www.gutenberg.org/files/2707/2707-h/2707-h.htm.

Hobbes, Thomas, *Leviathan* (1651; Project Gutenberg eBook, 2002), https://www.gutenberg.org/files/3207/3207-h/3207-h.htm.

Hume, David, *Essays, Moral and Political* (1742; London: Grant Richards, 1904), https://archive.org/details/in.ernet.dli.2015.45548.

Huysmans, J. K., *À Rebours* (Paris: 1884).

Jones, H., *The Epicurean Tradition* (London: Duckworth, 1989).

Jung, Carl, *Collected Works* (Princeton, NJ: Princeton University Press, 1957–79).

Kahneman, Daniel, *Thinking Fast and Slow* (London: Penguin, 2011).

Kant, Immanuel, *Critique of Pure Reason*, trans. P. Guyer and A. Wood (Cambridge: Cambridge University Press, 1999).

——, *Groundwork of the Metaphysics of Morals* (1785), trans. Mary Gregor (Cambridge: Cambridge University Press, 1997), https://cpb-us-w2.wpmucdn.com/blog.nus.edu.sg/dist/c/1868/files/2012/12/Kant-Groundwork-ngopby.pdf.

——, *The Critique of Practical Reason* (1786; Project Gutenberg eBook, 2004), https://www.gutenberg.org/ebooks/5683.

——, *The Conflict of the Faculties* (1798), trans. Mary Gregor (New York: Abaris, 1979), http://la.utexas.edu/users/hcleaver/330T/350kPEEKant ConflictFacNarrow.pdf.

Kierkegaard, Søren, *Fear and Trembling*, in *Selections from the Writings of Kierkegaard*, ed. L. M. Hollander (Austin, TX: University of Texas, 1912), http://www.sophia-project.org/uploads/1/3/9/5/13955288/kierke gaard_fear.pdf.

Laërtius, Diogenes, *Lives of the Eminent Philosophers*, trans. Pamela Mensch (Oxford: Oxford University Press, 2018).

Le Guin, Ursula, 'The Ones Who Walk Away from Omelas', in *The Wind's Twelve Quarters* (New York: Harper and Row, 1975).

Leibniz, G. W., *Theodicy*, trans. E. M. Huggard (Project Gutenberg eBook, 2005), https://www.gutenberg.org/files/17147/17147-h/17147-h.htm.

Levi, Primo, *If This Is a Man* (1947; London: Abacus, 2014).

Lewes, G. H., *A Biographical History of Philosophy* (1845; Cambridge University Press, 2013).

Li, Chenyang, 'Chinese Philosophy', in William Edelglass and Jay L. Garfield (eds.), *The Oxford Handbook of World Philosophy* (Oxford: Oxford University Press, 2011).

Libet, Benjamin, et al., 'Time of conscious intention to act in relation to onset of cerebral activity (readiness-potential) – The unconscious initiation of a freely voluntary act', *Brain*, vol. 106, no. 3 (1983), pp. 623–42.

Locke, John, *Essay Concerning Human Understanding* (1691; Project Gutenberg eBook, 2004), https://www.gutenberg.org/files/10615/10615-h/10615-h.htm.

Long, Anthony A., *Hellenistic Philosophy: Stoics, Epicureans, Sceptics* (Berkeley: University of California Press, 1971).

——, and David Sedley, *The Hellenistic Philosophers* (Cambridge: Cambridge University Press, 1987).

Longerich, Peter, *Heinrich Himmler: A Life* (Oxford: Oxford University Press, 2012).

Lucretius, *De Rerum Natura*, trans. W. H. D. Rouse, rev. Martin F. Smith, Loeb Classical Library 181 (Cambridge, MA: Harvard University Press, 1924).

Luscombe, D. E., *Medieval Thought* (*History of Western Philosophy*): Vol. 2 (Oxford: Oxford University Press, 1997).

Lynd, Robert, 'On Not Being a Philosopher', reprinted in W. E. Williams (ed.), *A Book of English Essays* (London: Penguin, 1942).

Maimonides, Moses, *A Guide for the Perplexed*, trans. M. Friedlander (London: Routledge and Kegan Paul, 1904), https://ia902705.us.archive.org/22/items/guideforperplexe00maimiala/guideforperplexe00maimiala.pdf.

Mandeville, Bernard, *The Fable of the Bees* (1714; Early Modern Texts eBook, 2017), https://www.earlymoderntexts.com/assets/pdfs/mandeville1732_1.pdf.

Manetti, Giannozzo, *On the Excellency and Dignity of Man* (n.p., 1453).

Mann, Thomas, *The Magic Mountain* (1924), trans. H. T. Lowe-Porter (London: Random House, 1996).

Marcuse, Herbert, *Reason and Revolution* (New York: Oxford University Press, 1941).

May, Simon, *Love: A History* (London: Yale University Press, 2011).

Mill, John Stuart, *Utilitarianism* (1732; Early Modern Texts eBook, 2017), https://www.earlymoderntexts.com/assets/pdfs/mill1863.pdf.

Mitsis, P., *Epicurus' Ethical Theory* (Ithaca, NY: Cornell University Press, 1988).

Moeller, Hans-Georg, *The Philosophy of the Daodejing* (New York: Columbia University Press, 2006).

Montaigne, Michel de, *Essays*, trans. M. A. Screech (London: Penguin Classics, 2004).

Moore, G. E., *Principia Ethica* (Cambridge: Cambridge University Press, 1903).

Nagel, Thomas, *Mortal Questions* (Cambridge: Cambridge University Press, 1991).

Nietzsche, Friedrich, *Human, All Too Human* (1878–80; London: Penguin, 1994).

——, *Thus Spake Zarathustra* (London: Wordsworth World Classics, 1997).

——, 'Maxims and Arrows No. 12', *Twilight of the Idols* (1888), trans. Anthony M. Ludovici, https://www.gutenberg.org/files/52263/52263-h/52263-h.htm.

——, *Gay Science*, Book VI (New York: Random House, 1974).

——, *Ecce Homo*, 'The Birth of Tragedy'.

——, *Selected Letters*, ed. and trans. Christopher Middleton (New York: Hackett, 1997).

Nietzsche Circle (ed.), *Nietzsche and Epicureanism* (The Agonist, 2018).

Nixey, Christine, *The Darkening Age: The Christian Destruction of the Classical World* (London: Picador, 2017).

Nussbaum, Martha, *The Fragility of Goodness* (Cambridge: Cambridge University Press, 1986).

——, *The Therapy of Desire* (Princeton, NJ: Princeton University Press, 1994).

Nyiszli, Miklos, *Auschwitz: A Doctor's Account* (1946; London: Penguin, 2012).

O'Connor, Timothy, and Christopher Franklin, 'Free Will', *Stanford Encyclopedia of Philosophy*, https://plato.stanford.edu/entries/freewill/.

Olafson, F., *Principles and Persons: An Ethical Interpretation of Existentialism* (Baltimore: Johns Hopkins University Press, 1967).

Ovid, *Amores* 1.5, https://www.gutenberg.org/files/47676/47676-h/47676-h.htm#link2H_4_0006.

Paley, William, *Natural Theology; or, Evidences of the Existence and Attributes of the Deity* (1802; Early Modern Texts eBook, 2017), https://www.earlymoderntexts.com/assets/pdfs/paley1802_3.pdf.

Pangle, Lorraine Smith, *Virtue Is Knowledge: The Moral Foundations of Socratic Political Philosophy* (Chicago: University of Chicago Press, 2014).

Pascal, *Pensées*, https://www.gutenberg.org/files/18269/18269-h/18269-h.htm.

Pater, Walter, *The Renaissance* (1873; Project Gutenberg eBook, 2000), https://www.gutenberg.org/files/2398/2398-h/2398-h.htm.

——, *Marius the Epicurean: His Sensations and Ideas* (n.p., 1885), http://www.ajdrake.com/etexts/texts/Pater/Works/mar_85_2.pdf.

Pearson, Lionel, *Popular Ethics in Ancient Greece* (Stanford: Stanford University Press, 1962).

Perloff, Marjorie, *Wittgenstein's Ladder* (Chicago: University of Chicago Press, 1996).

Pico della Mirandola, Giovanni, *Oration on the Dignity of Man* (1487), trans. A. Robert Caponigri (Chicago: Henry Regnery, 1956), http://www.andallthat.co.uk/uploads/2/3/8/9/2389220/pico_-_oration_on_the_dignity_of_man.pdf.

Pinker, Steven, *The Blank Slate* (New York: Viking, 2002).

——, *The Better Angels of our Nature* (New York: Viking, 2013).

——, *Enlightenment Now* (New York: Viking, 2019).

Plato, *Apology, Gorgias, Protagoras, Meno, Laws, Phaedo, Republic, Phaedrus*, trans. Floyer Sydeham and Thomas Taylor (London: Thomas Taylor, 1804), https://archive.org/details/PlatoThomasTaylor.

Plotkin, Henry, *Evolutionary Thought in Psychology: A Brief History* (Oxford: Blackwell, 2004).

Plutarch, *Essays* (London: Penguin, 1992).

Polderman, Tinca J. C., et al., 'Meta-analysis of the heritability of human traits based on fifty years of twin studies', *Nature Genetics*, vol. 47 (2015), pp. 702–9.

Posner, Richard, *Sex and Reason* (Cambridge, MA: Harvard University Press, 1992).

Powys, Llewelyn, *Skin for Skin* (1925), *Glory of Life* (1934), *Love and Death* (1939); Powys' works are all out of print, requiring second-hand book searches; but *Glory of Life* can be found at https://archive.org/details/in.ernet.dli.2015.86872.

Reeve, C., *Nicomachean Ethics* (Indianapolis: Hackett, 2014).

Rist, John, *Stoic Philosophy* (Cambridge: Cambridge University Press, 1969).

——, *Epicurus: An Introduction* (Cambridge: Cambridge University Press, 1972).

—— (ed.), *The Stoics* (Berkeley: University of California Press, 1978).

Robinson, Geoffrey, *The Killing Season* (Princeton, NJ: Princeton University Press, 2018).

Rogers, Ben, *AJ Ayer: A Life* (London: Vintage, 2000).

Russell, Bertrand, *The Conquest of Happiness* (New York: Liveright, 1930).

Saint-Exupéry, Antoine de, *The Wisdom of the Sands* (New York: Harcourt-Brace, 1950).

Samkange, Stanlake, *Hunhuism or Ubuntuism: A Zimbabwe Indigenous Political Philosophy* (London: Graham, 1980).

Sartre, Jean-Paul, *Existentialism is a Humanism* (Paris: Gallimard, 1946; published in English, 1948).

——, *Anti-Semite and Jew* (New York: Shocken Books, 1948).

Schopenhauer, Arthur, *Parerga and Paralipomena*, 2 vols. (Cambridge: Cambridge University Press, 2015).

Seneca, *Epistulae Morales ad Lucilium* (aka *Moral Essays* and *Letters to Lucilius*), trans. Richard Mott Gummere, Loeb Classical Library (1917–25), https://topostext.org/work/736.

——, *Moral Essays*, Volume I: *De Providentia. De Constantia. De Ira. De Clementia*, trans. John W. Basore, Loeb Classical Library 214 (Cambridge, MA: Harvard University Press, 1928).

Sharples, R. W., *Stoics, Epicureans and Sceptics: An Introduction to Hellenistic Philosophy* (London: Routledge, 1996).

Snell, Bruno, *The Discovery of the Mind: The Greek Origins of European Thought* (New York: Harper, 1960).

Sprigge, T. L. S., *The Vindication of Absolute Idealism* (Edinburgh: Edinburgh University Press, 1983).

Steinvorth, Ulrich, 'Hegel's *Sittlichkeit*', in *A Secular Absolute* (London: Palgrave Macmillan, 2020), pp. 73–126, https://link.springer.com/chapter/10.1007/978-3-030-35036-9_3.

Stendhal, *On Love* (1822; Project Gutenberg eBook, 2016), https://www.gutenberg.org/ebooks/53720.

Swift, Jonathan, *A Tale of a Tub* (1704; Project Gutenberg eBook, 2003), https://www.gutenberg.org/ebooks/4737.

Tawney, R. H., *Religion and the Rise of Capitalism* (London: John Murray, 1926).

Taylor, Gabriele, *Pride, Shame and Guilt* (Oxford: Oxford University Press, 1985).

——, *Deadly Vices* (Oxford: Oxford University Press, 2006).

Tiwari, Kedar Nath, *Classical Indian Ethical Thought* (Delhi: Motilal Banarsidass Publisher, 1980).

Tolstoy, *Anna Karenina*, trans. Richard Pevear and Larissa Volokhonsky (London: Penguin Classics, 2000).

Ure, Michael, and Michael Sharpe, *Philosophy as a Way of Life* (London: Bloomsbury, 2020).

Vlastos, Gregory, *Platonic Studies: Second Edition* (Princeton, NJ: Princeton University Press, 1981).

Warnock, M., *Existentialism* (Oxford: Oxford University Press, 1970).

Weber, Max, *The Protestant Ethic and the Spirit of Capitalism* (Oxford: Oxford University Press, 2011; from rev. edn., 1920).

Wilde, Oscar, *The Picture of Dorian Gray* (1890; London: Penguin, 2003).

Williams, Bernard, *Moral Luck* (Cambridge: Cambridge University Press, 1981).

Wilson, Catherine, *Epicureanism at the Origins of Modernity* (Oxford: Oxford University Press, 2008).

Wittgenstein, Ludwig, *Tractatus Logico-Philosophicus* (London, 1921).

Xenophon, *Memorabilia*, trans. Amy L. Bonnette (Ithaca and London: Cornell University Press, 1994), https://philocyclevl.files.wordpress.com/2016/09/xenophon-memorabilia-or-the-recollections-cornell.pdf.

Notes

Preface

1 People are not of course wholly passive; that the relation of individual agency and social phenomena is reciprocal is evidenced by the way significant individuals or influential groups can prompt palpable changes in society's patterns of behaviour and attitudes. Something very like 'structuration' in Anthony Giddens' sense explains this: Anthony Giddens (1984). A view which emphasizes the degree to which society is agent-like in *imposing* its norms is taken by Foucault in advancing his 'repressive hypothesis'; see his (1981).

2 A. C. Grayling (2019).

3 One could wax polemical on a general point of which this is an instance; how the academic professionalization of the humanities divided them up, put them into silos, invented rubrics for them ('Answer three questions, at least one from Section A'), borrowed ideas from the sciences (thinking and scholarship became 'research', mainly focused upon minutiae, its fruits career-influencing publication in journals) – one could, alas, go on.

4 My efforts in this respect are to be found in the following: Books: *The Future of Moral Values* (Weidenfeld, 1997); *What Is Good?* (Weidenfeld, 2003); *Among the Dead Cities* (Bloomsbury, 2006); *The Choice of Hercules* (Weidenfeld, 2007); *The Good Book* (Bloomsbury, 2011); *Friendship* (Yale, 2013); *The God Argument* (Bloomsbury, 2013); *War: An Enquiry* (Yale, 2017); *Democracy and Its Crisis* (Oneworld, 2018); *The Good of the World* (Oneworld, 2022). Essay collections: *The Meaning of Things* (Weidenfeld, 2001); *The Reason of Things* (Weidenfeld, 2002); *The Mystery of Things* (Weidenfeld, 2004); *The Heart of Things* (Weidenfeld, 2005); *The Form of Things* (Weidenfeld, 2006); *Against All Gods* (Oberon, 2007); *To Set Prometheus Free* (Oberon, 2009); *Ideas That Matter* (Bloomsbury, 2009); *Liberty in the Age of Terror* (Bloomsbury, 2009); *Thinking of Answers* (Bloomsbury,

2010); *The Challenge of Things* (Bloomsbury, 2015); (as editor with Andrew Copson) *Humanism* (Blackwell, 2015). Some of these *discuss* ethical ideas, some of them *apply* ethical ideas to problems in our world. Either way, they all involve the inescapable and ultimate question of value.

5 '*La morale? Cela t'intéresse? Eh bien, il nous semble, qu'il faudrait chercher la morale non dans la vertu, c'est-à-dire dans la raison, la discipline, les bonnes mœurs, l'honnêteté, mais plutôt dans le contraire, je veux dire dans le péché, en s'abandonnant au danger, à ce qui est nuisible, à ce qui nous consume. Il nous semble qu'il est plus moral de se perdre et même de se laisser dépérir, que de se conserver. Les grands moralistes n'étaient point des vertueux, mais des aventuriers dans le mal, des vicieux, des grands pécheurs . . .*' Thomas Mann (1996), pp. 338–9.

Introduction

1 Herodotus, *Histories*, trans. G. C. Macaulay (London and New York: Macmillan, 1890), https://www.gutenberg.org/files/2707/2707-h/2707-h.htm.

PART I

Chapter 1: The Question

1 Goya, *I Am Still Learning* (1826), https://www.museodelprado.es/en/the-collection/art-work/i-am-still-learning/foc1615c-8c5f-4e80-b7bc-702ec9f4d2f3.

2 Robert Lynd (1942), pp. 279–84.

3 See e.g. Llewelyn Powys, *Skin for Skin* (1925); *Glory of Life* (1934); *Love and Death* (1939).

4 Quoted in S. L. Budin and J. M. Turfa (eds.) (2021).

5 Ovid, *Amores* 1.5, https://www.gutenberg.org/files/47676/47676-h/47676-h.htm#link2H_4_0006.

Chapter 2: 'We' and Human Nature

1 A. C. Grayling (2021), Pt III, Ch. 4, 'The Mind and the Self', pp. 320–35.

2 An overview of the fascinating array of twins studies is Tinca J. C. Polderman et al. (2015), pp. 702–9. A well-known example is the study by

Benjamin Libet and colleagues purporting to establish that 'brains decide before "we" do': Benjamin Libet et al. (1983), pp. 623–42.

3 An excellent overview of the free-will debate, and a comprehensive bibliography, is provided by Timothy O'Connor and Christopher Franklin, 'Free Will', *Stanford Encyclopedia of Philosophy*, https://plato.stanford.edu/entries/freewill/.

4 Kant, *Critique of Pure Reason*. For a summary, see Grayling (2019), pp. 256–7.

5 See e.g. 'The Müller-Lyer Illusion', https://www.illusionsindex.org/ir/mueller-lyer; I. C. McManus et al., '*Science in the Making: Right Hand, Left Hand*: II: The duck–rabbit figure', *Laterality*, vol. 15, no. 1–2 (2010), p. 166; Peter Brugger and Susanne Brugger, 'The Easter Bunny in October: Is it disguised as a duck?', *Perceptual and Motor Skills*, vol. 76, no. 2 (1993), pp. 577–8; 'The Monkey Business Illusion', https://www.youtube.com/watch?v=IGQmdoK_ZfY.

6 See Grayling (2019), pp. 534–53.

7 Ibid., p. 541.

8 Ibid., pp. 529–33.

9 Edward H. Hagen, 'Controversies surrounding Evolutionary Psychology', in David Buss (ed.) (2005) is a good survey, though Hagen's attempt to revise the nature-nurture debate into a body-mind debate is unpersuasive. See also Henry Plotkin, *Evolutionary Thought in Psychology: A Brief History* (London: Blackwell, 2004); J. C. Confer et al., 'Evolutionary psychology: Controversies, questions, prospects, and limitations', *American Psychologist*, vol. 65, no. 2 (2010), pp. 110–26.

10 It is noteworthy that John Locke, to whom the 'blank slate' metaphor (he did not use this actual phrase) is owed, acknowledged by the end of his *Essay Concerning Human Understanding* (1691) that we have to think of the mind as a cupboard with pigeon-holes and drawers ready to receive the inputs of experience – that is, that the mind can compare, infer, remember, categorize, and so on, in preparation for receiving and processing inputs of sensory data.

11 Leda Cosmides and John Tooby (1997), https://www.cep.ucsb.edu/primer.html.

12 Steven Jay Gould and Richard Lewontin, 'The spandrels of San Marco and the Panglossian paradigm: A critique of the adaptationist

programme', *Proceedings of the Royal Society of London B.*, vol. 205 (1979), pp. 581–98.

13 Ibid.

14 Steven Pinker (2002).

15 See Noam Chomsky (1986).

Chapter 3: The Schools of Life

1 See Genesis 3.5 on the original sin of pride (seeking knowledge; seeking to be as gods) and St Augustine on the question of thinking for oneself, 'Understanding is the reward of faith; seek not to understand that you may believe, but believe that you may understand', Augustine of Hippo, *Tractate 29 on John 7.14–18* in *Nicene and Post-Nicene Fathers* (Edinburgh: T & T Clark, 1886), 7:184–5.

2 Recall Immanuel Kant on the reason to 'Dare to know!' in his essay *What is Enlightenment?* (1784): 'On all sides I hear: "*Do not argue!*" The officer says, "*Do not argue drill!*" The tax man says, "*Do not argue, pay!*" The pastor says, "*Do not argue, believe!*"' *https://users.manchester.edu/Facstaff/SSNaragon/Online/texts/318/Kant%20Enlightenment.pdf*.

3 Despite the controversies over how dark the 'Dark Ages' were, there is no question about the Christian culturecide of the millennium preceding its triumph: Christine Nixey (2017) *passim*.

4 William Paley, (1802, 2009), *Evidences of Christianity* (1794), https://www.gutenberg.org/ebooks/14780.

5 See e.g. David Cook (2006), https://core.ac.uk/download/pdf/10180565.pdf.

6 Desiderius Erasmus, *Convivium religiosum* (1522); *Ciceronianus* ('The Ciceronian') (1528). See also Hume's four essays on happiness, in *Essays, Moral and Political*, Vol. II (1742), and discussion of its Ciceronian inspiration: https://open.conted.ox.ac.uk/sites/open.conted.ox.ac.uk/files/resources/Create%20Document/EDH-Happiness.pdf.

7 Étienne Gilson (1955), D. E. Luscombe (1997).

8 Note that deontology – associated with Kant in the eighteenth century CE – and utilitarianism, associated with Jeremy Bentham and John Stuart Mill in the nineteenth century, are moral theories providing guidance

about *how to act*, not ethical theories about one's character and outlook; they are not in the business of providing answers to Socrates' question.

9 I concentrate here on the three major schools of ethical thinking: Stoicism (developed from Cynicism), Epicureanism, and the ethical doctrines in Aristotle's Peripatetic philosophy, with mention of the Cyrenaics because of the frequent conflation of Cyrenaicism and Epicureanism in the writings of hostile critics of the latter. For completeness it should be mentioned that Diogenes Laërtius, quoting a lost work by Hippobotus, *On Philosophical Sects*, lists the names of nine schools: Megarian, Eretrian, Cyrenaic, Epicurean, Annicerean, Theodorean, Stoic, Old Academic and Peripatetic. Missing from this list is Scepticism. Very little is known about the Eretrian school, which was closely identified with the Megarian school, whose ethical teachings are only sketchily known – the Megarians are chiefly remembered for their work in logic – though the founder of the Eretrian school was Phaedo, a pupil of Socrates (his name is the title of one of Plato's dialogues), and occasional mentions of the Eretrians in the doxologies attribute to them the idea that the Good is One and indivisible and is the same thing as truth. Annicereans and Theodoreans (the latter named for Theodorus the Godless) are sub-branches of Cyrenaics, whose views are described in the main text here. Neither of the main branches of Scepticism – the Academic Sceptics and the more extreme Pyrrhonian Sceptics – offered systematic ethical systems, reserving judgment about all things including any final dogmatic utterances on the good; but followers of the Academy like Cicero were able to apply the sceptical stance in epistemology to a pragmatically eclectic adoption of views – for a chief example, from Stoicism – in matters ethical.

10 See Grayling (2019), Part I: 'Ancient Philosophy'.

11 In other respects, Aristotle and his school, the Peripatos, were not so keen on Socrates, because they were interested in science, about which Socrates was dismissive. Aristotle's own few remarks about Socrates are somewhat sceptical.

12 Plato, *Apology* ; *Gorgias* ; *Protagoras* ; *Meno* ; *Laws*. And see Lorraine Smith Pangle (2014).

13 Grayling (2019), pp. 51–7.

14 Xenophon, *Memorabilia*, 11.1.1, https://www.gutenberg.org/files/1177/ 1177-h/1177-h.htm.

15 For Plato's theory of the Forms, see his *Phaedo*; *Republic*; *Phaedrus*; and *Parmenides*. See also Gregory Vlastos (1981).

16 This is at very least an implication of Plato's view about knowledge and the Form of the Good – see his Allegory of the Cave in the *Republic* and his likening of the charioteer's (i.e. reason's) task in attempting to control the heaven-tending and earth-tending horses in the *Phaedrus*.

17 For the following accounts of the Hellenistic schools of ethics, see Diogenes Laërtius, *Lives of the Philosophers* (as relevant); Christopher Gill, 'Cynicism and Stoicism', in Roger Crisp (ed.), (2013); Aristotle, *Nicomachean Ethics* (350 BCE), trans. W. D. Ross, http://classics.mit.edu/ Aristotle/nicomachaen.html, and trans. C. Reeve (Indianapolis: Hackett, 2014); John Rist, *Stoic Philosophy* (Cambridge: Cambridge University Press, 1969) and *Epicurus: An Introduction* (Cambridge: Cambridge University Press, 1972); Keimpe Algra, et al. (eds.), *The Cambridge History of Hellenistic Philosophy* (Cambridge: Cambridge University Press, 1999). Note that Aristotle's name is attached to two treatises on ethics, the *Eudemian Ethics* and the *Nicomachean Ethics*. They are the first systematic studies of ethical questions in the history of Western philosophy. These titles were bestowed by their editors – respectively, Aristotle's friend Eudemus and his son Nicomachus. Aristotle himself described them as treatises 'on character' (*ta ethika*). The *Nicomachean Ethics* is the fuller and undoubtedly later work than the *Eudemian Ethics*. A third work, the *Magna Moralia*, is attributed to him but is probably a collection of notes taken by students.

18 Seneca, 'On Care of Health and Peace of Mind', *Letters to Lucilius*, No. 104, https://en.wikisource.org/wiki/Moral_letters_to_Lucilius/Letter_104.

19 Epictetus, *Discourses*, http://classics.mit.edu/Epictetus/discourses.html.

20 This is discussed at length in Chapter 13.

21 Marcus Aurelius, *Meditations*, https://www.gutenberg.org/ebooks/ 2680.

22 Aristotle actually says 'all free males'.

23 Primo Levi, *If This Is a Man* (1947; English translation 1959).

24 For the Atomism of Democritus and Leucippus, see Grayling (2019) pp. 47–51.

25 Lucretius, *De Rerum Natura*. A somewhat glutinous verse translation can be found at http://classics.mit.edu/Carus/nature_things.html; more advisable is the Loeb parallel text translated by W. H. D. Rouse (revised by Martin F. Smith), Loeb Classical Library 181 (Cambridge, MA: Harvard University Press, 1924).

26 Following Aristotle's celebration of it in the *Nicomachean Ethics*, friendship became a major topic in ethical discussion. See A. C. Grayling (2014).

27 Friedrich Nietzsche, *Human, All Too Human* (1878–80; London: Penguin Classics, 1994).

28 Catherine Wilson (2008).

29 Sources for the following remarks include Kedar Nath Tiwari, *Classical Indian Ethical Thought* (Delhi: Motilal Banarsidass Publishers, 1998); Chenyang Li, 'Chinese Philosophy', in William Edelglass and Jay L. Garfield (eds.), *The Oxford Handbook of World Philosophy* (Oxford: Oxford University Press, 2011); David L. Hall and Roger T. Ames, *Thinking Through Confucius* (Albany, NY: State University of New York Press, 1987); Hans-Georg Moeller, *The Philosophy of the Daodejing* (New York: Columbia University Press, 2006). See also Grayling (2019), Part V, *passim*.

30 For a summary of these views, Grayling (2019), pp. 514–53.

31 Ibid., pp. 542–3.

32 Thomas Hobbes, *Leviathan* (1651), https://www.gutenberg.org/files/3207/3207-h/3207-h.htm.

33 Bernard Mandeville, *The Fable of the Bees: or, Private Vices, Publick Benefits* (1714), https://www.earlymoderntexts.com/assets/pdfs/mandeville1732_1.pdf.

34 'Taoism' is an older Anglicization of the term which unhelpfully represented the 'd' sound by a 't'. 'Daoism' more accurately reflects the pronunciation.

35 The Daoists' state of nature is therefore the opposite of Hobbes' and more like Locke's: there are easy models for the Daoist conception in the lives of those animals who live untroubled by predators at the top of a food chain.

36 The parallel with Pyrrhonian scepticism is striking; Pyrrho of Elis visited India in the train of Alexander the Great's army, and might have learned his distinctive outlook from its 'naked philosophers', the

gymnosophists; these would almost certainly have been Jains, whose most assiduous devotees wore no clothes. A convincing case for the connection is made by Everard Flintoff in 'Pyrrho and India', *Phronesis*, vol. 25 (1980), pp. 88–108.

37 Caricatures of today's representations of these positions would see tattooed skateboarders as Cynics and Daoists, prigs as Stoics, people who like freebies and jollies and never work too hard as Epicureans, middle to senior management as Aristotelians, and vegetarians who care about the climate as Buddhists.

38 These words were written to the sound of the Mediterranean breaking on the shores of the Côte d'Azur. I mention this because self-deception is not unknown even among philosophers, so it needs to be said that what the writer of these words finds attractive in the views of the various schools is repeatedly run through the filter of reflection with that sobering fact in mind. At the same time, these conditions were those experienced by the Hellenistic philosophers themselves, which might explain why some of them considered a life of, or equivalent to, beachcombing was a genuine option. But at this juncture it is important to note that the 'we' of the ancient philosophers was not *everyone*; it was the self-selected group of (mainly male) individuals capable of putting the teachings into effect, not just because the climate of the Mediterranean lands permitted it but because the conditions of life generally, and their own resources, enabled it. A poor and uneducated individual of the day who lived as (say) a Cynic did without doing so on avowed Cynic principles was just a tramp.

Chapter 4: Avoiding a Wrong Turning

1 I provide a systematic analysis of religion and religious claims in (2013).
2 See Ursula Le Guin (1975).
3 It is hard to imagine any rational person persisting in religious convictions after reading Randel Helms (1988). What Helms demonstrates about the creation of the Christian story can be generalized *mutatis mutandis*; this, conjoined with the powers of emotion and tradition, says it nearly all.

PART II

Chapter 5: Happiness, *The Pursuit of* –

1 The annual World Happiness Reports are informative on this: https://worldhappiness.report/archive/.

2 Philippa Foot makes the same point: see (2001), Chapter 6, *passim*.

3 Bertrand Russell, *The Conquest of Happiness* (1930); Sigmund Freud, *Civilisation and Its Discontents* (2002).

4 Jonathan Swift, *A Tale of a Tub* (1704), Section IX.

5 *Journal of Happiness Studies*, https://www.springer.com/journal/10902.

6 Actually this is not so surprising: both countries are home to highly superstitious syncretistic cultures centred on popular forms of Christianity that have absorbed aboriginal polytheistic and animistic elements, promoting belief in earthly rewards of wealth for faith, and with posthumous salvation being easily attainable.

7 The perennial problem with social science methodology is that, however careful and ingenious a study's research design, what it reveals is correlations rather than causes. Social unrest could cause or be caused by personal dissatisfaction; noting that the two are covariants does not say which is responsible. In this area, one would like causal explanations.

8 G. E. Moore (1903), https://www.gutenberg.org/files/53430/53430-h/53430-h.htm.

9 Croesus, by the way, was the king who decided to attack Persia, but first enquired of the Delphic Oracle what the outcome might be. The Oracle replied, 'You will destroy a great empire.' Delighted, Croesus attacked; and destroyed his own empire thereby.

10 Grayling (2001).

11 John Stuart Mill (1861–3), Chapter 2, https://www.earlymoderntexts.com/assets/pdfs/mill1863.pdf.

Chapter 6: The Great Concepts

1 Cologne Digital Sanskrit Dictionaries; Benfey Sanskrit-English Dictionary; Monier-Williams Sanskrit-English Dictionary.

2 Matthew 5:1–12.

3 The *Oresteia* was first performed in 458 BCE. Socrates was born *c.* 470 BCE, Confucius died shortly beforehand in 479 BCE. Siddhartha Gautama, known as the Buddha, was their close contemporary; he either died or was born within a decade of Socrates' birth. His dates are very uncertain, but he was in effect either a direct contemporary of Confucius or a direct contemporary of Socrates.

4 Athena gives the Furies a bribe: agree to this and stay with us in Athens, she says, and we will honour you with sacrifices, and call you 'the Kindly Ones' (*Eumenides*) and no longer the Furies. The three Furies – Alecto, Megaera and Tisiphone, daughters of Uranos who sprang from the spilled blood and semen resulting from his castration by his son Cronos – accepted.

5 The sterling virtues of Rome's republican heroes continued to be extolled, and held up as examples, to schoolboys of the Empire into living memory – though we who read these stirring tales and discussed them in class, and learned at least portions of Macaulay's *Lays of Ancient Rome* by heart, are a dwindling band, which many will think a good thing – and in many respects they are doubtless right. Latin ceased to be a requirement for university entry in the 1960s; two consequences were a diminution of knowledge and interest in classical civilization and a noticeable change in the nature of formal English prose styles – the kind used in non-fiction, reports, official documents and serious journalism. As an example, no one who knew about the ablative and dative could misuse 'who' and 'whom' – but given the evolution of language use, always in the direction of simplification even if a loss of expressive power results, the question will be asked: who cares?

6 It was said of the notorious New York financial fraudster Bernie Madoff that his mistake was not to heed the example of the Church by promising returns on investment in the *next* life rather than this one.

7 Peter Brown, *The Body and Society: Men, Women and Sexual Renunciation in Early Christianity* (New York: Columbia University Press, 1968).

8 Friedrich Nietzsche, *Thus Spake Zarathustra* (London: Wordsworth World Classics, 1997), p. 16.

9 Actually, Homer says that Priam was driven to the camp by Idaeus, his charioteer, and took a heap of treasure as a gift – or bribe – for Achilles. Homer also says that Priam was accompanied by the messenger god Hermes disguised as a Greek soldier, which, if Priam knew this, meant

that he was probably unafraid. But considering the story in its purely human aspect, Priam's visit to Achilles certainly deserves the name of 'courage'.

10 Trooper Mark Donaldson, VC Act of Gallantry, https://www.pmc. gov.au/act-gallantry.

11 The translations of Tolstoy's *Anna Karenina* by Constance Garnett (1901) and David Magarshack (1961) were among those best known until the spate of more recent translations, including those by Richard Pevear and Larissa Volokhonsky (2000) and Marian Schwartz (2014).

12 G. W. Leibniz, *Theodicy* (1710), https://www.gutenberg.org/files/17147/ 17147-h/17147-h.htm.

13 R. D. McIntosh et al., 'Wise up: Clarifying the role of metacognition in the Dunning-Kruger effect', *Journal of Experimental Psychology: General*, vol. 148, no. 11 (2019), pp. 1882–97.

14 Aristotle, *Nicomachean Ethics*, ed. Jonathan Barnes (Princeton, NJ: Princeton University Press, 1984), Book V, 1137b1-6.

15 Ibid.

16 Jean-Paul Sartre (1948).

17 Third Earl of Shaftesbury (1711), https://www.earlymoderntexts.com/ assets/pdfs/shaftesbury1711book1.pdf.

18 See Chapter 4, note 2. Hans Castorp's hallucination or vision, described in the chapter 'Snow' of *The Magic Mountain*, is of an horrific child sacrifice in a temple standing apart from the idyllic Arcadian scene of lovely youths and maidens enjoying themselves beside the sea, as if the gory sacrifice were a condition of the idyll. Both in the chapter itself and in Mann's subsequent comments on his novel, the message is explained as being that a condition of knowing how to live is that one must have an understanding of (through experience of) illness and death. The parallel with Le Guin is therefore not exact; in 'Omelas' the sacrifice is the condition of the city's happiness, not of the possibility of an individual ethics. But a parallel remains: that there is a contract with a horror for the possibility of life.

19 Kant's (1785) and (1786) are the major texts setting out a deontological view, to the effect that being moral consists in doing one's duty. The latter is available at: https://www.gutenberg.org/ebooks/5683.

20 Note that deontology and utilitarianism are moral theories providing guidance about *how to act*, not ethical theories about one's character and

outlook; they are not in the business of providing answers to Socrates' question.

Chapter 7: Death

1 See Plato, *Phaedo*, 67e; Cicero, *Tusculan Disputations*, 30.74–31.71.5; Michel de Montaigne, 'That to Study Philosophy is to Learn to Die', *Essays*, trans. Charles Cotton, ed. William Hazlitt (1877), Chapter XIX, https://www.gutenberg.org/files/3600/3600-h/3600-h.htm.

2 Most religions, in premising an afterlife, teach that it begins with a judgment bringing punishment or reward. Such notions are very useful for controlling the living. Some people find such notions psychologically supportive, others find that they make death more terrible – for them death becomes a strange country ruled by dangerous powers, into which we venture ill-prepared. Sometimes the more devout a believer is, the more dreadful immortality can seem. Plato said that belief in a blissful afterlife should be encouraged so that the citizens, not fearing death, would be good soldiers. Many forms of religious fanaticism share this view. Even respectable religions can be militaristic; some even promise that death in battle grants direct entry to paradise. In such cases also, therefore, superstitions about death prove useful to priests and princes.

3 Think here of the Feigenbaum constant of period-doubling bifurcations.

4 See, for example, David San Filippo, 'Historical Perspectives on Attitudes concerning Death and Dying', Faculty Publications, vol. 29 (2006), https://digitalcommons.nl.edu/faculty_publications/29.

5 Jorge Luis Borges, 'Funes the Memorious', *Ficciones* (2000).

Chapter 8: Love

1 See, for example, Angela Kwartemaa Acheampong and Alhassan Sibdow Abukari, 'Nurses' and midwives' perspectives on how the pursuit for the "perfect" body image affects their own breastfeeding practices: A qualitative study in Ghana', *International Breastfeeding Journal*, vol. 16 (2021), article 74, https://internationalbreastfeedingjournal.biomed central.com/articles/10.1186/s13006-021-00421-0.

2 Both are Puccini operas; he was a master in this regard. Others include Mozart's 'Voi che sapete' in *Nozze di Figaro*, Verdi's 'Celeste Aida' in *Aida* and Dvořák's 'Mesicku' ('Song to the Moon') in *Rusalka*.

3 Richard Posner (1992).

4 Stendhal, *On Love* (1822), https://www.gutenberg.org/ebooks/53720.

5 Grayling (2001), Chapter 12.

6 Marie de Vichy-Chamrond, Marquise du Deffand, was in her beautiful and scandalous youth an habitué of the Duc d'Orleans' notorious nightly orgies, at which unspeakable lubricities occurred. She had been a recalcitrant girl whose parents tried to rescue her from atheism (she preached it to the other girls at her convent) by sending the great theologian Jean Baptiste Massillon, Bishop of Clermont, to correct her. He failed, muttering as he left the convent, '*Mais elle est charmante!*'

7 Guibert was a significant figure; he correctly predicted major changes in the nature of warfare, not least in the involvement of civilian populations both in supporting war efforts, morally and materially, and in suffering war's effects.

8 It will perhaps astonish some to know that Julie de Lespinasse's letters to the Comte de Guibert were published by his wife, Madame de Guibert, in 1809. Julie died in 1776.

9 In the film version of the book, Mildred is memorably played by an early-career Bette Davis; Philip by the then-established cinema heart-throb Leslie Howard.

10 Actually, these romantic flights would not now be so well regarded; at the time of Shelley's elopements with Harriet and then Mary, each was aged only sixteen. In that era girls of that age were regarded, and regarded themselves, as nubile young women. From medieval times the age of sexual consent in England was twelve, raised to thirteen in 1875 and then sixteen in 1885. In the US, the age of consent varies by state, generally sixteen in Southern and Midwestern states; seventeen or eighteen elsewhere, noticeably in California and New York.

11 This was how things were until a decade or more after the Second World War in Western countries – hence, within living memory.

12 Simon May (2011).

13 I repeat the reference to my *Friendship*, which is a survey both of the history of debates about the subject and a discussion of the concept itself.

14 The passages quoted here are from an edited version of Cicero's *De Amicitia* as it occurs in Grayling (2011).

Chapter 9: Luck and Evil

1 Massacres perpetrated since 1945: Partition of India in 1947 (2 million dead); 100,000 Harkis (Muslims who supported France in the Algerian War) in 1962–3; the Zanzibar Revolution of 1964 (3,000 dead); the slaughter of Igbo in Nigeria in 1966 (30,000 dead, followed by a million or more civilian dead in the following Biafran war); the massacre of anyone associated with the political Left in Indonesia in 1966–7 (half a million killed in a few months, many others in inhumane concentration camps); the massacre by Pakistani troops of Bangladeshis in the Liberation War of 1971 (2 million dead, and the rape of 300,000 girls and women); the murder of 2 million people in Cambodia between 1975 and 1979; massacres in the Guatemalan civil war of 1981–3 (nearly 200,000 dead); the Rwandan genocide of April–May 1994 (800,000 dead); the July 1995 massacre of Bosniak Muslim men and boys in Srebrenica (8,000 dead) – and this list is incomplete. It is not as if no one had noticed the Holocaust; Equatorial New Guinea under the murderous presidency of Francisco Macías Nguema was known as the 'Auschwitz of Africa' because Nguema's reign of terror killed or drove out one-third of the country's entire population in the decade of the 1970s. Nor is it the case that these atrocities were confined to what was once known as the 'third world'; there is evidence that the UK and USA assisted the Sukarno regime in Indonesia by supplying names of Leftists; see e.g. Geoffrey Robinson, *The Killing Season* (Princeton, NJ: Princeton University Press, 2018).

2 Primo Levi (2014).

3 Viktor Frankl (2008).

4 In the two days 29–30 September 1941, 33,771 Jews, citizens of Kyiv, were massacred and their bodies cast into the ravine of Babi Yar outside the city. The victims were shot dead by members of Sonderkommando 4a and the 45th Battalion of the German Order Police. The site continued in use as a massacre location where Soviet soldiers, Roma, Ukrainian nationalists and others, numbering a further 50,000–100,000 victims, were killed over the period from 1941 until the German defeat

by the Soviet army at the Battle of Kiev in November–December 1943. Efforts to conceal the fact that the massacres had taken place were made by Sonderaktion 1005, the project of effacing all traces of 'Operation Reinhardt', code name of the plan to exterminate Jews in the areas behind the Eastern Front.

5 Edward B. Westermann, 'Stone cold killers or drunk with murder? Alcohol and atrocity during the Holocaust', *Holocaust and Genocide Studies*, vol. 30, no. 1 (2016), pp. 1–19.

6 Ibid.

7 Martin Gilbert (1985), p. 191. See also Peter Longerich (2012), p. 457.

8 Elissa Mailänder Koslov, 'Work, violence and cruelty: An everyday historical perspective on perpetrators in Nazi concentration camps', *L'Europe en formation*, no. 367 (2010), pp. 29 *et seq*.

9 Ibid. According to Iris Murdoch's biographer Peter Conradi, Canetti – who was Murdoch's lover for a time – was sadistic and manipulative, exerting a hold of power over Iris; the latter's husband, John Bayley, also took this view, describing Canetti as a 'tyrant and dominator'. Perhaps Canetti's analysis of power, not least as experienced by individuals over other individuals, was informed by a personal perspective.

10 Hannah Arendt (1963).

11 Frankl, *Man's Search*.

12 Miklos Nyiszli (2012).

13 The contemporary discussion of moral luck began with a debate between Thomas Nagel and Bernard Williams, pursued further by Martha Nussbaum and others. Nagel (1979); Williams, *Moral Luck* (1981); Nussbaum (1986).

14 Nagel, ibid.

15 Friedrich Nietzsche, 'Maxims and Arrows No. 12', *Twilight of the Idols* (1888), trans. Anthony M. Ludovici, https://www.gutenberg.org/files/52263/52263-h/52263-h.htm.

Chapter 10: Duties

1 F. H. Bradley, 'My Station and Its Duties', in (1927); Henry Sidgwick, 'My Station and its Duties', *International Journal of Ethics*, vol. 4 (1893), pp. 1–17.

2 See Ulrich Steinvorth, 'Hegel's *Sittlichkeit*', in *A Secular Absolute* (London: Palgrave Macmillan, 2020), https://link.springer.com/chapter/10.1007/978-3-030-35036-9_3.

3 Sir Edward Dyer, sixteenth-century courtier and poet.

Chapter 11: Living Among Others

1 Although an old concept, the contemporary salience of *Ubuntu* is owed to advocacy of it by the writer Jordan Kush Ngubane in the 1950s, and its adoption by Archbishop Desmond Tutu in his chairmanship of the Truth and Reconciliation Commission after the end of apartheid in South Africa. C. B. N. Gade in 'The Historical Development of the Written Discourses on *Ubuntu*' traces its use back to at least 1846. Ngubane's discussion of *Ubuntu* occurs in his novels and the magazine *African Drum*. Expressly philosophical discussion of the concept is attributed to Stanlake Samkange (1980).

2 Jan R. Magnus et al., 'Tolerance of cheating: An analysis across countries', *The Journal of Economic Education*, vol . 33, no. 2 (2002), pp. 125–35.

3 This is the point of Richard Dawkins' *The Selfish Gene* (1976).

4 Frans de Waal's famous experiment with monkeys on this point can be viewed here: https://youtu.be/meiU6TxysCg.

5 A classic example is afforded by the responses of those who viewed footage of the incident in which basketball player Akil Mitchell's eye popped out during a match; one example is at https://youtu.be/otZIMl-E_Gg.

6 Ben Thomas, 'What's so special about mirror neurons?', *Scientific American*, 6 November 2012, https://blogs.scientificamerican.com/guest-blog/whats-so-special-about-mirror-neurons/.

7 J. M. Kilner and R. N. Lemon, 'What we currently know about mirror neurons', *Current Biology*, vol. 23, no. 23 (2013), https://www.ncbi.nlm.nih.gov/pmc/articles/PMC3898692/.
  In this respect, the modest aims of the Epicureans in their Garden might have been a better example of ambition's target.

8 The Aché of Paraguay kill old women when they cease to be useful, by breaking their necks. The old men they exile from the tribe, leaving them to fend for themselves. Tim Harford, 'What happens when we're

too old to be "useful"?', BBC News, 22 January 2020, https://www.bbc.
co.uk/news/business-50673645.

9 Moses Maimonides, *A Guide for the Perplexed*, first published in 1190, is an
attempt to marry Aristotelian philosophy with Jewish rabbinical
thought. Maimonides is the Jewish Aquinas in this respect.

10 My former colleague Gabriele Taylor at St Anne's College, Oxford,
provides a subtle and absorbing account of these emotions of self-
assessment in her *Pride, Shame and Guilt* (1985). In her *Deadly Vices* (2006)
she examines the Christian sins of sloth, envy, avarice, pride, anger, lust
and gluttony, which in that outlook are designated as what brings 'death
to the soul', and argues – independently of the theological background –
that they are indeed well bracketed as deadly in that, in anything beyond
moderate form, they are 'destructive of the self and prevent flourishing'
(p. 1). Note the contrast: the philosophers of antiquity said the same
thing of the effect of the normal avocations and aims of social life; these
latter were the things 'deadly' to peace of mind. One might say that
their *ataraxia* is the earthly heaven for which the theologies of later centuries substituted an immaterial one, together with an alternative set of
impediments to attaining it. But in fact the Stoics and Epicureans had
already dealt with the likes of gluttony and avarice, by dealing with
excess: for them any excess, just in virtue of being such – and therefore
including a yet wider range of what can be done to excess – would destroy the self and its flourishing.

11 Ludwig Wittgenstein (1921), proposition 7. See Grayling (1988), and
https://www.youtube.com/watch?v=-7Pcwx7oFWs, recorded in an
especially hirsute phase.

Chapter 12: 'The Meaning of Life' and 'A Life Worth Living'

1 P. G. Wodehouse's pig character Empress of Blandings appears in all the
Blandings Castle novels starting with *Blandings Castle and Elsewhere*
(1935).

2 Arthur Schopenhauer, 2 vols. (2015). See 'Ethics' and 'Additional Remarks
on the doctrine of the affirmation and negation of the will to life' in Vol.
2. See also Byron Simmons, 'A thousand pleasures are not worth a single

pain: the compensation argument for Schopenhauer's pessimism', *European Journal of Philosophy*, vol. 29, no. 1 (2021), pp. 120–36.

3 If a life were outstandingly negative in its consequences on the world, such that it would have been better if the individual had not lived, it would still be 'meaningful', but not – obviously – worthwhile.

4 R. H. Tawney (1926); Max Weber (2011; from rev. edn, 1920).

5 Carl Jung, *Collected Works*, Vol. 11, p. 497.

6 Ibid., Vol. 8, p. 686.

7 Schopenhauer, *Parerga and Paralipomena*.

8 Nietzsche, *Gay Science*, Book VI (1974). In *Ecce Homo*, 'The Birth of Tragedy', 3, he says that the doctrine of eternal recurrence was first stated by the Stoics. In *Thus Spake Zarathustra* the prophet ends by celebrating recurrence.

9 For a good introduction see Kevin Aho (2020).

10 At first the great ebullition of ideas focused on magic, Hermeticism, the Cabala, alchemy, astrology, and the like; René Descartes and Francis Bacon were leaders in showing how the right methods of enquiry would separate genuine science from nonsense within and among these endeavours. See Grayling (2016).

11 Pascal, *Pensées*, 131, https://www.gutenberg.org/files/18269/18269-h/18269-h.htm.

12 Ibid., 192.

13 Jean-Paul Sartre (1948).

14 Albert Camus, *The Myth of Sisyphus* (1942; London: Penguin, 2013).

15 Herbert Marcuse, *Reason and Revolution* (New York: Oxford University Press, 1941); cf. Hegel, *Science and Logic*, Vol. 1 (2020), p. 404.

16 Cardinal Richelieu once said, 'Give me six lines written by the hand of the most honest man, and I will find something in them to have him hanged.'

17 Martin Heidegger (1962).

18 This idea relates to the more developed thesis in Sartre's *Being and Nothingness* about the relation of the self to others, and the distant root of the conception lies in Hegel's 'master-slave' dialectic. Whereas this latter premises the notion of a primal conflict in the reciprocal act of mutual creation, and whereas the *Being and Nothing* account identifies the risk in another's 'objectification' of oneself *as* an other – which he says is

something we realize through the experience of shame – Sartre in 'Existentialism is a Humanism' makes mutual recognition both positive and necessary, in a way reminiscent of the idea in southern African culture of *Ubuntu*, 'I am because you are'.

19 Of course the extremely particular relationship of the Jews to Yahweh long predates Christianity, but two factors make citation of Judaism inapt in this connection. The first is that the Jews were a small and local people who did not proselytize and whose religion was just one among a number in the Near East of pre-Christian times. The second is that the relationship of Yahweh to his chosen people is most accurately expressed as, at best, that of a herder to his sheep, and at worst, as that of a bully to a crowd of captives. Obedience is front and centre in the Hebrew bible – mentions of Yahweh's love and kindness in Hosea, Isaiah, the Psalms and elsewhere never quite effacing its conditional nature and the ferocity of punishment 'to the third and fourth generation' for disobedience.

PART III

Chapter 13: Philosophy as a Way of Life

1 Pierre Hadot (1995). Martha Nussbaum (1994). It is a special pleasure to record that my first introduction to Hadot came from Joe Palumbo, my friend and long-ago fellow student in philosophy at Oxford.

2 An excellent survey of the 'philosophy as a way of life' concept, with discussion of the ethical schools and Hadot, is given by Michael Ure and Michael Sharpe in (2020).

3 Nussbaum, *Therapy of Desire*, p. 3.

4 Nussbaum, 'Introduction' (1986).

5 Hadot (1995), p. 11.

6 Quoted from the Hadot papers in the Collège de France archive by Arnold Davidson, 'Introduction', ibid., p. 2.

7 In this way, Hadot is rather like the brilliant classicist of the sixteenth century Isaac Casaubon, who demonstrated from philological principles that the Hermetic texts dated from the first centuries of the Common Era, and not, as many wished to believe, from a remote past supposed to be the time of Moses, around 1600 BCE or earlier.

8 And not least, by way of aside, a significant slice of its calendar of saints from pagan deities (on the principle 'if you cannot beat them, join them', worshippers of a locally favourite deity were easier to convert if the deity could be reconfigured as a saint of the Church) and perhaps even its Mariolatry from the cult of Diana, virgin goddess, whose shrine at Nemi (ancient Aricinum) is claimed by James George Frazer in *The Golden Bough* to be its source. An example is St Hippolytus, a supposititious personage easily confused with the person of a myth who was dragged to death by horses; the fact that Greek for 'horse' is *hippos* gives the game away. The general method of these transitions is suggested by the way the *vera icona* or 'true image' on the cloth that wiped Jesus' sweating face on the way to Calvary became St Veronica.

9 This happened as a result of Rome's victory in the Macedonian and Achaean wars (ending 148–6 BCE).

10 Hadot (1995), p. 5.

11 Hadot, *La Citadelle Intérieure* (commentary on the *Meditations*), (Paris: Fayard, 1992), p. 62.

12 Ibid., p. 10.

13 Ibid., p. 268.

14 Hadot, 'Wittgenstein, Philosophe du Langage', quoted (1995), pp. 17–18.

15 As in the case of eighteenth-century thinkers such as Shaftesbury and Hume: the former premised his views about tolerance and good humour on the fact that human beings are social animals possessed of a *sensus communis* to which he explicitly appeals; the latter argued in similar vein that benevolence is natural to humanity. Neither offered a metaphysics in support, Hume expressly disavowing even the possibility of such.

16 See Grayling (2019), pp. 103–7.

17 Correlatively, there is the remark, variously attributed to Lichtenberg or Schopenhauer, that 'a book is a mirror; if a donkey looks into it you can't expect to find an angel looking back'. However, education is the hope that the faces looking back from the mirror of a book will, with attentive and thoughtful reading, grow fit for Botticelli's pencil.

18 Hadot (1995), p. 27.

19 Lord Chesterfield, *Letters to his Son* (1774), https://www.gutenberg.org/ebooks/3361.

20 The reference is to the Third Earl of Shaftesbury (1671–1713); distinguishing which earl is which is necessitated by the prominence of the name in British history from the seventeenth to nineteenth centuries. This one is also of course the author of the *Characteristics*.

21 In Walter Pater's conclusion to (1873).

22 Lawrence Klein 'Introduction', in Anthony Ashley Cooper, Third Earl of Shaftesbury (2003), http://library.mibckerala.org/lms_frame/eBook/ Shaftesbury%20-%20Characteristics%20of%20Men,%20Manners,%20 Opinions,%20Times%20(CUP).pdf.

23 Nussbaum (1994), p. 490.

24 Ibid., p. 491.

25 Ibid.

26 Daniel Kahneman (2011).

27 Plutarch, *Essays* (1992). Plutarch was a Platonist critical of both Stoics and Epicureans, though chiefly on the ground of their materialism, which meant that they did not agree with Plato's view that the source of morality is the intelligible world, as described in the *Timaeus*. Much of his writing on the practice of a philosophy of life shares a great deal with the views of the major ethical schools.

28 Withdrawal from engagement, given the nature of the world's pressing problems, seems scarcely an option in our age. See Grayling (2022).

29 As regards 'detachment from external contingencies': it is of course relevant to remember that the idea of philosophy as a practice is expressed even more fully and familiarly in the Indian traditions: see J. E. H. Smith, 'Philosophy as a distinct cultural practice', in J. Ganeri (ed.) (2017).

Chapter 14: A Life and Its Philosophy

1 Most Epicureans of the modern era were so in virtue of their attraction to the materialism of Epicurean physics, as set out in Lucretius' *De Rerum Natura*. Thomas Jefferson is an example. He liked the physics, not so much the ethics. Lucretius' remarkable poem, a work of great literary value as well as philosophical interest, was nearly lost to history; Stoics loathed Epicurean ethics and Christians loathed Epicurean materialism, so it is only because of the literary qualities of the poem that it survived

the centuries, thanks to a few connoisseurs dotted across their span. It was rediscovered in a single copy in the Renaissance by a professional manuscript hunter sent out by Poggio Bracciolini, an avid collector, to scour the monasteries and libraries of Europe.

2 The town of Ferney has been renamed Ferney-Voltaire.

3 When my *Wittgenstein* was published in the Past Masters series (later 'Very Short Introductions') by Oxford University Press in 1996, I sent a copy to my brother John. He wrote back, 'I didn't read your book, as you'd expect, but I did look at the last couple of pages to see if the boy gets the girl or not – and I notice that he doesn't.' It was an astute remark.

4 Even worse has been the uncritical and incomprehending parasitism and fawning of some – too many – in the 'critical theory' movement in literary studies, for whom Wittgenstein, with his deliciously foreign clever-sounding name, has been a dressing-up box of ideas (as with the literary theorists' ignorant riffs on terms and tropes from quantum theory in science). Here is an example from Marjorie Perloff's *Wittgenstein's Ladder* (1996): she quotes the *Tractatus* 6.54, 'My propositions are elucidatory in this way: he who understands me finally recognizes them as senseless, when he has climbed out through them, on them, over them. (He must so to speak throw away the ladder, after he has climbed up on it.)' and then writes: 'This famous metaphor, which has given me my title, contains in embryo three critical aspects of what I take to be a distinctively Wittgensteinian poetics. First, its *dailyness*: for Dante's purgatorial staircase, for Yeats's "ancient winding stair", Wittgenstein substitutes a mere ladder – a ladder, moreover, whose origin (unlike that of the ladder in Yeats's "Circus Animals' Desertion") is as equivocal as its destination. Second, the movement "up" the ladder can never be more than what Gertrude Stein called "Beginning again and again" – a climbing "through", "on", and "over" its rungs that is never finished. Hence Wittgenstein's suspicion of generalization, of metalanguage, indeed of *theory*.' This hangs an excessive weight of allusion onto Wittgenstein's borrowing (without acknowledgement) of Schopenhauer's ladder metaphor. You would think Perloff had neither understood the *Tractatus* – offered as a definitive solution to 'the problems of

philosophy' (yes, all of them) – nor looked into the *Philosophical Investi-gations* which repudiates it, nor *On Certainty*, which by implication repudiates the *Investigations'* claim that there are no genuine philosophi-cal problems. 'Critical theory' – the least self-critical of the disengaged cogs of intellectual playground machinery prompted by the mutually causative relationship of postmodernism and higher education that pro-liferated in the last third of the twentieth century – relies on promiscuous quotation to generate clouds of apparent meaning; in Perloff's 'ladder' cadenza, nothing is added to the original metaphor other than a display of her own range of reading. Her 'Preface' to *Wittgenstein's Ladder* fur-nishes an index to those who have appropriated Wittgenstein without understanding him or the philosophical context of his writings, bran-dishing amputated quotations from the *Tractatus* without appearing to know that the basis of his later philosophical work was the explicit rejection of its theses. There is no rational way of engaging with the allusion-mongering displays that pass for discussion in literary theory, but one can point to factual errors, which abound: for example Perloff says Wittgenstein was 'a Jew baptized in the Catholic church, with strong leanings toward Protestant piety', when in fact his family had converted to Catholic Christianity two or three generations before he was born, and he himself preferred Tolstoy's recension of the Gospels to the originals; which is consistent with the fact that he appears to have read very little in philosophy or outside it, his work remarkably bare of input (one can only be sure of some overheard fragments of Schopen-hauer and what he learned from Russell) – one consequence being (as *On Certainty* shows) his impressionistic reinventions of some philosoph-ical wheels.

5 The 'neck-top computer' allusion comes from my colleague Dan Den-nett.

6 My father, Henry Clifford Grayling (1909–1988), was emphatically not one of these. He went to Africa north of the Zambezi – a territory then quite recently annexed as a 'British protectorate' – as a young bachelor in the 1930s in search of adventure, hunting big game (after the war he became an ardent game preservationist and regretted his hunting days) and in love with the trackless immensity of that amazing continent.

Because he was in a reserved occupation he was not allowed to join up in 1939 despite traipsing all over London in an effort to get into any branch of any armed service that would have him – but without the advantages Evelyn Waugh gives to Guy Crouchback in the same dilemma. He took my mother to Luanshya on the Copperbelt on what is now the Zambia–Zaire border in 1940. I was born there in 1949, some years after my two siblings whom my parents regarded as having completed the family; my mother, not one to eschew frankness on some matters, gave me a clear idea of her feelings on discovering her late unplanned *grossesse* when I was old enough to appreciate them.

7 A particular incident is recorded at https://youtu.be/DcUyMM7y1Z4.

8 The two schoolmasters about to be described were verdant islands in an otherwise turbid sea. I derived little benefit from my various schools, apart from an intense dislike of arbitrary authority, capital punishment, and the awfulness of ignorance and bigotry when it has power. My housemaster at Falcon College at Essexvale in Rhodesia was an especially unpleasant example of the stupid bully put in charge of boys over whom he had despotic sway, and upon whom – most especially me; I held the record for the number of beatings received – he liberally applied the cane. My salvation, such as it was, was that I was a reader, enormously self-educated by voracious reading; but if I had had the benefit of wise preceptors to give some guidance, to challenge what notions I formed, to alert me to further possibilities and to discuss and dilate upon them, I should have arrived ten years earlier at the point where the organized benefit of education began to tell. I had grown a forest on the land I was to plough, and had to go back and forth to put it in order for planting. To put the matter more directly: by the time I had completed two undergraduate degrees, I was ready to begin as an undergraduate.

9 G. H. Lewes, *A Biographical History of Philosophy* (2013).

10 T. L. S. Sprigge (1983).

11 The argument in question concerns the re-identification of particulars, the possibility of which is necessary to the unity of the spatio-temporal framework within which the particulars exist. It is an argument directed at refuting the epistemological sceptic, since it offers a proof of the continued existence of perception-independent things. Since, as the sequel here shows, this was then a primary focus of my own philosophical

concerns, I was intensely interested in this argument. I found a flaw in it – as stated it relies on an assumed verification principle – which I unearthed, and then restated the argument in an alternative form which is, so I argue, more effective. The details are first developed in my DPhil thesis at Oxford, 'Epistemological Scepticism and Transcendental Arguments', and successively developed further in my books *The Refutation of Scepticism* (London: Duckworth, 1985) and *Scepticism and the Possibility of Knowledge* (London: Bloomsbury, 2009).

12 Ben Rogers (2000).

13 On only one occasion of many that I set Austin's book as reading for a tutorial did the student return the following week having read Jane Austen's *Sense and Sensibility*, saying that though he had enjoyed it enormously he could find no relevance in it to the subject of our tutorials. He might have been having me on, but I played along. This reminds me of a time I set an essay from W. V. Quine's collection of essays called *From a Logical Point of View*. The student, already bewildered by the many new long words he was having to master in the study of philosophy, threw his hands up in despair on hearing me name the book, and said, 'But what's fromology?' The title of Quine's book comes from a song made popular by Harry Belafonte in which the chorus is, 'From a logical point of view you should marry someone uglier than you.'

14 Freddie had a fabulously undistinguished military career. He was no good at soldiering, but in any case was obviously better suited to the Intelligence Corps than anything that involved shooting. He was sent to Sierra Leone to be Britain's eyes and ears there – it has been pointed out that the real reason was to get him as much out of the way of the real war as possible – and while there he contracted a dangerous fever. He told me that at the height of his delirium he understood with perfect clarity what Kant was on about; but had forgotten his insight by the time he recovered.

15 A. J. Ayer, 'Has Austin refuted the sense-datum theory?', *Synthese*, vol. 17, no. 1 (1967), pp. 117–40.

16 Out of caution, fearing for their possible effects on the brain, I never took illegal psychoactive drugs, though I have always been of the view that they should be decriminalized.

17 Indeed the book was so successful in this respect that for a long time it was known as 'the Holy Grayling'.

18 These are discussed in essays in (2008), especially numbers 2, 8 and 9: respectively, 'Metaphysically Innocent Representation', 'Understanding Realism' and 'How Not to Be Realistic'.

19 The BBC World Service series in question is *Exchanges at the Frontier*, still available from the archive. The series, which I devised and hosted, began under the auspices of the Wellcome Trust and continued as a joint enterprise between Wellcome and the BBC. In it I interviewed leading scientists to get them to explain their work clearly for a lay audience, and then to discuss with them the social impact of what they were doing.

20 *The Meaning of Things* (2001), *The Reason of Things* (2002), *The Mystery of Things* (2004), *The Heart of Things* (2005), *The Form of Things* (2007), *To Set Prometheus Free* (2009), *Thinking of Answers* (2010), *The Challenge of Things* (2015).

21 *Towards the Light* (2007), *The Age of Genius* (2016).

22 *Ideas That Matter* (2009).

23 *Liberty in the Age of Terror* (2009), *Democracy and Its Crisis* (2017), *The Good State* (2020), *For the Good of the World* (2022).

24 A *New Yorker* article appositely remarked, 'No one expects contemporary philosophers to be more than mildly eccentric. Creatures of the modern academy, they have careers, not vocations. Some mixture of incentive and professional obligation keeps them productive. They can cultivate the odd quirk – elbow patches or, naughtily, a cigar habit – but more outlandish idiosyncrasies are ruled out by the institutions that discipline them into tameness'. Nikhail Krishnan, 'How queer was Ludwig Wittgenstein?', *New Yorker*, 9 May 2022.

Appendix 1: Three Instances: Stoic Justice, Epicurean Experience, Athens versus Jerusalem

1 Seneca, *De Clementia*; and see also *De Ira* (Cambridge, MA: Harvard University Press Loeb Classics, 1989).

2 Richard Bauman (1996).

3 Ibid., p. 82.

4 Ibid.

5 Part of the opposition to the infliction of the full punishment arose from considerations not of clemency or mercy, but economics; the

household of Pedanius was left without any slaves, and had to start over to acquire the scores that had evidently been necessary to run it. Other slave-owning families doubtless recognized that so flinty an application of the law might likewise cost them dear if a household slave murdered one of the family; they would suffer twice over.

6 Seneca, *De Ira*, and Bauman, *Crime and Punishment*, p. 80.

7 Bauman, *Crime and Punishment*, p. 88.

8 Pater, 'Conclusion', *The Renaissance*.

9 Another influence on Wilde and other 'decadents' of the time was J. K. Huysmans, *À Rebours* (1884), about the eccentric ultra-aesthete Duc Jean des Esseintes. Wilde admired it enthusiastically; it figures in his *Picture of Dorian Gray* (1890) as 'a poisonous book . . . the strangest book that he had ever read. It seemed to him that in exquisite raiment, and to the delicate sound of flutes, the sins of the world were passing in dumb show before him.' Doubtless Proust had the idea of his nocturnal life in a cork-lined room from the example of the Duc's house and lifestyle at Fontenoy.

10 Oscar Wilde (1890; 2003).

11 Walter Pater (1885; 2016).

12 Karl Marx, 'The Difference Between the Democritean and Epicurean Philosophy of Nature' (1902), https://rowlandpasaribu.files.wordpress.com/2013/09/karl-marx-the-difference-between-the-democritean-and-epicurean-philosophy-of-nature.pdf; Friedrich Nietzsche, *Selected Letters*, ed. and trans. Christopher Middleton (1997).

13 Nietzsche Circle (ed.), *Nietzsche and Epicureanism* (*The Agonist*, 2018).

14 King James Version. It happens that God's promises about multitudinous seed had already been made to Abraham earlier in Genesis at least twice (Chapters 12 and 16), so this very severe test of Abraham's faith appears arbitrary – either that, or it is evidence of vacillation on the deity's part. In the imagination of that era, having numerous offspring was the great desideratum, for economic reasons and the security of one's old age; great social status was attached to the father of a big family. Genesis promises as a reward what was then highly valued; if Genesis were being written now, what choice desire would it hold out as the reward for faith? Money? A super-yacht?

15 Immanuel Kant (1798), http://la.utexas.edu/users/hcleaver/330T/350k PEEKantConflictFacNarrow.pdf.

16 Søren Kierkegaard (1843), http://www.sophia-project.org/uploads/ 1/3/9/5/13955288/kierkegaard_fear.pdf.

17 This, as an aside, introduces a few little complexities for the Christian story also, given what happens in it to the son of God.

18 Charles I. Glicksburg (1960), p. 12.

19 William K. Clifford, 'The Ethics of Belief', https://people.brandeis. edu/~teuber/Clifford_ethics.pdf.

Appendix 2: A Technical Aside to Chapter 14

1 Grayling (2007), *passim*.

2 This part of the argument derives from Donald Davidson's 'On the Very Idea of a Conceptual Scheme', *Proceedings and Addresses of the American Philosophical Association*, vol. 47 (1973), pp. 5–20.

3 Grayling (2021), pp. 7–9 and Part I, Chapters 3 and 4 *passim*. *The Metaphysics of Experience* is in progress at time of writing – a project many years in development following the volume publication referenced in the last but one footnote.

Index

Notes are indexed by page numbers followed by the letter 'n' and the respective note numbers.

Index

403

Gestapo 138, 196

Gianni Schicchi 164

god/God 5, 7, 24, 249, 250, 256, 262
  creation of a perfect world 126
  vs. evils 84–5
  and the Genesis story 340–43,
    387n14
  good 316
  grace of 26
  happiness and 71, 109, 110
  logos as 47, 54
  and love 84, 91, 121, 182
  and meaning of life 238
  mercy and justice conflict 130
  nature and 85–7
  punishment by 162, 179
  slaves of 92
  young 119
  see also deity/deities

Goethe, Johann Wolfgang von 176,
  196, 221, 241

Goldsmith, Oliver 185, 186

Gonatas, Antigonus 50

good life, the 41, 58, 63, 67, 68, 108,
  189–92, 207, 215, 239, 277, 279,
  291, 292–3, 294

good person 60, 206

goodness 24, 76, 109, 110, 141, 182, 190,
  207, 316

Gorgias 39, 42, 296

Gould, Stephen Jay 29, 30

Gramsci, Antonio 126–7

Gray, Thomas 180, 244

Grayling, Henry Clifford 304, 383n6

Grayling, John Richard 306, 382

Greece xv, xvi, 34, 38–9, 51, 118, 119,
  259, 281, 295, 297

greed 17, 25, 74, 138, 225, 229, 233, 264

Greek (language) 6, 17, 38, 42

Greek myths/Greek mythology 5, 221,
  293, 306–7

Greeks 24, 39, 121, 162–3, 179, 216

Green, T. H. 214–15, 309, 310

grief 11, 13, 17, 124, 190, 232, 247, 258,
  277, 290, 324
  and death 8, 12, 149, 152–3, 154, 156
  of losing a friend 186, 187–8

Guibert, Comte de 174–5, 373n7,
  373n8

guilt 67, 133, 141, 150, 234, 252, 277, 335

habits 60, 61, 195, 197, 220, 284, 287,
  291, 293–4, 331, 337

Hadot, Pierre 275, 280–84, 286–90,
  293, 318, 379n1, 379n2, 379n7

Hamann, Heinrich 196

Hamlet 52, 156, 208

happiness xiii, xvi, xvii–xviii, 16, 140,
  209, 327
  in afterlife 99, 114
  Aristotle on 59, 62, 70, 97, 100 *see
    also* eudaimonia
  ataraxia and 109, 116, 234, 240–41
  in the city of Omelas 141–2
  cultural differences in 104–5
  definitions of 97, 104
  from desires 99, 100
  doing worthwhile things 107–8
  Epicurean view on 66–7, 69
  as an epiphenomenon 100, 106
  from family 105, 107, 115
  'feeling happy' 97, 99, 103, 106, 116
  from goals 98, 99, 100, 103, 106–7,
    108, 111, 116
  and god 71, 109, 110
  and harm 104, 113
  as the highest good 59, 109, 111
  Mill's views on 112–13
  neurotransmitters associated with
    115 *see also* serotonin
  nostrums for 37
  from obedience to god 71, 99

THE FRONTIERS OF KNOWLEDGE:
WHAT WE KNOW ABOUT SCIENCE, HISTORY AND THE MIND
A. C. GRAYLING

From the bestselling polymath, a gripping history of science, life on earth and the human mind – and what we might know in the future.

In very recent times humanity has learnt a vast amount about the universe, the past and itself. But through our remarkable successes in acquiring knowledge we have learnt how much we have yet to learn: the science we have, for example, addresses just five per cent of the universe; pre-history is still being revealed, with thousands of historical sites yet to be explored; and the new neurosciences of mind and brain are just beginning.

What do we know, and how do we know it? What do we now know that we don't know? And what have we learnt about the obstacles to knowing more? In a time of deepening battles over what knowledge and truth mean, these questions matter more than ever.

Bestselling polymath and philosopher A. C. Grayling seeks to answer them in three crucial areas at the frontiers of knowledge: science, history and psychology. This is a compelling and fascinating tour de force, written with verve, clarity and remarkable breadth of knowledge.

'Grayling brings satisfying order to daunting subjects'

Steven Pinker

'This book hums with the excitement of the great human project of discovery'

Adam Zeman, author of
Aphantasia

THE HISTORY OF PHILOSOPHY
A. C. GRAYLING

**Authoritative and accessible, this landmark work is the first
single-volume history of philosophy shared for decades.**

The story of philosophy is an epic tale: an exploration of the
ideas, views and teachings of some of the most creative minds
known to humanity. But there has been no comprehensive
history of this great intellectual journey since 1945.

Intelligible for students and eye-opening for philosophy readers,
A. C. Grayling covers with characteristic clarity and elegance
subjects like epistemology, metaphysics, ethics, logic and the
philosophy of mind, as well as the history of debates in these
areas, through the ideas of celebrated philosophers as well as
lesser-known influential thinkers.

The History of Philosophy takes the reader on a journey from
the age of the Buddha, Confucius and Socrates. Through
Christianity's dominance of the European mind to the
Renaissance and Enlightenment. On to Mill, Nietzsche, Sartre,
then the philosophical traditions of India, China and the
Persian-Arabic world.

And finally into philosophy today.

> 'A cerebrally enjoyable survey, written with great clarity
> and touches of wit'
>
> *Sunday Times*

> 'Grayling's accessible omnibus will provide a stepping
> stone for the student or novice'
>
> *Kirkus Reviews*